NONE SO BLIND

D1328346

SIR ROBERT VANSITTART IN 1933

IAN COLVIN

NONE SO BLIND

A British Diplomatic View of
the Origins of World War II

HARCOURT, BRACE & WORLD, INC. · NEW YORK

Copyright © 1965 by Ian Colvin

All rights reserved. No part of this book may be
reproduced in any form or by any mechanical means,
including duplicating machine and tape recorder,
without permission in writing from the publisher.

First American edition
Published in Great Britain under the title
Vansittart in Office
Library of Congress Catalog Card Number: 65-23972
Printed in the United States of America

To Sarita,
Lady Vansittart,
who shared in his
endeavour and conflicts,
this story of a great
civil servant
is dedicated

ACKNOWLEDGEMENTS

THIS book, though written without the assistance of the Foreign Office, contains personal reminiscences of individual members of H.M. Diplomatic Service from Sir Harold Caccia downwards. It was not to be expected, or indeed desirable, that a Government Department should participate in an independent biography of this sort. My guide to Vansittart's period as Permanent Under-Secretary of State for Foreign Affairs, to his thoughts and actions in office is derived from notes by himself of his advice and opinions. These were carefully kept in calendar order, some in his own handwriting, in his country home, Denham Place, where he spent the last years of his life writing an autobiography, *The Mist Procession*. They can be read in connection with the main published documents of the same period and subject. Some of these notes appear to have been abbreviations of his official opinions, paraphrased to omit internal and departmental detail, but the thought and the prose is undoubtedly contemporary to the events and stresses of his ten years at the centre of affairs in the Foreign Office. It is Vansittart labouring to avoid war, or to enter war at least prepared, in letters, memoranda and summaries of advice, whether written at the Foreign Office, 44 Park Street or Denham Place. Here and there I have been able to quote from an original document of his composition published in the series of Documents on British Foreign Policy.

My thanks are in the first place due to Lady Vansittart for making the Vansittart papers available to me in their entirety. I could not have filled out numerous gaps but for the kind assistance of Sir Alexander Cadogan, his successor in the office of Permanent Under-Secretary for Foreign Affairs. Others who have been helpful to me are Sir Clifford Norton, Sir Reginald Leeper, Sir Laurence Collier, Sir Horace Seymour, Sir Horace Wilson, Sir Donald St. Clair Gainer, Lord Gladwyn, and Lord Strang to mention former colleagues of the Foreign Office, and Brigadier Humphrey Stronge, former British Military Attaché in Prague. My special thanks are due to Lord Avon for giving me access to original letters of Sir Robert Vansittart in his archives, and to Lord Salisbury for recollections of Sir Robert in office. Ava Lady Waverley has kindly assisted me with recollections of the period 1935-36 and the personality of Ralph Wigram. I am grateful to Lord Norwich and Mr. Rupert Hart-Davis for permission to read and quote from the unpublished diary of Sir Alfred Duff Cooper. I have to acknowledge kind permission of the Crown to quote the advice tendered to King George V by Sir Robert Vansittart on foreign affairs, and to thank Mr. Robert Mason, Chief Librarian of the Foreign Office, and Mr. Rohan Butler, historical adviser to the Foreign Secretary, for their assistance. Mrs. Sylvia Jaxa has given me great help and inspiration in the labour of travelling again over this period of history.

To W. N. Medlicott, Martin Gilbert, Richard Gott, David Dilks, Geoffrey Warner and Donald Watt, I am grateful for advice and expertise, and to the librarians of the Royal Institute of Foreign Affairs for access to various publications. The cuttings library of the *Daily Telegraph* has been invaluable for checking various references and recollections not otherwise in print.

21.10.64.   IAN COLVIN
S.W.1.

CONTENTS

Principal Characters in the
Order of Their Appearance

SIR ROBERT VANSITTART: *born 1881, died 1957.* Permanent Under-Secretary of State and Head of the British Foreign Office 1930–38, Chief Diplomatic Adviser to the Government 1938–41. Created Baron Vansittart of Denham on retirement in 1941.

STANLEY BALDWIN: *born 1867, died 1947.* Thrice Prime Minister between 1923 and 1937 and Leader of the Conservative Party. Created Earl Baldwin 1937.

RAMSAY MACDONALD: *born 1866, died 1937.* Prime Minister 1929–30, 1931–35, Leader of Labour Party.

SIR JOHN SIMON: *born 1873, died 1954.* National Liberal politician, Foreign Secretary 1931–35, member of Chamberlain Cabinet 1937–40. Created Viscount Simon 1940.

SIR WINSTON CHURCHILL: *born 1874, died 1965.* Conservative statesman, First Lord of the Admiralty 1939–40, Prime Minister 1940–45, 1950–55.

SIR SAMUEL HOARE, Baronet: *born 1880, died 1959.* Conservative politician, Foreign Secretary 1935, member of Chamberlain Cabinet 1936–40, Ambassador to Spain, 1940–44. Created Viscount Templewood 1944.

ANTHONY EDEN: *born 1897.* Conservative politician, Foreign Secretary 1935–38, resigned from Chamberlain Cabinet, Prime Minister 1955–56. Created Earl of Avon 1957.

EDWARD WOOD, Viscount (later Earl) Halifax: *born 1885, died 1959.* Foreign Secretary 1938–40, Ambassador in Washington 1941–46.

NEVILLE CHAMBERLAIN: *born 1869, died 1940.* Conservative leader, member of National Government from 1931, Prime Minister 1937–40.

SIR AUSTEN CHAMBERLAIN: *born 1863, died 1937*. Conservative statesman, half-brother to Neville Chamberlain, Foreign Secretary 1924–29.

PHILIP KERR, 11th Marquess of Lothian: *born 1882, died 1940*. Liberal politician, Ambassador in Washington 1939–40.

CHARLES VANE-TEMPEST-STEWART, 7th Marquess of Londonderry: *born 1878, died 1949*. Secretary of State for Air 1931–35.

IVAN MAISKY: *born 1884*. Russian diplomat and historian, Soviet Ambassador in London 1932–39.

SIR WARREN FISHER: *born 1879, died 1948*. Permanent Secretary to the Treasury and Head of H.M. Civil Service 1919–39.

SIR MAURICE HANKEY: *born 1877, died 1963*. Secretary to the Cabinet 1919–38, Secretary to Imperial Committee of Defence 1912–38. Created Baron Hankey 1939.

SIR HORACE WILSON: *born 1882*. Chief Industrial Adviser to the Government, 1930–39, Permanent Secretary to the Treasury and Head of H.M. Civil Service 1939–42.

JOACHIM VON RIBBENTROP: *born 1893, executed 1946*. German Ambassador in London 1936–38, Reich Foreign Minister 1938–45.

BARON KONSTANTIN VON NEURATH: *born 1870, died 1956*. German Foreign Minister 1933–38.

COUNT DINO GRANDI: *born 1894*. Italian Ambassador in London 1932–39.

PIERRE LAVAL: *born 1883, executed 1945*. French Prime Minister 1935–36, Foreign Minister 1934–35, Prime Minister 1940–44.

DR. KARL GOERDELER: *born 1885, hanged 1944*. German Opposition Leader.

YVON DELBOS: *born 1885, died 1956*. French Foreign Minister 1936–37, 1937–38.

GEORGE AMBROSE, 1st Baron Lloyd of Dolobran: *born 1879, died 1941*. Conservative politician, Secretary of State for the Colonies 1940.

SIR ALEXANDER CADOGAN: *born 1884.* Adviser on League of Nations Affairs 1929–33, Permanent Under-Secretary of State for Foreign Affairs 1938–46.

ROBERT CECIL, 5th Marquess of Salisbury: *born 1893.* As Lord Cranborne, Parliamentary Under-Secretary for Foreign Affairs 1935–38.

ALFRED DUFF COOPER: *born 1890, died 1959.* Conservative politician, First Lord of the Admiralty 1937, resigned 1938. Created Viscount Norwich 1952.

SIR NEVILE HENDERSON: *born 1882, died 1942.* Ambassador to Germany 1937–39.

DR. KURT VON SCHUSSNIGG: *born 1897.* Austrian Chancellor 1934–38.

KONRAD HENLEIN: *born 1893, died 1945.* Leader of the Sudeten-German Party in Czechoslovakia.

EWALD VON KLEIST-SCHMENZIN: *born 1888, hanged 1944.* Prussian monarchist member of the German Opposition after 1933.

GEORGES BONNET: *born 1889.* French Foreign Minister 1938–39.

DR. EDUARD BENES: *born 1884, died 1948.* President of Czechoslovakia 1935–38.

COLONEL JOSZEF BECK: *born 1894, died 1944.* Polish Foreign Minister 1932–39.

MAXIM LITVINOV: *born 1876, died 1951.* Soviet Commissar for Foreign Affairs 1930–39.

VYACHESLAV MOLOTOV: *born 1890.* Soviet Commissar for Foreign Affairs 1939–46.

FOREWORD

WHEN Sir John Wheeler-Bennett in 1962 encouraged me to undertake a book about the causes of the Second World War, he had in mind that I should relate my own part in the events immediately preceding it. He had already made reference to me in his own history of the period, *The Nemesis of Power*. Relating to the origins of the war, a vast quantity of documents had been published: the records of the International Military Tribunal at Nuremberg; the entire German Foreign Ministry archives—though not the archives of the Ribbentrop office; the documents of British Foreign Policy in H.M. Stationery Office series—though these have not, twenty years after the end of the war, been completed for the critical years 1936–37. Memoirs are numerous and various—those of the victors, including Sir Winston Churchill and Lord Avon; those of the vanquished, von Papen, General Halder, Erich Kordt. British Cabinet ministers in office during the thirties, the Earl of Halifax, Viscount Simon and Lord Templewood, wrote their own defence of appeasement in those fateful years; but Neville Chamberlain, the central political brain during the last three years of peace, left no considerable document to show what his innermost thoughts were as Prime Minister when Great Britain was playing her leading world role for perhaps the last time. After the war of 1914–18, the Liberal Prime Minister, Herbert Asquith, defined in his memoirs the five points that governed British policy then:

1. We have no obligation of any kind to France and Russia to give them military or naval help.
2. We must not forget the ties created by our long-standing and intimate friendship with France.
3. It is against British interests that France should be wiped out as a Great Power.
4. We cannot allow Germany to use the Channel as a hostile base.
5. We have obligations to Belgium to prevent its being utilised and absorbed by Germany.

I could find no such definition of British or Allied aims in 1939 other than the statements of an obligation to go to the aid of certain countries in case of aggression. Cabinet papers and internal memoranda of the British Foreign Office, as well as the proceedings of the Committee of Imperial Defence, are not open to scrutiny. It did not seem to me at first that I could add very much to the versions of recent history already told, or explain the origins of what Sir Winston Churchill has called "the unnecessary war". How was it unnecessary and why was it fought? I could myself relate the story of repeated warnings given from Germany of Hitler's plans for aggression; warnings that have been recalled in detail by the survivors of the German opposition. How could men be so blind, the reader of history may ask today? Were Allied statesmen blind or were they calculating? During some of the negotiations of 1938 and 1939, the men engaged in them appear in the documents as simpletons, as extremely shallow men or extremely devious. A. J. P. Taylor in his *Origins of the Second World War* even reaches the startling conclusion that "in principle and doctrine Hitler was no more wicked and unscrupulous than many other statesmen". The Oxford lecturer in history was tempted to this assertion after reaching the conclusion that "the war of 1939, far from being premeditated, was a mistake, the result on both sides of diplomatic blunders", and that Hitler was simply following an "historical necessity".

It seemed to me therefore essential to add to my study of the pre-war years some documentation that would show how British statesmen really thought and acted. I had myself seen three elder Ministers in their moments of indecision, in March 1939 after the policy of appeasement had failed, seeking to return to their country's traditional policy of the balance of power. In rapid succession I spoke then with Lord Simon, Lord Halifax and with Neville Chamberlain himself on the great issue whether to seek allies in Europe and at a late hour construct a system of collective security. It was a brief encounter and I never returned to the subject with them. But in the years after the war, I had made the acquaintance of a bigger man who, because he served them for ten years as their principal adviser on foreign policy, was able to form an intimate picture of the Cabinet at work and the fates at their elbow. Sir Robert Gilbert Vansittart was

Permanent Under-Secretary of State for Foreign Affairs from 1930 till 1938, and then Chief Diplomatic Adviser to the Government until 1941. After several conversations with him in the last year of his life, I asked Lady Vansittart in 1962 to let me use his posthumous papers to write the story of the years that led to the Second World War.

Over many years I had caught glimpses of Lord Vansittart first in his official work and then in public life, speaking in the House of Lords. I have likened him to a ploughman seen from a distance in a nearby field and admired for the straightness of his furrow.

Between 1935 and 1939 I was a journalist in Germany serving the London daily *News Chronicle*, and owed allegiance to no other masters than my editor and Fleet Street. I never worked for Sir Robert Vansittart at any time, though he did read some warning reports of mine on the intentions of Hitler, sent in 1938 and 1939 to friends in British political life. "Van" was in those pre-war years accessible to many journalists; for he believed in influencing the press in the interests of his country. Yet it was late in his life that I sought him out, doing so with a feeling of assurance that he had reached a plateau of calm, from which he could look back and speak freely of events long wrapped in official secrecy.

His post was that of a senior civil servant. It was, of course, not a political office. Whenever a general election gives office to a new Prime Minister, his Cabinet finds in the various ministries a complement of permanent civil servants whose function it is to effectuate whatever the policies of His Majesty's new Government shall be and to provide continuity of administration. The Chief Librarian of the Foreign Office, Mr. Robert Mason, tells me that Vansittart was the eighteenth in the line of Permanent Under-Secretaries of State for Foreign Affairs, an appointment first created in 1790. Mr. Mason writes:

"The history of this particular office is unfortunately, like so much of our administrative history, not particularly clear. The Order in Council of 21st August 1841 which settled the establishment of the Foreign Office and which is the earliest official document to mention the 'Permanent' Under-Secretary seems in this matter to have sanctified a practice already old.

"There seems always to have been at least two Under-Secretaries and for most of the time since the creation of the Foreign Office in 1782 one of them was a permanent appointment. It is this official who in the rolls of Under-Secretaries published in *Foreign Office Lists* and in other sources later than 1841 is described as '(Permanent)'. They were not so called but were in fact permanent officials."

Sometimes the term Permanent Head of the Foreign Office is used to describe the office of Permanent Under-Secretary. To Sir Robert in this post all foreign intelligence flowed. He was the Head of the Intelligence Service as well as being the senior executive official of the Foreign Office. The appointments of H.M. Ambassadors abroad were recommended by him, and to him foreign Ambassadors came for interview. He prepared reports for the Cabinet on State policy and the future. He had to forecast as far as ten years ahead whether there was likely to be a major war and where. It was his duty to inform and advise the Government on foreign affairs, and at the discretion of the Secretary-of-State for Foreign Affairs he was also able to keep the Leader of the Opposition informed of Foreign Office business. Some others have held this office for longer periods, though none recently. The era of permanent officials long in high office belongs to the past. John Backhouse was Head of the Foreign Office from 1827 to 1842, and Lord Hammond from 1854 to 1873. Sir Arthur Nicolson was Permanent Head from 1910 to 1916, a period of stresses comparable to that during which Vansittart held the same office.

My research decided me to limit my study to the years 1933–39. The year 1933 was that in which Hitler came to power. G. M. Young, in his biography of the British Prime Minister Stanley Baldwin, writes of 1933 as the year "after the Lausanne Conference when German reparations were swept up and thrown away and the whole German press burst into a demand for rearmament". Mr. Young thought this the point "the historian might perhaps choose for the beginning of the war of 1939". The appointments of Sir Robert Vansittart coincide with this entire period. I began in 1962 by using the Vansittart papers simply as a guide to events and a check on published material. But Vansittart was not a subordinate character. He seemed rather larger than human size. His impatient prose leaped out of the official foolscap sheets, and the book with each revision became more and more a book about him. If I have not attempted a biography it is because he wrote his own autobiography, *The Mist Procession*, though it fails to convey the importance of the man. Death ended his book abruptly before he was able to describe the climax of his career—the year 1937. In that year—the year of the American Neutrality Act—Neville Chamberlain decided to forsake irrevocably the policy for which Vansittart stood, the European balance of power. Anthony Eden, then Foreign Secretary, raised no objection to "dropping the pilot". The beginning of the end of British greatness lay in that decision.

The man who stood as an obstacle to their change of policy was an Englishman of orthodox thinking, the most brilliant of their career diplomats. His family was of Dutch origin and had inhabited the Rhineland Duchy of Juliers until 1598, when William Van Sittart fled to Danzig to avoid religious persecution. In 1670 Peter Van Sittart, a wealthy merchant, moved to England, where during the next century and a half his descendants flourished, bought land and manors and distinguished themselves in the service of the Crown. Nicholas Vansittart, Lord Bexley, was Chancellor of the Exchequer from 1814 to 1827. The Vansittarts intermarried with various landed families, and it is possible to trace a kinship between Robert Gilbert Vansittart and T. E. Lawrence (of Arabia), who had Vansittart blood through his grandmother, Louisa Vansittart. Of much greater interest is the suggestion of a Palmerston strain in the ancestry of Vansittart, though there is no more than presumptive evidence of a family friendship between two neighbouring country houses in the 1820's. Between that masterful English statesman of the Victorian era and the Under-Secretary of State for Foreign Affairs of four generations later there are some points of resemblance. "More like a Secretary-of-State than a permanent official", is the apt description applied to Sir Robert Vansittart by Lord Avon, who as Foreign Secretary in 1937 and 1938 had experience of his forceful personality.

I should record the circumstances in which I became the first person to write a biographical work about a British Permanent Under-Secretary of State for Foreign Affairs. For the life, personality and written work of the Permanent Head of the Foreign Office has hitherto been regarded as "not for publication". Lord Vansittart met with a refusal from the Foreign Office in 1948 when he asked for permission to write the story of his life in office. It is perhaps for this reason that his autobiography is written in a somewhat cryptic and reminiscent style. He was engaged in the last chapters of *The Mist Procession* when I met him in 1956, "and I don't think I'll live to finish it", he said. He had in fact written the last chapter in advance of some others in anticipation of this. That evening he arrived at Claridges Hotel for dinner rather breathless from the House of Lords where he had taken part in the debate. It was Winston Churchill who had put forward his name in 1941 for a peerage on his retirement, and thereafter Vansittart had devoted himself in Parliament to many causes of merit, particularly those of the victims of Nazism and Bolshevism—the refugees, the homeless, those whom the victors had forgotten in their peacemaking. He was sorry to have kept us waiting, he said, and ordered his favourite vintage champagne for dinner. I turned the conversation again to Germany, to the pre-war years, to his relations with the men of the Chamberlain Cabinet, and said that I wanted to write a book about him.

This seemed to surprise "Van". For this outstanding public servant, who in his day made and unmade Cabinet ministers, had begun to consider himself a failure. "Mine is a story of failure", he wrote in the ultimate chapter of his autobiography, "but it throws light on my time which failed too, partly because one good may oppose another, whereas evils unite."

He signified that such a book by me might come later. Then he fell to outlining the main reasons for the Second World War, as he had known them. In reliving those years he may have excited old tensions, for suddenly there was a heart attack. Lord Vansittart, however, positively refused to be taken home and directed the head waiter to place a screen round him, reclining on a sofa and still presiding at his dinner party with particular anxiety that his guests should be well entertained. I saw him again in his country home at Denham, soon recovered, though he lived only a few months longer. There he told me of an important warning to the Cabinet on Germany which—it hardly seemed credible—Anthony Eden had refused to circulate for fear of causing trouble. This paper must have been obstructed, so I surmised, in the period when the appeasers were driving a wedge between the Foreign Secretary and his chief permanent official. I last saw Lord Vansittart late in 1956 and his death occurred early in 1957. With him, for me, died an age, as much as for most people an age died with Winston Churchill.

Vansittart had known Churchill for forty-five years. They were like minded, both believing in the greatness of their country and in its rightful position of world influence. During the years of inertia, from 1934–1938, when Churchill was a rejected Conservative leader, Vansittart was a disregarded prophet. They met sometimes by stealth and sometimes openly, and Vansittart informed Churchill on the menace to Europe of "the half-mad, ridiculously dangerous demagogue Hitler". Both these Englishmen were of uncomfortable stature among their contemporaries.

Five years after the death of Lord Vansittart I returned to England from a long assignment in Africa and the Middle East, and made my way again to Denham Place, the gracious seventeenth-century house of brick and stone, where I had last seen the unheeded prophet. Lady Vansittart led me through the quiet old rooms—nothing altered here, so it seemed, since the days when Lord Vansittart sat and wrote his last recollections of diplomacy. In a Dutch tallboy I found his carefully ordered papers and, almost first among them, the warning report on Germany that he had not been allowed to send to the Cabinet in 1937. Lady Vansittart said: "So you have found it! I think he must have meant you to write the book about him."

It is difficult fully to convey in these pages the warm-hearted greatness of the man and his passionate sincerity in the service of his Government. I have taken for this book the title *None So Blind* from the saying of Jonathan Swift: "There is none so blind as they that won't see", which corresponds to the agonised comment of Vansittart: "nothing seems any good; it seems as if nobody will listen to or believe me".

It is appropriate to mention also how well informed Vansittart was on American problems. He assessed the dilemma of the United States in 1932 in a minute written at the height of the Shanghai crisis on a State memorandum:

"It is universally assumed (here) that the U.S. will never use force.

"I do not agree that this is necessarily so. Same was said of the U.S. in the Great War. Eventually she was kicked in by the Germans. Japanese may end by kicking in the U.S., if they go on long enough kicking as they are now.

"By ourselves we must eventually swallow any and every humiliation in the Far East. If there is some limit to American submissiveness this is not necessarily so."

When the European war began and the British Ambassador in Washington, the Marquess of Lothian, reported on September 6th, 1939 that the U.S. Government could not define its attitude in the event of war between Japan and Great Britain, Vansittart scrawled across his copy of the Ambassador's dispatch "Characteristic!" His policy of containing Germany had suffered a severe setback through the U.S. Neutrality Act of May 1937. He understood, however, the American dislike of dictators and was quick to remind the British Cabinet, whenever it seemed to waver, that American opinion would react strongly against deals with Hitler. His forecast of the eventual issue in the Pacific proved correct, just as his forecasts of trouble with Germany were correct ten years before war occurred.

Although the situation in the Far East is referred to, this book is concerned mainly with the European storm centre. My effort, with the guidance of the Vansittart papers, is to get nearer to the facts that are not yet known, adding them to those that are well known and often repeated. The duplicity of Hitler and Ribbentrop is well known. What is less known is how far and for how long the British were taken in by it. The anxiety of Neville Chamberlain to avoid war is well known. What is less well known is at what cost, and for how long, the British Government supposed that this was possible. President Roosevelt, it is evident from the documents, had no illusions at the outset of the war, though he was polarised between the Neutrality Act and its opponents.

Professor Alfred North Whitehead, writing to Lord Halifax from Harvard University in October 1939 on American attitudes towards England and France between 1931 and 1939, thought that "both in the East and in the cities of the Middle West, these attitudes have presented a double aspect throughout this period". His report, which Sir Robert Vansittart read attentively and underlined, spoke of a common literary and cultural background between Americans and English, but a "profound American distrust of our historical role and national characteristics. . . .

"The growing fear of German totalitarianism during the last two years or so has done little to diminish the desire of Americans for an isolationist policy, but it has convinced them that it is the manifest duty of England and France to rid the world of this danger. Opinions have been emotionally held on this point and culminated in an outbreak of almost hysterical anger and disappointment with England at the time of the Munich conference last year. Significantly it was recognised in responsible papers that the obligations of France to Czecho-slovakia were far more definite than were ours. Nevertheless it was we, rather than the French, who disappointed the Americans. From that day to this there has been no widespread confidence that we would stand by our obligations."

This was a fair analysis of both American opinion and the harmful effect upon it of recent British policy. So Europe slipped into war.

This war, then, began over a free city and a corridor, but not long after peace was restored human rivalries were again at work, forming another free city and tracing another corridor. Danzig ceased to be a powder keg and Berlin became one. This repetition of history, with its implicit lesson, has moved historians of the Second World War into the realms of philosophic speculation upon its origins, debating whether determinism or accidentalism rules human affairs, whether our stars or ourselves.

The champion of the theory of accidentalism in these pages is evidently Sir Nevile Henderson, the last British Ambassador in Berlin, and Sir Robert Vansittart wrote a sonorous contradiction of his views a month after the outbreak of war. From this it is evident that having seen all prescriptions for peace fail, he inclined to believe that the great issue was decided by manifest destiny.

I believe that I have been able to gather and add considerable detail to what some may call the accidental course of history and others the march of fate. Whatever the final verdict of history may be on the attempts to avert the Second World War, the ultimate moral of this book remains that it is best to rely, when making unalterable decisions, on the wisdom of the constitution, with its rules of Cabinet responsibility, rather than seek to manage the destinies of a nation through a cabal of Ministers. There is a ringing comment in the diary note of their principal civil servant, Sir Alexander Cadogan, when he wrote on the fateful September 13th, 1938 after Chamberlain had decided on his trip to Berchtesgaden: "Cabinet to be told what has been done". He underlined this in two spoken words to me twenty-five years later—"Quite unconstitutional!" When school children, years hence, come to study that period of lapse from greatness, the picture will be of an upright old Prime Minister, earnestly endeavouring to keep the peace of Europe, faced with a megalomaniac in charge of a vast war machine. By and large this will be the picture; but it tends to convey a dangerous simplification. Those who assume the responsibilities for today and tomorrow must not be content with half the truth. Without vision the people perish.

Ian Colvin

London, 1965

CHAPTER I

PERMANENT HEAD

On a Sunday evening in the year 1933, before dictators had begun to spoil the English week-end, little moved in between the brick front of 10 Downing Street and the stone façades of the Foreign Office. Both buildings, nearly empty except for resident clerks and door-keepers, stared at each other, as if appraising each others' secrets. On many such a Sunday, a car drove up and Sir Robert Gilbert Vansittart stepped out in the courtyard and ran briskly up the steps of the Foreign Office to have copies of the telegrams brought to him in the big room of the Permanent Under-Secretary overlooking St. James's Park. "Van" was already then something of a legend. For he had startled "the Office" out of a period of complacency in 1930, when at the age of forty-nine he became its Permanent Head, by daring to assert in official print that the world was in a retrograde period and that progress was not just round the corner.

Those in the Foreign Office who mistrusted the League of Nations, and wished for stronger and more traditional lines of British policy saw in him a leader. He was talked about as a Permanent Secretary with a literary flair, and chiefly because of the memorable paper in which he attempted in 1930 to answer the perennial question whether British policy might be founded on the usual assumption of "no major war for ten years". In 1930 he already struck a new note, declaring that *Homo sapiens might yet truly come to pass*, "but alongside and concomitant . . . goes the old Adam".

This phrase—the old Adam—recurs in his private and official papers and drafts throughout the succeeding eight years, and throughout his warnings to the Cabinet too, "the old Adam—whom I first mentioned in 1930". For even the pact of Locarno signed in 1925 he regarded as a "misleading achievement", if held up as the elimination of war. The national pride of Germany, he warned, demanded other achievements.

These he forecast in 1930 as:

1. Re-establishing Germany as a world power with colonies and mandates.
2. Anschluss with Austria.
3. Rearmament to a level of parity at least with Poland.
4. Drastic alterations to the Polish frontiers of Germany.

Since the man whom he described in 1930 as "the half-mad and ridiculously dangerous demagogue Hitler" was not yet near power, these were prescient views indeed to commit to writing in a memorandum tendering advice on foreign affairs.

The young men of the Foreign Office, the clerks, the door-keepers who had never read these papers, admired him for other reasons. Six foot one, a strongly jawed face with a twinkle of humour in his eyes, he seemed alert, comprehending and straightforward in an occupation tending to the devious and the obscure. He was besides a versatile man, with a brilliant past, and a great swell even among contemporaries who were used to wealth and fastidious living. He was an eccentric, a poet and a dramatist, and withal a successful senior civil servant. From 1920-24 he had been principal private secretary to Lord Curzon, and suffered with others from his overbearing qualities. "Lord Curzon has killed me," were the last words of one expiring Foreign Office copy clerk; and to another over-whelmed by Curzon's rudeness, Vansittart said "never mind, learn to cultivate a duck's back, as I do". He reflected that "it was from Curzon that I learned that there is no such thing as great men". "Van" had crossed Downing Street to become principal private secretary to Stanley Baldwin in 1928 and in 1929 to Ramsay Macdonald. In 1930 he became Permanent Under-Secretary of State for Foreign Affairs, being promoted over some senior men.

His formative years were at Eton, where he excelled at foreign languages, became Captain of the Oppidans and was remembered as a Captain who by firmness of personality sup-pressed bullying. His early impressions of Germany were formed at an unfortunate time. During the Boer War he spent a few months in Germany and sampled the Anglophobe hostil-ity of the master race. Birds he loved, more than shooting birds, with childhood memories of noiseless owls flying out of the elms of a noiseless Kentish countryside; and others as a young man of potting with a pistol at a butcher bird from a ship's rail in the Caspian, because it was tearing smaller birds to bits. An eccentric undoubtedly, and brilliant at languages. As attaché in Paris he had written a play in French which ran for four months. He spoke fluent French, German, Turkish, Spanish and Arabic. He had caught the spirit of James Elroy Flecker, written a cycle of poetry in his style entitled the *Singing Caravan*, written also two plays for the London stage, played bridge well, gambled for high stakes, knew everybody that there was to know in London Society. With all this he was not aloof from the less spectacular in "his service", became Vice-President of the Civil Service Boxing Club, and when he married Sarita, widow of Sir Colville Barclay in 1931, founded a welfare fund for the dependants of the Foreign Office. On the distaff side Robert Vansittart was related to T. E. Lawrence of Arabia, whose grandmother was Louisa Vansittart. One of the Vansittarts, Nicholas, Lord Bexley, had been Chancellor of the Exchequer in 1815 and bewigged portraits of other Vansittart notables hung round the tall panelled rooms and up the staircase of the Buckinghamshire manor of Denham Place. There among tapestries and silver he entertained his friends in the Cabinet after tennis with talk over the champagne. "He was much more a Secretary of State in mentality than a permanent official," wrote Lord Avon in recollection of games of tennis and listening to "Van" on foreign affairs. And Permanent Head he remained from 1930 till 1937, under three Prime Ministers and five Foreign Secretaries, himself responsible for continuity in the foreign policy of Great Britain.

Sir Robert, described by a German diplomat as immensely industrious, used to foreshorten the week-ends of his eight years in office, read the telegrams, drive on to his town house at 44 Park Street and arrive on Monday morning at the office again, having slept on that knowledge which his departmental heads had not yet assimilated.

Of British diplomacy in his early career he retained two impressions—a magisterial memorandum by Sir Eyre Crowe in 1907 had clearly defined the threat of German military power to Europe, but the Cabinet had not been sufficiently impressed by it. In 1911 the Foreign Secretary, Sir Edward Grey, had failed, so Vansittart thought, to bring home to the Commonwealth prime ministers the imminence of the danger in Europe. These lessons Vansittart had laid up in his heart.

When the year 1933 began with the accession to power of Adolf Hitler in Germany, Ramsay Macdonald was the Prime Minister of Britain in a Coalition Government, Stanley Baldwin Lord President of the Council, and Sir John Simon Foreign Secretary. The Prime Minister was abstractly interested in international affairs. The Lord President abhorred them. Sir John believed that his own legal brilliance would necessarily enable him to master foreign problems. These were the years when disarmament and rearmament overlapped and the nations still wavered between the Covenant of the League of Nations and air power as the alternative guarantees to their security. Mr. Anthony Eden as Under-Secretary in the Foreign Office, and later as Lord Privy Seal, was specially entrusted with League affairs; and the League itself, having failed in the Manchukuo dispute, was in its first real functional crisis. The British Cabinet at these crossways in history should have looked to Vansittart for advice. His advice was insistent. Rearm.

His assessments of Hitler in 1933, and the two probable causes of war, Czechoslovakia and Poland, were terse and accurate and remarkable. But he was reporting to a failing Prime Minister; in Ramsay Macdonald the spark was dying; what Baldwin felt and thought we shall shortly see. The Foreign Secretary Sir John Simon, was forever legalising the issues, confessedly unaware of what men were thinking. As for Eden, he looked to be the coming young man; but in the year that Hitler emerged to power, it was Eden's misfortune to be labouring in Geneva at a new draft Disarmament Convention on the shaky premiss that "since we were so weak in air power any international limitations were bound to be to our advantage".* The world still thought in terms of large navies, but had turned also to fleets of military aircraft. Russia led numerically with an estimated 1,890 machines, France was second in strength, the U.S.A. third, Italy fourth, Japan fifth and Britain sixth; while Germany was still supposed to have no Luftwaffe. Supported in his efforts by Alexander Cadogan,† Anthony Eden had been pursuing with tenacity his purpose of making the League of Nations work, though many Englishmen of his day mistrusted the League, very much as they later mistrusted the United Nations Organisation. Still Eden persevered.

* *Facing the Dictators*, p. 29.
† The Hon. Alexander Cadogan, British Representative at the League of Nations.

Sir Robert in May 1933, seeing from Berlin dispatches how in the past three months Hitler had consolidated his internal power, made a relatively cautious assessment that "only the future can show whether aggressive militarism is an essential element in this policy of national regeneration". He did not leave the future long in doubt; for by July, after reading more dispatches from the strong pen of Sir Horace Rumbold, British Ambassador in Berlin, his comments were unmistakeably clear. While reaffirming that British policy was founded on the League and its Covenant, he estimated that the League of Nations had fallen into "increasing discredit".

Among a score of solemn commitments and treaties binding Britain all over the world, the untried League Covenant had been given first place in the foreseeable future.

The Treaty of Locarno, coming next in importance to the Treaty of Versailles, committed Britain to maintain the existing territorial arrangements in that area with which the signatories' interests were most closely bound up, "namely, the frontier between Germany and her Western neighbours". Germany, Belgium, France, Great Britain and Italy severally and collectively guaranteed:

    (*a*) the territorial *status quo* resulting from the frontiers between Germany and Belgium and Germany and France;
    (*b*) the inviolability of those frontiers;
    (*c*) the demilitarisation of the Rhineland.

The Treaty of Versailles had entitled France to make war, if Germany in any way violated articles 42 and 43 of that treaty. The Locarno Treaty limited this right to the case of a flagrant breach of article 42 or 43; that is, an aggressive concentration of German forces in the demilitarised Rhineland. The Locarno Treaty modified Britain's commitments to uphold the Versailles Treaty, and significantly left Germany's eastern frontiers unguaranteed, a cause of latent suspicion to Russia, to say nothing of Poland and Czechoslovakia.

The Daladier government in France declined in 1933 to consider the question of revision of European frontiers. France maintained its treaties with Yugoslavia, Poland and the Little Entente. I find in his personal notes that Sir Robert thought "relations between Germany and Poland are little changed", and "it would be erroneous to suppose that Germany has in any way become reconciled to the Polish Corridor and its separation from Danzig". Czechoslovakia he described as having "an Achilles heel in the presence of 2 million Germans within her borders and her constant obsession was that an *Anschluss* between Germany and Austria would mean physical and economic encirclement". Of Italy his 1933 assessment presented an interesting conclusion, that became a key to his diplomacy in the next two years.

Despite a disclaimer by Mussolini that any traditional friendship existed with Britain, "it is a fact that direct conflict between the interests of the two countries is rare; and the likelihood that this country will be drawn into hostilities with Italy, save in virtue of our obligations under the Covenant of the League of Nations, may still be said, as heretofore, to be remote". At the same time he noted that Italy had "joined the expansionist powers".

Sir Horace Rumbold from Berlin sent him reports on the *Machtübernahme* and subsequent consolidation of Nazi power that lacked nothing in frankness and clarity. Sir Eric Phipps, his successor in the Berlin Embassy, and later Sir Nevile Henderson, the third and last British Ambassador to the Third Reich, failed to represent the changing scene with the same force and vision as Rumbold, whose appointment ended, however, that same year of 1933 under the sixty year rule of retirement. Vansittart was strict in applying the rule, as he was in his view that diplomats should go where they were sent and not argue for other posts. It must seem that every rule ought to have its exceptions.

Sir Horace, in his dispatch 425 of April 25th, 1933, summed up·Hitler's achievement in the first three months of power as negligible in the economic field, but politically full of menace. The Germans had to rearm on land and lull their opponents into security so that they could be attacked one by one. On this Sir Robert commented: "The present régime in Germany will, on past and present form, loose off another European war just so soon as it feels strong enough. . . . The conclusion is that if we wish to avoid the disaster for which Hitlerism is working, we must keep as close as possible to the United States, to France, and, if possible, also to Italy and bring the last two together."

On May 10th 1933 he described the possibilities to Sir John Simon as:

1. Collapse of Hitler through economic failure, followed either by a military dictatorship or Bolshevism.
2. Success of Hitler, followed by a European war in four or five years' time.
3. A preventive war on Germany before Germany is strong enough to attack anyone else. This would undoubtedly rally the German nation to Hitler, as Sir Horace Rumbold had pointed out, "but it would *at present* rally it in vain— which he (Sir Horace) does not say. These are singularly uninviting alternatives."

The idea of preventive war in 1933 had also occurred to Brigadier Arthur Temperley, British military representative at the League of Nations, who produced a memorandum early in May arguing that Germany was like a mad dog that must be destroyed or locked up before it could do harm. Vansittart forwarded his memorandum to the Cabinet but "to no effect".* Temperley was at this time engaged with Eden in trying to negotiate a draft Disarmament Convention with Germany, to whom the memorandum was shown before Vansittart sent it to the Cabinet. Germany "is powerless before the French army and our Fleet," wrote Temperley. "Hitler, for all his bombast, must give way." Of the Temperley memorandum there is no word in Lord Avon's memoirs. In a letter at the time Eden reported to Baldwin the difficulties of getting progress with disarmament.†

The Nazis sensed the mistrust that was building up against them abroad. Goering had tried to allay it in 1931 in conversations with Arthur Yencken, a British diplomat, during which he emphasised that a Nazi Germany would not equip Soviet Russia industrially, an assurance calculated to allay British dislike of the emergent party. Hitler was also sensitive to reactions against his anti-Semitic excesses.

The Counsellor of the German Embassy, Gottfried von Bismarck, brought Hitler's Minister for Germans Abroad, Dr. Alfred Rosenberg into the Foreign Office on May 11th, 1933 to meet Vansittart, who told him forcibly of the strong feelings aroused in England by Nazi behaviour towards the Jews. Rosenberg argued the Nazi case, drew a picture of Communist plots to seize power in Germany, gave the numbers of those in

* *Mist Procession.*   † *Facing the Dictators.*

concentration camps as only 12,000 and defended the National Socialist programme as "social" rather than militarist. On this same morning Hitler was passionately haranguing Sir Horace Rumbold in the Berlin Chancellery and explaining the Rosenberg visit to London. "Never" he shouted at the British Ambassador, "will I agree to the existence of two kinds of law for German nationals. There is immense unemployment in Germany. . . . The Jews must suffer with the rest. . . . If Jews engineer a boycott of German goods abroad, I will see that this hits the Jews in Germany." The shrewd conclusion of Sir Horace was that "it would be a mistake to believe that anti-Semitism was the policy of his wilder men whom he has difficulty in controlling".

Hitler was himself a fanatic on the subject, said Rumbold. In Whitehall Dr. Rosenberg laid a large wreath on the Cenotaph inscribed to the dead of the Great War. An unknown man removed it and threw it in the Thames.

Signor Mussolini confided in Sir Ronald Graham, the British Ambassador, on May 13th as they sat watching an Italy versus England football match in Rome that "he was doing all he could to be friendly to Germany, but Germans made it very difficult to be friends".* Herr Tauschitz, Austrian Minister in Berlin, discovered the same thing in Berlin three days later, when Hitler stormed at Austria for suppressing Nazi subversive activities, and threatened economic reprisals. "It is all terrible" exclaimed Baron von Neurath to the Austrian, gently closing the door behind them and putting his hands to his head in a gesture of despair. This year it seemed that there might be the crisis that happened only in 1938. A British Foreign Office memorandum of May 30th, 1933 discussed the possibility of a "pacific blockade (without declaration of war) of the German coast". It found such action not precluded by the Locarno Treaty. On land there could only be invasion of Germany by a unanimous vote of the League Council. Even the "pacific blockade" could only be imposed after putting the dispute to the League Council or The Hague International Court. This meant that a massive violation by Germany of the Rhineland demilitarised zone was the sole possible move that could be quickly and effectively countered without recourse to League and treaty procedure and delays.

* Documents on British Foreign Policy, Series II, Vol. V.

Late in July, the Austrian Minister to the Court of St. James, Herr von Franckenstein, called on Vansittart and recalled to him an anxious discussion of Nazi aggressive policy held with Dr. Dollfuss during the Austrian Chancellor's visit to London. Herr von Franckenstein now reported Nazi subversion in Austria as intensifying and said that it included incursions by leaflet-dropping aircraft from Germany. "The moment had come," he said, "when the Austrian Government felt entitled to ask interested Governments to support Austria openly."

Sir Robert Vansittart's hand appears forcefully in the ensuing instructions to the British Ambassadors in Paris and Rome, proposing three-power representations to Germany on this "entirely justifiable request". But there was a cautious response from Mussolini, of whom Sir Ronald Graham commented "so far as I can interpret ... Signor Mussolini, owing to the affinity between National-Socialist Germany and Fascist Italy can exercise a special influence in Berlin which ... he ... could lose by joining a common front with Great Britain and France."

To a suggestion from one Foreign Office colleague that the Nazis *might* still be better than the German Nationalists whom they had displaced, Vansittart observed that "all proof is yet to come". By July 7th, 1933, he had made up his mind on the argument often repeated in that year that Hitlerism was less dangerous than Communism.

This was not an argument to be found in Foreign Office papers, but it was a familiar topic of Club and City dinner conversations, linked with the reasoning that Nazi excesses were on a far smaller scale than those committed in Bolshevik Russia. Sir Robert has preserved his 1933 comments: "It does not help us," he wrote to Sir John Simon, "to compare the internal excesses of Hitlerism with those of Bolshevism: the latter of course are vastly greater at present. But that is beside the point. We cannot take the same detached and highbrow view of Hitlerism as we can of Bolshevism or Fascism, precisely because these are not really and vitally dangerous to us, and Hitlerism *is* exceedingly dangerous. Fascism has never presented the least danger to this country, and Russia has been too incompetent a country to be really dangerous, even under Bolshevism. But Germany is an exceedingly competent country, and she is visibly being prepared to external aggression.

I do not think that anything but evil and danger for the rest of the world can come out of Hitlerism, whichever way the dice fall in Germany."

Not all his colleagues shared this outlook. Mr. Basil Newton, later to be British Minister in Prague in the crucial years 1937-39, in a letter from Berlin of August 30th to Orme Sargent in the Foreign Office described the Nazi movement as "a movement of youth . . . which . . . may have rather overshot the mark of what is typical for Germany. . . . I think that we should try to reserve judgment on tendencies in Germany until the present régime has been in power at least a year, if not longer."

But Vansittart's mind was clear. On August 28th, 1933 he submitted to Sir John Simon an important "Memorandum on the Present and Future Position in Europe", making plain the dangers of a *Putsch* in which Austria would be annexed by Germany, either forcibly or by threat of force.

"A glance at Hitler's past will suffice to show that Austria is for him the psychological obsession of the renegade. But it is more than that: it is his first trial of strength with the forces of a detested stability, and on the success or failure of this will to domination, the success or failure of his régime may in large measure hinge.

"Hitler may vary his methods, but he will not abandon—save under compulsion—his firm intention of destroying Austrian independence and creating a *de facto* 'Anschluss'.

"All Europe would be affected by this event, but Italy more than anyone else. We have no official knowledge how she would meet it; but there is a distinct possibility that she would meet any irruption from Germany by an irruption from Italy—however ill this would square with League principles.

"I do not doubt that Italy is most truly and heartily at one with us in our desire to preserve Austrian independence. At present—let us make no mistake about it—we are all backing a losing horse in Austria. That is no reason for not pursuing to the best of our ability a vital policy, the more so when we ask ourselves what if and when the horse has lost? Italy still clings to the vanishing asset of her 'special position'. She has not yet the vision or the courage to face the facts, which are quite clearly that Germany is playing with her.

"If this estimate of Hitlerism is correct, nothing but a change of heart can avert another catastrophe; and that change of the German heart is unlikely to come from within, for the true German nature has never changed. Its effectual semblance can only be induced from without. The means of such inducement will be dealt with later. Austria has only been chosen for the first break through, because it is the easiest and weakest point. The next move will be upon the Polish Corridor; and the Germans, elated by the success of their first trial of strength, and encouraged by the Japanese demonstration that the League will only talk, will only delay the move until her armaments are sufficient to enable her to cope with Poland. Practically no German doubts that the Corridor must and will be regained. 'There is no doubt whatsoever about the ultimate intentions of the Nazis.' The Polish Minister for Foreign Affairs has recently used almost these words.

"But Poland is in no yielding mood. The Corridor is, and has been for nigh 2,000 years, ethnologically almost pure Polish. Those who have swallowed the persistent German propaganda on the subject have followed, consciously or subconsciously, the normal human instinct to get rid of a bone of contention between a weaker and a stronger Power by a settlement in favour of the latter—the same instinct as is now prompting Soviet Russia to get rid of the Chinese Eastern Railway spontaneously.

"But the position is now that the Poles will cede nothing while the Germans demand everything. The moment for compromise thus seems to have passed—barring that change of heart, which, politically so rarely comes from within. Poland will fight; but—a few years hence—will 30 million human beings be able to hold 60 m.? Of course not, alone. But if Poland is destroyed and if Italy is out of the picture, as she may well be on the assumption of preceding paragraphs in this memorandum, Germany will, a few years later, be able to do the very thing that she could never hope to do in 1914— to fight on one front, for, by herself, Czechoslovakia would hardly count on the second front."

Such was his view in August 1933 and in the six ensuing years what need would there have been to alter a word of it?

He advocated an economic squeeze to keep Germany lean.

"We can ill afford to let Hitlerite Germany prosper. The Trades Union Congress is also of this opinion, though for different motives—see their recently announced boycott of German goods. If the foregoing views are sound, it is, however, a not unwelcome announcement. Ought we not to wish strongly enough to see Hitlerism fail, to be prepared at least to risk the consequences, which could hardly be more dangerous to European peace? German communism has never seemed a menace to any observer who k ows the German character, and is not gulled by German propaganda as to the fictitious 'dangers' from which Hitlerism saved a Germany that required no saving. The collapse of Hitlerism should leave Germany too weak and disordered for external aggression. That is the essential point. We are now at a pass where 'peace in our time' (and even in Eastern Europe) must be the first consideration."

Reference to the League could and would lead to economic pressure. Would it be effective? Hitler might trade with Russia, not a member of the League. Many considerations must be weighed. "But we find ourselves always back at the point where we have to consider, in the face of *every* consideration, whether this grave matter ought to be kept from the League: whether the League can afford another failure, whether *we* can afford a world in which the League would have been practically destroyed by a triumphant Hitler, whose real doctrines are all incompatible with the League. What would be the fate within a decade of a world so situated, and of this country in particular?" He recommended to the Cabinet that economic pressure on Germany might either be confined to the Austrian issue or that they should "tackle Germany's already existing secret armaments concurrently".

But in the mood of Britain and France at that time, his proposal was fated to run into the sand. Of the three solutions considered by the French preventive war and unilateral rearmament were ruled out. (Economic sanctions against Germany were not mentioned.) When he met Eden on September 18th, 1933, Daladier preferred to work for a triple accord with Italy and Britain.* Although then much concerned with Geneva, Eden does not refer in his memoirs to the Vansittart proposal to arraign Germany before the League in 1933. Would there be an arms race with Germany to maintain Britain's lead in air

* *The Mist Procession.*

strength? This seemed the last grim alternative after the Vansittart proposal of August 28th was disregarded.

On September 6th, the British military attaché in Berlin forwarded a detailed report on expansion of Nazi para-military organisations, on which Sir Robert commented:

"The aims of Germany are quite clear: and already a formidable force has been half constructed for their realisation. In a relatively brief while the reconstruction will be complete." He directed that this information must be forwarded to Mr. Eden at the Geneva disarmament talks.

In October 1933 the German delegation walked out of the Disarmament Conference. With preventive war and economic sanctions rejected, to rearm more quickly or to keep the Allied armed services "lean" were the two remaining courses. All that could recommend the latter course was the hope that Germany would not embark on an arms race. Here was an opportunity for Sir Robert Vansittart to reinforce his demand for massive rearmament. For this was the first open act of Germany on the path towards war.

But at this moment a small event intervened in the shape of a British by-election. In East Fulham, one Alderman William Waldron, President of the Conservative Constituency Association, had managed to get himself adopted as Conservative candidate without any other name being considered for interview. His opponent of the Independent Labour Party, Mr. John Wilmot, was a strong candidate. The mood of the East Fulham by-election shows how the National Government in 1933 drifted towards Appeasement. Five days after the German walk-out from Geneva, Baldwin's electoral message to Alderman Waldron said nothing of rearmament. In Fulham Town Hall on October 23rd, Mr. George Lansbury leader of the Parliamentary Party, raised the spectre of war and accused the Conservatives of wanting it. Unemployment, the dole, the means test, the war bogy, the personalities of the candidates were all factors in the ballot.

The upshot was that a Conservative majority of 14,500 in East Fulham at the previous election became a Socialist majority of 4,800—a landslide of 19,400 votes. Mr. Wilmot regarded his victory as "a message of hope to all who are working for peace in every country". This was the fifth by-election of twenty-four since the General Election to be won by the Socialists. The swing so impressed Stanley Baldwin, himself deeply pacifist at heart, that he read into it perhaps more importance than was necessary. He sent for Vansittart.

Lord Vansittart related to me in some detail what happened between him and the Lord President of the Council.

"You are the most powerful man in the country, Van, and you can boot me out if you like," Baldwin began: "but I cannot go to the country on rearmament. Look at these East Fulham results".

Vansittart protested: "I have no power, Sir, in that way, as you must know. I am a civil servant and the tradition is that I do as I am told."

Baldwin looked at him, an eyebrow cocked as if in disbelief, his broad sagacious face downcast.

"Well, I can't take rearmament to the country."

Vansittart spoke familiarly in the language of the gaming tables. "You have a *caisse de jeu* to make any gambler's mouth water. You can lose a packet and still have a majority of 250."

"Baldwin reminded me that he knew much more about this sort of thing than I did. . . . British ministers did not neglect rearmament, but handled it gingerly. In the year after Fulham, they nerved themselves for an increase in the Air Estimates that was promising but insufficient."

Mr. Baldwin found foreign affairs tedious, and he mused that "the man who says he can see far ahead is a charlatan". As the years went by, Vansittart found that he counted less with Baldwin, and the Prime Minister's week-end visits to Denham Place became more infrequent. There were other less inconvenient advisers.

Germany left the League of Nations in December 1933. The British Government instructed the British Ambassador in Berlin to raise the question of Storm Troop formations privately with Hitler. This Sir Eric Phipps, successor to Sir Horace Rumbold did on December 8th. He reported, "Hitler assured me that the S.A. and S.S. might be compared to the Salvation Army." The Ambassador noted that "here I regret to say I laughed". Sir Eric, brother-in-law of Vansittart, was the last British Ambassador who could laugh at Hitler. The Chancellor assured the Ambassador that he was willing to sign non-aggression pacts with all neighbouring states, especially France, Poland, Czechoslovakia, Yugoslavia and England.

Sir Robert commented on the dispatches of this time that he shared the scepticism of Sir Eric Phipps in doubting the value of Hitler's signature, but that British policy seemed to offer no option other than a solution seeking ostensible faith in signatures. There was the alternative of an armaments race and its likely though not inevitable end, a race in which moreover Britain would, in the existing condition and temper of the country, be left far behind. As to such international signatures, Vansittart noted that: "I shall remain a resolute sceptic as long as this intensive militarisation of the entire German race is carried on with its present speed and bitterness. The explanaation that all this is needed against Communism is ridiculous. And there is only one other explanation." A dispatch from the British Embassy in Paris of December 6th* confirmed Vansittart's misgivings on the growing strength of Germany and the inability of France and her allies to do anything about it. Colonel T. G. Heywood, the British military attaché in Paris, wrote that the French General Staff expected Germany to have a more powerful army than France by 1938, with more modern equipment and aircraft, and a more mobile war industry.

Vansittart commented on the anxieties of the French General Staff contained in this dispatch.

"According to this, Germany is going to be far more powerful than France (and far more powerful than in 1914) by 1938. For there is no question of preventing Germany from rearming. They have only talked. And so the moment for choosing has passed, even if they were disposed to act, which I still do not think they are. Personally I do *not* believe in the sincerity of Hitler's pacific professions. In that case the attitude of our people may cost them dear by 1938."

As a forecast in the year 1933 of what befell in the year of the Munich Agreement, this was no overstatement.

* Documents on British Foreign Policy, II, VI.

CHAPTER II

ENCIRCLEMENT OR APPEASEMENT?

At one of the evening courts at Buckingham Palace in 1933, Sir Robert and Lady Vansittart were watching a diplomat and his wife walking about the State rooms among the levée of glittering folk. He was of short stature, pale complexion and wore a small, *impériale* beard. This dark tag on his chin made Ivan Maisky, the Russian Ambassador to the Court of St. James, an easily recognisable figure during his many years in London. The simple court dress of his wife was also a sign that these two did not feel that they fitted entirely in this royal occasion. Nor did others think so, for there was no nod or pause to exchange a few words, and when they sat for a moment on one of the wall sofas, a Peeress sitting next to Madame Maisky twitched up her skirt and walked away. It was at this moment that Lady Vansittart felt moved to sit down beside the Russian Ambassador's wife and begin an animated conversation. So that when in the year 1934 it became necessary to think of practical steps for the security of Europe, Sir Robert and Lady Vansittart were already familiar friends of the Maiskys. The house at 44 Park Street was the first in London where Ivan Maisky was entertained, and Lady Vansittart used to go to the Soviet Embassy for tea with Madame Maisky, who occasionally entertained her guests with Russian folk songs.

There is no indication in his papers that Vansittart felt it politic to befriend the Maiskys. It seemed to arise in the nature of things that he would go ahead of others and on his own responsibility. Maisky, an economist and one of the former Menshevik party, was sensitive to kindness. Of his reception by King George V in November 1932 he spoke to Lady Vansittart with some wonder—"the King was so kind", Maisky hesitated . . . "I thought he would look upon me as a . . . murderer. But it was quite different from what I expected."

Sometimes Maisky grew impatient of the continued prejudices of London society . . . "after all, if we are regicides, if we killed Czar Nicholas, you killed King Charles and the French sent Louis XVI to the guillotine".

"Yes", exclaimed Lady Vansittart, "but that was two centuries ago and more, and you killed the entire imperial family. Why!", she added with a characteristic English reflex, "you even killed their dog!"

Maisky liked frankness and sincerity, and the friendship flourished into 1934. Of Vansittart he wrote:* "a clever and cultivated man, of course flesh of the flesh of the ruling class of Great Britain. His divinity was the British Empire. Vansittart was a warm supporter of the rebirth of the Entente, and took advantage of his position in the British machinery of Government really to do a great deal in this direction." He spoke of Vansittart helping Louis Barthou to work for a triple Entente.

Insistent for rearmament, Vansittart had worked all that winter in the Defence Requirements Committee with Sir Warren Fisher, Permanent Head of the Treasury, and Sir Maurice Hankey, Secretary of the Imperial Defence Committee, to amend British defences. Meanwhile the politicians discussed the British draft disarmament plan at Geneva, and Germany clamoured for the conceded right to rearm to new levels, privily doing so all the time.

The decision was near at hand whether it was to be encirclement of Germany or appeasement of her claims. There were those in the Conservative Party in England, and in the amorphous social strata beneath it, who saw Germany as the future policeman of Europe, while others thought that Hitler could be turned conveniently eastwards to exhaust his energies in conflict with Soviet Russia. Such idiocy existed, Winston Churchill explained to Maisky in the summer of 1934, but it was not his way of thinking or that of Sir Robert Vansittart. Nor were the Conservatives alone to blame. To many in the Socialist ranks France was still the embodiment of reactionary Continental power in 1934. The British Ambassador in Paris reported disquiet in French Government circles at the prospect of Britain detaching herself from France and assuming a balancing position between her and Germany. In Cliveden House, the home of Viscount Astor, which became conspicuous at that time as a social centre for those who believed in the policy of appeasement, the purposeful adherence of Vansittart to the French alliance was noticed. One of this circle, the Welsh philanthropist and Downing Street habitué, Tom Jones, managed to slip

* *Who helped Hitler?*

in a word against Vansittart in April 1934 when Baldwin remarked to him that, "Vansittart hates the Germans." Jones interposed that, "diplomats should have nothing to do with hatred of anybody. It is both silly and dangerous." Baldwin replied: "I've always said you were a Christian." Jones noted: "I keep on and on preaching against the policy of ostracising Germany, however incalculable Hitler and his crew may be, and the duty of resisting Vansittart's pro-French bias."*

In fact when Tom Jones made his insinuations, Baldwin had already been sent a paper by Sir Robert, dated April 7th, 1934, which adequately replied to them:

"It may perhaps be asked", he wrote, "whether the Defence Requirements Committee, in its recent report, was justified in taking Germany as the ultimate potential enemy. It is possible that such doubt may be entertained, if no opportunity has been given to see as a whole the evidence on which such a conclusion is based; and this paper is written to supply that deficiency."

He proceeded to a review of German policy and political literature from 1925 onwards including the unexpurgated 1925 edition of Hitler's *Mein Kampf.* "The foundation of Herr Hitler's faith is that man is a fighting animal. Pacifism is therefore the deadliest sin. Had the German race been united in time, Hitler argues, it would now be master of the globe. The new Reich must therefore include all the Germans in Europe. This would mean not only Austria but South Tyrol, Memel, Czechoslovakia, Eupen, Malmedy, Luxemberg, Slesvig, German Switzerland." Sir Robert had already alluded to Danzig, the Polish Corridor and Upper Silesia. "But Germany must not repeat the mistake of fighting all her enemies at once. She must single out the most dangerous in turn and attack him with all her forces.

"The French are right as regards the demilitarised zone. It is only a question of time, at most until Germany is strong enough to prevent reoccupation by France, before some overt breach of treaty obligations occurs there—a matter directly concerning this country. . . . If we have taken Germany to be a potential enemy we are in the company of most of the political minds in Europe. Everywhere in fact, is to be found the anticipation that within strictly measurable time Germany will be practising a policy of blackmail or force. . . .

"I have heard it suggested, particularly in the City, whose

* *Diary with Letters,* Oxford University Press.

feeling in respect of Germany has been a millstone round the neck of this country, that the Foreign Office is anti-German and pro-French. It goes without saying that no capable or trustworthy public servant can be pro- or anti- any foreign country. It is his business to think of the feeling and interests of his own country and of the Government that directs it. It is his responsibility, however, to record facts, however unpalatable, nor is it his fault or desire that the facts should all point in one direction. To many including myself it may indeed not seem unnatural that Germany wishes to recover part at least of what she had, and I have in the past made no secret of my view that a long-range policy must aim at the reconciliation of revisionist ideas with anti-revisionist fears. But Nazi Germany has rudely disturbed the atmosphere. Her citizens are being innoculated with the fanatical doctrine that force is not only the sole but the intrinsically noble and desirable means of realising her ambitions. That is why Germany left Geneva. Even if she returns under prayers and pressure, these ambitions and these consequences will not be changed, unless she changes her heart and her teaching to the rising generation. There lies the only acceptable test."*

Baldwin disliked being drawn into foreign affairs. He came to solace himself with the advice of the fourth of the senior civil servants, Sir Horace Wilson, the Chief Industrial Adviser to the Government, "wise, calm, serene", in preference to Vansittart.† The Lord President did bestir himself in March 1934 when the Air Estimates were taken. He stated that the Government's policy was "no inferiority to any country within striking distance". He put forward in 1934 a programme of 41 new air squadrons, but spread over five years—too long a period for safety, Vansittart thought.

Plainly then since Colonel Heywood's dispatch had pointed the danger, and since the combined military power of Britain and France was not sufficient to deter Germany from rearming to her own requirements, there must be another road to safety. The issue was in the crudest terms encirclement or appeasement. At this moment emerged for a period tragically short the mobile and persuasive figure of Louis Barthou, Foreign Minister of France.

Safety in the mind of Louis Barthou lay in adding an Eastern

* Documents on British Foreign Policy, Series II, Vol. VII.
† *Mist Procession.*

Pact in Europe to the Locarno Treaty. He divulged this plan to Eden in May 1934, after talks in Geneva with M. Litvinov, explaining that he aimed also at the entry of Russia into the League of Nations. Eden noted with some misgivings that Barthou envisaged the Pact as based mainly upon Russia and France. The British reaction was that an Eastern Pact ought to include Germany, just as Germany had been included in the Locarno Pact of 1925. That this was a very different Germany in 1934 seemed not of decisive importance to Sir John Simon. Accordingly the French were told of British views and the French Ambassador in Berlin was instructed to inform the German Foreign Ministry that the Eastern Pact could be extended to include Germany. M. François-Poncet explained on June 7th that this offer was being made to avoid the impression of a policy of encirclement. Herr von Hoesch, the German Ambassador in London called on Vansittart on June 12th to tell him of this approach and added that Germany was not likely to accede to an arrangement which would put her inside a combination of states, in which "she would not be sure of getting fair treatment".*

Vansittart noted the remarks of the German Ambassador, and divined the real misgivings behind the objections. He determined to pursue his own diplomacy as to the Eastern Pact, and Ivan Maisky described as "a very curious one" the form of initiative that Vansittart took a few days later.

A luncheon party was arranged at 44 Park Street, at which Maisky found himself seated on the right of Lady Vansittart while His Majesty's Principal Secretary of State, Sir John Simon, sat on her left. This was actually in keeping with the protocol, but the table arrangement seems to have impressed Maisky. On this same day, on instructions from Vansittart, Lord Chilston called on M. Litvinov in Moscow to enquire "as to the precise nature and extent of the proposed Eastern Pact".† The British Ambassador found Litvinov "a little ruffled and disappointed that his ideas did not receive from some powers more attention and approval in Geneva".‡

At lunch that day Maisky was also impressed at the confidential manner of Lady Vansittart when she asked him how he

* Documents on British Foreign Policy, Series II, Vol. VI.
† *Who helped Hitler?*
‡ Documents of British Foreign Policy, Series II, Vo. VI.

liked it in London. He in reply touched on his "great difficulties".

"I suppose it's my neighbour on the left who is making these difficulties," she murmured, turning away from Sir John. Maisky nodded.

"Then why should you not have a frank talk about this with Van?"

Maisky had already observed that Simon and Vansittart did not see eye to eye, but he replied to her that he hesitated to take such an initiative.

"I will undertake it myself," Lady Vansittart volunteered. Somewhat to his astonishment Maisky was telephoned two days later from the Foreign Office and on July 3rd Sir Robert and he had the first of several talks about Anglo-Soviet relations and the proposed Eastern Pact. Before the month was out Vansittart had invited Winston Churchill and Maisky to the same dinner table at 44 Park Street and after the ladies had left them Churchill unfolded his grand design in words which Maisky recalled:

"Now I consider that the greater danger to the British Empire is Germany, and therefore now I am the enemy of Germany. At the same time I consider that Hitler is making ready to expand not only against us but to the east, against you. Why should we not join forces to combat our common enemy?"*

At another of their meetings Churchill avowed to Maisky that there were people in Britain who argued that Germany should be allowed to carve out an empire for herself in eastern and south-eastern Europe "but I am firmly convinced that in the long run the victory will be, not with the supporters of western security, but with those who, like Vansittart and myself, consider that peace is indivisible."†

The French Ambassador, M. Charles Corbin, handed to Vansittart on July 7th, a draft of the proposed Eastern Pact, and on July 9th, 1934, began a series of meetings at the Foreign Office between M. Barthou and a French delegation and Sir John Simon and his advisers:

"Do the British Government think it good to try to turn Russia with its population of 160 millions towards peace?" M. Barthou asked Sir John Simon, in probable knowledge of Sir John's prejudices.

* *Who helped Hitler?*   † Ibid.

Sir John in his guarded replies pointed out that whereas this was a proposal for an Eastern Pact of Russia, the Baltic states, Poland, Germany and Czechoslovakia, it was also proposed that Russia should guarantee her help to France in case of need. Sir John evidently thought that this smelled of the "encirclement" of Germany. He doubted whether Germany would adhere to such an agreement. He argued that Russia was brought in to the advantage of France but not to the advantage of other countries. He made it plain that he still had hopes that Germany would adhere to a disarmament plan. "If the Eastern Pact was merely a proposal for more security in Central and Eastern Europe, then opinion (in Britain) would be very critical," said Sir John.

Vansittart interposed that it would be desirable to present the Eastern Pact "as a preface to a new start in the Disarmament Conference".

After this meeting Vansittart worked out a formula which Barthou and Simon agreed—that the Eastern Pact, with Germany included, would be a starting point for a convention providing for a reasonable interpretation of German claims to equality in armaments. Thus far they had succeeded, although Barthou returned to France exasperated at the manner and suspicions of Sir John Simon. Vansittart worked on and Russia was brought into the comity of the League of Nations on September 17th, 1934, by the invitation of fifty nations.

"Well, now, we have become members of one and the same club", remarked Vansittart to Maisky.*

But the initiative towards an Eastern Pact failed on the obdurate attitude of Poland. This was a setback to the policy of defensive encirclement. Meanwhile, Germany had been thrown into a state of confusion by the purges of June 30th among Hitler's Storm Troops, and still further by the failure of the *Putsch* in Austria in July 1934 in which Dr. Dollfuss was brutally murdered.

On July 30th Baldwin came forward with his most memorable saying that, "when you think of the defence of England, you no longer think of the chalk cliffs of Dover, you think of the Rhine". The year might have seen the most emphatic discomfiture of Hitler, but for a calamitous act on October 9th, when terrorists assassinated King Alexander of Yugoslovia on his

* *Who helped Hitler?*

arrival in Marseilles and mortally wounded Louis Barthou at his side. The Frenchman in the minutes of panic bled to death without medical attention.

With the death of Barthou a driving impulse was lost, and although Russia sat in the League, there was no progress towards a system of collective defence. The forces in favour of not isolating or pinioning Germany were powerful in Britain. And if 1934 was a year of endeavour for European alliances, 1935 became the year in which appeasement of Germany gained ground. While Vansittart laboured to arrange a visit to Moscow for Eden, Sir John Simon pursued the course of understanding with Germany. Upon that British policy put the greater emphasis.

"It is becoming more and more clear", wrote Sir John to King George V on January 19th, 1935, "that the early months of the present year may offer the opportunity for a definite improvement in European relations, in which there is every reason to believe that Your Majesty's Government will be able to play an important, and, indeed, the leading part. . . . The coming year is likely to be a vital year in the sense that if European improvement is *not* secured and some element of German reconciliation effected, the world may enter into a most dangerous future. The point which Sir John has been pressing is that the practical choice is between a Germany which continues to rearm without any regulation or agreement, and a Germany which, through getting a recognition of its rights and some modification of the Peace Treaties, enters into the comity of nations, and contributes in this and other ways to European stability. As between these two courses, there can be no doubt which is the wiser."[*]

This is the earliest evidence that I find in a document of state of the appeasement policy, about which so much has since been written. Eden admits to having used the word "appeasement" occasionally in speeches or Foreign Office minutes before the beginning of 1936,[†] but not, he tells us, in its later and pejorative sense. The policy had its beginnings here in Sir John's report. Appeasement took more than one form. There was the laudable attempt to get a general settlement in company with France, mindful of Central and Eastern Europe.

---

[*] *King George V*, H. Nicolson, Constable and Co., p. 522.
[†] Lord Avon, *Facing the Dictators*, p. 324.

There was also the course of embarking on a two power policy with Germany to the exclusion of France, and this brought with it the attendant idea of "letting Germany go east". As Churchill told Maisky, he and Vansittart accepted the former and fought against the latter conception as fraught with peril and unreality.

Early in 1935 there was a flow of insinuations from the Ribbentrop office that Germany on land and Britain at sea could rule the world. This idea of an Anglo-German deal was never seriously advanced in any accepted British document on foreign policy; but it was talked about in clubs and City luncheons, and at the country house parties of Cliveden and Blickling Hall to listening Ministers by men without the responsibilities of office.

One of this sort was Philip Kerr, 11th Marquess of Lothian, who sought an interview with Hitler in January 1935. A Liberal in outlook, an optimist by nature, a believer in generosity and gratitude as impelling forces in human affairs, Lord Lothian had worked for Lloyd George on the terms of the Versailles treaty after graduating in Lord Milner's political "Kindergarten" of brilliant young men.

After spending more than two hours with Hitler, Lord Lothian had reported to Sir John Simon that in January 1935 no one in Germany was thinking of war, "at any rate for the next ten years"; that Hitler would agree not to interfere with Austria by force; that it was contrary to Nazi principles to incorporate non-Germans (Czechs or Poles) in the Reich; that there was a chance of political settlement that would keep the peace for ten years on condition of a frank discussion between Great Britain and Germany. If Britain and Germany reached agreement, Hitler would not raise insuperable objections to French defensive treaties in Eastern Europe. He wrote: "The central fact is that Germany does not want war and is prepared to renounce it absolutely as a method of settling her disputes with her neighbours provided she is given real equality."*

These opinions could not have been more wrong, and they were circulated to a Cabinet which was already on the path of error. Early in February 1935, two men very different from Louis Barthou, the French Prime Minister Etienne Flandin and Pierre Laval his Foreign Minister, visited London for three days

* Sir J. R. M. Butler, *Lord Lothian*, p. 336.

to discuss "a general settlement freely negotiated between Germany and the other powers" . . . said the communiqué, "which in the case of Germany would replace the . . . limiting . . . provisions of the Versailles Treaty." These talks aroused the suspicions of Maisky that the British and French were adhering to the Locarno front in the West, but had abandoned any thought of an Eastern Pact.

"So far as in me lies", wrote Vansittart on February 13th, "I am doing all that is possible to further the policy of helping Russia—by friendly response—out of the dangerous, indeed, fatal, path that would lead to Berlin" . . . "We must help M. Litvinov to the utmost of our power."*

But plans for British talks with Hitler went forward. Eden found Baldwin uneasy about proposals that whereas both Simon and Eden should visit Berlin, only Eden should proceed to Warsaw and Moscow. "To me the odd part of the business was that Simon showed no wish to go further than Berlin," wrote Lord Avon.† According to Maisky the powerful Vansittart had to work hard to achieve the Eden visit to Moscow. Reports reached Whitehall in February 1935 of German preparations to militarise the Rhineland and Vansittart commented that "if we let matters drift, which is the usual and easy course, we shall one day have a crisis out of this. The Germans are always professing a desire for good relations with us. We should be committed to no action if we intimated to them that a violation of their obligations in this respect would be a handicap to such relations."‡ He recommended on February 28th that the subject be taken by the Cabinet before the Berlin talks.

Meanwhile, senior British officials, fearing that Britain would suddenly be faced with a vastly stronger Germany, had decided to urge the Cabinet and particularly Baldwin towards a clearer policy.

Sir Warren Fisher, Sir Maurice Hankey and Sir Robert Vansittart had prepared a draft White Paper to accompany the 1935 defence estimates. Their object was to warn the British people of increasing peril, the growth of German military strength and the need for a great defence effort. It was an outspoken draft that Vansittart showed to the Lord President, in which Germany and its leadership were named.

* Vansittart Papers.   † *Facing the Dictators*, p. 126.
‡ Vansittart Papers.

"I am going to mention no names", said Baldwin after reading it, and though Warren Fisher joined Vansittart in protest, and Vansittart worked "all winter" to get the danger clearly stated, the only strong words that survived were in a reference to the spirit of growing militarism in the training of German youth.

The final draft did not satisfy Vansittart, though Eden found its language "rougher stuff than anything that had been officially written of German behaviour hitherto".* It introduced on March 4th, 1935 an increase of only £10,000,000 in the Services estimates, and apart from the reference to militarism, spoke only of "a situation where peace may be in peril", and "the general feeling of insecurity which has already been incontestably generated".

The visit to Berlin, on which Sir John Simon in his letter to King George V reposed such great hopes of appeasement, was due on March 8th, 1935. Hitler after reading the preamble to the British Defence White Paper simulated a cold and asked for the Simon visit to be postponed. He then delivered his counter stroke to the British White Paper. Hermann Goering announced on March 9th, 1935 the existence of a German Air Force, and Hitler announced on March 16th compulsory military service and a standing army of 36 divisions.

Britain, France and Italy entered separate protests, the result of unwillingness in the British Cabinet to follow three-power procedures just before the Berlin visit. Vansittart thought that the visit should still take place, but urged that Eden should visit Paris first. He himself saw Maisky again to try and allay Soviet suspicions that there was any intention to come to a separate agreement with Germany.

After a suitable pause, Hitler agreed to Sir John Simon and Mr. Eden visiting him on March 25th and 26th. The White Paper had annoyed Hitler, without frightening him and without really arousing the British people. In their talks extending over two days Sir John spoke strongly for Germany re-entering the League, and referred to Locarno, though avoiding the subject of the demilitarised Rhineland zone, on which Vansittart had advised that a warning should be given. Hitler may have noticed the avoidance of this subject. He did not wish to state a claim for colonies, he said, for he was not in a position to

* *Facing the Dictators.*

defend territories overseas, though in concert with Britain he might well be able to help defend her territories too. When Simon came to the question of air strength Hitler claimed parity with his neighbours, and when Simon put in his key question as to the present air strength of Germany, Hitler answered quietly: "We have reached parity with Great Britain."

This exaggerated claim made an ominous impression on Anthony Eden at the time, but the word parity was confusing to assessments of air strength. A naval parity of ships of the line means something. Parity could be reached and maintained between navies, but as we shall later see in discussing air strength it was the rate of production that really mattered.

Hitler's interpreter, Dr. Paul Schmidt, found Eden throughout more sceptical than Simon, on whom Hitler formed a favourable opinion, noting with disapproval that Eden with a small staff was continuing his exploration to Warsaw and Moscow on the night of Tuesday, March 26th.

Both Eden and Simon wrote reports of their Berlin visit. Simon thought Germany "determined to go her own course in rearmament . . . expects in time to get all Germans within her borders, including Austria, and has no intention of joining in collective security". Eden found himself in the next few days answering such uncomfortable questions in Moscow from Mr. Litvinov as . . . "If Hitler is now saying that he is not interested in the West and has his eye only upon the East, is not this simply because he thinks his policy acceptable to Great Britain and other powers?"*

Simon reached London on the Wednesday afternoon, having had, as far as can be ascertained, no further formal talks with Hitler and prepared a full memorandum for the Cabinet. The *Daily Telegraph* diplomatic correspondent, evidently in close touch with the British delegation, had given a circumstantial account of the four official talks. The newspaper on Friday, March 29th, referred to "the strong appeal which Herr Hitler undoubtedly made to Sir John Simon for an Anglo-German alliance".

There is no record of such an offer in the official documents published, though it was evidently much in Hitler's mind. Sir John apparently did not wish to reveal details of the talks and told the House of Commons on the Friday that "these were a

* *Facing the Dictators.*

series of visits of exploration and enquiry. In these circumstances it will be obviously undesirable to make a full statement. Unauthorised speculations should be disregarded."

Meanwhile, Vansittart, impatient at the report that Hitler had reached air parity with Britain, looked over the twenty-page report of the talks that Simon had classified as Secret.

"This claim to air parity should be made known," he told Rex Leeper, Head of the News Department. "We need to support our own air estimates. If the Secretary of State complains to you, I will take the responsibility."

So Leeper in his briefing of the British press mentioned it to trusted correspondents. In the *Daily Telegraph* and other London newspapers on March 29th, a report was published that "Herr Hitler is said to have admitted that the German Air Force is already as large or slightly larger than the Royal Air Force". A German *démenti* was promptly issued, on the consideration no doubt that the words "or slightly larger" had never been spoken. The B.B.C., which was involved in the leakage, broadcast a commentary on March 30th on the German *démenti*—"it is now learned, however, that actually there is good reason to believe that the German air force has now attained equality with our own". The German Ambassador, who called on Sir John that day, reported: "I derived the impression that he in no way approved of the fantasies of the Press and, of course, is in no way responsible for them, but he is afraid that in putting individual points right he will be drawn away from the principle that the Berlin talks be kept confidential."*

On April 3rd, Sir John had to answer a question in the House of Commons and admitted the accuracy of the report that Hitler had claimed to have air parity with Britain already. Back in the Foreign Office he called for Mr. Leeper and the following conversation took place:†

"Mr. Leeper, can you tell me how these reports in the *Sunday Times* and other newspapers came to the knowledge of the Press?"

He held up the cuttings pasted on Foreign Office entry sheets and lying on his desk.

"Yes, I think they may have gathered this in conversation with me."

* Documents on German Foreign Policy.
† Related by Sir R. Leeper to the author.

"And this one, too?"

"Yes, this may have been also gathered from conversation with me."

"And do you think, Mr. Leeper, that you are in any way authorised to divulge from Secret Print?"

"No, sir, of course not."

"Then, Mr. Leeper, I fail entirely to understand."

The Foreign Office News Chief replied:

"Secretary-of-State, it was being said both here and in newspapers abroad that you had discussions with Herr Hitler behind the back of Mr. Eden. It was necessary to inform the Press on what really happened."

Sir John was so visibly taken aback by this rejoinder that although Sir Robert Vansittart himself entered the room at that very moment, and although the culprit cuttings lay on the desk, the Foreign Secretary made not the slightest further allusion to the matter.

The only positive outcome of the Berlin talks was that discussions of an Anglo-German naval agreement on a 100:35 ratio were continued. Otherwise the omens all pointed to a need for strengthening the Western Alliance.

A week later the Heads of Government of Britain, France and Italy met at Stresa to proclaim what was to be a very temporary unity of purpose—soon after dislocated by the Abyssinian crisis. Plainly there was little to be achieved by talking of air pacts with Germany, or devising new ways of re-affirming the Locarno Agreement with her. But the western triple alliance was, though it left eastern questions open, an alternative to unguarded appeasement.

From the Stresa talks, Sir Robert Vansittart travelled to Geneva and saw for the first and only time the League of Nations in action. It had to deal in special session with the results of the Stresa conference. Vansittart remarked to Rex Leeper, who accompanied him, on the unreality of the Geneva atmosphere. The main interest of his visit was a private meeting with Maxim Litvinov, disappointed of his Eastern Pact, whose awareness of the Nazi danger to Europe impressed him.

At last Ramsay Macdonald stood down in June 1935 from the premiership, and the long day of Sir John Simon in the Foreign Office came to an end. As Maisky divined, Vansittart had found him "impossible" in foreign affairs. Simon had

retained a quality of innocence in his thinking combined with a
testy legality and owned himself that he found it hard to understand the thoughts of others. At the time of the Stresa conference
Sir Robert said of him and Ramsay Macdonald: "You can't
make two empty sacks stand upright." Simon in the Home
Office and later in the Treasury became one of the "Inner
Cabinet" who gave a disreputable meaning to the word
"appeasement".

The appeasement policy assumed more dangerous dimensions
in 1936 and 1937 after it had become apparent that Italy was
estranged and hopes of a triple alliance to hold Hitler in check
had receded. But in 1935 the struggle of policies was already
being fought round the Foreign Office. Sir Eric Phipps continued the critical line of Sir Horace Rumbold in his dispatches
from Berlin, and received a heartening message from Lord
Wigram, Secretary to King George V, who wrote in March
1935 that His Majesty felt "that we must not be blinded by the
sweet reasonableness of the Germans".* In 1936 Tom Jones
recommended to Baldwin the removal of Phipps as an obstacle
to better relations.

Distressed at the policy of *The Times*, edited by Geoffrey
Dawson and influenced by Lord Lothian, Vansittart wrote to a
friend in May 1935 that: "Only *The Times* and the weaker-
minded members of the House of Lords could fail to be impressed by Germany's avowed military intentions."

In July 1935 he commented on British air estimates "that
Germany will be ready for trouble before 1939"—"It becomes
far more dangerous if we are to alienate all our prospective
friends and allies. . . . This alienation has of late years been
largely influenced by the desire to placate Germany. In reason
that is well. But it goes beyond reason; and in ministerial
quarters too, all other ends but the German end tend to be
overlooked."†

However much he recorded the danger of being cool towards
France and cold towards Soviet Russia, the fatal attraction of
this course gathered impetus in the social world around him.
The Anglo-German naval agreement of June 1935 gave it
acceleration, and so did discussion of an air pact on the same

* *King George V*, H. Nicolson. The phrase is identical to a passage in one of the
Vansittart memoranda on Germany.
† Vansittart Papers.

lines. After considering such proposals on July 30th, 1935, he warned Sir Samuel Hoare, the new Foreign Secretary:

"The surest way of making Laval court Germany, as Caillaux did, would be to follow the separate naval agreement with a separate air agreement with Germany. It would be high folly to drive a wedge between ourselves and our eventual ally. A further separate agreement with Germany would be neither an election winner, nor a safe move internationally."*

"At this time I was thinking particularly of an air pact, towards which Hitler was favourably disposed," wrote Joachim von Ribbentrop in his memoirs. . . . "Hitler proposed a meeting on board a ship in the North Sea and even declared he was ready to fly to Chequers to see the Prime Minister. I was told that Mr. Baldwin was not unfavourably inclined, but that he was well known to take time before making decisions.

"Then I learned that Mr. Baldwin had declared that he must first talk to 'Van', that is Vansittart. Finally Mr. Baldwin sent me a message through his friend Mr. T. Jones that 'more preparations were needed for such a meeting. . . .' I was told over and over again that British diplomatists led by Sir Robert Vansittart were exercising strong pressure on the British Cabinet with a view to blocking any further negotiations outside the Versailles system. . . . Why did British diplomacy and those influential circles surrounding men like Churchill, Vansittart and Duff Cooper adopt this negative attitude towards Germany? The answer to this question also explains the outbreak of the Second World War. The answer is: The balance of power in Europe was in danger."

For the rest of 1935 and increasingly in 1936 Ribbentrop, as Head of Hitler's Foreign Political Office, shortly to be Ambassador to Britain and later Foreign Minister of the Reich, deployed his persuasions in London. He met whomever he could who had pretensions to influence, still arguing that Britain and Germany must be friends for ever, but that Germany must be free to settle her Eastern claims in her own way.

The big houses of England where political men were entertained would be open to him in the following year— Londonderry House, the Park Lane home of Lord Londonderry, former Secretary of State for Air, in which during the premiership of Macdonald, social patronage had been wielded

* Vansittart Papers.

by the determined Marchioness; Blickling Hall and Cliveden, where Viscountess Astor talked politics incessantly. Even Polesden Lacy, home of Mrs. Ronald Greville, where there was no political line, could be used to propagate talk of Anglo-German friendship, as all the Cabinet could be found there, though Mrs. Greville's shrewd Scottish tongue sometimes made Ribbentrop wince. There was Brocket Hall too, home of Mr. Chamberlain's friend, Lord Brocket, and at 7 Grosvenor Square, the town house of Lady Maud Cunard, "Emerald", people could be met, and sometimes the Prince of Wales himself, susceptible to arguments for Anglo-German co-operation. The debate on British Continental policy went on between politicians, Dons and Fellows at All Souls College in Oxford, where such subjects as the balance of power or the alternative of an Anglo-German policy were discussed by candle-light as the port went round. Mr. Baldwin went hardly at all in these years to Denham Place, and instead Vansittart had for company a few chosen friends in politics and the Press who were at one with his outlook. He was open in these friendships. Rex Leeper sometimes came upon him in his room at the Foreign Office in full conversation on the telephone with Winston Churchill, of whom it was being said that, like David Lloyd George, he would never return to office, though Maisky thought in 1934 that he might very soon be Prime Minister.

"Of course I tell him whatever I know", said Vansittart to Leeper. "It is so important that a man of Churchill's influence should be properly informed."

But Churchill remained in political isolation, and Eden as Foreign Secretary did not think it amiss to frequent Cliveden, a circumstance which Tom Jones observed to be worrying Baldwin* and which Vansittart noted also with disquiet. For it had come to his ears that in the Cliveden circle, it was being said that Vansittart was the only obstacle to an understanding with Germany, "and we are going to have him out".†

"The seat of Government has been shifted from Downing Street to Cliveden," joked Lloyd George. Vansittart spoke to Eden about his continued visits there while animosity was running high against the Permanent Head of the Foreign Office. It seemed perhaps unreasonable to have expostulated, thought Vansittart looking back, and anyway the Eden visits continued.

* *Diary with Letters.*   † *Mist Procession.*

By the end of October 1935 the persistent clamour round Baldwin for an understanding with Germany prompted King George V to ask Sir Robert Vansittart for more expert advice. In October the King received him in audience and asked what the possibilities were of reaching such an understanding. Sir Robert pondered his remarks and on November 7th wrote to Lord Wigram, the King's secretary, a letter summarising his views:

"I do not think it would be profitable to undertake any serious attempt to an agreement with Germany until our own national re-equipment is well under way. It is clear that since agreements are always matters of bargain, you can drive a much better bargain when you are strong than when you are weak. Secondly, it would be essential that any such exploration should be undertaken *à trois* and not *à deux*; in other words, that we should have to act with the French. If we did not do so, the French would be all the time going behind our backs at Berlin, and we correspondingly should be compelled to go behind theirs. The result would be that Germany would play one Power off against the other and raise her terms accordingly. In fact the terms might be too high to be payable.

"This question of terms brings one right up against the central difficulty. Any arrangement with Germany will have to be paid for, and handsomely paid for. Otherwise it will not even work temporarily, let alone hold permanently, and nothing that will not fulfil the latter requisite is really greatly worth while. Now I am convinced that modern Germany is highly expansive and will become highly explosive if it is sought to cramp her everywhere. But the inevitable expansion can only take place either in Europe or Africa. Therefore, if we are to undertake eventually and seriously any negotiation, we must be prepared to pay in one of these two quarters. If the expansion were to be in Europe, it would be at other people's expense. If it is to be in Africa, it will be at our expense.

"I do not think there can be any question that it will have to take the latter form. Any attempt at giving Germany a free hand to annex other people's property in central or eastern Europe is both absolutely immoral and completely contrary to all the principles of the League which form the backbone of the policy of this country. Any British Government that attempted to do such a deal would almost certainly be brought down in ignominy—and deservedly. It would have been of no use to run the risks that we have recently been running to stand up for the League if we ourselves were going to destroy it later.

"Any suggestion that a British Government contemplated leaving, let alone inviting, Germany to satisfy her land hunger at Russia's expense would quite infallibly split this country from top to bottom, and split it just as deeply and disastrously as France is now split, though on rather different lines. This is an undoubted fact, whatever we may think of it, and I hope it will always be in the minds of our political folk.

"We therefore come down to the basic fact that if any lasting agreement is to be made with Germany, some expansion will have to be allowed for, and that expansion can only take place by restoring to her some of, not all of, her former colonies. This conclusion will no doubt raise considerable objection on the Right in this country, but it will have to be faced in the long run."

On a dispatch written from Berlin the same day, in which Sir Eric Phipps reported the expansionist aims of Germany, Sir Robert reflected in a comment to which he attached a copy of his letter to Lord Wigram:*

"It is highly probable that Germany will want to have it both ways—to expand in Europe *and* in Africa. That is precisely why we are going to, and must, rearm. But there is still a chance that—if we don't waver and halt too long between two opinions—she might be content to expand in Africa only. On this my own mind is quite clear, and I shall not change it: it is the lesser of two evils. Even against that we might stand out if we were going to rearm further than I think we shall. Otherwise we shall have to make up our mind. I agree that we should make up our minds negatively, if we can't get a proper price; and I agree that we alone should not have to pay the counterpart. But I have always said that any

---

* It was apparently this letter that led to the joint reproof from Ramsay Macdonald and Sir John Simon after the King's serious illness and convalescence that Sir Robert was not to depress His Majesty with gloomy forecasts, even if asked for them. *The Mist Procession*, p. 350.

agreement would have to be tripartite, i.e. include the French. We had better leave the Portuguese and Dutch out of our minds. Settling at other people's expense in Africa or East Indies is on the same plane as settling at other people's expense in Europe."

King George V was of all men the least likely to be deceived by illusory promises of goodwill in exchange for abandoning friends and so appeasement at any price made no immediate progress in Court circles. But his reign was drawing to its close in the cold January of 1936.

With the new reign of Edward VIII, new influences were exerted. I find no such intimate correspondence between Vansittart and the new king. Ribbentrop towards the end of his Ambassadorship in London told Hitler that his main hope of an understanding with Britain had focused on the personality of Edward VIII and faded after the abdication.

In November 1935 the Foreign Office was exercised with the question whether a lasting agreement could be achieved with Germany. Disillusion with Italy over Abyssinia gave the partisans of an Anglo-German understanding their opportunity for advocating "co-operation on an equal footing" as a means of "modifying German expansion".

The views of Vansittart were unaltered on the colonial question, in which he agreed that it was the only matter in which Britain had any moral right to make concessions, even though not in her own interest. He repeated that it would be disadvantageous and dangerous for Britain to be drawn into discussions of Germany's Eastern ambitions. As to showing "readiness to co-operate with Germany on an equal footing" . . . so as to be "in a better position to influence German designs in Central and Eastern Europe", he asked how could there be such co-operation, since Germany was already superior in strength. He did not believe that Germany could be dissuaded from expansionist aims or have those aims "modified" by partnership with Britain. Was she to have Austria and Memel, and not Czechoslovakia and Russia? As to wishing for a strong Germany, he did not wish to see her strong in her present mood. These views, given on December 1st, 1935, effectively slowed down the encroachments of appeasement in the Foreign Office.

But the German question was real and insistent, and Vansittart declared in the same commentary: "I reject of course the policy of drift." He wanted to have a little pause, only until a strong beginning was made with re-equipment of the armed forces; for that was anyway an unalterable necessity. Then a cautious examination of the possibilities of an agreement.

The question of appeasement reached the Cabinet in February 1936. Sir Robert presented Eden with a lengthy report in which he discussed "Britain, France and Germany". Eden's comments on this report, in which he summarised the alternatives of British policy, are interesting, because they admit an argument for making some attempt to come to terms with Germany even if it resulted in failure. For such a failure could reasonably be expected to show the intransigence of Germany, and the need for British rearmament and the strengthening of collective security.

This reasoning was politically not very different from that on which Mr. Chamberlain founded his 1938 journey to Berchtesgaden and Munich; but in putting this view forward Eden could not have dreamt of such a colossal failure. Smaller prizes were still to hand, such as the naval agreement with Germany, the proposed air pact, access to raw materials, colonies and occupation of the Rhineland by a limited German military force.

Sir Robert having in mind the intensive rearmament of Germany saw the problem as removing Germany's grievances "by the process of give and take before Germany took the law into her own hands. . . . This policy is still the constructive one. The alternative of permanent drift is avowedly a counsel of negation and despair: and there are grave and obvious dangers in a policy of encirclement. Economic sanctions on Germany would be a dangerous delusion a few years hence." But Sir Robert distinguished between "collective security" and encirclement, because the former would "be combined with an elastic policy of settlement". He could no longer assume that Italy would form part of a counterpoise to Germany (for the Abyssinian crisis had followed upon Stresa and broken the triple accord). "This new uncertainty renders any prospect of an effective encirclement of Germany even more doubtful than before."

It had been conceived that Germany might be kept quiet by

eliminating the demilitarised Zone while the League scored an effective victory over Italy. But this would impress Germany very little and would gain no time for rearmament. "For rearmament, like the elimination of the demilitarised Zone must form part of *any* policy that we may adopt."

It would seem that the Government must resume its attempt to come to honourable terms with Germany, but how? They must move soon or not at all, and the difficulty was that Germany would demand territorial changes.

He passed on to examining the chances that Germany might attack the West after lulling their suspicions and mentioned fears of the Polish General Staff "of a German drive eastward in a couple of years". He noted the sudden coldness of Hitler towards England as soon as the Abyssinian crisis arose. Sir Eric Phipps had been told by Hitler that since France had concluded a treaty with Russia, it would be impossible for Germany to accept an Air Limitation Agreement. Prospects for coming to terms were far from promising. Any agreement must be as broad as possible and not just an agreement between Great Britain and Germany. A settlement with Germany to be effective must be European.

The approach might be made by way of a revision of the Treaty of Locarno—the elimination of the demilitarised Zone was "a nettle which we should be wise to grasp before it stings us". Revision of the League Covenant might be discussed as a means of tempting Hitler back to Geneva. But none of many openings by itself would lead to a real settlement. A bargain could only be achieved at a price and no latitude could be allowed Germany in Europe. "We cannot make a stand for Abyssinia and connive at the spoliation of Lithuania, or Czechoslovakia, or Austria." Yet Sir Eric Phipps was explicitly warning the British Government that the question in Germany was no longer "whether she shall expand but where and when". Vansittart explained to the Cabinet the plan to incorporate all German-speaking people in Germany, as outlined in Hitler's book, *Mein Kampf*, which most of them had not read. In certain circumstances expansion in the East might be carried out by Germany in co-operation with Russia and not against her, he warned. As for colonies, Germany would in the long run only be satisfied by getting all her former colonies back, and might yet pursue European claims as well. Hitler appeared to be hesitating and a strong line by Britain now might prove decisive. It would be best to satisfy aspirations before they became demands, but to show that Britain was strong at the same time. He summed up that it would be well to come to terms with Germany if possible, and in good time, paying a high price but not at the expense of others. Expansion could only be "at our own expense" by restitution of former German colonies in Africa, and it should be coupled with a return of Germany to Geneva and arms limitation.

Reflecting early in 1936 on Anglo-German problems he thought that: "We should do all we can to secure better treatment of German minorities. And I would certainly dispose of the demilitarised zone in Germany's favour. And I would restore her colonies to Germany.

"All this I regard as part of the political settlement which must precede the economic considerations . . . in return for these offers we should extract from Germany a return to Geneva disarmament and a formal renunciation of any territorial designs in Europe, including aims at absorption of Austria and Czechoslovakia. This is, of course, incompatible with the idea that we should disinterest ourselves in the fate of Austria."

He emphasised that Britain would have to strengthen herself to get into a bargaining position at all. Such was his serious proposal in February 1936; but the Cabinet did not grasp this nettle then. It was left for Mr. Chamberlain to grasp it more than two years later in a vaguely remembered quotation of Hotspur's words in Henry IV. In 1936 British Conservatives had formed a strong Colonial lobby. There was also a policy of economic containment of Germany to be weighed, which conflicted with colonial restitution.

I find Vansittart later conceding that there were "excellent reasons" why the Cabinet decided against colonial restitution about this time. Those reasons, advanced by the Board of Trade, were that Dr. Schacht's economic plan for self-sufficiency was likely to fail, and the pace of German rearmament therefore to flatten out. These were, to Vansittart, reasonable assumptions, provided that Britain was rearmed to a minimum of safety.

When eventually colonies were offered to Hitler, it was through Sir Nevile Henderson just before the fall of Austria in 1938, and then a slice only of British mandated territory with a promise of slices of Belgian and Portuguese territory, too—

exactly what Sir Robert advised against in 1935, and Hitler refused the offer indignantly. It will surprise some that Vansittart, the preacher of strength against Germany, advised colonial restitution in early 1936. He may have known that his masters were considering it; and so he proposed an offer large and honourable, and tied it to strict demands for security. Most important of all, he made it a condition that there should be no betrayal of European states.

The disadvantage in any discussion of Anglo-German understanding was how to suggest concessions to Hitler as a possibility without making it perfectly clear that he could help himself to them. If negotiation was tried, and failed, Vansittart warned, Britain being weak "would be in a terrible position".

Thus about the time that the great reign of King George V ended the Cabinet talk had turned from collective security to appeasement. There was no mention any more of an Eastern Pact. Litvinov came to London and walked in the State funeral procession among the Kings and princes. Marshal Tuchachevsky, Deputy Commissar for Defence, marched in the Soviet delegation, unaware of the terrible doom that German intrigue was preparing for him and the Russian officer corps. Heads of nations and Ambassadors followed behind the royal bier from a Europe that would soon be no more. Vansittart thought of the dead King as his friend, of his gruff "I have read your report, but not all of it", of a royal intervention when his own position in the Foreign Office had been strongly assailed, and the King had said he would have no interference with "my senior civil servants". Lady Vansittart who noticed much, saw tears in the eyes of Ivan Maisky as he walked in the obsequies of the cousin of the Czar.

"Of those I saw, it was you who shed tears!" she said.

"Yes," replied Maisky, "he was very, very kind to me. I shall never forget it."

CHAPTER III

DIVIDING THE DICTATORS

"The international politics of this time would not be intelligible without some reference to the part played by Sir Robert Vansittart," wrote Lord Avon looking back at 1934-37 during which he was Lord Privy Seal, Minister for League Affairs and then Foreign Secretary. "Vansittart held decided views and his instincts were usually right," thought Eden, but his sense of political methods was "sometimes at fault". Seeing the menace of Nazi Germany "he was determined to keep the rest of Europe in line against Germany and would pay almost any price to do so. He did not discern that to appease Mussolini beyond a certain point in Abyssinia must break up the alignment that Italy was intended to strengthen."* There spoke the League of Nations advocate on a choice of evils that will remain the subject of unsolved controversy. His appraisal of Vansittart was that he had "never known . . . a head of department . . . to compare with Sir Robert as a relentless, not to say ruthless, worker for the views he held strongly himself . . . much more a Secretary of State in mentality than a permanent official." If we turn to *The Mist Procession*, we see how "young Eden" appeared to his Permanent Head. "Anthony and Cranborne†were not only correct but straightforward in pinning faith on the League. That was our rightful policy. But I could never see the League's components tackling an aggressor of weight. So I laboured under a dualism which might look like duplicity. . . . My real trouble was that we should all have to choose between Austria and Abyssinia."‡ Their differences were "amicable but defined", and Eden's "instincts harboured few enthusiasms except for the League", which by the time real aggression came in Europe had become a discarded instrument, of which nobody spoke any more. Sharply defined was their difference of attitude over supplying arms to Abyssinia, as Eden wished to do, whereas Vansittart made certain that Britain adhered to the French policy of "arms to neither side".§

* Lord Avon, *Facing the Dictators*, p. 242.
† Lord Cranborne, Under-Secretary of State in the Foreign Office.
‡ *Mist Procession*, p. 522.   § *Facing the Dictators*.

Eden and Vansittart disagreed on a great question in history —whether the two dictatorships could be kept apart at a price acceptable to the democracies. To both men it was clear that Italy did not wish Austria to be annexed by Germany; but, as Eden put it, "Mussolini had probably convinced himself that he could win his war in Africa and yet uphold the *status quo* and the fabric of peace in Europe. In this he was wrong. At that time, it would have been possible to uphold international order in Europe, but not while abusing it in Africa. No man could play these two parts, not even the Duce."* This opinion is significant as it esteems Mussolini as something other than a junior partner in European aggression, and so the Duce did appear after alerting his troops on the Brenner Pass at the time of the abortive Nazi putsch in Vienna in July 1934. His laurels not yet tarnished by his Abyssinian exploits, he seemed in the spring of 1935, though a dictator, a possible partner against aggression in a period when Britain cherished good relations with several established dictators.

The grand question whether Italy could have been kept as an ally cannot be properly assessed from the contemporary British diplomatic documents without taking into account that many of these secret documents were available to Mussolini soon after they were written. It must make a foreign power seem less formidable, if you can read its diplomatic correspondence while you are dealing with it. In sad fact, the leakages that took place in the years between the Stresa conference and the out-break of war, traced since to the British Embassy in Rome, were in quantity and importance far more serious than the more publicised exploits of "Cicero" during the war, when a valet photographed the papers of the British Ambassador in Ankara. Sir Robert in 1935 got wind of these leakages. At first he thought that the Foreign Office was itself insecure, and made a personal tour of it from Downing Street to the adjacent India Office in the company of his private secretary, Clifford Norton. In its portentous stone walls he discovered no fewer than five un-controlled exits, one of them a cellar cover large enough to have admitted a cabin trunk. But he was still on the wrong scent. From the Ciano diaries it appears that Guido Schmidt, Austrian foreign minister, warned the British of leakages and intercepts, but to little avail. Vansittart sent "the Head of our Secret

* *Facing the Dictators*, p. 243.

Service" to Rome, "who soon got ample confirmation".* It seems that Sir Eric Drummond took official papers out of the Chancery in a Foreign Office dispatch box, and that the key had been duplicated by his butler or valet. This source of leakages was revealed when the Ambassador locked his wife's tiara in the box one night after returning from a ball and found it empty in the morning. It is quite possible that the tiara, subsequently recovered, was removed by a British Security Officer to impress the incredulous Ambassador that official boxes are not really secure and Italian butlers not really trustworthy; but confirmation of this aspect of the theft will not be forthcoming. The upstairs staff of the Embassy was not alone in purloining papers. The boilerman-stoker who was meant to shovel confidential waste into the furnace found it more profitable to take it away and hand it to the Italian *Siguranza*. The first leakages were detected early in 1935. In January 1936 a report circulated by Eden on German expansionist aims was also purloined and was passed on by Mussolini to Hitler nine months later. The German diplomat Theo Kordt, Counsellor of the Reich Embassy in London in 1938-39, revealed after the war to the Nuremberg tribunal that in December 1939 he had been selected to go to Italy and examine the signatures on documents of the British Embassy in Italy, of which there were "two hand suitcases full". This suggests that for five years before the Second World War under successive Ambassadors, the British Embassy in Rome was a sieve through which official secrets filtered to Mussolini and Hitler. The amazing self-assurance of the Duce during the Abyssinian crisis is easier to understand when we consider that he and Count Ciano very often knew the instructions of Sir Eric Drummond in advance of his audiences with them, and that among the papers that fell into the hands of Mussolini was a copy of the Maffey Committee report containing the British Chiefs of Staff Committee opinion, in which it was clearly stated that Britain had no essential strategic interest in Abyssinia.† "Such knowledge was fatal to compromise," reflected Vansittart as he looked back over the years of leakage. He was himself well aware of the underworld to diplomacy in which duplicate keys and micro-films were the stock in trade, but every Ambassador abroad was responsible for the security of his own establishment. Ambassadors

* *Mist Procession.*   † *Nine Troubled Years.*

were often tetchy and autocratic and Lord Perth, who in his later life seemed to have an aversion for Vansittart and his opinions, may have found his advice on security matters unpalatable even in 1935.

There was no thought of these leakages at the time of the Stresa conference in April 1935. Mussolini still seemed very much a friend; but Eden in his sick bed before the Stresa conference urged upon Sir John Simon that Mussolini should be warned against an Abyssinian adventure. Secure at Stresa in his knowledge of British documents, Mussolini may not have felt the need to raise the subject himself. Vansittart, with whom the responsibility lay for briefing the Prime Minister and the Foreign Secretary for Stresa, advised Sir Eric Drummond to press his own view on the two Cabinet ministers "that we should begin by warning the Duce of our wrath should he attack Abyssinia". Vansittart himself preferred to reach a general agreement with Mussolini first (over Europe) and then tell Mussolini that it would "go for nothing if he embroils himself in Abyssinia". Vansittart did not press for the subject of Abyssinia to be openly discussed in conference, nor yet did Sir Eric do so. Macdonald and Simon were silent about this uncomfortable hypothesis. Although Lord Avon has told me that both of them promised to warn him about Abyssinia, it was discussed only between expert advisers.* One of them, Geoffrey Warner, came to Vansittart at Stresa with intelligence that Italian Foreign Ministry officials expected such an adventure. Sir Robert arranged for Warner to breakfast with Sir John Simon, but somehow their conversation did not reach this awkward subject.

Until the official record is available, the best evidence that I can find of the actual moment of failure at Stresa is the verbal account given by Ralph Wigram on his return home† of the final session at which the communiqué was approved. At the conference table sat the British Prime Minister Ramsay Macdonald, Sir John Simon, Vansittart, the French Prime Minister Etienne Flandin, and the French Foreign Minister Laval. After agreeing with Mussolini and his delegation its six points on European security and embodying an Anglo-Italian declaration of intent to honour Locarno obligations, there was a Final Declaration.

"The three Powers, the object of whose policy is the collective

---

* *Mist Procession.*   † Related to the author by Lady Waverley.

maintenance of peace within the framework of the League of Nations, find themselves in complete agreement in opposing, by all practicable means, any unilateral repudiation of treaties, which may endanger the peace, and will act in close and cordial collaboration for this purpose."

Just before the last clause was read, Mussolini spoke: "Let us say here 'which may endanger the peace *of Europe*'," he proposed.

There was an uneasy silence. Macdonald turned to Simon. Vansittart looked quickly towards him. Simon between them sat immobile and said not a word in objection. The meaning was fairly clear: for this added phrase seemed to exclude the three-power 1906 treaty on Abyssinia. What was going on in the mind of Sir John Simon? The communiqué was completed in that form, though Flandin grumbled to the British afterwards and Count Grandi came to Vansittart and Wigram saying:

"The Duce has turned on me and told me that all my warnings about your attitude over Abyssinia are wrong—'for I have altered the communiqué in that sense and they have accepted it'." In Foreign Office papers since, the Stresa Conference has become a standard example to illustrate the danger of leaving a warning unspoken. The illness of Eden, the silence of Simon had an incalculable effect on the future relations of the Allies. "It is true," reflected Lord Avon, "that the Italians had a number of warnings before Stresa from Vansittart, myself and others, but there still remains some substance in the complaint that Mussolini should have been confronted on this occasion when the leading statesmen of the three nations were in council together for four days."*

According to Mussolini, at his earlier meeting with Laval in Rome in January 1935, the French Foreign Minister had given him a "free hand" in Abyssinia, though Laval argued later that he had only conceded that Abyssinia should be within the Italian sphere of economic influence. At the price of not wrangling over Abyssinia a common front of the three western allies was achieved at Stresa in April 1935 against German expansion. The German Ambassador in Rome, Herr von Hassell, assessed Italian feelings at this time in a dispatch to Baron von Neurath. "It must never be forgotten that . . . the

* *Facing the Dictators*, p. 180.

basis of the tension here is fear . . . above all of a forcible solution of the Austrian problem."*

"Does Mussolini seriously believe that we propose to occupy Austria? Then his intelligence service, to say the least, must be bad," commented von Neurath. But von Hassell explained that the German proclamation of March 16th, 1935 on rearmament was seen in Rome as an overt threat to Italy. At their Venice meeting Mussolini had thought he possessed Hitler's assurance that the policy of annexing Austria would be abandoned. Von Hassell explained, "Then came the murder of Dollfuss. Mussolini who was expecting a visit from Dollfuss, whom he held in special sympathy and respect and whom he regarded as a pillar of the present Austrian régime, was deeply affected psychologically, especially by the presence of Frau Dollfuss in Italy, and by the necessity of breaking the news to her himself."

Signor Cerrutti, the Italian Ambassador in Berlin, told the German Foreign Minister on May 2nd, 1935 that "the only question of any difficulty is Austria". Von Neurath recorded his post-Stresa impression that "Signor Mussolini is now striving to improve the atmosphere with Germany somewhat. He is obviously most anxious . . . to settle if possible the question of non-intervention and so free his rear in Europe for his adventure in Abyssinia."

On May 14th von Hassell thought that "Mussolini's whole manner confirmed the assumption, which is also supported by information received from within the British Embassy, that the British and French are exerting pressure on Italy in the Abyssinian question." Reading that France had signed a treaty of mutual assistance with Russia, Mussolini told a German diplomat at a reception on May 26th that he "hoped for a gradual and systematic rapprochement of Germany and Italy". By May 30th the German Ambassador reported that "one might almost speak of a reversal of Italy's former attitude to Germany". Mussolini had said that "the only outstanding question between Germany and Italy is that of Austria". The German Ambassador assessed Italian foreign policy as "tentatively feeling its way . . . completely dominated by the Abyssinian question. . . . Italy's foreign relations with other European powers are considered in the light of their attitude in the Abyssinian question. This applies above all to Britain. . . ." The

* Documents on German Foreign Policy, Series C, Vol. IV, p. 3.

Ambassador thought the British press campaign against Italy of "unprecedented violence".*

Such was the position in Europe when Sir Samuel Hoare took over the Foreign Office for a brief but notable period in June 1935. It was a change of personality and outlook from Sir John Simon. Member of a wealthy banking and merchant family, long associated with the port of Bristol, who landscaped their estates in the West of England in sedate ostentation, Sir Samuel, of a cadet branch, had settled on the coast of Norfolk. He was small of stature, active, mentally agile, a determined tennis player and an accomplished skater, who tried perhaps too hard in office, but did not lack experience or aptitude. He had been Secretary of State for Air for five years and Secretary of State for India during the passage of the India Bill, when he made no fewer than 166 speeches during its committee stages. This grinding performance had left him much exhausted and in need of a rest. He was subject to recurrent fainting fits. But public ambition was strong in Sir Samuel and he accepted the office.

For every Foreign Secretary chosen in any Ministry there were always several disappointed candidates, and though Warren Fisher and Vansittart spoke for Eden, when Mr. Baldwin came to weigh up, he decided for the older man. Eden remained Lord Privy Seal and was found the title of Minister for League Affairs.

Sir Samuel Hoare recorded in his autobiography† that the first of a long list of questions that needed answering was his relations with Eden "who had established for himself so notable a place in Geneva and Westminster that his loss would have been very serious to the world at large". Baldwin stood aside from this competition of personalities and asked Hoare in a pencilled note to settle details of their respective competence "direct with the young man".‡ In consequence there was, in the attempt to maintain good relations with Italy in June 1935, a sort of duality of ministerial authority, just as the policy of Great Britain was dually founded on the double basis of established treaties and the League of Nations Covenant. Sir Samuel found the pertinacious Sir Warren Fisher, Head of the Treasury, critical of Foreign Office organisation; but equally he

---

* German Documents, Series C, Vol. IV, p. 231.
† *Nine Troubled Years*, Lord Templewood.   ‡ Ibid.

remembers him in 1935 as "wholeheartedly engaged with Vansittart as his chief colleague in preparing plans for intensifying British rearmament". Of later divergences between Fisher and Vansittart there was then no hint, and no record either in the Vansittart papers. Lord Avon recollected that sometimes when the dominating personality of Vansittart overbore Hoare in counsel, the Foreign Secretary "would answer tersely". Of terseness there is no word in Hoare's memoirs. He willingly admits the ascendancy of Vansittart's mind . . . "the repeated failure of a foreign policy without adequate force to support it . . ." was felt intensely by Vansittart. "From the first moment I came under the influence of his singleness of purpose. His creed was short and undeviating. He firmly believed in the reports of Hitler's aggressive plans. . . . Once convinced . . . I threw all the influence I possessed into the double campaign for more arms and more time. . . . Vansittart's fertile mind and unequalled knowledge of European politics were invaluable to me, whilst my more conventional methods may have been useful to him as a supplement to his sparkling tours de force. . . ."

Before setting about improving relations with Italy, Hoare and Vansittart had between them to finish the last work begun in the Secretaryship of Sir John Simon by Sir Robert Craigie and get the Anglo-German Naval Agreement signed on June 18th. Ribbentrop, who came to London for this purpose, thought Vansittart responsible for a last-minute "hitch", when the Foreign Office tried to make ratification dependent on the agreement of other Versailles treaty powers. He protested at this condition as not envisaged during the negotiations, and noticed that when it was waived and the signatures completed, Sir Robert Craigie took him aside and asked him not to call on Vansittart. Ribbentrop, who did not easily accept advice, recorded in memoirs written shortly before his death that "I also called on the Permanent Under-Secretary at the Foreign Office, Sir Robert Vansittart, but could not discover his real opinion. Although he welcomed the agreement in general terms, he seemed to be extraordinarily nervous, and I had the impression that he did not like the course which events had taken. I knew Sir Robert only slightly, and on the few occasions when I had called upon him in the past I had always found him very reserved. I could not escape the impression that he cared far less for improved Anglo-German relations than I did myself, and I wondered whether the reason was that he was such a pronounced Francophil. He wrote poems and plays in French, but this could not altogether explain his negative attitude, for after all I too was a Francophil.

"The decisive factor was that from the very beginning Vansittart was an advocate of the thesis, originally proclaimed by Sir Eyre Crowe, the Englishman with the German mother, that Britain must never make a pact with Germany. Sir Robert stuck to this policy until Germany was destroyed—his great moment of triumph. All the attempts which I and others made to change his mind failed. In those years he was undoubtedly the great opponent of all German aspirations and throughout the world 'Vansittartism' has become the symbol of hatred of the Germans, but it is questionable whether history will pass a favourable judgment on his policy.

"Vansittart clearly showed his uneasiness over the signing of the Naval Agreement. His attitude was made plain by the fact that, after the signing, Mr. [sic.] Craigie had taken me aside and asked me not to call on Sir Robert. Friends later told me that Vansittart had objected to the Naval Agreement coming into force immediately and that the difficulties on the last day before its signature had originated with him. Whether or not this is so, Vansittart, usually so self-assured, appeared to be decidedly nervous when I called on him, and he showed his special courtesy by seeing me down the steps of the Foreign Office and to my car in Downing Street, probably a very rare occurrence. I decided then to do what I could to establish friendly contact with this important man, but unfortunately I never succeeded.

"Even in those days there were forces at work in Britain which rejected any German proposal, however reasonable. The position established by this agreement guaranteed Britain, if she really wanted peace, a 100:35 ratio, in other words, a naval supremacy, which she had not had in the *Tirpitz* era. But Vansittart and his circle stuck to Versailles and are therefore mainly responsible for the subsequent developments which again drove Germany and Britain apart.

"After the Naval Agreement, I concentrated on building further on this foundation; I wanted to create even closer relations and possibly bring about an alliance with Britain. For this was Hitler's ardent wish, and also my own."*

* *The Ribbentrop Memoirs.*

Early in June 1935 Sir Samuel spent two afternoons in long discussions with Vansittart, one at his own house in Cadogan Gardens, the other in the quiet house and park of Denham Place, going over the European problem in all its phases. "The basic facts were stark and ineluctable. Hitler's strength was becoming daily more formidable and his intentions more unabashed. Secondly Japanese aggression threatened us with war in the Far East. Thirdly it was essential to Britain to have a friendly Italy in the Mediterranean. . . . Fourthly Mussolini was at the time on very bad terms with his fellow dictator, Hitler. . . . Perhaps we were too optimistic. . . . Perhaps we did not sufficiently realise the contrast between Mussolini's outlook and ours."

So it was decided that Mr. Eden should visit Mussolini and speak to him those words about Abyssinia which were omitted at the Stresa conference. That was one side of his mission to Rome of June 1935; but there was another, less well remembered and overshadowed by the Hoare-Laval episode that succeeded it six months later. Hoare, Vansittart and Eden met on June 16 at Trent Park, seat of Sir Philip Sassoon, and agreed to propose a redistribution of territory. Eden was to propose ceding to Abyssinia a corridor to the sea in British Somaliland in return for concessions of territory in the Ogaden to Italy. The scheme was doomed to failure after a leakage which led to its publication in a Sunday newspaper, and a good deal of unfavourable comment. Sir Robert would have preferred the Abyssinian question to be quietly explored by Sir Eric Drummond in Rome. He foresaw little hope of progress in the Eden visit. Lord Avon has left us in his memoirs a fairly full account of his talks with Mussolini on two successive days, during which the Duce without bombast explained his African ambitions— that he intended to detach its non-Amharic (Somali and Arab) territories from Ethiopia, and asserted that M. Laval during his January visit to Rome had conceded that Italy was to have "a free hand in Abyssinia".

"I returned to the charge several times", recalled Eden, but Mussolini remained quiet and emphatic about his plans. On the second day he said that "if he accepted a settlement without war, he would require all the territories that had been conquered by Abyssinia". After a somewhat mild expostulation expressing his disappointment and anxiety, Eden ended his rejoinder by thanking the Duce for his attention. Afterwards he concluded that the British cabinet "would now have to determine their course between upholding the League and [so] losing an ally, or undermining the foundation of peace in Europe".* He thought that as almost all pacts and agreements related to the League, to defy it in this issue would weaken peace everywhere. Peace was, to his mind, indivisible. The same dilemma vexed Vansittart, but the Permanent Under-Secretary thought that though the League might be useful against Italy, it was not effective as a weapon against Germany any longer, and could not become effective in the future.

On July 4th Sir Warren Fisher saw Mr. Baldwin and Mr. Neville Chamberlain and they discussed the heightening tension with Italy over Abyssinia. A letter written by Sir Warren to Baldwin next day showed that he shared the misgivings of Vansittart.

"I confess feeling very disquietened as a result of our talk yesterday," wrote Sir Warren. "If Italy persists in her present policy, is England really prepared not merely to threaten, but also to use force, and is she in a position to do this successfully?"

What would be Britain's motives—safeguarding her African interests, or championing the League of Nations? Britain had not intervened on behalf of China when Japan seized Manchuria nor was she likely to do so if Germany were to seize Memel.

It was questionable whether the cause of the League of Nations would be advanced by a course of action which resulted in Italy leaving the League. Germany, Japan, Italy and the United States of America would then all stand outside it.

Sir Warren thought that the worst blow to the League would be any disaster to Great Britain in the course of the next twenty years. The League's interests were intimately bound up with British influence, but Britain could not in the foreseeable future make the League the effective conscience and policeman of the world. He thought that the threat of or use of force in the crisis over Abyssinia had nothing to commend it.

The League could not be made a reality by spasmodic resort to force in cases in which Britain deemed it could be safely applied.

* *Facing the Dictators.*

At this time, then, there was no difference in outlook between Sir Warren and Sir Robert.

On his way home from Rome, Eden had to defend to Laval his own attempt to reach agreement with Mussolini without having first informed France. In his Warwick constituency on July 5th, 1935 he spoke in defence of Government policy in the abortive Somali strip plan—it had been "a risk . . . but the gravest risk would have been to sit idly and watch conditions deteriorate". He asked for the Cabinet to repeat his warning to Mussolini and though a draft was made, the dispatch was held back by the deliberate consideration in the minds of Sir Samuel Hoare and Sir Robert Vansittart that a strong warning would disincline Mussolini from taking part in three-power talks. On August 6th at a meeting at 10 Downing Street, Baldwin and Hoare decided that Eden and Vansittart should represent Britain at the tripartite Paris talks that Sir Warren had recommended and take stock of her obligations under the League Covenant first with the French. When the Wal Wal incident occurred in the previous December (in which Abyssinian and Italian Askari troops clashed in the Ogaden with severe loss of life), Lord Chatfield, First Sea Lord, had sent warning notes from the Admiralty to Vansittart. He had warned that the Mediterranean Fleet was not up to strength in face of an Italian threat and recorded the main weaknesses—shortage of anti-aircraft ammunition and lack of air cover.

"We shall have to be exceedingly cautious in Paris," observed Vansittart, recollecting Admiralty advice. Eden added: "but we must be clear. No use in going otherwise."* He wrote to a Cabinet colleague that he dreaded this visit with such vague instructions, lest some attempt be made to foist an unjust settlement on the Abyssinians. On August 14th, Eden and Vansittart met Laval in Paris and tried to explain to him how important it was that the League should prevail. They failed to draw Mussolini into three-power talks. Baron Aloisi arrived from Rome with no clear mission and Mussolini refused to have him discuss an economic solution to his claims on Abyssinia. Eden returned to London and Vansittart set off to Aix-les-Bains to acquaint Mr. Baldwin with the failure of the conference.

Between August 17th when the Paris talks ended and

* *Facing the Dictators.*

September 12th, British policy swung away from negotiating with the adamant Duce towards a tougher line. On September 12th Sir Samuel Hoare made an impressive and solemn speech to the League of Nations Assembly. It was a memorable and fateful challenge to Italy.

Lord Avon told me in after years that neither he, nor Lord Cranborne assisting him in League affairs, doubted that this speech meant anything else than that Britain was in earnest. Yet if we read again those resounding phrases, the escape clauses are apparent. It was composed by Sir Samuel Hoare and Sir Robert Vansittart together in the hope of "putting new life into the crippled body of the League".* It was not entirely bluff, in that it only pledged Britain to act if other League powers did so. It was not drafted as the result of a full Cabinet meeting. But in response to an appealing letter from Sir Samuel dated August 14th, Neville Chamberlain, then Chancellor of the Exchequer, returned from Switzerland, having persuaded the lethargic Mr. Baldwin to convene a meeting at the end of August of those ministers who were within reach of London. Even so Baldwin did not seriously concern himself with its contents. He was in Chequers when it was completed, and all that he found to say about it was:

"You have got a speech to make. Let me have a look at it," and after a quick glance, "That is all right. It must have taken you a long time to make it up."

Before it was delivered, Sir Samuel sent a private message to Mussolini on September 3rd that "Britain in no way desired destruction of Italian prosperity, of Fascism or of Mussolini's personal position," reported Herr von Hassell, German Ambassador in Rome, in a dispatch to the Foreign Ministry in Berlin.†

September 12th, 1935 was a memorable day for collective security, so many observers at Geneva thought. Sir Samuel read his speech to the Assembly from carefully prepared notes:

"The League stands and my country stands with it for the collective maintenance of the Covenant in its entirety, and particularly for steady and collective resistance to all acts of unprovoked aggression."

He repeated the last phrase, striking the desk of the rostrum with his hand.

* *Nine Troubled Years.*
† Documents on German Foreign Policy, Series C, Vol. IV, p. 687.

"One thing is certain," he continued, "if risks for peace are to be run, they must be run by all. The security of the many cannot be assured solely by the efforts of the few, however powerful they may be. I can say that the British Government will be second to none in their intention to fulfil, within the measure of their capacity, the obligations which the Covenant lays upon them.

"We believe that small nations are entitled to a life of their own . . . and that backward nations are entitled to expect that assistance will be afforded to them by more advanced peoples in building up their national life. . . . The justice of a claim is not necessarily in proportion to the national passions which are roused in support of it. They may be deliberately roused by what I regard as one of the most pernicious features of modern life—Government propaganda."

Lord Avon in after years thought there was an element of bluff in the speech and Lord Templewood claimed that if there was, bluff was both "legitimate and inescapable". Thus their historical feud continued though their names had changed. Two days after the speech a large part of the Home Fleet moved to Gibraltar. Sir Samuel had previously agreed during his talks with Pierre Laval in Paris on the 10th and 11th September that, "we both excluded the idea of war with Italy as too dangerous and double-edged for the future of Europe.* We also agreed that we must, if possible, avoid provoking Mussolini into open hostility." This being the Allied decision, it might be argued that it would have been better if the speech of September 12th had never been delivered.

In London the Left called to the Right and the echoes went round every political club and public house. It heartened the body of Anglican opinion against the Abyssinian adventure. The Bishop of St. Albans praised Sir Samuel in his diocesan magazine in the words of the 15th psalm

> He that sweareth unto his neighbour
> and disappointeth him not,
> Even though it were to his own hindrance.
> Whoso doeth these things shall never fall.

On the same day as this laud was published, September 24th, Sir Eric Drummond handed the Duce a privy message of

* *Nine Troubled Years.*

friendship from Sir Samuel. After a short period of stimulation in the League of Nations on the Abyssinian question, came the relapse when Sir Samuel telegraphed to Eden at Geneva— "I trust you will not allow any haste on the [League] Council in regard to the discussion of sanctions." The Abyssinians pressed for the arms embargo to be lifted. By the end of September the Negus found it necessary to mobilise his army and he let it be known that he was not averse to employing white mercenaries. News that Italy had begun warfare against Abyssinia was conveyed to Sir Robert at the Foreign Office on October 3rd by Signor Dino Grandi, Italian Ambassador to the Court of St. James. He described it as a forward movement of Italian troops to increase their military security. The Abyssinian war had begun, and the warning of September 12th had failed. "We were not as earnest as we thought," wrote Vansittart. "We assumed postures contrary to our intentions."* At a critical moment, with war between Italy and Abyssinia imminent, Sir Robert Vansittart had written on September 30th, 1935 an urgent warning to his Foreign Secretary against pressing too hard in pursuit of League policy. He argued a danger that Poland, Hungary and Yugoslavia would regroup themselves with Germany and cease to look towards Italy. He wrote to Sir Samuel that:

"In these circumstances . . . it becomes more difficult and alarming for France to break hard and definitely with Italy . . . we ourselves have now additional food for thought in our unarmed condition. We have all long been agreed that we must play for time. Time is indeed a vital necessity to us. We are in no condition for any adventures.

"I write this note of warning in advance of our discussions with Mr. Eden. This development is likely to make France even less whole-hearted in the Italo-Abyssinian question than hitherto. And by France I mean France and not individual members of the French government.

"I go further and add that in unfortunately existing circumstances i.e. a strong Germany and a weak England—it is not to *our* interest either to force this burning question anywhere near a conflagration if it can be by any means avoided.

"I conclude that the Council must make a further and enlarged effort for peace, and not on the contrary narrow itself

* *Mist Procession.*

as MM. Titulescu and Litvinov would have it do for varied and unavowed motives; and that the form of the enlargement, or extra inducement, must be the change of territorial satisfaction which we have propounded. . . . The Council may not like this, but the European situation is full of potential menace."*

On October 5th Signor Grandi reported to Rome that Mr. Baldwin was alleged to have delivered to a French personage (probably the French Ambassador M. Corbin) the following weighty utterance: "The British people have always countenanced dictatorships as long as the dictatorships concerned themselves with the domestic affairs of their own countries. When dictatorships have shown an urge to sally forth from home, to poke their noses beyond their own frontiers, and to disturb the peace, Great Britain has been compelled sooner or later to intervene in order to free the world from the danger of the dictatorships. That is what England did with Napoleon. That is what England did with Wilhelm II. That is what England will do with Mussolini now. . . ." The contents of this dispatch† apparently inspired an article from the Rome correspondent of the *Deutsche Allgemeine Zeitung* alleging that Britain wished to smash Fascism. Sir Robert thereupon instructed Sir Eric Drummond to seek an interview with Mussolini and endeavour to dispel this embarrassing impression. Mr. Baldwin may have spoken in this vein, but it did not suit British foreign policy that he should be taken seriously. Drummond assured the Duce that Britain was not going beyond economic sanctions and would impose no blockade. So by uneasy use of bluff and blandishment in turn British diplomacy tried to turn Mussolini from his purpose. It might have worked, but his self-confidence was inflated by his relationship with Laval and his own knowledge of the British Embassy archives in Rome. Nervous of the effect of empty threats, with Laval acting as a brake on any genuine initiative, to the detriment of British relations with Italy, Sir Robert arranged for Sir Samuel Hoare to restate British policy both to Grandi and to the German Ambassador, Herr von Hoesch. Sir Samuel said that despite a surprising unanimity of British public opinion against Italy, the British government were not pursuing any

* Vansittart Papers.
† Documents of German Foreign Policy, Series C, Vol. IV, p. 763.

73

imperialist aims of war with Italy, and was in no way encompassing the downfall of Mussolini. To the German Ambassador Vansittart spoke critically of M. Laval's endeavours to obtain "selective" application of the League provisions, though he must have spoken with a degree of simulation; for his own inclination too was to temper League action against Italy in order to keep the front against Germany in being.

On the 16th October Laval was informed of the minimum Italian demands. He then prevailed on Baldwin and Hoare to send Mr. Maurice Peterson, Head of the Abyssinian Branch of the Foreign Office, for talks with the Comte de Saint-Quentin, Head of the Africa Division of the French Foreign Ministry. These two in late October compared the British demands with the Italian claims and found them still wide apart. Britain would favour ceding East Tigre province to Italy but not West Tigre. In the first half of November there were Italian successes in the field, which made the Duce stiffer, but in the second half the rainy season began to delay Italian transport, and it may have been this factor rather than Mr. Baldwin's victory in the November General Election that seemed to bring Peterson and Saint-Quentin closer together at the end of November to an agreement which Italy might accept. Although Vansittart in some of his early published works maintained the elaborate cover under which the Hoare-Laval talks were planned, it is clear now from the documents that theirs was no casual meeting on December 7th and 8th. For a month earlier Herr von Hoesch reported on a lunch with Vansittart at which, the Permanent Under-Secretary put it that, "things had started to move. Vansittart does not reckon with the possibility of a solution before sanctions against Italy come into effect on November 18th, but he did mention the second half of December as a possible date when prospects of a solution might eventuate."* He could not have been so frank with Herr von Hoesch unless there was an equally frank attitude with Signor Grandi. If there was, a lot of the sound and fury of British movements against Mussolini were without significance.

Maurice Peterson who was mysteriously withdrawn during election time and sent back to Paris on November 21st after the British General Election was over, recorded that "one conviction I carried back with me to Paris, that in no circumstances

* German Documents, Series C, Vol. IV. Nov. 8th, 1935.

74

would the Baldwin government go to war for Abyssinia".*

"I decided to take a holiday," Vansittart wrote of the Hoare-Laval meeting, looking back in 1943 in *Lessons of My Life*, "Unwisely I took a busman's." Sir Samuel Hoare entered the same excuse, and in the aftermath of criticism Mr. Baldwin entered it for him too. But to quote Herr von Hoesch again, the German Ambassador in London reported on December 12th to Berlin that "Vansittart informed me on December 6th before he left for Paris that the forthcoming visit by himself and Sir Samuel Hoare stemmed from the desire to clarify what possibilities of a solution might exist before the situation possibly took a more acute turn. Apparently the British representatives then found that a plan existed in Paris which had been more or less agreed between Laval and Mussolini. . . ." Once more Vansittart had told the Germans something, but not all that was in his mind. Dino Grandi, who remained a good friend and a frequent visitor to Denham Place in the years between 1935 and 1939, said to an Italian journalist in February 1946 that "the Laval-Hoare plan of 1935 was nothing more or less than the Grandi-Vansittart plan".† Lady Vansittart clearly remembered the secretive atmosphere of a "busman's holiday" in which Sir Robert and she left Denham Place for the Hotel Ritz in Paris, and Anthony Eden, who had "dreaded" his own August talks with Laval in Paris, saw them go with some misgivings. He said to Sir Samuel, "don't forget that in Paris 'Van' can be more French than the French." He has also recorded for him Sir Samuel's answer. "Don't worry! I shall not commit you to anything," replied Hoare, "It would not be fair on my way through to my holiday."‡

Before leaving for Paris Vansittart called Rex Leeper, Head of the News Department, and Ralph Wigram to his room at the Foreign Office, and asked them:

"How long will it take to alter public opinion on the Abyssinian issue?"

The Election had been fought on the issue of collective security, a measure of rearmament and no truck with the aggressor. Rex Leeper thought that it would take three weeks to prepare the public mind for a negotiated settlement instead of sanctions.

* *Both Sides of the Curtain.* Sir Maurice Peterson.
† Forte, "Dino Grandi Racconta", in *Secolo* XIX, March 7th, 1946.
‡ *Facing the Dictators.*

"We have only three days," said Vansittart.

A week before their departure for Paris, Vansittart wrote to Sir Samuel about ideas then current in Whitehall of Britain standing firm against Italy and of reaching a general agreement with Germany, including colonial restitution. This may not have seemed at that time so wildly improbable to some partisans of Anglo-German understanding. For the successful negotiation of the Anglo-German naval agreement suggested that there might be yet other fields for treaty revision, such as the colonies, an air pact and the demilitarised zone of the Rhineland which Germany at that time had not yet openly reoccupied. Some in the Foreign Office emphasised the weakness of France as a treaty partner. Vansittart countered to Sir Samuel:

"I propose if I go to Paris to make plain the unpleasant truth —that unless France stands by us in deed as well as in words she will be abandoned by the United Kingdom, Russia, the Little Entente and Poland and will count as nothing in Europe except as an incitement to German aggression. . . . On present form her support of Czechoslovakia against Germany would be most improbable, if she had not even the courage to fight Italy with the United Kingdom."

He did not accept the view that Britain could "co-operate with Germany on an equal footing in the task of maintaining peace in Europe". "How?" he asked. "Germany cannot co-operate in maintaining peace if she is to expand in Europe." He did not believe that British influence could "modify" German expansion.

He could not agree to delaying the military re-equipment of Britain, and while he acknowledged the argument for a strong Germany rather than a weak one, he did not care to see Germany stronger .until her mentality was altered for the better. . . . "Till then I do not care to add to her strength." Expansion of Germany in Africa might not stop expansion in Europe. Britain would then probably have to fight. "Unless we run away from the sanctions which we are now imposing against Italy," he reflected, "we shall certainly have to do so."*

At this time, the pressure to do deals with Germany during the temporary clouding of relations with Italy was evidently hard to resist. But he plainly intended to resist it, and since it was not in his policy to stiffen the front against Italy at the risk

* Vansittart Papers.

of throwing her into the arms of Germany, his promised admonition of the France of M. Laval most probably was not uttered in the drastic form that his comments outlined. "It was neither easy nor effective to lecture others even privately, when our own armaments were so backward."* He was in reality going to Paris to keep the front against Germany in being at the expense of Abyssinia, which was anyway a lost cause.

* *Lessons of My Life*, p. 53.

CHAPTER IV

CRISIS IN THE ALLIANCE

If the departure from Victoria Station in London had the appearance of the beginning of a holiday, the arrival in Paris was of an official nature. Sir George Clerk, the British Ambassador, and French officials met the Secretary of State and Sir Robert Vansittart. They drove at once to the Quai d'Orsay and there elbowed their way through a crowd of journalists and photographers outside Laval's room. It was an inauspicious start to a confidential exchange of views, and the French Foreign Minister did not seem to be embarrassed by the publicity.

According to Sir Samuel Hoare, Laval began by saying that France had no intention of going to war with Italy, and that attempts at a compromise must be made, since an oil embargo would drive Mussolini to desperation. When Hoare asked whether Britain could count on French assistance if Italy attacked the British forces in the Mediterranean, Laval's answer was "in general terms satisfactory", but he suggested that any joint defence precautions, other than staff talks, would depend on the immediate agreement to be reached on Anglo-French policy. The joint plan for a compromise in Abyssinia which Eden had outlined to Peterson in November, and which had been under discussion in Paris since, must be extended, he said, if there was to be any chance of Italian acceptance. Since the provisional plan had been made, Mussolini had seized a considerable part of the Tigre province. Laval appeared to have a direct telephone line to Mussolini and occasionally made use of it during the meeting, though Vansittart was inclined to doubt whether he talked with the Duce himself. The meeting went on until late on Saturday afternoon. It was adjourned until Sunday, December 8th, and a short interim communiqué declared that there was complete agreement between the two ministers in seeking a basis for a friendly settlement of the Italo-Ethiopian dispute. Eden, who was spending a vigilant week-end in London, saw this communiqué and a record of the

Saturday conversations next day. His close attention suggests that he was apprehensive. He was further disturbed on Sunday afternoon by a telegram from Sir Samuel Hoare, asking that a Cabinet meeting be held on Monday.

Hoare and Laval had met again with Vansittart and Leger, Head of the French Foreign Ministry, that Sunday morning, but left outside the Abyssinian experts, Maurice Peterson and the Comte de Saint-Quentin. Eden was worried, and his disquiet communicated itself to Mr. Baldwin "who agreed that we ought to obtain more news". Eden telephoned to the British Embassy in Paris in the late Sunday afternoon, only to be told that Sir Samuel was resting, and that Sir Robert was staying at the Ritz and could not be called to answer the telephone. Eden was insistent for information. An Embassy secretary returned a few minutes later with the cryptic message that "the Secretary of State and Sir Robert Vansittart are well satisfied with the day's work". Obviously there could be no detailed discussion on an open telephone line and as Maurice Peterson would arrive in London next morning with the draft agreement, there was nothing to be said. A rather fuller communiqué, issued in Paris after the conference had ended, stated that "in the spirit of conciliation, formulae have been sought as a basis for a friendly settlement which, once the British government have agreed to it, could be submitted to the interested governments and the League of Nations."

What had happened meanwhile at the Quai d'Orsay? Hoare and Vansittart pressed for a solution whereby Italian troops would withdraw from the Amharic territories that they had occupied and be compensated with other Somali-populated lands. The agreement eventually reached was that Abyssinia should be given an outlet to the sea through British Somaliland, though without the right to build a railway (since the French-owned Addis-Djibuti line existed already and Laval was mindful of its interests). A large part of Tigre province and some lands in the east and south-east should be ceded to Italy, which would also have the monopoly of economic development under League of Nations direction in a large zone of south and south-west Abyssinia. Ethiopian sovereignty in territories not ceded was to be reaffirmed.

These were stiff terms and when Eden at breakfast time on Monday morning read the draft in French initialled S.H./P.L., it seemed to him that the Emperor was being asked to surrender about half his territory.

"I didn't think you would like it," said Peterson as the surprised Eden expostulated. In his memoirs, however, Peterson asked the question whether it was better to prepare against Germany by sacrificing part of Abyssinia, or seal the fate of Abyssinia by rejecting the plan.

Sir Samuel thought the terms "in striking contrast to Mussolini's earlier demands for all non-Amharic districts and an Italian mandate for the rest of Abyssinia."* At the time and afterwards Vansittart's opinion did not change: "every victor wants to keep his conquest. It was a question of getting back something or losing everything."† Hoare recorded that at the end of the talks, Vansittart and Sir George Clerk "congratulated me on having re-established the Anglo-French front". Vansittart recollected the French saying *"de deux choses l'une"*, which served for his motto on this occasion—at the expense of nearly half Abyssinia he sought to keep the Stresa front alive. It was not a just solution, but one that British interests, as laid down in his 1933 outline of foreign policy, seemed to require. He pressed Peterson to explain to Eden the necessity of accepting the Hoare-Laval agreement in face of the imminent German menace.

There may be an impression that Vansittart lingered on in Paris and left Eden in the dark as to developments in the next three days. I am indebted to Lord Avon for the contents of a letter written by Vansittart to him on December 10th from the British Embassy in Paris, reporting contacts with the Italian Ambassador, who had raised the question of another visit to Mussolini.

British Embassy,
Paris
December 10th, 1935

My dear Anthony,
    Please see the telegram recording my interview with the Italian Ambassador in Paris.
    At the end of our interview the Ambassador asked me plainly whether, in case of need, I would still refuse the personal contact which I had refused in August. I replied that I had refused because Signor Mussolini had then decided

---

* *Nine Troubled Years.*   † To Lady Vansittart.

upon war, but I had never refused any service in my power
to the cause of peace. We left it at that. I have let the P.M.
know of this, but no one else.

yours ever
Van.

The Right Honourable
Anthony Eden, M.C., M.P.

"The rest of the tale is known," Vansittart wrote afterwards.
"The storm broke and blew away all prospects of further
negotiation."* There were leakages before the Foreign Secretary could see the draft, but what long remained unknown is
how the leakages occurred. Vansittart suspected Laval who
gave a parting lunch to the British on Sunday the 8th and
"began talking and talked quite a lot". Others suspected that
Alexis Leger, head of the French Foreign Ministry, was unable
to contain the secret of the draft agreement until the British
Cabinet had pronounced upon it. Sir Samuel Hoare remembered the crowd of photographers and diplomatic correspondents pressing round Laval's door on the Saturday when the
British arrived. He also confessed to having briefed "several
correspondents who wished for an interview" in the office of
Sir Charles Mendl at the British Embassy on the Sunday evening and asked them "not to comment in any detail" on the
"very general idea" that he gave them. He added that "they
appeared ready to fall in with my request".† The tortuous
motives that Vansittart ascribed to Laval appeared in after
years even to Vansittart himself over-ingenious. It was perhaps
in the very nature of these negotiations that they would leak,
and the fact that two newspapers hostile to the Foreign
Minister, the *Oeuvre* and the *Echo de Paris*, printed the entire
text, suggests that there were forces in France wishing to em-
barrass Laval, who was obliged to resign a fortnight later. He
certainly summoned Vansittart in the middle of the night to the
Quai d'Orsay after the leakages occurred, bleary eyed himself
in a soiled nightgown, and asked him to explain to the British
government by telephone the merits of the draft agreement.

Sir Samuel was already in Switzerland before he was aware
of the leakages. When he first ventured on to the ice at Zuoz
near St. Moritz next day, Sir Samuel was confident of his skill

* *Lessons of My Life.*   † *Nine Troubled Years.*

at figures. In the middle of a turn he fell unconscious from one of his periodic black-outs and badly fractured his nose in two places. His doctor ordered him to rest for several days before travelling, and it was not until December 16th that he reached London, still unfit for strenuous business, but committed to answer for the Hoare-Laval agreement on December 19th in a Parliament increasingly impatient of the deal.

Rex Leeper, head of the News Department of the Foreign Office, found himself being assailed with questions from all sides about the Hoare-Laval proposals. He telephoned to Zuoz and found Sir Samuel convalescing and surprised at the uproar.

"I advise you to come home at once, in your interests," said Leeper. Sir Robert was back in London four days ahead of the Secretary of State. He was met on December 12th at Victoria station by his own friends in the Department, Rex Leeper among them and his Personal Secretary, Clifford Norton. They told him that a storm appeared about to break on the head of Sir Samuel Hoare, the fiercer because to the British public the Hoare-Laval plan seemed to be a new departure in policy and a breach of election pledges. Vansittart seemed amazed at the uproar.

"I thought we did a pretty good job in Paris," he said. "Come to dinner and we'll talk it over."

He continued in surprise at the rising storm that Leeper and Norton predicted. "We'll have to ride it out," he said imperturbably.

"It will bring down the Government," they warned him. "You must go and see the Prime Minister."

"When?"

"Now."

It was 9 p.m.

All three went down to the House of Commons, and as Vansittart talked to Baldwin in the Prime Minister's room, the secretary carried in a sheaf of telegrams of protest at the change of British policy. It seems that Vansittart had heartened him; for when he came out, Norton saw Baldwin throw up the whole bunch of papers into the air, where they floated for a moment like a cloud of pigeons.

"Tell the Press that we must have more aeroplanes," said Stanley Baldwin.

Van came out smiling and said: "He is all right." They were

still dubious. When Norton had spoken earlier to Cabinet officials of the need for the Prime Minister to brief the Press, his Parliamentary Private Secretary, Thomas Dugdale, had exclaimed, "He mustn't touch it."

So it turned out. Under the stresses of parliamentary faction Baldwin saw the gravity of his own position and decided that he would not seek to explain the apparent change of policy to any but *The Times*. He fended off parliamentary questions on the plea that the proposals had not been discussed with other governments. Next morning Vansittart rang up Leeper and said:

"It is no use. S.B. intends to let it rip." Sir Robert had urged that the Prime Minister should make it plain that Sir Samuel's action simply continued the negotiations with France that had been going on for several weeks and upon which the Cabinet had been informed at every stage. Vansittart described his reception in London as "my icy return".

"I urged him to take the Press into his confidence, but he only sent for Dawson."*

To the Commons Baldwin "instead of insisting that the plan had been made at the request of the League as a basis of compromise to stop war, talked mysteriously of facts that, if they were fully known would convince the whole House of the wisdom of what had happened."† "My lips are not yet unsealed," he said, and afterwards he told his crony Tom Jones that he had been thinking of the unpreparedness of Malta against an Italian bombing attack when he said that "if the facts were known nobody would go into the lobby against him". His mysteriousness also covered the progress already achieved in the Peterson–Saint-Quentin talks, which made his Foreign Secretary appear to be taking a new initiative in his meeting with Laval.

At its first meeting on Monday, December 9th the Cabinet had actually adopted the draft plan and agreed to forward it to the League for consideration. It was telegraphed to the Emperor of Abyssinia. Eden said flatly that neither the League nor the Negus would accept it.

"That lets us out," grunted Baldwin.‡

While the turmoil began to rise around the unfortunate

---

* *Mist Procession*, Geoffrey Dawson, editor of *The Times*.
† *Nine Troubled Years*.   ‡ *Facing the Dictators*.

Hoare, Mr. Eden went to Paris and travelled on with Laval to Geneva. There Eden said in a speech to the Committee of Eighteen on Abyssinia: "These conversations in Paris were begun with the approval of the members of the League and neither the French Government or ourselves had at any time any other intentions than to bring the outcome of our work to the League for its information and judgment. The proposals are neither definitive nor sacrosanct. They are suggestions which, it is hoped, may make possible a beginning of negotiations. The Policy of His Majesty's Government remains today that any final settlement must be acceptable to the League as well as to the parties in conflict."

But Hoare lingered in Switzerland and that was his downfall. When he returned on December 16th, two damaging debates had already taken place in the House of Commons. On December 17th Neville Chamberlain came to see him in bed at his house in Cadogan Gardens and agreed to defend the agreement reached. The same afternoon Baldwin called, listened and said: "We all stand together." But after another Cabinet meeting Neville Chamberlain came back "with a very different story". Sir Samuel must recant on the Hoare-Laval plan as a mistaken initiative. In the meantime Sir Austen Chamberlain, Neville's half brother, had played an unwitting role in the downfall of Sir Samuel Hoare. Many Conservatives trusted him as a leader more than the lethargic Baldwin. Eden, who stood vexed and righteous near the head of the Conservative revolt, was mindful to serve with Sir Austen either as Premier or Foreign Secretary. Other more powerful men had long felt that the Prime Minister must go. To Baldwin, as Hoare lay in bed, came rumour of the rebellious mood of his Party. He saw in Sir Austen a danger to himself, sent for him and spoke a few well-chosen words:

"Austen, when Sam has gone, I shall want to talk to you about the Foreign Office."

Sir Austen took this hint to mean that he would return to his beloved Foreign Office which he had left after illness in 1928. He hurried round to see his friends Ralph and Ava Wigram* at their home in Lord North Street and confided in them.

It was noticed by Neville Chamberlain that Austen first made a speech to the Conservative Party Foreign Affairs

* Narrative, Lady Waverley.

Committee supporting the Hoare-Laval plan as the least bad of several alternatives, but that he found Conservative opposition to it so strong that he ended by condemning it. This seemed to Hoare to decide the whole coalition against the Government policy. But when requested by Neville Chamberlain:

"I told him at once that I was not prepared to make any such recantation," wrote Sir Samuel.* "I was convinced that nothing short of the proposals would save Abyssinia and prevent Mussolini from joining the Hitler front." This was also the view of Vansittart, who "asked some friends if they would be so bellicose if the aggressor were Germany. . . . I thought that there was still a chance of saving most of Abyssinia. It was not to be. The whole was lost." On December 19th Sir Samuel made his speech, not from the dispatch box but from the back benches, having resigned from office and handed in his seals, and so came Eden. "I should have liked to resign," wrote Vansittart; but he received friendly advice from an unexpected quarter, Lord Beaverbrook, who told him that it was not for civil servants to resign on public issues. Sir Samuel went alone.

It was then for Baldwin to summon Sir Austen Chamberlain and this he did, as he had promised. Sir Austen related his words to Ralph Wigram immediately afterwards.

"Austen, I said I wished to see you about the Foreign Office after Sam Hoare's resignation. If you had been ten years younger, there would be no doubt in my mind but that you should have it. As it is, and I am sure you will admit my choice, I have decided to offer it to Anthony."

Every man is a victim of the circumstances in which he comes to power. Hoare fell in an attempt to retain Italy in the western alignment. The manner of succession of Anthony Eden inhibited thereafter attempts to revive the triple front of Stresa. Of the agitation against the Hoare-Laval agreement Vansittart summed up that thus "we lost Abyssinia, we lost Austria, we formed the Axis. We made certain of Germany's next war." In what measure was he at fault in his determination to keep the continent aligned against Germany? For that he was the driving force behind Sir Samuel Hoare, there was no doubt. "Vansittart never ceased to hold up my arms while the storm was raging," wrote Lord Templewood.†

* *Nine Troubled Years.*   † Ibid.

Vansittart did an unusual thing when he noticed the strength of opposition to the Hoare-Laval agreement by calling together all his Heads of Department in his room and discussing with them the policy and intention of the Foreign Office. He invited criticisms and two of them, George Rendel then Head of the Eastern Department, and Laurence Collier, Head of the Northern Department spoke up and criticised what they held to be an over-credulous acceptance of Italian strength.

"I expected to be sent to South America," said Sir Laurence Collier to me looking back in retirement, "but I noticed on the contrary that the Permanent Head of the Foreign Office treated me rather better after my intervention than he did before."

It is said that Mr. Baldwin was urged by the partisans of Anglo-German understanding to get rid of Sir Robert Vansittart at this juncture by sending him to an Embassy abroad. There were reports published of his impending removal, but it is reliably said that King George V was emphatic that a senior civil servant could not be made the victim of a minister's error, though he thought it a mistake to have altered the helm so suddenly after a General Election. Lord Avon, twenty-eight years afterwards, seemed to me inclined to think that Vansittart could not be blamed and that Sir Samuel, the politician, should have known to what extent he could rely on British public opinion to follow him.

"If the League action against Italy had succeeded," Lord Avon told me in his retirement at Fyfield Manor in 1963, "we would have fought Germany over Czechoslovakia and not over Poland." He evidently thought that the sword of the League could have been effectively whetted on Italy, a possibility that Vansittart never ceased to doubt.

So they stood at the end of the Hoare-Laval crisis, Foreign Secretary and Permanent Under-Secretary on the threshold of 1936 and greater stresses. In his first paper to the Cabinet in that year Vansittart chose as his text an extract from the dispatch of Sir Eric Phipps from Berlin of November 6th 1935:*

"The present Ethiopian imbroglio is mere child's play compared with the German problem that will, in some not very distant future, confront His Majesty's Government." "Hitherto," Vansittart wrote, "it had always been assumed that Italy would form part—indeed an indispensable part—of any

* Dispatch No. 1129.

counterpoise to Germany. That position was reached at Stresa; but the assumption is no longer possible. No one can foretell what either her tendencies or her capacity will be as a result of her war with Abyssinia and her quarrel with the League. All we can say is that this view certainly renders any prospect of an effective encirclement of Germany even more doubtful than before."

He considered what quietening effect a League victory over Italy would have on Germany and thought that Hitler would only judge and be impressed by the strength and readiness of the component parts of the League, "and these clearly still leave much to be desired". He visualised a situation in which "we and our League associates may within a respite of years grow to a position where defence can make attack too hopeless to be worth while. But no member of the League has embarked on this course in time and Germany will be ready first."

It was inevitable that his thoughts should revert to reviving friendship with Italy. Dino Grandi, the Italian Ambassador in London, much in his confidence, believed that it could be done. Some of his Foreign Office colleagues believed it too. The crux of British policy in early 1936 was how to pursue an orthodox League of Nations policy of sanctions against the aggressor Italy, without making it easy for Germany to unbalance the *status quo* in Europe; and how after the collapse of Abyssinian resistance to seek renewed friendship with Italy without seeming to condone aggression. Vansittart admitted that both the new Foreign Secretary, Mr. Eden, and the Under-Secretary of State, Lord Cranborne, maintained a correct attitude towards Italy, whereas his own laboured under a duality of purpose. He saw what he wanted. He was impenitent.

Impenitent, and the history of relations with France after the fall of Laval late in January 1936, seemed to bear out his misgivings. For it was not only Pierre Laval who remained firmly opposed to a policy of sanctions. Eden thought that "while there could be no going back on sanctions",* the League had been so shaken by the Hoare-Laval affair that it would be some time before its strength could be rebuilt. But he found Etienne Flandin, the new Foreign Minister in the Sarraut government as cautious about an oil sanction against Italy after February 26th as Laval had been at their last meeting on

* *Facing the Dictators*, p. 318.

January 20th. Flandin "argued the Fascist case with blatant confidence"* and said that an oil embargo would not work. American oil companies were then increasing their exports to Italy. Eden pressed for a date to be named on which to impose the oil sanctions, while Flandin thought it time for a new peace move in Rome. "Flandin's attitude was indistinguishable from Laval's. . . ." Here was the situation, reflected Lord Avon, that would confront him again and again in the next two years. Sir Eric Drummond thought, and Flandin thought, (and Vansittart with a body of opinion in the Foreign Office believed also) that the Duce would become more reasonable if timely concessions and appeals were made. "I thought not," wrote Lord Avon, "I considered that strength, economic or military, was the factor which carried most weight with Mussolini." This strength, as Vansittart had pointed out on innumerable occasions, Britain had not really got, in view of the rising might of Germany. Eden saw Count Grandi and as the new Foreign Secretary assured him that he harboured no personal antipathy towards the Duce and Fascist Italy. Grandi seemed much relieved to hear it and earnestly argued that if neither side insisted on a complete success for itself, agreement could again be reached. The wrangle with France over sanctions dragged on and Flandin on March 3rd finally presented Mr. Eden with a document which went to the heart of the matter. Would Britain fulfil her engagements under the Locarno Treaty, if necessary alone? He said that without such an assurance France could not agree to an oil sanction. Mr. Eden could go no further than an undertaking to consult the Cabinet. The misgivings of Flandin were well founded. For Germany was to reoccupy the Rhineland four days later.

This happened during a period of schism between Britain and France, brought about by the disagreement over Italy and Abyssinia and deepened by French suspicion, with some justification, that Britain wanted the Rhineland question out of the way. The Cabinet had formed its opinion on this and Vansittart's references to it make it plain that revision was accepted as desirable, if it was embodied in a general settlement.

The schism enabled Hitler to settle the Rhineland question by itself. Herr von Hoesch, in presenting the unpalatable *fait accompli* to Eden, came with Hitler's tempting promise that if

* *Facing the Dictators,* p. 328.

Britain accepted the German move, Germany would shortly consider re-entering the League of Nations.

There was little real indignation in Britain. The public were too bewildered at the multiplicity of belligerent states, Japan, Italy, Germany. There was also no contrition among those British politicians who saw a possibility of leaning on Germany and separating from the Latin bloc. In Foreign Office circles there was division of opinion over the wisdom of making Italy pay for aggression. The matter of League commitments and the official conscience continued to perplex them.

In the early days of April 1936 the Abyssinian armies began to face defeat. Harassed by poison gas attacks and continuous bombardment they fell back on the northern front. An Abyssinian delegate reported to Mr. Eden a very grave situation. Vansittart in London and Eden in Geneva argued with the French for a League enquiry on allegations of gas warfare, but even that Flandin wished to avoid. By April 9th, without effective support, moral or material, the Abyssinians still declared through their representative in Geneva that they would not accept such terms as the Hoare-Laval plan contained,* and Eden returned to England to tell Mr. Baldwin of the imminent collapse of Abyssinian resistance. By June, a month after the Emperor had left his country, Eden found some readiness among League supporters in London and a few small Mediterranean states for Britain to close the Suez canal. A memorandum on this course of action was drawn up in the Foreign Office. But in April Vansittart had already expressed himself emphatically against any such course.

"I do not think it is of any use at this stage to speak of closing the Canal," wrote Vansittart to Eden. "It is highly improbable that the Government would consider it, and a very serious situation would be created for the Government in the country, particularly if the war (for of course it would lead to war) did not go well in the opening stages. There would have been a great deal to be said for closing the Canal at the beginning of this unhappy affair. The reason we were not in a position to do so is that for fifteen years we have starved our fighting services and made a virtue of it. We cannot behave as if those fifteen years had not been."

The criticism of backwardness applied, Vansittart thought,

* *Facing the Dictators*, p. 377.

not only to Britain but to every Member of the League of Nations. Behind this immediate emergency, whatever form it took in its first stages, there did undoubtedly lie the danger, indeed probability, of a much wider conflagration. The risk might have been run if Britain had started her military re-equipment three years earlier when Hitler first came to power.

He wanted the maintenance of existing sanctions and the extension of financial or armaments facilities to Abyssinia. If Britain could not carry the League with her in that, he saw little hope of it following her effectively into a war. He feared anyway the utmost trouble with Italy in Africa, if not in Europe. But that prospect was less unpleasant than the danger of setting fire to a fuse in the powder barrel of Europe.

Neville Chamberlain may have had wind of this conflict of policy within the Foreign Office. In a speech to a Conservative club on June 10th the Chancellor of the Exchequer described continuation of sanctions or intensifying them against Italy as "the very midsummer of madness". Eden protested, but Baldwin denied responsibility and even the Foreign Secretary had to admit that "the sanctions front was now out of joint", and that sanctions would soon have to be lifted.

There had been in the British Cabinet "those who wanted the Stresa Front and those who wanted the League".* Eden had for weeks past been pressed to raise sanctions and win back Mussolini from the side of Hitler. Neither counsel prevailed, though he realised that many countries were already in breach of their sanctions undertakings. Sanctions everywhere were gradually dropped after his speech to the House of Commons on June 17th making it plain that Britain would abandon them.

What dragged on was an indeterminate British attitude. Sir Eric Drummond reported in December 1936 from Rome on the worsening economic plight of Italy after the Abyssinian war and the likelihood that Italy would be more amenable to British influence in consequence. This report was taken up with alacrity by the school in the Foreign Office that thought the Stresa front could be revived, though by then Italy had joined the Anti-Comintern pact and sent troops to Spain, an action which the British interpreted as unfriendly to their interests.

* *Facing the Dictators.*

A junior official suggested that it would not be wise to "keep all the hungry powers lean at the same time". He seems to have borrowed this phrase from the Vansittart vocabulary of style, and argued that after all, compared with Germany, Italy was only a petty thief. British public opinion should be prepared gradually for some such action as a loan or credits to Italy some time in the first half of 1937, to keep her out of the company of "other international toughs".

Mr. Orme Sargent, Assistant Under-Secretary of State, thought this a useful opinion. An indirect approach from Mussolini to British government circles in December 1936 gave him to suppose that Italy sought a *rapprochement* and would soon seek a system of credits. He thought that any settlement concluded should be based on the broader field of European politics and economics. Vansittart expressed his strong agreement, but when the proposal was put to Eden, the Secretary of State reacted forcibly. He did not agree so strongly, he replied. What was this argument that everything should be done to ease Italy's path and nothing to ease Germany's? If Italy were so poor a creature, why repeat the tragic mistake of autumn 1935 of overrating her? Italy would sell herself always to the highest bidder, and though less formidable than Germany her recent record was worse. He thought that towards both dictators the British attitude should remain steadfastly the same—they would be aided economically and financially if they changed their political behaviour, not otherwise—in return for acts not promises.

Vansittart expostulated that the Foreign Office did not advocate lending "blind" to Italy.

"Why," he reminded Eden, "I mentioned to you the other day the probability that Italy was shaky internally, and would be driven to borrow, and you said:

"Then she will have to pay for it." All that the Foreign Office wished to do, Vansittart argued, was to think ahead in case Italy made such an approach in 1937, so that she could be detached from extreme complicity with Germany.

Eden replied tersely that the proposition thus stated was rather different from that first put to him. Lord Cranborne, Under-Secretary of State, interjected that the Government must be wary of a policy of trying to bribe Italy away from Germany. Under the present régime he regarded Italy as a natural born crook. "Any assistance given to her in her present frame of mind will be used to further her crooked purposes." As he saw it, Italy and Germany had themselves to create the atmosphere in which loans would be possible. Britain possessed the sinews of prosperity, and without economic assistance, neither state could ever recover its full strength. He would like to see the United States enter an agreement not to give loans to either Germany or Italy unless in some sort of general settlement, and no assistance given merely in vague hope of buying either of them off. This seems to have been the last initiative for the time being from within the Foreign Office to make a bargain with Italy. The stubbornness of Mussolini in maintaining intervention in the Spanish Civil War gave no hope of the sort of behaviour that Mr. Eden and Lord Cranborne thought indispensable to a *rapprochement*. This lively exchange of views on the attitude to Italy, recorded in the Vansittart Papers, explains much. Eden was highly sensitive to public opinion on the subject of Italy. After all, that same public opinion had brought him to this high office at the age of thirty-eight. He was also incensed at the flouting of the gentlemen's agreement on Spain by Mussolini. Vansittart as a civil servant was less sensitive to public opinion. He sensed, moreover, that Britain could only with safety have taken strong action against Italy after the precaution of an understanding with Germany. The Cabinet would never have risked action otherwise, and it was a price that Vansittart was unwilling to have them pay.

CHAPTER V

POINT OF NO RETURN

"Such were these odd days that my wife and I found cordiality suddenly limited," wrote Vansittart.* After the Hoare-Laval crisis he was the target of press attack—"the man behind it all", the *News Chronicle* called him. There could have been no immediate harmony of views between Vansittart and the new Foreign Secretary, Mr. Eden, in January 1936, at any rate on British policy towards Italy, and before the year was out Eden was consulting with Mr. Baldwin to transfer Vansittart to the Embassy in Paris. The Vansittart hand is less evident in the Foreign Office documents of January and February 1936, but it was his good fortune to have in Sir Orme Sargent, Assistant Under-Secretary, a man who pursued the same courses by less visible paths—"Moley" he was called. And the Head of the Central Department, Ralph Wigram, possessed the same informed mistrust of German intentions, but managed to express himself with a calm detachment that was a welcome change in manner to Cabinet Ministers though not varying in matter from the uncomfortable advice of his master. The mind of Ralph Wigram, a brilliant intellect within a body wasted by infantile paralysis, appears in a delaying action early in 1936 that had to be fought while the League of Nations was in disarray, France and Britain mistrustful of each other in the aftermath of the Hoare-Laval crisis and Italy estranged by sanctions. "He seemed a very gentle, almost shy person . . . with his youthful looks and quiet voice and few words."†

So a Foreign Office colleague described him and so he may have appeared to Herr von Hoesch, the German Ambassador, and Prince Bismarck, Counsellor of Embassy, when they called at the Foreign Office in January and February. But his close friends knew him as the man who had discovered significant omissions from the English translation of Hitler's book *Mein Kampf* and had them specially circulated to members of Parliament. He was not afraid to meet Winston Churchill socially, to have Sir John Simon know it when he was Foreign

---

* *Mist Procession.*   † *Bound for Diplomacy*, Valentine Lawford.

Secretary, or for that matter to inform the eminent back bencher on the more serious reports from Germany—a heavy responsibility for a junior official to assume. He had also handed secretly to British newspapers in 1934, with the permission of Vansittart, some of the disturbing reports reaching them of German air strength.

On January 30th Herr von Hoesch reported from London to the German Foreign Ministry two long and confidential conversations with Wigram. The British diplomat had told him of a French offer to Britain of a bilateral air pact early in 1935, to which "the British General Staff had decisively opposed agreement", preferring supposedly to work for an "Air-Locarno". Wigram sought to explain to von Hoesch that there was nothing singular in a triangular air agreement which, in the event of a German infraction, would give Britain the right to use French airfields.

It must have required all Wigram's serenity to expound this embarrassing feature, on which Sir Eric Phipps in the autumn of 1935 had failed to convince Hitler. On February 4th there was another meeting between Wigram and von Hoesch, with Wigram denying that after the funeral of King George V there had been any secret talks with Mr. Litvinov about a political agreement—"such a *rapprochement*," he said, "would create the conditions prevailing before the [First] World War."* He sought to reassure the German Ambassador that Britain was really as undecided and unallied as she unfortunately was.

Prince Bismarck continued these visits on February 12th, drawing attention to hostile British press comments on Germany, and Wigram seized the occasion to point out that the German press was accusing Britain of taking part in "encirlement", whereas there was no such intention. He then hinted that he had been instructed that very morning by the Cabinet to begin drafting "a working agreement" between the three Western powers, Great Britain, France and Germany, for which "the chief requirement was a common basis between Britain and Germany". He added that "it was seriously believed that there was a danger of Germany proceeding to a military occupation of the demilitarised Rhineland zone". Two days later a Polish diplomat in London told Bismarck that Mr. Eden had given a "juridical answer" to a question from Litvinov

* German Documents, Series C, Vol. IV, p. 1,089.

about British intentions if the Rhineland zone were re-occupied by Germany; and on that very day, February 14th, Eden reported to the Cabinet that it was improbable that France would fight for the Rhineland, and so "it would be preferable for Great Britain and France to enter betimes into negotiations with the German Government".* On February 17th Lord Cranborne, Under-Secretary of State, tried his hand at quietening the German diplomats, and on February 25th Herr von Neurath instructed Herr von Hoesch, "in your next conversation unobtrusively ask if the British have formed a more concrete idea of a working agreement", to which the reply came that "Eden is not in the position at the moment to make any concrete proposals", as he would shortly be seeing M. Flandin. A more concrete attitude was meanwhile reported from Rome on February 22nd by Herr von Hassell that "Italy would not take part in action by Britain and France if Germany violated the Locarno treaty." On February 28th Herr von Hassell was more explicit—Mussolini expected intensified sanctions over Abyssinia, and "a participation of Italy with the other Locarno powers in the event of an alleged breach of Locarno is extremely unlikely". The way into the Rhineland seemed clear.

Flandin in Geneva early in March, aware of the mood of Mussolini, engaged Eden in long arguments against an oil embargo on Italy, and on March 3rd clinched them with a document asking Britain for a written undertaking that she would fulfil her engagements to France under the Locarno treaty, if necessary alone. All Eden could do was to undertake "to consult my colleagues". The incongruity of asking France to embroil herself further with Italy was not at this moment apparent to him, though Flandin expressed his acute fears about the Rhineland zone and stated its value as a deterrent to Germany attacking Czechoslovakia or Belgium.

Eden was intent on making the League the working machinery of peace. He returned to London on March 5th and at once reported to the Cabinet that evening on the anxieties of Flandin. They decided against an open warning to Germany and even, as we shall see, a private warning. Instead Eden suggested drawing the Germans into discussion of some topic between the Locarno powers "to forestall the growing threat of occupation". He invited the German Ambassador to the

* *Facing the Dictators*, p. 335.

Foreign Office on March 6th and asked Herr von Hassell to
refer to Hitler the possibility of opening serious discussions on an
Air Pact. "I judged that the matter of the demilitarised Zone
would certainly be raised early. The French could then be
drawn in, and the whole matter peaceably settled." The
memoirs of Lord Avon are not explicit on what he told Herr von
Hoesch. As for the dispatch that Herr von Hoesch sent reporting
his conversation of March 6th with Eden, I have been unable
to find it in the copies of the German Archives now available in
the British Foreign Office Library and Public Record Office.
It was first included, but then omitted from the compiled British
edition of the German documents, Series C, Vol. V, so that
either the editors thought Mr. Eden's last attempt to avert the
German occupation of the Rhineland of merely marginal
interest, or there is some other explanation for the absence of
the Ambassador's report. Since it has not yet been published, I
quote from it here,* as being of more than passing interest and
evidence of how far the British Government was prepared to go
to prevent re-occupation of the Rhineland.

"Eden asked me to call on him in the afternoon," wrote the
Ambassador in a telegram that reached Berlin next day. ". . . I
spoke on the telephone to Dieckhoff† and sent a reply that as I
expected an important instruction from Berlin could we postpone till Saturday morning. Eden replied . . . he wished urgently
to see me this afternoon too.

"I therefore visited him at once. He began by expressing his
great satisfaction at the Anglo-German naval pact. . . . The
Foreign Secretary went back to his conversation with me of
February 27th on an Anglo-German working agreement. He
wanted after seeing Flandin in Geneva to discuss it with me
further." Eden then expounded the idea of a triple Air Pact.
"Of course there was a wish to see Germany return to the
League of Nations; but it was clear to Mr. Eden that this could
not be expected of the Reich government at this moment, and
he would refrain from pressing that point." Mr. Eden then
discussed details of the proposed Air Pact including "a basic
exclusion of bombing". He spoke of collateral pacts, which
Germany regarded with suspicion, but assured Herr von
Hoesch that any entered into by Britain would not create

* From a copy in the Bonn archives.
† Under-Secretary in the German Foreign Ministry.

unbalance between the signatories and would contain no secret clauses. Talks on this basis would certainly create an atmosphere of confidence in Western Europe. I limited myself mainly to receiving this communication. . . . Mr. Eden asked me whether newspaper reports were true that the Fuehrer shortly intended an important political declaration of the Reichstag. I said that I had not been informed." In the whole conversation there was no hint of a British warning against a breach of Locarno or an intrusion into the Rhineland zone.

Herr von Hoesch repeated to Eden at the conclusion of their talk that a courier was on the way from Berlin with a special message for Eden from Hitler. Could they meet again next day so that he could deliver it? Von Hoesch was not speaking the truth in saying that he had not been informed. For a Most Secret code message of March 3rd* had been sent from Berlin to German embassies in London, Paris, Rome and Brussels informing them that the Fuehrer would reply to the recently ratified Franco-Soviet pact of mutual assistance by re-establishing German sovereignty in the Rhineland. They met again next day and the news was given to Eden that German troops were entering the Rhineland. The note which Herr von Hoesch delivered at their encounter on March 7th contained affirmations that Herr Hitler would not fortify it for the time being and was ready when the Rhineland question was out of the way to re-enter the League of Nations. He had no intention of doing so, but this had been one of the conditions which British Cabinet Ministers had discussed together as part of a general settlement attaching to a permitted German "occupation" of the demilitarised zone.

The sequel is well known. Hitler never did. Wigram had vainly hoped, as his friend Valentine Lawford recalls,† that this time the Hitler bluff would be called once and for all. Instead a comment was spoken around that is quoted by Mr. Eden in his memoirs as repeated to him by a taxi-driver that "the Germans were only going into their own back garden". This homily was really of less humble origin, having been put into circulation by the assiduous Marquess of Lothian, who quickly called on the German Ambassador to discuss how Hitler's move could be made acceptable to the French.

* German Foreign Office Documents, Series C, Vol. IV.
† *Bound for Diplomacy.*

The British attitude had been cautious from the start. Eden had instructed the British Ambassador in Paris in February that Britain expected to be told the French attitude in the event of a violation of the zone, but not to have "to discuss the matter on the basis of the British attitude".* As soon as Herr von Hoesch had left Eden on March 7th, Eden summoned his chief advisers, Vansittart, Orme Sargent, Wigram, and Rex Leeper. He showed them the Hitler note. Vansittart spoke of it without illusion, and dismissed the German claim for an unfortified zone on the French side as a piece of rhetoric. The rest of them had the impression that Hitler's offer to discuss returning to the League did not deceive Eden. He turned to Leeper and asked the Head of the News Department:

"What will the Press say tomorrow?"

"I think they will say that Germany is on her own territory."

"I was afraid that would be your answer," Eden replied. He was in a position hardly less difficult than Vansittart. For like Sir Samuel Hoare before him, he was fresh in office when the crisis came. Having staked his reputation on the campaign to make the League work over Italy, here was a much greater menace in a much less assailable form, and British foreign policy was out of joint. Eden knew how disinclined Baldwin was to become involved in the Continent. When *The Times* pronounced on the following Monday, it was in an editorial article entitled "A Chance to Rebuild". "British opinion will be nearly unanimous in its drive to turn an untoward proceeding to account," it wrote. "The old structure of European peace, one sided and unbalanced, is nearly in ruins. It is the moment, not to despair, but to rebuild." After this departmental conference and before seeing the Cabinet, Eden took the precaution of summoning the French Ambassador. His message for the French government expressed the hope that France would do nothing to make the situation more difficult, and that there must next be a "steady and calm examination". To the Cabinet he wrote a sceptical comment on Hitler's good faith, but added that "owing to Germany's growing material strength and power of mischief in Europe, it is in our interest to conclude with her as far-reaching and enduring a settlement as possible while Herr Hitler is in the mood to do so". He thought that in this instance Britain should press for a formal condemnation by the League of

* *Facing the Dictators.*

the Rhineland zone violation, but not ask for financial or economic sanctions. Eden sent this Cabinet paper to Vansittart on Sunday, March 8th, and records that he described it as "lucid, dispassionate and realistic". There is no note of this exchange in Vansittart's aide-memoires, but there is no reason to doubt it. He was not in a position to advise sanctions on Germany when he had resisted them against Italy in the previous year on the grounds that Britain was too weak to risk enforcing them. His personal position was too shaken to permit a *volte face* then, or for him to endanger his weakened influence.

"Don't bother about Vansittart, he's done for," said an English friend to Flandin when the French Prime Minister, visiting London in the course of the March talks, thought to press the French case in that quarter. After Eden and Halifax had heard from Flandin in Paris on March 9th that he envisaged military action the British switched the talks to London. It fell to Wigram to insinuate to Flandin that he would gain more effective British support by holding the League Council talks in London—a suggestion that proved to be untrue and which Wigram did not relish making.

Lawford saw Wigram at the St. James's Palace Conference, at which the League Council surveyed the shattered Locarno Agreement. Wigram was "constantly at the Foreign Secretary's side, inwardly increasingly disillusioned and depressed". His sense of doom is more strongly on record on this occasion than Vansittart's. In his autobiography foreshortened by death, Vansittart hardly refers to the Rhineland crisis in the last chapter, nor does it figure in *Lessons of My Life*. It was Ralph Wigram who worked behind the scenes of the St. James's Palace Conference of the League Council, to stiffen British public opinion; and he and his wife as friends of Flandin from Paris Embassy days were able to invite to their house in North Street an audience of British politicians and journalists to hear Flandin say what he thought of the Rhineland crisis.

"If you do not stop Germany now, all is over," said the French Foreign Minister in the quiet of Mrs. Wigram's drawing room to those assembled, "France cannot guarantee Czecho-slovakia any more, because that will become geographically impossible. . . . If you do not stop Germany today, war is inevitable."

Wigram suggested to Winston Churchill that a meeting

between Baldwin and Flandin be arranged, and this happened on March 19th at 10 Downing Street. Flandin said afterwards that he proposed a French police operation, for which he required only the moral support of Britain. The outcome was that Baldwin said: "You may be right, but if there is even one chance in a hundred that war would follow from your police operation, I have not the right to commit Britain—England is not in a state to go to war."*

For Wigram there was the unpleasant duty of accompanying Flandin to Victoria Station at the end of his mission of failure. After which Wigram returned to his house in Westminster and spoke those prophetic words which his wife preserved and Winston Churchill perpetuated—"War is now inevitable and it will be the most terrible war there has ever been. . . . I don't think I shall see it, but you will. . . . Wait now for bombs on this little house."†

This contrasted somewhat with Mr. Eden's proposal to the Cabinet for an agreement with Hitler "while he is in the mood to do so". From my own observations two years later, I consider it exact that Hitler had not the ascendancy over his generals in 1936 that would have enabled him to survive a sudden upsurge of French and British determination in March 1936, and the precipitate military retreat from the Rhineland that he would then have been obliged to order.

But the British cabinet in 1936 was in perhaps a more dangerous mood of illusion than in 1938, because it believed so much more in the possibility of peace that it was prepared even to discard such action as entailed a minimum risk. Sir John Simon hotly attacked the idea of Staff talks with France and Belgium, and Mr. Kingsley Wood told Mr. Baldwin that the back benchers objected to them—"the boys won't have it". Ribbentrop came over at the end of the conference, March 19th, to state the German case and hear a formal resolution condemning the German action. He stayed about London after Flandin had left and argued to Eden that if Anglo-French Staff talks were pursued they would preclude further negotiations with Germany.

Lord Avon recollects the endless conversations with Ribbentrop and his angry protests at the declaration that there would be Staff talks with France and Belgium. On March 25th

* Flandin to Winston Churchill.   † *Gathering Storm.*

Ribbentrop even tried to dissuade him from mentioning Staff talks in his speech next day, but Eden proceeded to explain to Parliament the loss that France and Belgium suffered to their security, for which Staff talks of limited scope were intended to compensate. He reminded the House that when France evacuated the Rhineland it had been on the understanding of an Anglo-American guarantee, which the United States had never ratified.

Ribbentrop recalled that "happily Mr. Eden did not make things more difficult for me",* though he had "rough passages" with him. "Before leaving London I was invited to the home of Sir Robert Vansittart, whom I went to see in the company of the German Ambassador, Herr von Hoesch." He described Denham Place as a "solid old English country house. Its well-kept appearance was in rare harmony with its choice modern interior, which was in good taste and had probably been chosen by his American wife."

The "choice modern interior" of Denham Place is a misnomer. For it is furnished entirely in the styles of the eighteenth century with some tapestries and pictures of earlier date. This was a curious lapse of memory in a man who was so fastidious in his modernity that he even had the Adam ceilings of the German Embassy at Carlton House Terrace encased to indulge his craving for undecorated surfaces and concealed lighting. He was also wrong in describing Lady Vansittart as American, and omits a detail that the Vansittarts never forgot. Going in to dinner he did not wait to be assigned his place at the big Jacobean table but strode round and put himself on the right of Lady Vansittart in the place which was that of the Ambassador.

Herr von Hoesch stiffened and turned dusky red, taking the chair on her left. This was a symbolic usurpation. For Herr von Hoesch had already been noticed by Himmler and the extremists as a non-Party man and probably an anti-Party man, and it was a matter of time before his recall. "During our meal we talked little about politics," continued Ribbentrop. "I particularly welcomed this invitation and had gladly accepted it, because I still considered it my most important task to establish lasting friendship with Britain, and because Sir Robert Vansittart still undoubtedly continued to occupy a key position *vis-à-vis* Anglo-German understanding. I had a long

* *The Ribbentrop Memoirs.*

talk about this with Herr von Hoesch as we drove back. He agreed that Vansittart was an important man who was sceptical of Germany, difficult to understand and hard to win over. Hoesch confirmed Vansittart's strong influence on the other [sic] members of the Cabinet."

Ribbentrop wrote that he found Herr von Hoesch, "who was not always well disposed to me, almost friendly on this occasion". It was their last meeting. Herr von Hoesch died suddenly a few days afterwards of reported heart failure, and Ribbentrop was chosen to succeed him as Ambassador some three months later. An air of mystery surrounded the death of Herr von Hoesch. The Ambassador's valet, Lady Vansittart tells me, suspected that he had died of poison, since his master had never spoken of any heart trouble. If there was an autopsy, it was performed by a German doctor. On April 15th, two Secretaries of State in full ceremonial dress, Simon and Eden, walked with Vansittart behind the funeral cortège of Herr von Hoesch in London. His coffin was received at the quayside in Germany without ceremony or honour of any kind.

Eden had to face criticisms that the Government had left the French in the lurch and allowed Hitler one more triumph. Of course his handling of the situation had been cautious and in line with Cabinet policy. General Gamelin's own account of the Rhineland crisis has since shown that although it had been long expected, no French counter plan to the German intrusion existed on March 7th, and it was March 12th before his own appreciation of what could be done was presented to the French cabinet. The three French Services had decided that they could not safely deal with the German move unless the Government ordered a full mobilisation.

Vansittart took these facts into account in writing an understanding letter to Eden after the crisis had subsided a little.

March 22

Denham Place,
Denham,
Bucks.

My dear Anthony,

I hope you will not be disheartened because men—including states-men and press-men—are blind. You have extricated your country, with great skill, from a position in which it might have been either dishonoured and isolated, or forced into dangerous courses. And you have avoided, with equal wisdom, a head-on collision with old associates, who constitute no danger to us, before we know what the future portends from the only quarter that may be, and certainly is still, full of danger in this day of our weakness. To have done that would indeed have seemed criminal two years hence, in view of all the information in our hands. (There are as many red lights as if the road was "up" to the horizon.)

Yet some of our acquaintance would do so. You have had the foresight and the firmness to grasp the central fact. We have *got* to be cautious, and not be carried away prematurely, or we may pay for it with our national existence. What you have accomplished is a skilful survival of the first round—with a good margin of manœuvre for the second. If that had *not* been accomplished there would have been no second without disaster. You and your colleagues indeed deserve praise. Don't worry if you don't get it all now. The future will bear you out right enough—and you have such a long personal future still. If they don't give you *enough* credit *now*, you will have to open out on them (I still wish you had begun the other day) and tell them the world as it is and not as they—and we—would have it. (I shall always feel that the Government ought to have done this sooner, as the Defence Requirements Committee urged in 1934.) Nobody who knows the full facts could fail to pay a tribute to your work. And if not enough people know the facts, you are now the man to put that straight. You will be justified to the hilt in due time, even if "Men are unwise and curiously planned."

Yours ever
Van.

Don't pay too much attention to the kind of things that Beaverbrook and Garvin have written today. I will tell you more about that tomorrow and I will try to get hold of Rothermere tomorrow.

In this review of the first three months of Eden as Foreign Secretary he brought out the same considerations as had prompted him to counsel Hoare against risking any kind of conflict in the previous autumn.

Staff talks started in London on April 15th with France and

Belgium, and Eden drafted a questionnaire to Hitler, presented in the second week of May, asking pointedly whether Germany had reached a stage where she was able to respect the existing territorial and political status of Europe. Eden also noted in his diary on May 20th that Mr. Baldwin was asking him to get "on better relations with Hitler than with Mussolini". He was to wait all summer for a formal reply from Hitler to his questionnaire, but already on May 17th Vansittart reported on a "discouraging reaction" through the British Embassy in Berlin —"I never expected anything but this—let us briefly summarise. Hitler rejects a pact with Russia. He is not, in his own view, in a position to conclude 'equal' and enduring treaties . . . I wonder if anyone really expected any other attitude than that. He will play for time to avoid, on any pretext, giving us a clear and reassuring answer. He does not even want a ministerial visit from us . . . I trust we shall not humiliate ourselves by pressing a visit on the Germans."* Of Hitler's admiration for Mussolini he wrote:

"We must do all we can to keep these two beauties apart, and we shall not succeed unless the Abyssinian trouble is liquidated with reasonable speed.

"We shall have to go on with this exploration, though without illusions. If this is the spirit, there can be no question whatever of any colonial restitution." His earlier advice on the colonial question was directed only toward a general comprehensive and abiding settlement, but to obtain that "our rearmament is not proceeding fast enough or notoriously enough".

He returned to this subject, commenting to Ralph Wigram that though "Hitler has never meant business, it will be necessary to 'play' him for some time—because we need time more than anyone to make up deficiencies in our equipment, . . . but . . . on no account whatever must we allow ourselves to be separated from France." This commentary on June 1st, 1936, was followed with another on June 24th when the Plymouth Committee had decided quietly to shelve the question of restoring colonies to Germany. He seemed to doubt that the colonial question could prudently be "pigeon-holed" without speedier re-armament.

The outcome of these uncertainties, and the apparent

* Vansittart Papers.

reluctance of Hitler to receive a visit from Eden or any other British Cabinet Minister at this time led that summer to a visit to Berlin by Vansittart himself. Ribbentrop had already decided that he wished to cultivate this "important man" and sent him an invitation to the Olympic Games held in August 1936 in Berlin. Lady Phipps, wife of the British Ambassador in Berlin was indisposed, and this gave a reasonable excuse for Lady Vansittart to take her sister's place at the Embassy entertaining that must accompany the games. Thus Vansittart ventured into the lair of the beast. But Europe was already beyond the point of no return, and Baldwin in the years of meditation that remained to him after retirement gave the opinion that the Rhineland crisis of 1936 was the last occasion on which Hitler could have been effectively stopped. This did not happen, less because Italy had fallen out of step than because some British minds had become conditioned to the idea at this very time that a general settlement could still be reached with Hitler.

CHAPTER VI

THE OLYMPIAD 1936

From the high tribune of the Olympic Stadium in Berlin, Adolf Hitler swung his binoculars along the rows of distinguished visitors, till they came to rest on the determined profile of Sir Robert Vansittart. Enough was known in Germany about his strong views for a picture to have formed of the Permanent Head of the Foreign Office as an arch-enemy of the Reich, and three times Baron von Neurath had blurted out at their first courtesy meeting that he had never expected to see Sir Robert in Berlin. Dr. Goebbels, Minister of Propaganda, recovered soon enough from the shock of their arrival to send a bowl of orchids to Lady Vansittart at the British Embassy where she was soon busy helping Sir Eric Phipps in entertaining the many Olympic guests. After his first scrutiny in the stadium Hitler told Ribbentrop that he wished to meet this visitor.

It was August 1936. Hitler's March venture into the demilitarised Rhineland had been resented and nearly forgotten. Proposals for sanctions had been discussed and discarded; for how could there be sanctions simultaneously, even if ineffective, against both Germany and Italy? France, Britain and Belgium had since the Rhineland intrusion conferred at great length on a substitute for the Locarno Agreement with associated pacts of mutual Western assistance, but by the summer of 1936 there was neither a firm system of Western alliances, nor yet a substitute for Locarno. The Germans kept the future open.

Before making his excursion to Berlin, Vansittart had summarised in a memorandum* the courses open to Britain and France as the Rhineland crisis subsided. He favoured removing sanctions and opening negotiations with Italy, "the same policy as that to which we are already committed in the case of that other treaty-breaker Germany". What would be the real advantage to Britain of a collapse of Italy? It would cut both ways, he argued, in taking pressure off Britain in the Mediterranean and North Africa, but also weakening an important

* May 21st, 1936. The Future of Anglo-Italian relations and the League.

counter-weight to Germany in Central Europe, as M. Litvinov, Soviet Foreign Commissar, had already remarked in Geneva. "Italy may become dangerous," wrote Vansittart, "but has not yet the same striking force or resolve or reserve of power as Germany. Mussolini has made his first advances to his fellow dictator across the Alps; but unless we drive him into an active and offensive co-operation with Hitler, we are entitled to hope that he will not be anxious to take the high road to Berlin. We shall have to compromise with Mussolini, for we can never compromise securely or even live safely with Dictator Major, if we are at loggerheads with Dictator Minor." These were views that fastened more strongly in the mind of Neville Chamberlain than in the mind of Eden. The entire British Cabinet was, however, of the persuasion that some form of understanding must be sought with Germany. But what sort of understanding should it be? Eden had correctly defined British policy on June 18th, 1936 with the words "nothing less than European settlement and appeasement should be our aim". By this he plainly meant a general settlement binding Germany to keep the peace with all. But the more invidious idea of appeasement without general settlement was in the minds of some of the Cabinet. The Foreign Office dissented.

Its attitude was that even if failure was probable, the attempt to bring Germany into a general settlement should not be abandoned. It might well be that the development of events would make it impossible to resist German designs in Central and Eastern Europe; but that was no reason why there should be any spectacular or sudden abandonment of the policy which Britain had, up till then, consistently pursued. How could it be known that Germany would not involve herself in great difficulties with Poland and Russia? Wisdom suggested that where so much was uncertain, it would be right to play a waiting game and abstain from any course of action which would indicate that Britain was disinteresting herself in Central and Eastern Europe. It would surely be better if the breakdown of the policy of a general settlement should be laid clearly at the door of Germany and not attributed to eleventh hour default or perfidy of Britain. The only conceivable reason for abandoning the policy of general settlement would be to secure a definite and immediate advantage to Britain, so great as to outweigh international disadvantages

such as loss of allies, but from an immediate agreement with
Germany confined to the West no real advantage would ensue,
and might be coupled with German demands that Anglo-
French-Belgian Staff talks should cease. If Britain dissociated
herself from the affairs of Central and Eastern Europe, far
from causing a *détente*, the tension in Europe would be increased.
Nor would that satisfy Germany if her colonies were not also
returned to her. The advantages from local settlements were
thus illusory and taken by itself appeasement would be fatal.

Such were the insoluble problems of Europe. The Foreign
Office came nearer than most to analysing them and what was
actually to happen. In the midst of this argument the Spanish
Civil War broke out, adding to previous complications. Spain
was the new subject of conversation everywhere in Berlin
around the Olympic visitors.

"The sporting events offered a very favourable opportunity
to make contacts with politicians and prominent men in the
most diverse camps," Ribbentrop wrote. He was glad that Sir
Robert and Lady Vansittart had accepted his invitation. His
own appointment as Ambassador to the Court of St. James was
announced on the day of Herr von Ribbentrop's reception for
the Olympic guests. Vansittart congratulated him, and Ribbentrop was gratified to notice that the Vansittarts stayed on and
danced at his Dahlem villa and seemed to enjoy themselves.
Ribbentrop invited him to lunch at the Hotel Kaiserhof next
day and told him that Hitler was anxious to meet him.

Of the luncheon Ribbentrop wrote: "I tried my very best
to be persuasive. I urged Vansittart to understand that the
presence of the Führer, who alone had the sole sovereign
authority to decide, offered a unique opportunity for a really
enduring association between Germany and Britain, which,
built solidly on mutual confidence and common interests,
would redound to the advantage of both. The Führer was
ready for a sincere understanding based on equality.

"It was unfortunate that I had to do most of the talking;
I felt from the start as if I were addressing a wall. Vansittart
listened quietly, but was not forthcoming and evaded all my
openings for a frank exchange of views. I have spoken to
hundreds of Englishmen on this subject, but never was a
conversation so barren, never did I find so little response,
never did my partner say so little about the points which really

mattered. When I asked Sir Robert to express an opinion on certain points and to criticise frankly what I had said, or to explain where exactly we differed in matters of principle or of detail, there was absolutely no reply except generalities. In the following years I often looked back on this conversation.

"One thing was clear, an Anglo-German understanding with Vansittart in office was out of the question. Only once again did I have a similar feeling after a conversation. That was in 1937, after a talk with Mr. Churchill, when I was Ambassador in London, except that while Vansittart had expressed no opinion whatever, Mr. Churchill was considerably more frank.

"Vansittart, I felt, had completely made up his mind. This Foreign Office man not only advocated the balance of power theory, but was also the incarnation of Sir Eyre Crowe's principle: 'No pact with Germany, come what may.' I gained a firm impression that this man would never even attempt a *rapprochement*, and any discussion with him would be in vain. The Führer said later that Vansittart must also have been influenced by other reasons, by questions of ideology. I do not know; I do not think so; but this will never be explained. Whatever influences he may have been subjected to, the main thing was his basic attitude: 'Never with Germany.'

"There are those who contend that Vansittartism and the hatred of Germany which this word implies were a result of Hitler's policy. To this I reply—and I believe with a better right: Hitler's policy was a consequence of Vansittart's policy in 1936."

It is noteworthy that these lines were not written in 1936, but exactly ten years later in the cell at Nuremberg, and we must set against them the words that Vansittart recorded at the time from their lunchtime conversation, a dour reminder from Ribbentrop that "if England did not give Germany the possibility to live, there would eventually be war between them and one of them will be annihilated".

Ribbentrop had told the Führer in private that the time an alliance with Britain could have been obtained was past, but he recorded in his last memoirs that he had looked forward to his London mission.*

Vansittart's impression in 1936 of Ribbentrop as future Ambassador was that "with this gentleman we shall have

* *The Ribbentrop Memoirs.*

more trouble. I fear that he is shallow, self-seeking and not really friendly. No one who studies his mouth will be reassured. He was most markedly unenthusiastic about his appointment to London, of which I spoke to him many times with never a flicker of response. Frau von Ribbentrop on the other hand is genuinely delighted at their new appointment."

After their Kaiserhof luncheon Ribbentrop conducted Vansittart to the Chancellery. Hitler stared with surprise at Vansittart as Ribbentrop showed him into his study. There was a long and embarrassed pause. His aides had told Hitler to expect a "small man of Jewish appearance", and Vansittart's solid six foot one did not conform with the fable, while his fluent German made Hitler uneasy. Vansittart began by expressing the hope that Hitler would not pay too much attention to travelling "light weights and busybodies" on Anglo-German relations, having in mind no doubt the visit of Lord Lothian and others. He had then to listen to a long complaint from Hitler that Germany was "misunderstood" in England. Hitler gave the impression of "a sly rotund, ascetic bourgeois . . . able to impress himself so strongly that he impresses himself on those standing in tangible awe around him. . . . Of his talk nothing could have been more friendly, but nothing could have been more general."

But the talks with Hitler were prolonged affably, and he seated the Vansittarts in the place of honour at a banquet in the Chancellery, a cause for pique to the French president of the Olympic games. Eating vegetables and drinking water, the Führer talked, as he had done to Eden a year earlier, of a British film that had so impressed him, "The Lives of a Bengal Lancer". He admired the British Empire, he said, feared the Communist menace to Europe and said that he supposed that the Left would win the Spanish civil war. After kissing Lady Vansittart on the hand and arm, he talked to her at length of friendship with Britain.

"Oh, how lucky to have dined with the Führer," exclaimed Unity Mitford, a daughter of Lord Redesdale, enthusiastic about Germany, who was asked in for coffee afterwards. Small coincidences at this time had their later effect in history; for Lady Vansittart introduced the Marquess of Clydesdale, as captain of the British Olympic boxing team, to Hitler's deputy, Rudolf Hess—a clue to the mysterious demand of Hess when he parachuted into Scotland five years later that he should be instantly taken to the Duke of Hamilton.

Another chance encounter at this time is of interest. Away from the glitter of Olympiad entertaining, through the side door of the British Embassy a stealthy visitor called on Vansittart during his Olympics visit, Wilfrid Israel, described in the 1940 Wehrmacht Confidential Book on Britain as a British agent. His story was of the shadows behind the façade, persecution, suicides, despair among the Jewish population of Germany. Could nothing be done for them? Vansittart replied that any intervention by himself at this time would do more harm than good. Perhaps in the autumn there would be an agreement at Locarno with Germany, after which there could be intercession for those persecuted. He did not relish this interview and long remembered "the thin transparent profile with high forehead and frightened eyes, who came and spoke in whispers," and yet remained in Germany till 1938 helping to smuggle refugees away from the death camps, and was still engaged in refugee work between London and Lisbon when in 1943 he perished in an airliner shot down over the Bay of Biscay.

In a summary of his impressions, at the end of this Berlin visit, Vansittart wrote that: "Those in authority would clearly like to come to an understanding, perhaps even something closer, with us—on their own terms. They would far sooner reach it with us than the Italians. Germans have long memories and though Lloyd George is obviously cultivating them they have not forgotten his record and say so. The Germans would sooner deal with us alone, but I doubt whether they retain any serious hope of dividing us from the French. . . . There is no hope of any acceptable limitation of air forces. There is also no prospect of inducing Germany to conclude any Convention with Russia. A Western agreement is attainable by itself. A proper settlement in Central Europe is also just possible, if we are tactful and determined enough. British minimum conditions should be for a Western multilateral agreement, *without limitation* of armaments." For Germany had left Britain too far behind in that race, he asserted, and limitation "would concede vast and undue superiority to Germany". Any new pact would have to be an "Act of Faith" and must be accompanied by continued British rearmament. The pact would not have a serious chance of success if the colonial question was met "by half measures", which would give this gamble for understanding only half a chance of success. He would like to return to Germany some time later "and get down to details and plain speaking. For we shall have to come to that fairly soon."

As to the reasons for this Olympic trip, "I may say fairly during my visit that I succeeded in largely removing the idea that the British Foreign Office was peopled with professional anti-Germans. Herr Dieckhoff (the Under-Secretary for Foreign Affairs) asked whether I could come back in case of need (a similar suggestion was made by Herr Hitler to my wife). I replied that I would always make any contribution in my power to understanding, and that if we failed to agree it would be because of honest conviction or political impossibility and not because of any bias or ill feeling."

Few Germans today will recognise in these sentiments the personality of the man whom they quickly came to regard as their arch enemy. Mr. Baldwin read his report and dallied with the idea of appeasement, but not in time to make it work or in anything but "half measures". The Spanish war, a side-show in Europe, became the main diplomatic preoccupation. The Franco-Soviet assistance pact, the Popular Front of M. Blum remained irritant factors to Germany. It seemed preferable to Hitler and his advisers to continue rearming without seeking a new Locarno arrangement.

Not a "light-weight" by any means, but the sort of surface investigator with no official position or party following, David Lloyd George, whom he instinctively mistrusted, arrived in Germany soon after Vansittart left. The elder statesman travelled with Tom Jones, whom Vansittart had seen already to be one of the Cliveden circle, and whose "wisdom" he knew Baldwin preferred to his own. Tom Jones left an account of the meeting at Berchtesgaden* at which Lloyd George spoke up for better understanding between Britain and Germany and Hitler exclaimed "I agree with all my heart."

"The immediate business before us is the forthcoming conference of the Five Powers," said Lloyd George. "We should concentrate on making 'Locarno' a success. Consolidation of the West can be brought about on a basis of equality."

* Diary with Letters.

Hitler: "The peoples of the West wish to see the conference succeed, but there are certain sections in certain countries infected with Bolshevism."

Afterwards Lloyd George told Tom Jones that he had covered all the points that he intended: "We must insist on keeping Locarno to Locarno and leaving the East for separate consideration." This was a less careful assessment than that of Vansittart, full of trust and optimism.

Going on without Lloyd George to the 1936 Nuremberg Party Congress, Tom Jones found Ribbentrop there, impatient and intense, relating that Hitler had since been asking in tears what were the chances of bringing Stanley Baldwin over to meet him. Jones told Ribbentrop that Baldwin would not quit London in winter and that the Coronation would fill the spring of 1937. The impressions of Lloyd George were printed late in September 1936 in the *News Chronicle* and were repeated by him to Tom Jones on September 25th. "Hitler is arming for defence, not for attack. For at least ten years war between Russia and Germany is impracticable. The German army is not in a position to attack anybody. It is formidable for defence—it has machine guns, the most useful defensive weapon. Hitler and his people want friendship with the British. But we have no leadership to exploit this desire." These were echoes of the same assurances given to Lord Lothian eighteen months previously.

Tom Jones on September 17th rejoined Mr. Baldwin at Blickling Hall, which the Marquess of Lothian had lent to the Prime Minister for the second stage of convalescence from a condition of nervous exhaustion, which left him limping about and unable to concentrate on work. He admitted to being much better, but "now I shall be shortly shouldering things again. It is responsibility that kills". He spoke of the good administrators in his Cabinet, Neville Chamberlain, Sir Samuel Hoare, Lord Swinton and Kingsley Wood. . . . He thought Vansittart had "got on fairly well with Dieckhoff during his visit to the Olympic games." . . . Evidently Baldwin had read that report at any rate. It was late November before Jones saw fit to remind Baldwin, finding him visibly improved in health, that Herr Hitler still hoped for a visit from him.

"Well, it's not outside the bounds of possibility," replied the Prime Minister.

It may have been partly in hopes of Mr. Baldwin's visit to him that Hitler kept Britain waiting for his next Ambassador to arrive. On September 25th, when Britain had been without a German Ambassador for more than five months, Vansittart wrote to Eden at Geneva:

> My dear Anthony,
> I hear that Ribbentrop, who was by way of coming to take up his post at the beginning of October, now says that he will not be coming until November as he is in need of a holiday. This may be the real reason; there may also be others. The postponement in any case offers food for thought, as it looks rather like a confirmation of what we have thought for some time, that is that the Germans will be in no hurry about the Five Power Conference but will rather play for time.
> Yours ever
> Van.

On September 30th, Vansittart had something further to add in a letter that reached Eden in Geneva just before he left for a holiday.

> My dear Anthony,
> I wonder whether the breathing space is not going to be rather longer than we expect. None of the five Powers seems in a particular hurry to answer our last communication, and I feel that it is more than ever likely that the Germans, and now also the Italians with all their talk of clarification, may cause considerable delays and we may well find ourselves in the new year before anything happens, even if we really meet then. The political signs all point that way, so perhaps you may think it well not to stint yourself for a day or two extra if you feel like it.
> Not only the political signs point that way but some rather interesting and entertaining private ones. I told you the other day that Ribbentrop was apparently postponing his arrival till November, and that did not look like haste. There have been some rather curious developments since then. To begin with, when I was in Germany Ribbentrop and his wife asked me to do what I could with the Head-

master of Eton to get their boy, who is over fifteen, admitted
to Eton. I said I would do my best and took it up with
Elliott when I got back. After some time Elliott said it was
really impossible, owing to the boy being too old and to there
being no vacancy anyway, but he strongly recommended
Stowe and thought there was something to be done there if
I knew Roxburgh, the headmaster. I did know Roxburgh,
and wrote to Ribbentrop at once saying I would do my best
to get the boy in there if he wanted this. A month has now
elapsed and I have not had an answer. I don't think that
Ribbentrop would be likely to be either rude or forgetful
on a matter of this sort, and I arrive at the conclusion that
he has not answered because he does not know his own mind.

And then yesterday came a curious little development,
which is really curious if read with the otherwise uninterest-
ing episode I have just recounted. Yesterday we got
an indirect but perceptible feeler as to whether the fact that
Frau von Stoehrer had divorced her first husband would be
any obstacle to their coming here as Ambassador. Stoehrer
was for long Minister in Cairo and afterwards Ambassador
in Madrid. . . . Does not all that look just a little as if Ribbentrop was beginning to waver again and as if the postponement to November might possibly portend a change of
mind? On the other hand they have taken the Chancellor's
house in Eaton Square,* and Hitler kept on telling Lloyd
George what a compliment he was paying to London in
sending there his chief confidant. I suppose Ribbentrop still
will come, but there does not seem to be any empressement
as there doubtless would be if the Germans intended to
co-operate with us quickly over the conference. . . . .

The preparatory talks for a Locarno meeting with Germany
dragged on that autumn, and would drag into the spring of
1937. There were two good reasons why they came no nearer
fruition. Hitler had partially freed himself of anxiety about
Russia through a secret pact with Japan, negotiated between
Herr von Ribbentrop and General Hiroshi Oshima, the
Japanese Military Attaché in Berlin and already concluded
at the time Vansittart visited Berlin. This provided for political

* This was 37 Eaton Square, which Ribbentrop rented from Neville Chamberlain, then Chancellor of the Exchequer. Ribbentrop did arrive in November, and
pondered over the events of the abdication "in Chamberlain's little study".

consultation between Japan and Germany on all political acts relating to Europe, Russia and the Far East, and an exchange of military information. It gave Germany a Far Eastern lever against Britain and if need be against America. This secret convention, negotiated over twelve months, was known to Russia through photostats of documents almost as soon as completed.* The many rumours about it during 1936 prompted Hitler to conceal it behind a brief public document known as the Anti-Comintern Pact, which Italy joined in 1937. Litvinov made open reference to the terms of the German-Japanese agreement speaking to a Congress of the Soviets on November 28th, 1936.

Further relief came to Germany through a visit of Count Galeazzo Ciano. In October 1936 the Italian Foreign Minister came to Berlin with a powerful weapon, some of the stolen British documents from the Embassy in Rome dated January 1936, in which Mr. Eden had circulated the strong views of Sir Eric Phipps on the Nazis as "a band of adventurers". Ciano presented this document just five months after Mr. Baldwin had told Eden that he wanted "better relations with Hitler than with Musso". This had evidently become apparent to the Duce and he was administering the antidote.

"According to the English, there are two countries in the world today which are led by adventurers," exclaimed Hitler, after reading it, "Germany and Italy. But England too was led by adventurers when she built the Empire. Today she is governed merely by incompetents."†

Lord Avon refers to this purloined document‡ and Ciano often speaks hereafter of cipher "intercepts". Clearly it was difficult for Britain to separate Italy and Germany, if its secret policy documents could be discussed together by both those powers. In 1936 Hitler was wavering in his attitude towards Britain. The Cabinet document was already nine months old, and his big move for the year—the Rhineland military re-occupation—had been made. But the sight of it encouraged him to do rather more than "react unfavourably", to quote Lord Avon's description. Hitler told Ciano in Berchtesgaden on October 24th, 1936 that the understanding between the democracies must be opposed by another between Germany

---

* *I was Stalin's Agent*, Walter Krivitsky, 1939
† *Ciano's Diplomatic Papers.*   ‡ *Facing the Dictators*, p. 323.

and Italy. "We must take up an active role. We must go over to the attack. And the tactical field on which we must execute the manœuvre is that of anti-Bolshevism."*

Mussolini would send another fifty aircraft and two submarines to Spain, said Ciano. It was more than an ideological field on which the friendship of the two dictators would be tempered. Spain became a dump for obsolete arms and a testing ground for new weapons. In that the venture in Spain held Italy effectively out of the Stresa front, it suited Hitler to have Mussolini committed there.

Having deep social causes the Spanish Civil War was no product of foreign adventure. Yet its effect on European alignments was profound. Historical accident lay in the purloined documents which Mussolini had kept to himself for so long and only now decided to share with his friend. It was going to be made difficult for Vansittart to separate Dictator Minor from Dictator Major.

Vansittart noted that at a Ministry of Propaganda briefing for the German press after the Ciano visit, it was stated that "the time is past when it seemed necessary to run after England".†

In November 1936 he found an echo of this change of sentiment in the minds of the British Chiefs of Staff. Eden had already noted with concern that the military men were importuning the Cabinet with papers attempting to analyse foreign political questions.‡ Vansittart sometimes referred to the three Chiefs of Staff as "the amenable trio". Their attitude now confirmed him in that impression. For he noted that they spoke of "repeated rebuffs and lost opportunities" having weakened the German desire for friendship with Britain. The Chiefs of Staff continued to urge that British foreign policy should be directed to keeping out of any war that did not involve "a vital British interest".

It seems that the Foreign Office reaction was to ask the Services Chiefs for a definition of rebuffs and lost opportunities. "I don't think they know what they are talking about," said Vansittart: "but we may as well see." As to their statement about keeping out of war, "I know the answer and it is just sheer weakness; so it is no good pursuing that [point]. I think the Chiefs of Staff might have agitated a lot more in the past

* *Ciano's Diplomatic Papers*, p. 57.   † Vansittart Papers.   ‡ *Facing the Dictators.*

to get our weakness rectified. My experience over seven years is that this agitation has been mainly left to the Foreign Office, and that the Chiefs of Staff have dubbed me alarmist."*

Aware of this weakening mood in the Government, a parliamentary deputation and its military advisors called on Mr. Baldwin and Sir Thomas Inskip, Minister for Co-operation of Defence, at the end of 1936. It consisted of Lord Salisbury, Sir Austen Chamberlain, Mr. Churchill, Admiral of the Fleet Lord Keyes, Marshal of the R.A.F. Lord Trenchard and Field-Marshal Lord Milne. Mr. Baldwin had met them once already before the summer recess. The Prime Minister simply sat in. Sir Thomas Inskip spoke, assuring the deputation that everything was being done for defence that could be done without causing public alarm and despondency or upsetting industry. The emphasis on these last words meant all the difference between security and peril. The deputation went morosely away.

Soon after his convalescence at Blickling Hall an event overtook Baldwin—and Britain—which was to add to the confusion of British policy in Europe, and for a time obliterate all Government business, prompting Baldwin to ask Eden "not to trouble me too much with foreign affairs just now".† Between October 18th and December 12th, the crisis of the abdication of Edward VIII was "with the Prime Minister day and night. . . .‡ The one topic continues to dominate all conversation, Parliament and Press. It is impossible to escape from it. Spain, Italy, Germany, Japan, all forgotten."§ Although the crisis of abdication was over in the first week of December 1936, on January 19th, 1937 Mr. Baldwin was still discussing it. He had by then decided to resign from office but only on May 20th, a resolution which he stretched another week. When we sum it up, here were five months at a time when Britain was in dire need of every expedient to win time and use time for its defence when nothing of immediate importance was done either in rearmament or in foreign affairs. This was the time of drift, which brought Chamberlain face to face with the fateful decisions of 1937. Tom Jones, still ignorant of the nature of the Berlin-Tokyo agreement, called '36 a year of diplomatic reverse for Hitler, and that may have been a general impression. Sir Robert Vansittart penned to his old

---

* Vansittart Papers.　　　　† *Facing the Dictators.*
‡ Tom Jones, *Diary*, December 8th, 1936, p. 290　　§ Ibid.

friend and Chief, the Prime Minister, a gloomier picture in a Christmas letter on the world situation in 1936. "Time was when Japan was thought to be our chief danger," he wrote. "Foreshadowed events have changed all that. While Japan is generally considered likely to await a war in Europe, Germany has become the recognised storm centre of the earth. It is a thousand pities for Germany presents the human animal at its most efficient."

He assessed the Japanese-German pact, which Litvinov after seeing photostats of the Axis documents had already described rather fully in a speech to the Congress of Soviets on November 28th.*

The agreement, thought Vansittart, clearly introduced Japan into the orbit of European affairs at a delicate and dangerous stage. It would be impossible to import American munitions early in a Second World War. "Our own supplies will have to be more plentiful and *timely*." The question of time was everything, "and it is the principal preoccupation of the Foreign Office since time is the very material commodity which the Foreign Office is expected to provide in the same way as other departments are expected to provide *other* war material.

"The year 1939 is the first in which we shall be able to breathe even with comparative relief, although much will yet remain to be taken in hand. We shall not even then have reached safety. Germany is admittedly not yet ready for war on a considerable scale, either militarily, economically or politically. The Army wants time, must have time, to create a better balance between the purely military preparations and the essential economic preparations—raw materials and food supplies for the nation. These are facts of great import and comfort. But on any showing Germany will be ready for big mischief at least a year—and probably more—before we are ready to look after ourselves. To the Foreign Office therefore falls the task of holding the situation at least till 1939, and the foregoing account of the world shows that there is no certainty of our being able to do so, though we are doing our utmost by negotiating with Germany."†

If Britain was not going to hasten its steps towards remarmament, the colonial door would have at least to be kept ajar.

* Walter Krivitsky, *I was Stalin's Agent*.   † Vansittart Papers.

Britain was having to "manufacture time", and in this respect "we have a good and improving position in the United States of America. . . . The perennial question of the war debt is still against us . . . but our prestige is still high and the United States of America are generally and strongly opposed to dictatorships and therefore inclined towards our fellow democracy. They might be further so inclined if Mr. Roosevelt carried out his vague idea of calling a 'World Peace Conference', rendered abortive by the dictators. Such a step on his part might, indeed, help us in manufacturing time." Vansittart told Baldwin that in Central Europe at the end of 1936 "everybody fears war, but they do not know what war. . . . Schuschnigg, Kanya and Ciano all feel that events are moving slowly towards war; but even they no longer foresee where or how."

Germany was creating an international anti-Bolshevik front as a vehicle for ultimate expansion. Czechoslovakia was under threat of disintegration, and the Danube and Balkan countries threatened with complete German domination.

This campaign could at will be turned against Britain, as chief obstacle to Germany having "means to live".

Politically the Foreign Office was working to ensure a friendly Italy, and obtain a Five Power Agreement, first for a Western settlement and then for a Central European settlement. Thus an intermediate barrier of treaties would keep Germany and Russia apart. But the latter endeavour was not likely to materialise. "Treaties can, at the best, be acts of faith, but cannot alone preserve the peace."

Britain must act and state her case in such a way as to retain American sympathy at all times. The possibility of ceding a colony to Germany should therefore not be ruled out of a political settlement. People in America and in Central Europe could never understand a British mentality which they saw as "a horror of the *status quo* in Europe with a determination not to surrender anything that Britain gained in the war". Some economic easement for Germany might have to be found. He urged rearmament at a quickened pace, that no concessions, financial, economic or colonial, be made without reliable returns in security, and avoidance of any heavy-handed action that might unite Germany under the Nazi régime. Only this procedure could give the moderates in Germany a chance.

These were weighty views even if he sought to state them

simply. Baldwin in the winter of 1936-37, rusticating with his eyes on "this dear, dear land of elms in the evening sun, of the ploughman and his team . . . the peace of the countryside" may have laid them aside as too heavy to digest. Van was for ever writing lengthy papers. Tom Jones wrote from Cliveden on January 3rd, 1937 that "Stanley Baldwin is at Astley feeling happy and contented with the conclusion of the Palace crisis."

When he had written the last words of this Christmas epistle Vansittart returned to Denham Place to see in the year 1937. Something recollected must have prompted him to want to speak to Ralph Wigram, whose calm and determined personality had supported him in the past year of shaken authority. But when he telephoned to the little house in North Street, where Flandin had spoken during the Rhineland crisis, it was Ava Wigram who answered him and as she seemed to be fending him off,—"so you think you can speak to Ralph"—he did not persist, knowing that his friend was an invalid and that it was already late. But just before the year ended, she it was who telephoned him at Denham Place to say that Ralph Wigram was dead. She heard the telephone fall with a clatter from Vansittart's hand, and when he picked it up and spoke, she remembered him saying: "I don't think I have the strength to go on without him—alone."

CHAPTER VII

THE AIR DETERRENT

LORD Vansittart in his latter days wrote of his lifework with a sense of failure. Had he looked back at his labours in the field of air rearmament alone, he would have had to admit to an excess of modesty. Sir John Slessor pays a tribute to him* as the high official, of whose support the Air Staff did not take advantage soon enough. It was to Vansittart that the first reports of German air rearmament came before reaching the Cabinet. He took on his own initiative the first diplomatic steps to oppose it in 1933, and his insistent hand is everywhere in the battle to keep British air strength, as laid down in Cabinet policy "not inferior to any power within striking distance".

The idea of a British air deterrent, which would effectively protect the British Isles from surprise attack and deter aggression elsewhere in Europe, was discussed by British statesmen as early as November 1932. Hitler had not yet come to power, and Germany was still without an air force under the terms of the Versailles treaty. "The only defence is in offence," said Baldwin then, considering the role of bomber aircraft, "which means that you have to kill more women and children more quickly than the enemy if you want to save yourselves." It was a subject of controversy, in which the estimates of destruction were much overstated. "I certainly do not know how the youth of the world may feel," reflected Baldwin; "but it is not a cheerful thought to the older men. . . . When the next war comes and European civilisation is wiped out as it will be."† Lord Robert Cecil wrote about this time to a fellow pacifist, Lord Allen of Hurtwood, who had been a conscientious objector in the First World War: "My objection to bombing from the air is not so much that it amounts to an attack on the civilians as well as the military as that it is essentially and typically an aggressive action."‡

Nevertheless it was the action that must commend itself to a Britain wishing to have some military influence in Europe

---

* *The Central Blue.*   † Stanley Baldwin, November 28th, 1932.
‡ Lord Robert Cecil to Lord Allen of Hurtwood, July 15th, 1932.

without maintaining a large continental army, and it was also essential to have a large air force for home defence. Therefore when Baron von Neurath published the German case for re-armament in the form of an open letter to the press on May 11th, 1933, the telephone rang between London and Geneva and Sir Robert Vansittart was soon talking to Mr. Anthony Eden in the British delegation to the Disarmament Conference. The German Ambassador to the Court of St. James, Herr von Hoesch, had quickly called on Vansittart that morning to insinuate that agreement on the Draft Disarmament Convention was "very nearly reached".

"My information is that your delegate, Herr Nadolny, has been making impossible demands," retorted Sir Robert. "He has in fact asked for an equality of *materiel* for Germany within the lifetime of the present Convention."

"In principle perhaps, but not in practice," parried von Hoesch, and he urged that "more conciliatory instructions should be sent to Mr. Eden."

When Vansittart telephoned to Geneva, Eden told him that it was "quite untrue that agreement had been practically reached". As for the Neurath article, it looked to Eden as if Germany was claiming a free hand in her programme of avia-tion and artillery. Eden and Vansittart were at this time working on two different principles. For Eden then and as late as 1935 was pressing for "a straight and steady course in support of the League and collective security", whereas Vansittart described the League in a memorandum of May 19th, 1933 a week after this telephone conversation, as having fallen "into increasing discredit . . . with . . . its prestige now at the lowest point" and soon afterwards affirmed that the League was "the sick man of Europe".* He therefore turned increasingly to a collateral of air strength as the key to successful diplomacy. It was of special interest to him that a month after Baron von Neurath had stated the case for Germany rearming, Herr Bolle, the Under-Secretary in the German Air Ministry, gave strong hints to the British air attaché in Berlin that Germany was building military aircraft, and would continue to build them on a scale that could not be kept secret. In fact Germany at this time in 1933 wanted to build openly, in order to establish her right to an air force. On June 24th, 1933 an extraordinary

* Vansittart Papers.

German claim was published that unidentified "foreign aircraft" had dropped provocative leaflets over Berlin. Captain Hermann Goering, Minister for Air, promptly declared that "in no circumstances can we admit further postponement of the question of equality of rights in the air and on land".

Sir Robert took immediate action. In instructions to Mr. Basil Newton, Chargé d'Affaires in Berlin, he recalled that on June 10th, before ever this incident of intruder aircraft had been invoked, Herr Bolle had told the British military attaché that "the German firm of Arado had never built anything other than high powered military types of single-seaters, that it was useless to try and keep secret that Germany was arming in the air, and inevitable that a rearmament programme such as that now in progress should become known". Perhaps the building of military prototypes was not thought particularly dangerous . . . or . . . of sufficient importance to justify a protest. Herr Bolle had admitted that a risk was being taken, but spoke of the number of German military aircraft as "so small a total that they did not amount to a force of any consequence".

Sir Robert's dispatch* of June 28th instructed the Chargé d'Affaires to remind the German Under-Secretary for Foreign Affairs, Herr von Bülow, of this German admission and to inform him that "His Majesty's Government . . . think that there must be a misunderstanding as to the statement made by the Secretary of State of the Air Ministry (Herr Bolle) to the British air attaché that Germany was already manufacturing military aircraft. His Majesty's Government would be glad to be assured that this view is correct. They could give no countenance or encouragement to the disregard of treaty obligations." Vansittart at once informed the British Ambassadors in Rome and Paris of this step. Mr. Newton, after suggesting some variation in his instructions to save Herr Bolle from possible embarrassment, proceeded to make an oral communication to Herr von Bülow on August 1st, 1933.

"I much dislike receiving this communication and feel that it was unfriendly of His Majesty's Government to make such representations," replied von Bülow. He saw "no reason for this show of anxiety, or any necessity for His Majesty's Government to cross these bridges before they come to them". He doubted whether the statements had ever been made by Herr

* Documents on British Foreign Policy, Series II, Vol. V.

Bolle . . . "no firm had built or is building military aircraft". But von Bülow then reminded Mr. Newton of the German declaration of December 11th, 1932 regarding military equality.

Once more Herr von Hoesch hurried round to tell Sir Robert on August 2nd how "profoundly pained" the German government were, "accustomed though they may be to this sort of thing on the part of the French, to see such an attitude adopted by Great Britain".*

"The German government left us no option but to take this action," answered Vansittart, "and it was taken in the most moderate possible way."

He noted that Herr von Bülow's reply was "not very satisfactory . . . what we asked for was an assurance that the statment of the Under-Secretary in the Air Ministry was not intended to suggest a German intention to disregard treaty obligations. We are still waiting for this assurance."*

The assurance never came. Yet discussion of the Draft Disarmament Convention dragged on at Geneva. Because of that, it was late in 1934 before designs for new British bomber aircraft were started. A new Committee entitled the Defence Requirements Committee was formed, of which the members were Sir Robert Vansittart, Sir Warren Fisher, Head of the Treasury, and Sir Maurice Hankey, Secretary of the Committee of Imperial Defence, together with the three Chiefs of Staff, General Sir Montgomery Massingberd, Admiral Sir E. Chatfield and Air Chief Marshal Sir Edward Ellington. Vansittart proposed an increase in the Royal Air Force of twenty-five squadrons, "but the amenable trio would not go beyond the five for which they were sure of sanction".†

His clear sighted opinion on Air Defence is nowhere better illustrated than by a sentence or two written on June 2nd, 1934 after reading the records of the Ministerial Committee on Defence Requirements.

"What was lacking in 1914 was common knowledge of our attitude and a deterrent to gambling. Europe remains in equal doubt both as to our policy and as to our capacity. Italy, Poland, Yugoslavia, Rumania are all tending to be drawn into the German orbit. We thus come to the deterrent; and here I venture to put the point very briefly. The execution by 1940 of an air programme approved in 1923 is no deterrent."

* Documents on British Foreign Policy.　　† *Mist Procession.*

Sir Warren Fisher, noted Vansittart, supported his proposal for twenty-five squadrons. The opportunity to maintain numerical superiority over the Germans existed then. He remained unsatisfied with five and argued for more to his Foreign Secretary, Sir John Simon, to Baldwin and to the reluctant Prime Minister Mr. Ramsay Macdonald. He was not concerned with types and design of aircraft, but insisted on air superiority. "On diplomacy I simply offered my advice. On matters of national security I pressed it upon them." By July 1934 he had been largely instrumental in a plan to increase R.A.F. strength by forty-one squadrons, though the expansion was to be spread over five years. "I have not won," he told a Foreign Office colleague, "the programme is spread over five years. It will come too late."* Even so, it needed a powerful speech by Mr. Winston Churchill on July 30th before a Socialist motion of censure was defeated and the programme was passed.

Who could tell in the conditions existing in the Third Reich how fast Germany was building up the Luftwaffe? Baldwin, who introduced the July 1934 expansion programme with bold words, speaking of the Rhine as Britain's frontier, hazarded the estimate on November 28th that by the following November Britain would still have a 50 per cent margin of air strength over Germany. Vansittart who thought the Air Ministry "weak, especially in Intelligence" relied on sources of his own, and thought differently. The Air Ministry analysis might be strictly correct without being realistic. For what mattered was the potential rate of expansion. Mr. Churchill contradicted the complacency of Mr. Baldwin in November 1934, declaring that Germany would soon reach parity in the air. He owed some of his information to Vansittart. Where did it originate?

"Apart from our Secret Service, I had been able to find sources of my own in Germany," wrote Vansittart, and among his papers there is a collection of reports on the German air force. "A few brave men there knew that I realised a war to be nearing. They thought that if they fed me with sufficient evidence, I might have influence enough to arouse our Government and so stop it. They would not have worked for a foreign intelligence, but they hoped to serve Europe by revealing the German conspiracy. . . . One of my sources was in the German

* *Mist Procession.*

Air Ministry. From him I got the German Air Estimates and particulars of construction. . . ."

This was an astonishing testimony from a man notorious for his outspoken mistrust of Germans. It showed that a contrary spirit was even then stirring against Hitler. For these brave men, according to his own papers, were providing him with information as early as 1935.

Who were they? We can only guess. He writes of having "a man in the German Air Ministry," but there is no indication of his name or position in the Vansittart papers, and every indication that Vansittart was absolutely determined to keep both a secret, even from the Chief of the Air Staff himself. It is a fair assumption that his informants belonged to what came to be the German Resistance. He names one of them only in his autobiography, Dr. Karl Goerdeler, the former Lord Mayor of Leipzig, once Price Commissioner for Germany and the man whom Dr. Brüning, on resigning, wished to recommend to President Hindenburg as the next Chancellor. But Lady Vansittart, who met the secret visitors to Denham Place, tells me that the Luftwaffe informant was a different person from Dr. Goerdeler.

"Why we went so wrong in the air cannot be explained," wrote Vansittart in retrospect.* British programmes sounded imposing, but the air estimates for 1934 were only £20,000,000, of which no more than £9,000,000.was for aircraft and equipment. The Churchill prophecy that Germany would reach parity in 1935 seemed to have come true in March 1935, when, as we have already seen, Hitler made an apparent admission to Sir John Simon that he had already reached parity with Britain. As I have recorded, German officials did not agree with this claim at the time and Sir John Simon for reasons of policy wished to keep the claim secret at least until he had fully discussed it with the Cabinet and subsequently at the Stresa Conference. Vansittart, however, acted on the impulse to reveal the Hitler claim in order, as he said, to support the case for British supplementary air estimates, even though Sir John told the House of Commons that he could not reveal details of his discussions. In a standard British work, *The Narrow Margin*, written from captured German documents, the Hitler claim is described as "certainly not justified". It was contradicted by

* *Mist Procession.*

reliable secret information at the disposal of the Air Ministry and by German officials including General Erhard Milch, Under-Secretary for Air. Germany had in fact 1,888 aircraft in May 1935, mainly trainers. "Of the first 9,000 military aircraft built in Germany nearly half were trainers", according to figures supplied to Vansittart by his German sources.

If Eden and Simon were dismayed at the time by the parity claim, the Air Ministry quite rightly did not at once accept it as fact. It was scrutinised in the interval between the Hitler meeting with Simon and the Stresa conference of April 20th, 1935, at which Britain, France and Italy met to discuss the growing menace of Germany to Europe. That Baldwin was not yet convinced of the need for an accelerated programme was indicated by his speech on April 8th, 1935 at Llandrindod Wells, where he said that: "I may hate the prospect of an increased air force as much as any of you, but . . . If I decide it is my duty to see that a greater deterrent is set up, and the way of the aggressor made harder, then I appeal to you to . . . respect the decision of the statesmen even if you do not agree."

Two days later on April 10th, 1935, two contradictory reports were produced for the Cabinet, one by Lord Londonderry for the Air Ministry, and the other by Sir John Simon for the Foreign Office. Sir John Simon put forward to Mr. Ramsay Macdonald the views of Sir Robert Vansittart and Mr. Ralph Wigram, head of the Central Department that "German superiority over all first-line machines in United Kingdom aerodromes under Air Ministry control now seems to be some 30 per cent. I can see no likely motive for the German Air Ministry deliberately to exaggerate . . . I understand that the Air Ministry now believes there to be 1,375 machines of military type in Germany . . . our secret reports give a total of 3,000 machines of every type now in existence. . . . Still more disturbing is the speed at which these aeroplanes are being manufactured. . . .

"The conclusion which might have to be drawn from the above figures, if they are correct, is that this country is open to the threat of sudden attack by a Continental Power in a degree to which it has not been exposed for hundreds of years."*

The other memorandum circulated by Lord Londonderry, Secretary of State for Air, to his Cabinet colleagues took a less

* *Facing the Dictators*, Lord Avon.

alarmed view of the German potential. It quoted an Air Ministry assessment of October 1934 that Germany would reach a first-line strength of about 1,300 aircraft by October 1936 and an eventual expansion to a first-line of 1,500 or 1,600 aircraft. He thought that "there is no ground for alarm at the existing situation. Whatever first-line strength Germany may claim, we remain today substantially stronger if all relevant factors are taken into account. But the future, as opposed to the present, must cause grave concern." At this point the Londonderry memorandum parted company with reality, for it assumed that the Luftwaffe would remain in the strength of about 1,500-1,600 first line aircraft in 1939, and it gave the Air Staff's considered opinion that "Germany will not be ready for and not intending to go to war before 1942".

In the light of history this was an extraordinary assertion, probably based on a calculation that Germany would reach in that year its peak of efficiency. The Ministerial Defence (Plans) Policy Committee in its 1936 Memorandum "Planning for a War with Germany" assumed that war would break out in the latter part of 1939. This was the year that Vansittart considered dangerous. He wrote on July 4th, 1935 that "in the Defence Requirements Committee at the beginning of 1934, I urged upon the Chiefs of Staff that they were not asking enough in the Air. 1935 has borne me out. And I am confident that I shall also be right in my repeated predictions that Germany will be ready for trouble before 1939." On reading the Londonderry memorandum he commented that its optimism was "shared by no one else in Europe". So the dispute went to and fro between Cabinet, Air Ministry and Foreign Office, accumulating minutes on either side, as in early April 1935 the Stresa conference assembled. The obstinacy of the Air Ministry had something to do with the professional caution of Sir Edward Ellington, the Chief of Air Staff, and a lot to do with the limited intelligence of Charles Henry Vane-Tempest-Stewart, 7th Marquess of Londonderry, a tall amiable man of fashion, whose wife kept at Londonderry House in Park Lane the last political salon of this age, and held magnificent receptions, the invitations to which were often scrutinised by the Prime Minister of the day. "Charlie" Londonderry had a reasonable case to defend; for Hitler *was* lying about his actual air strength. Where Londonderry failed was in making an issue of that, instead of gaining the utmost for the future. Vansittart had persuaded Ramsay Macdonald to go to Stresa himself, in order to have the opportunity of his support. German air strength was very much a subject for discussion. Among the British delegation was Ralph Wigram, Head of the Central Department, primed with the Foreign Office assessments of the Luftwaffe, and Wing Commander Charles Medhurst, Deputy Director of Air Intelligence, whose knowledge would be authoritative on the question of German air strength. On the boat train from Victoria Station, Medhurst and Wigram were already in conversation on their joint subject, and soon Vansittart and Rex Leeper, Head of the News Department, joined them. It was plain to Wigram and Vansittart that Medhurst took as anxious a view of comparative air strength and potential expansion as they did. Since the Londonderry memorandum should have been based on the intelligence available to Medhurst, this was interesting to Vansittart. "I want you to breakfast with the Prime Minister," he said to Medhurst, "Tell him what you have been telling me."

The airman realised his invidious position. His junior rank, he said, precluded him from stating the views of the Air Ministry to the Prime Minister; but Vansittart insisted, and at Stresa the breakfast took place. Macdonald was then in the cerebral twilight that closes in before Prime Ministers accept retirement. He was a deviating Socialist, a League of Nations man and a pacifist; and none of those qualifications would help him at Stresa to face realities fully. After a day at the conference table, he would slump in his chair and murmur at the weight of his responsibilities: "A' these people, dependent on me!" A solution must be found; but when a question bothered him, he would brush it off with, "Ask Van! Ask Lady Londonderry!" The world of 1935 was a blurred background to his own extraordinary career and guid conceit of himself. But at his lakeside breakfast with Medhurst the vision cleared, and within a few days of his return to London in May 1935, a further expansion of the Royal Air Force was decided.

One Sunday that spring Lord Londonderry button-holed Air Vice-Marshal Philip Joubert in Park Lane and complained bitterly to him that he could not make the Cabinet understand that the total number of aircraft did not represent what could be put into battle.

130

"Being of the opinion that the Germans were catching us up very fast," Joubert answered that "we must accept the dilution (of quality) involved in a rapid expansion." Londonderry argued further and "as we could not agree, we parted with our relations slightly strained".*

Londonderry remained obstinate in his view and after the Stresa conference burst into Vansittart's room at the Foreign Office.

"Van, you've been making a lot of trouble for me."

"Don't you worry, Charlie!" replied Vansittart. "We're going to make yours a great Department."

It would be great, but it would be great without Charlie. Baldwin, perhaps intentionally, was making heavy weather of it all. On May 22nd in speaking to the House of Commons he still accepted that Britain had a margin of 50 per cent superiority in October 1934. However, "where I was wrong was in my estimate of the future. There I was completely wrong. Neither I nor my advisers . . . had any idea of the exact rate at which production . . . was being speeded up in Germany." In the Cabinet reshuffle of June 1935 he moved Londonderry to the post of Lord Privy Seal, and chose Philip Cunliffe-Lister (Lord Swinton), a hard and competent Yorkshireman, to take over the Air Ministry.

Poor Charlie! He pursued his own course. Having failed to convince the Cabinet that the Air Ministry had not been taken by suprise, he began to cultivate Germans and attend Nazi functions, bringing back friendly assurances that there were no aggressive intentions in the mind of Hitler. He wrote plaintive letters to Baldwin: "Looking back (Stanley) I think that you, Neville and Ramsay lost confidence in me, because you were frightened by the propaganda of Winston and Rothermere which asserted that the Germans were overwhelmingly strong. You had refused to listen to our advice on rearmament and I am sure you became anxious lest the propaganda might be correct, and that then you would be confronted with the charge of having failed in your duty of establishing the security of this country. I think that is why you threw me to the wolves."†

Cunliffe-Lister was a man of different fibre. By marriage

* The Third Service, Air Chief Marshal Sir Philip Joubert.
† G. M. Young, Stanley Baldwin.

he had inherited an enormous fortune, estates in Yorkshire and some of the finest grouse moors in the British Isles. He was tough and practical and had powers of organisation. All this commanded a position for him in the Conservative Party. He accepted a peerage without scruple to free himself from the exacting business of the House of Commons and, as he told me, "to get on with the job". Both Baldwin and Chamberlain respected his ability. It fell to him to announce the Defence reorganisation in 1936, and as Chairman of the Air Sub-Committee of Imperial Defence, which became known as the Swinton Committee, had the prescience to invite Winston Churchill to become a member. In the period June 1935 to May 1938, Lord Swinton provided the shadow factories for aircraft production, accepted the aircraft designs put forward by industry to meet (and improve on) the Air Staff requirements, and developed the greatest asset of all, Radar. In these activities he continued until May 1938 when Mr. Chamberlain decided to replace him with Sir Kingsley Wood, on the grounds that Kingsley Wood could answer for air matters to the Commons, while Lord Swinton could not.

But the advent of Swinton did not immediately bring the accelerated production that Vansittart so urgently desired. Scheme A, as the air defence plan was called, was still being put forward by the Air Staff in July 1935 as its accepted rearmament programme, with the final stage to be reached in 1942.

Vansittart wrote at this time:

"We have laboured for years under the burden of these endless committees which spend nothing but time. The results are nearly always futile.

"My view is a short and simple one. Anything that fails to provide security by 1938 is inadequate and blind. Even Scheme A is inadequate and not what our situation and the situation of Europe require. And now apparently we do not seem to be getting even Scheme A after all this talking and writing. We may pay dearly for these futilities."*

This insistence in 1935—evident also in his departmental papers—that there must be air readiness by 1938 sets Vansittart apart from and above the men whom he served. None of them stood on the same intellectual ground, except perhaps Duff Cooper, then Secretary of State for War. None ever produced

* Vansittart Papers.

132

a more prescient written judgment than this smothered cry from a Permanent Official. When the shame of Munich was followed by the tattered glory of Dunkirk, he would remember it, and wrote to his secretary of these extracts—"Please keep them by me. The record is an insistent one, over the years."*

In its first transition from quality to quantity in 1935, the Air Council wanted an expansion that would advance the existing programme of getting 3,800 aircraft by 1939 and push it forward to 1937. This would have produced a different strategy, and probably a different political approach at the time of the Munich crisis: but Sir William Weir, who had been Director of Aircraft Production in the First World War, advised that so rapid a programme would put too great a strain on the rearmament capacity of the country as a whole. The programme was scaled down to 1,500 aircraft by 1937. As successive reports of German expansion came in, the Air Staff sought to accelerate production. Lord Swinton wanted to hurry, but he wanted also to be sure that his designs, taken fresh from the drawing board and omitting the prototype stage, were really superior to the German standard types of aircraft. "The Germans made the mistake of accepting the Heinkel 111 and Junkers 88 as the best aircraft some two years or more before the right moment to take this decision," wrote Joubert. "The British, either by chance or by skill, waited until better types were available, and so when war broke out were technically ahead of their enemy." But this also meant that the Spitfire and the Hurricane would not be available in the numbers required in 1938 and 1939 to support British foreign policy. Rapid expansion would affect the normal peacetime economy, and that the Treasury would not permit.

Nor was it only a matter of technical delays or production capacity. The Chiefs of Staff opinion that 1942 was the date of German readiness for war inhibited all British preparations in 1935. Vansittart wrote again in July that "1942 is all very much a matter of conjecture. Things will move more quickly than either the C.I.G.S. or the Air Staff believe. In any case we cannot delay our own preparedness beyond the end of 1938 at latest."†

"We do really need to hasten our measures of self-protection," he wrote in October 1935, and in November "the Germans

* Vansittart Papers.　　　　† Ibid.

are themselves giving us far clearer warning than we had before 1914; and we have the remedy of rearmament in our hands, if we are quick enough."*

In December 1935 and again in early 1936 his mysterious German informants brought Vansittart reports of Luftwaffe expansion. The first of these reports estimated German porduction capacity at 6,000 aircraft per annum, depending on availability of materials. Aware that his own strong views amounted to intervention in Air Staff policy, Vansittart preferred to pass these reports under elaborate conditions of secrecy to Colonel Sir Maurice Hankey, requesting him to hand them to Sir Edward Ellington personally, but resolutely refusing to disclose the identity or nature of the source. For, as he wrote, "intelligence was becoming increasingly hard to operate in Germany, because informants died slow and horrible deaths if detected". Even in sending the reports to Eden, who in late December 1935 became Foreign Secretary, the Permanent Under-Secretary asked for "the smallest possible circulation . . . as a matter of justice to a courageous man". Few would have suspected that Vansittart could be so protective with Germans.

To Medhurst as Deputy Director of Air Intelligence fell the task of analysing these reports. He thought that if the methods of analysis were reconciled with those of the Air Ministry, the results were not far out. He disagreed with the calculations of first-line strength and estimated output of aircraft as being on the high side. Sir Edward Ellington, the Chief of Air Staff, agreed that there was not a great deal of difference fundamentally. He thought that Vansittart's information about present and future types of German aircraft and engines was a very valuable contribution to knowledge on this subject.

Because Hitler had chosen to act unilaterally in sending troops into the Rhineland, Britain could not in 1936 enter into an air limitation agreement with Germany. But Lord Swinton attempted at least to find out the scale of German aircraft production. At a meeting in the autumn of 1936 with General Erhard Milch, Under-Secretary for Air, he proposed an exchange of air information, and to this Milch after some delay agreed. Consequently a British air mission visited Berlin in January 1937, including the Air Council member for Supply,

* Vansittart Papers.

Air Vice-Marshal Courtney. The technique of Milch was interesting; he must have been aware that the annual British air estimates were to be presented a month later. Milch told Courtney that, provided he brought no British Embassy official with him, he might visit the German Air Ministry and be shown the German air strength. Courtney did so, and Milch lifted down from his safes in conditions of dramatic secrecy clasp-locked confidential books and showed him the current pro-gramme. It appeared that by September 1938 Germany would have a first line of 1,755 aircraft. Compared with the British air strength in September 1938, forecast as 1,736, this did not seem to give grounds for alarm. And that, no doubt, was the object of the deception. Once the British estimates were presented to Parliament in March, it would be much harder to obtain parliamentary approval for increases, whereas German air production could be secretly accelerated with a stroke of the pen.

There had been an effort made in Britain in March 1936, after Hitler's march into the Rhineland, to quicken defence, when the Ministry for Co-ordination of Defence was called into being. It was still too leisurely. Lord Ismay recalls the first meeting of the Home Defence Committee in March 1936 when he recommended provision of "an additional hundred guns or so" for anti-aircraft defence of Great Britain. Each gun was allotted to a site or city in the effort to pass Treasury approval, and yet Neville Chamberlain, then Chancellor of the Exchequer, had said: "Was there to be no end to this importunity?" Scarcely a year ago there had been a substantial increase in air defence, and Chamberlain "hoped that this demand would really be the last".*

The British defence estimates in February 1937 amounted to £1,570,000,000 over a five-year period. This was an impressive figure; but the Cabinet had laid down that normal trade was not to be disrupted. This made it impossible to fulfil the pro-gramme. It was not so easy to open the throttle, with Labour leaders like Sir Stafford Cripps exhorting British ordnance workers, as he did in March 1937 to "refuse to make armaments ... that is the only way you can keep this country out of war". Sir Stafford made this speech at Eastleigh a month after a secret Defence Report showed the Foreign Secretary that by

* Lord Ismay, *Memoirs*.

May 1937 Germany would have 800 long range bombers whereas Britain would possess 48.*

In April 1937 Vansittart's informants sent him disturbing news that "the old programme of Luftwaffe construction which was to have been completed by the end of 1938 has already been replaced by one of greatly increased magnitude. The new programme was introduced and the supplementary construction work already commenced on March 15th, 1937," Vansittart forwarded this information to the Air Ministry. So much for the gentleman's agreement in January with Milch. On June 30th, 1937 he wrote that "it was quite obvious to me that Milch was lying from the start, and I pointed this out at the time. The *mise-en-scène* was so childish that I could never understand how anybody could be taken in by it." The Air Staff was now of the same opinion, and so also was General Milch himself, who obligingly sent over information that German aircraft production had been stepped up to a new target. The Luftwaffe was slipping numerically into the lead in the summer of 1937. A paralysis began consequently to creep over British diplomacy. There was a panic plan to offer Germany a colony, which Vansittart sharply criticised as useless—"with Germany in her present state of exaltation I do not think anybody believes she would pay any substantial price in Europe for the mere return of the Cameroons."†

The Chiefs of Staff Committee report on German military preparedness of February 1937 showed the Foreign Secretary a disquieting disparity of strength, with Germany snatching a lead of 800 against only 48 British long range bombers. Eden complained that this would not give British diplomacy much chance in 1938, but the Cabinet view was that Britain had only a limited liability to support its Allies.‡ The Air Ministry produced a memorandum in October 1937 in support of Scheme J, its "crash-programme" answer to the acceleration of German rearmament. This notable document was probably the last attempt to stabilise Europe by an earnest attempt to overtake Germany in air strength. It showed that by the end of 1939, the German first line air strength would be nearly twice that of the R.A.F. and demanded that the Cabinet abandon its rule that the national economy was not to be disturbed by rearmament. The October memorandum drew an historical

* *Facing the Dictators.* † Vansittart Papers. ‡ *Facing the Dictators.*

parallel with the position of Britain in 1912, when Sir Edward Grey, then Foreign Secretary, wrote of the situation created by German military strength: "You must not rely on your foreign policy to protect the United Kingdom. . . . If you let your margin of strength fall below that which may be brought to bear on you rapidly, you are setting foreign policy a task which you ought not to set it. The risk of an attack on the United Kingdom stronger in force than we could meet with the ships we keep in Home waters is not one to be settled by diplomacy." Vansittart showed this memorandum to Eden, who repeated to Chamberlain on November 8th the view already stated on November 1st that rearmament must go faster. The Prime Minister replied that he did not think anybody was going to attack Britain for the next two years. It was necessary, he said, to follow a very cautious foreign policy; but he promised discussion of the general situation a week later.* He had evidently missed the point of the Air Staff memorandum entirely, or did not wish to accept it.

Vansittart showed his concern at Chamberlain's obstinacy. He urged Eden to return to the attack. He began:

"You have read, I think, the Air Ministry's paper. There is not a man among us who does not feel that foreign policy cannot with any safety at all be continued on our present basis of material strength. Lord Grey is rightly quoted, and nothing on earth can ever alter that truth. You must not rely on your foreign policy to protect the United Kingdom. None the less, day by day the Foreign Office is tacitly expected to live in the teeth of that unalterable dictum, and it is criticised for obvious inability to perform the impossible. . . . I feel that you ought to point out to the Cabinet that it is becoming steadily more perilous to disregard the wisdom of Lord Grey. I have pointed out on many occasions from the beginning of 1934 that nothing can be guaranteed in Europe from the end of 1937.

"The moral is that the present scheme of the Air Ministry represents a rock-bottom minimum. Even so we shall be two whole years behind Germany. . . . Of course you will be told that the Foreign Office can and must help by lowering tension." Here Vansittart weighed that Lord Halifax was about to make an exploratory visit to Hitler, and in the view of the Permanent

* *Facing the Dictators.*

Under-Secretary it was necessary that such a gesture should be made to Mussolini as well.

"Of course the real answer is that if this country had had proper warlike resources there would have been no Abyssinian adventure. But it will be unprofitable to argue long about that. . . . The Foreign Office might well agree to pass a sponge over the past, if we get the Air Ministry's present proposals (through) and get them quickly. This time we should be earnest against a day's unnecessary delay, for we still have to live through four frightfully dangerous years. I only hope this programme will be discussed at once and accepted at once."

Vansittart reflected that some concession must be made to the inner cabinet, Neville Chamberlain, Sir John Simon and Lord Halifax in order that Scheme J should go through. The Treasury, in which Sir Warren Fisher wielded a diminishing, and Sir Horace Wilson, Chief Industrial Adviser, a growing, influence had the powers of refusal and delay. All that the Foreign Office could do was to try to maintain its own control of foreign affairs in the face of unofficial missions and private talks between Downing Street emissaries and the expansionist powers. Chamberlain badly wanted to placate and make a friend of Mussolini, but the Foreign Secretary with sceptical rectitude was blocking any gesture in that direction.

Why not give "the other side" what they want so much? suggested Vansittart. By "the other side" he meant Chamberlain, on the other side of Downing Street. In a Cabinet bargain, he thought, the Foreign Office could concede a visit to Mussolini in exchange for Scheme J—security in the air. After all, Lord Halifax was about to make a casual visit to Germany for talks with Hitler, so why not a similar visit to the junior dictator?

Eden may not have liked this last advice. For over the years he and Vansittart still differed on the wisdom of bargaining with Italy. Eden's memorandum to the Cabinet pointed out that the forces of diplomacy could not guarantee the safety of Britain except at the risk of "deep national humiliation". He wrote a fine description of Germany as "so fully prepared and showing such expectation of war, that it is not easily distinguishable from a will to make war". But over Italy he did not employ the lever tactics recommended by Vansittart. Eden stated in fact nearly the opposite—that the anti-Comintern pact witnessed the common desire of Germany and Italy to bring pressures to bear on Britain.* This was equivalent to saying that he saw no hope of detaching Italy. A position of rectitude appeared to him of paramount importance. The attempt to get through a crash programme of aircraft production failed. Scheme J was shelved. German air production forged ahead and British production never caught up with it in peacetime. The Cabinet decision in 1937 was to rely on diplomacy rather than on air strength. "We did not do enough soon enough," reflected Lord Swinton,† "the financial limits laid down were too rigid: we should have insisted on some power in peacetime to direct part of industry into war production." But who could insist? Swinton himself was to be removed in May 1938, and his successor at the Air Ministry, Sir Kingsley Wood, whose instincts were for accommodation with Germany, shelved the master plan for a Vickers shadow factory at Castle Bromwich which, as Lord Swinton told me, "would have given us another 1,500 Spitfires at the time of the Battle of Britain." Of the three men who fought for Scheme J in 1937 none would be in a position to influence decisions a few months later. Whatever else Mr. Chamberlain may have lacked, he had a cold grasp of power. He was impatient of Eden; not wholly sure of Swinton; but first he thought it advisable to deal with the formidable Vansittart.

* *Facing the Dictators.*   † *I Remember*, p. 118.

CHAPTER VIII

THE ADVENT OF CHAMBERLAIN

ON May 28th, 1937 Neville Chamberlain became Prime Minister. There had been no doubts about his succession. He was trusted both by the Court and the people. His promise from previous years was that of a shrewd and competent administrator, though his half-brother Austen once remarked to him at dinner in the presence of Anthony Eden that "of course you know nothing of foreign affairs". Even so, his notes in 1934 and 1935 show him to have been well aware of the need to rearm, and in his position as Chancellor of the Exchequer he was brought in those years into the close Cabinet counsels on peace or war. His mistrust and dislike of the Nazis was plain. The 1934 *Putsch* in Vienna moved him to write in his diary on the 28th July that he "hated Nazism and all its works with a greater loathing than ever. . . . What does not satisfy me is that we don't shape our policy accordingly." But that was not the entire horizon of Britain's responsibilities. The growing strength of Japan in the Far East perplexed him and he wrote about the same time that "we ought to know by this time that the U.S.A. will give us no undertaking to resist by force any action by Japan short of an attack on Hawaii or Honolulu."

He confessed to a certain weakness for seeking solutions. "Unhappily it is part of my nature that I cannot contemplate any problem without trying to find a solution to it."* Even this may have appeared a virtue in the spring of 1937 after the months of drift that followed the proclaimed decision of Baldwin to retire. But his impulse on becoming Prime Minister was a departure from his earlier and more measured judgments on foreign affairs: "if only we could get on terms with the Germans" he wrote.

Vansittart had no strong presentiment of disaster at the accession of Chamberlain. He noted that Chamberlain thought Germany could be "economically placated". It should also be said that the Prime Minister was equally interested in the idea that the aggressive powers could be economically contained,

* Keith Feiling, *Life of Neville Chamberlain*, p. 259.

and paid much attention as Chairman of the Imperial Committee of Defence to the work of the Advisory Committee on Trade Questions in the time of war (A.T.B.) which worked out blockade plans against the three hypothetical enemies, Germany, Italy and Japan. The A.T.B. was established within the Board of Trade, though subordinate in reality to the Chiefs of Staff Committee. Of the blockade planners, little mentioned yet in works of history, it should be said that A.T.B. targets were sometimes switched with great rapidity in response to some new surprise in the outside world, or a notion formed in the recesses of Mr. Chamberlain's mind. For as he told Lady Astor, the hostess of Cliveden, he meant to be his own Foreign Secretary.

The purpose here is to make Neville Chamberlain intelligible and to show not only how he failed, which has been made clear to the point of caricature, but also why he failed. How was it that the man of clear and cautious judgments in 1935—when he gave some support to Sir Samuel Hoare in the Abyssinian crisis—became an addict of wishful solutions? It seems that he made up his mind on high policy in the summer months of 1937, and nothing that happened between then and March 1939 altered him in his obstinate course. What were the events that helped him to make up his mind?

Continued tension with Germany in early 1937 led the Chiefs of Staff to draw up a report on "Planning for War with Germany", recommending that the Advisory Committee should draw up definite blockade plans for the contingency of war with Germany in 1939. It seems to have been implicit in this instruction that it would be unsafe to venture into war—even a war of blockade—any sooner than that, an opinion which the Service Chiefs repeated in more emphatic form in March 1938. But the prospect of being drawn into European war before 1939 was too evident to be ignored, and that was the grave issue before a meeting of the Commonwealth Prime Ministers sitting intermittently in London from May 14th to June 15th, 1937. Their decisions were influenced by that taken by America in May 1937 in passing the Neutrality Act—a grave setback to the Vansittart policy of strength in Europe.

In March 1937 we see for perhaps the last time the competent vigorous Neville Chamberlain pursuing a traditional English policy of containing the aggressor in Europe. He had much to contend with; for in February it was apparent from the conversation of Mr. Henry Morgenthau, U.S. Secretary of the Treasury, that Mr. Roosevelt was still thinking in terms of disarmament as a means of reducing tension. Then the President switched to the idea of a bold initiative by the U.S.A. and Britain, but how bold could they be with American neutrality legislation unaltered?

Mr. Chamberlain pointed this out in a frank letter which Eden approved, though he resented Mr. Chamberlain's discouragement of a similar initiative a year later in more urgent circumstances.

"The Chancellor of the Exchequer has received Mr. Morgenthau's important message", wrote Mr. Chamberlain, "with the greatest interest. He has discussed it with the Prime Minister and the Foreign Secretary and wishes to say how warmly all three appreciate this evidence of Mr. Morgenthau's—and as they understand—the President's urgent desire to find some way in which the United States—possibly in conjunction with the United Kingdom—can help in preventing the outbreak of another war. Beset as they are with the differences and risks inherent in the present political situation in Europe, the Chancellor and his colleagues have given their most anxious consideration to this message.

"In order to arrive at a proper appreciation of the possibility of averting war, it is necessary first to consider where the menace lies and what are the causes which keep it alive. These causes are both political and economic and it is sometimes difficult to disentangle them from one another. But Mr. Morgenthau is undoubtedly right in saying that the needs of armament programmes are responsible for a good deal of the economic troubles in Europe and these programmes are in turn the result of political consideration."

Here there appears a paragraph that breathes the spirit of Vansittart. Lord Avon disclaims authorship though he records his satisfaction at it.

"The main source of this fear of war in Europe is to be found in Germany. No other country, not Italy, since she has her hands full with the task of consolidating her Abyssinian conquests, not Russia with all her military preparation, certainly not France, England or any of the small powers, is for a moment credited with any aggressive designs. But the fierce propaganda against other nations continually carried on by the German Press and wireless under the instructions of Dr. Goebbels, the intensity and persistence of German military preparations, together with the many acts of the German Government in violation of treaties, cynically justified on the grounds that unilateral action was the quickest way of getting what they wanted, have inspired all her neighbours with a profound uneasiness. Even these Islands which could be reached in less than an hour from German territory by an air force with hundreds of tons of bombs, cannot be exempt from anxiety.

"The motive for this aggression on the part of German policy rises from her desire to make herself so strong that no one will venture to withstand whatever demands she may make whether for European or Colonial territory. With this intention in her heart she is not likely to agree to any disarmament which would deflect her purpose. The only situation which would influence her to a contrary decision would be the conviction that her efforts to secure superiority of force were doomed to failure by reason of the superior force which would meet her if she attempts aggression.

"It is because of the belief that British forces would be available against German aggression that British re-armament plans have been welcomed by so many nations in Europe by a sigh of relief and if they still feel anxious, their anxiety rises from their doubts whether this country's re-armament will be adequate or will be completed in time to act as a deterrent to German ambitions.

"This being the consideration in Europe as H.M.G. see it, they have no doubt whatever that the greatest single contribution which the United States could make at the present moment to the preservation of world peace would be the amendment of the existing neutrality legislation. Under this legislation an embargo would be imposed on the export from the United States of arms and munitions irrespective of whether a country is an aggressor or the victim of aggression.

"It is obvious that the existing neutrality law and, *a fortiori*, any extension of it so as to include raw materials, suits the requirements of a country contemplating an aggression which can and would lay in large stores of raw materials, with the knowledge that its intended victims will, when the time comes, be precluded from obtaining supplies in one of the greatest world markets. The legislation in this present form constitutes an indirect, potent encouragement to aggression, and it is earnestly hoped that some way may be found of leaving sufficient discretion with the Executive to deal with each case on its merits.

"Mr. Chamberlain realises that this question is, apart from its international aspect, a matter of domestic controversy in the United States, and that it may well be impossible for the United States Government to take such a step even if they desire it, but in view of Mr. Morgenthau's request for the Chancellor's views he has thought that the United States Government would wish to have them expressed without reserve.

"Mr. Chamberlain hopes that this frank exposition made in response to Mr. Morgenthau's message may prove helpful in clarifying the position and saying how it is regarded by H.M.G. He earnestly trusts that some form of collaboration may be found possible between our two countries since he is profoundly convinced that almost any action common to them both would go far to restore confidence to this world and arrest the menace which now threatens it."

In conclusion Mr. Chamberlain explained himself again. Since he has been criticised, and rightly, by Lord Avon and others for failing to grasp the Roosevelt offer of January 1938, it is fair to show how much he understood the issues in March 1937 and how little then America understood the nature of the problem.

The task of Vansittart was complicated at this moment by a crucially timed visit to Germany by the Marquess of Lothian who met privately on May 4th, 1937 with Hitler and Goering and on May 5th with Dr. Schacht. He circulated his views both to the British Government and the Commonwealth Prime Ministers—particularly to General Hertzog in South Africa, Vansittart noted—on the advisability of a deal with Hitler. The Lothian memorandum is summarised in the biography by Sir James Butler. He suggested that Germany should receive colonies and be entrusted with a European sphere of interest. Only thus could she be deterred from a war of desperation.

Lord Lothian obligingly drew the attention of Hitler and Goering to Mr. Eden's speech at Leamington on November 20th, 1936, and the passage in which the Foreign Secretary defined the only firm British military commitments as the defence of the Commonwealth, France and Belgium if they were attacked, Egypt and the Canal, and Iraq; whereas problems elsewhere were matters of concern more because the risk of war anywhere affected everybody. Hitler professed to Lord Lothian that the Czechs and others in Eastern Europe had a right to a national existence. Lord Lothian summed up in his memorandum to the Government that the first article of British policy should be "to avoid at any cost becoming part of an anti-German alliance, unless it is absolutely clear that she is organising an alliance (with Italy and Japan) not for justice but for attack and domination. . . . We ought to make it clear that we were not committed to defending the frontiers of Eastern Europe. . . ." A conference with the United States and all the colonial powers should examine how to relax the economic tensions of Germany. "If all this failed, the only chance of preventing a European war from becoming a World war would be for Great Britain to limit its commitments in Europe to the minimum necessary for its security" . . . and "for the whole Commonwealth to move much nearer to the American policy of armed non-commitment anywhere".

Mr. Orme Sargent noted that the Lothian memorandum had already had a deep effect on the Commonwealth Prime Ministers. On reading Lord Lothian's memorandum, Sir Robert interpreted this as conceding a German claim to absorb Austria and Czechoslovakia, to reconquer Danzig and Memel and to reduce other neighbouring states to military satellites.

"We fought the last war largely to prevent this," he commented, adding that France could not be expected to abandon Czechoslovakia for, as M. Yvon Delbos, the French Foreign Minister, had just reminded Mr. Eden on May 15th, that would "leave France a second-rate power". Not one Foreign Office senior official could be found to say a word in support of the deal that Lothian proposed and "America would execrate us if we took such a line", concluded Vansittart. A Foreign Office memorandum for immediate circulation to the Commonwealth Prime Ministers was written refuting the Lothian thesis, but it had begun a rot and when the Munich crisis came Geoffrey Dawson, editor of *The Times*, testified to streams of Canadian and Australian visitors coming to tell him that their countries would not fight for Czechoslovakia.*

In May 1937 the United States passed the Neutrality Act, divesting herself of the traditional rights of the neutral to trade with a belligerent. It was a heavy blow to Britain and France.

* K. Feiling, *Life of Neville Chamberlain*.

For it made it of questionable value to buy American military equipment in peacetime, since supplies could not be assured in war. In assuming the leadership of Britain, Chamberlain spoke of exchanging Bleak House for Great Expectations. But behind the closed doors of 10 Downing Street he had heard the Commonwealth Prime Ministers declare that they could not support Britain in a European war. Mr. Mackenzie King refused to have Canada made the rearward arsenal for the British rearmament effort. Mr. Robert Menzies pointed to the tensions of the Far East as making Australian participation in a European war impossible, and General Hertzog let it be known that South Africa could not take part in a war on Central European issues. This moment, with the ill fated intervention of Lord Lothian, seems a parallel to the year 1911, of which Vansittart noted* that Sir Edward Grey had failed sufficiently to warn the Commonwealth states of the imminence of war. Within a fortnight of becoming Prime Minister, Mr. Chamberlain must have made up his mind. Once upon a course he followed it with enormous tenacity. Nothing would deflect him, nor was he willing to revise his opinions along the way in the light of experience or fresh occurrences. Out of this necessity, as he saw it, to avoid war at all costs, arose a credulous philosophy that became so much a part of himself that the picture of him left to us is that of a bewildered and weatherbeaten old man. Yet he could be ruthless and masterful in putting his illusions into practice, and exercised a cold power through the Conservative party machine that has seldom been approached by any tenant of No. 10 Downing Street. The reign of Chamberlain is impossible to illustrate without dwelling on the personalities of his advisers. Sir Warren Fisher, for fifteen years Permanent Head of the Treasury and self-styled Head of the Civil Service, had suffered something of the eclipse of influence that overtook Vansittart after the Hoare-Laval crisis. Sir Warren then found it expedient to associate his fortunes with those of the rising man among the senior Civil Servants, Sir Horace Wilson, Chief Industrial Adviser to the Government, on whom Baldwin and Chamberlain had leaned increasingly since the Ottawa conference. Neither of these Civil Servants fully understood foreign policy, though Sir Warren had been strong in his mistrust of Germany. Sir Horace impressed me as having just

* *Mist Procession.*

sufficient knowledge of foreign problems to mishandle them.

"When Baldwin left I wanted to get away," Sir Horace told me in after years. "But Chamberlain wanted me to stay. So I did." Wilson had helped to defeat the General Strike in 1926, and the ascent of this quiet self-effacing man had been assured after that. A third man in a key position was Sir Nevile Henderson, in April 1937 appointed British Ambassador in Berlin, whose personality was probably the most calamitous of all at this time. Even Baldwin was grumbling about him before retirement, and the irony was that it was Vansittart who selected Henderson for this most important of all diplomatic posts. It happened in this manner at the end of 1936, as Sir Clifford Norton remembers. Three ambassadors came to Vansittart in the Foreign Office for interview to succeed Sir Eric Phipps in Berlin. They were Sir Percy Loraine, Ambassador in Ankara, Sir Miles Lampson, Ambassador to Egypt, and Sir Nevile Henderson, Ambassador to the Argentine and Paraguay. Eden enquired of Vansittart afterwards what had prompted the appointment and was told by the dismayed Permanent Under-Secretary that Henderson had been reckoned "a good shot" while in Yugoslavia and had got on well with King Alexander and Prince Paul. No doubt this was considered in his selection, but the final remark of Vansittart on reading their respective papers and finding their records of service otherwise equal was that:

"Sir Nevile has done his stint in South America. He shall have his reward."

How often before his failing mission in Berlin was completed must Henderson have wished himself back in the Argentine, and Vansittart wished him anywhere but in Berlin. Soon after the arrival of Neville Chamberlain at 10 Downing Street, Sir Nevile began to circumvent the regular Foreign Office channels and ply the Prime Minister direct with letters and visits to give his views on the form that policy with Germany ought to take, in terms that later moved Sir Robert to such comments as "I am afraid Sir Nevile's forecasts of the future are quite wrong and I am ready to bet him any sum that Germany will not settle down into a satisfied European."*

Mr. Chamberlain's tidy mind was already formulating his course in May 1937. Perhaps the Foreign Office was being too gloomy, he thought. He told the House of Commons that he

* Vansittart Papers.

refused to consider industrial conscription. He cautiously defined British interests as "1. the security of the United Kingdom, 2. defence of trade routes, 3. defence of British territories overseas, 4. co-operation and the defence of the territories of any allies." His private formula at the outset of his premiership was that:

"I believe the double policy of rearmament and better relations with Germany and Italy will carry us safely through the danger period, if only the Foreign Office will play up."* If only! His counsellors began to sap and underburrow the building on the other side of Downing Street. Sir Warren Fisher had a habit of inviting people to tea when he had something particular to say to them. Sir Horace Wilson one afternoon in May 1937 told Mr. Eden's Parliamentary Private Secretary Mr. J. P. L. Thomas, newly appointed in April, that he would like to take him to tea with Sir Warren who wished to meet him.

"I had no idea what this was about," wrote Thomas, "but it was soon made clear that both Fisher and Wilson were thoroughly dissatisfied with the Foreign Office and especially with Vansittart. They told me that Vansittart was an alarmist, that he hampered all attempts of the Government to make friendly contact with the dictator states and that his influence over Anthony Eden was very great. For this reason they had strongly backed the idea that I, whom Sir Horace knew well, should become P.P.S. at the Foreign Office, because I would be in a position to help them build a bridge between Downing Street and the Foreign Office and to create a better understanding between the two Departments. This might lessen the damage that had been done by the Foreign Office in general and by Vansittart in particular."

Thomas protested that this seemed to be an invitation to him to work behind the back of his own chief, and that he could only make complaints, if there should be any against Vansittart, to Mr. Eden and nobody else. Sir Horace left the room hastily. He returned next day to the subject and insinuated that there had been a failure on the part of Sir Warren to express his meaning clearly, but Thomas replied that Sir Warren's meaning had been made all too clear.

To a second tea party Sir Warren invited Lady Vansittart and this time he unfolded his ideas with a startling clarity after a few preliminary courtesies.

*K. Feiling, *Life of Neville Chamberlain*.

"I want you to tell Van not to write these long papers for the Cabinet. They don't like it and his predecessors didn't do it. He's exceeding his functions."

He referred to the series in which Vansittart periodically surveyed the international situation.

She said, distressed: "He's always done it, to sum up the year for them and the outlook. I can't tell him not to. He wouldn't understand."

"Well if he thinks he'll get his G.C.B. that way," snapped Sir Warren, "he's mistaken."

"Why should he want a G.C.B.?" she asked, and this guileless question about an honour to the fount of many honours disconcerted Sir Warren. The tea party petered to a close. On a third occasion Sir Warren and Sir Horace betrayed their close communion of ideas at a lunch with the Vansittarts at 44 Park Street in 1937. As Sir Robert developed his anxieties about Germany the two men exchanged amused glances. Lady Vansittart observed their smiles and afterwards warned her husband not to trust them, but he found only good words to describe his two colleagues. But either his views were being too forcefully and repetitiously expressed for the liking of the Cabinet, or the Senior Ministers were themselves entering a period of delusion and did not like to be shaken out of it. Lord Avon tells me that it was beginning to be difficult to get the views of Vansittart accepted.

"It was hard for Eden in Cabinet," Sir Clifford Norton thought. "When he tried to speak strongly on Germany, they used to smile to each other and murmur—'His Master's Voice'."—This was "the very great influence of Vansittart over Anthony Eden", to which Sir Warren had referred in his attempted intrigue with Mr. Thomas.

Under the strain of disbelief Vansittart had asked Austen Chamberlain at the end of 1936 whether to quit his permanent post and accept an Embassy, and Austen had replied:

"You had better go. You are getting rattled."

In his leisure moments as a younger man, Van had written poetry and plays, among them a successful play in French. His verse had something of James Elroy Flecker in it, a tinge of his Persian memories and occasionally a vivid epigram. To express his determination to remain at his London post he quoted* one

* *Mist Procession.*

of his own lines, which I find in a leather bound copy of his verses *The Singing Caravan* inscribed by the author to Anne Chamberlain, wife of the Prime Minister.

"My duty is to tug my oar—
so long as I am chained to it."

Should he have gone at this time to Paris, where his impelling strength might have served to keep the French Government to its Central European commitments, though, as we shall see, that was not exactly what Chamberlain and Sir Horace Wilson wanted? The duty of a Permanent Under-Secretary is to preserve his influence, but at what a price?

"It wasn't that I had lost confidence in him," Lord Avon told me. "I see that Van wrote in his *Mist Procession* that I said as much to my 'biographer', Lewis Broad, who wrote a book about me. I have never met Mr. Broad. The fact is that Van had been a long time in his post and he was becoming in-effective—no longer getting along with the other heads of Departments in Whitehall. He had always said that a diplomat should accept a new post but he did not do so himself."

It was a difficult Cabinet to influence—for both of them. Besides Chamberlain, Simon, the Chancellor of the Exchequer, Lord Halifax, the Lord President, Kingsley Wood, Minister of Health, and even Sir Samuel Hoare, now Home Secretary, held unreal views on the future. Their hope of scraping up a European solution was so great that it did not occur to them that time gained should be better used to rearm. From Germany in the summer of 1937 came a warning that their thinking in dealing with Hitler was fatally wrong, and a catastrophic misunderstanding near at hand.

Dr. Karl Goerdeler, chief Burgomaster of Leipzig, had resigned and retired on April 1st, 1937 after the statue of the composer Mendelssohn had been removed from its place in front of the City hall by order of the Nazi party. He thought for a time to take a position with Krupp in heavy industry, for which his talents as an economist would have fitted him, but after Hitler had informed Alfred Krupp von Bohlen that he disapproved of such an appointment for a man who had shown himself critical of National-Socialism, Goerdeler went instead to an advisory post with the Stuttgart industrialist, Robert Bosch. Concerned both with the economic risks that the Third Reich was incurring in its total rearmament plan and its extremist policy, Bosch readily agreed to Dr. Goerdeler making a world tour, upon which he would base an economic report and, at the same time, take soundings with prominent men in politics abroad about the collision course that Hitler was steering. This tour took him to Belgium, to England, to France and to the United States.

Sir Robert Vansittart's recollections of Goerdeler began in 1935, though there is no written mention of him in the Vansittart papers earlier than the summer of 1937. He is given honourable mention, though he retained "a transparent honesty and hankered still for the frontiers of 1914", not believing that the eastern frontiers of Germany with Poland could be permanent. A conspirator of German-Nationalist origins, "he was the only man with such a past that I ever liked".* He seemed to Vansittart the sole German conspirator against Hitler to be genuine.

The mission of Goerdeler had to be approved by the German Military Security Service of Admiral Wilhelm Canaris, Chief of the Abwehr. But before he could start Marshal Goering, as head of the Four Year Plan office, had to demand release of Dr. Goerdeler's passport from Gauleiter Mutschmann of Saxony who had confiscated it after the brawl over Mendelssohn's statue. Goering, who had misgivings about a war on two fronts, thought that Dr. Goerdeler could usefully assess the risks through other sources than those of the German Embassy in London, having himself no great liking for or confidence in Joachim von Ribbentrop as Ambassador. Goering exhorted Goerdeler to maintain "a German attitude" abroad and gave the project his blessing, while Dr. Hjalmar Schacht, the Reichsbank President, gave him letters of introduction to friends in the City. The ostensible purpose of his journey was to report on the economic potentials of the countries that he visited.

According to German sources, compiled by Gerhart Ritter in his work on *Carl Goerdeler and the German Resistance*, Dr. Goerdeler met in London during June 1937 with several important British personalities, Lord Halifax, Lord President of the Council, Mr. Eden and Sir Robert Vansittart among them. There is no mention of this visitor in the autobiography of Lord Halifax, *Fulness of Days*, nor yet in the memoirs of Lord Avon, which seem preoccupied in the summer of 1937 with the

* *Mist Procession.*

Spanish Civil War and relations with Italy. The assertions of German survivors that they warned Britain of Hitler's intentions in 1937 sometimes sound incredible. Fortunately Sir Robert has left some detailed notes of his meetings with Dr. Goerdeler and what was said, so that it is possible to bridge this chasm in history.

There is firstly his characterisation of Dr. Goerdeler, and as he imagined at the time of drafting it that he would be presenting the Goerdeler case to the Cabinet his lineaments must have been attentively traced.

"Herr Goerdeler is an impressive person, wise and weighty, a man of great intelligence and courage and a sincere patriot. He is a party-man and a friend of those in power, but an outspoken friend and well aware of the risks that he runs by his frankness. He told me that in 'offering' his advice and criticism at home, or in making any but blindly favourable comment abroad he was 'putting his neck in a halter'. The risk indeed is even greater than he knows. For it is probably only his friendships in the Army that have ensured his immunity from the Secret Police."

The arrival of Dr. Goerdeler in London and his two visits to the Foreign Office and to Denham Place were a fortunate occurrence. For Sir Robert was able to show him a document of remarkable interest that had fallen into his hands, a memorandum drawn up by the Association of Heavy Industries of the Rhineland and Westfalia on the economic potential of Germany and its programme of self-sufficiency, with particular emphasis on the shortcomings of the Four Year Plan. A copy of this document, drawn up at the request of Dr. Goerdeler himself, had been presented to General Baron von Fritsch, Commander-in-Chief of the German Army, in order to support him in arguments against risking a war in Europe. Fritsch had made some use of it in discussions with Field-Marshal Goering. A copy of the memorandum had somehow come into the hands of the British Legation in Prague and had been submitted to the Embassy in Berlin for an opinion on its authenticity. The Embassy assumed it to have been written for Dr. Schacht and rightly suggested that it was couched in rather too rudimentary terms for such an expert. Dr. Goerdeler now gave Sir Robert the proper explanation—that it had been prepared as a simple economic guide for the senior officers of the German General

Staff. He then unfolded his views on the disturbing economic and political situation of his country, and declared himself apprehensive of any agreement that might encourage the National-Socialist régime to continue in its evil courses—for that would lead to eventual disaster.

Continuing his talks at Denham Place, Dr. Goerdeler outlined the struggle for policy in Germany between a group in the Wehrmacht who wished for an understanding with Soviet Russia, and the group in which Dr. Schacht, the banks and industry wished for a peaceful settlement on colonies and raw materials with the western powers. Suspended between these two courses, the German economy was running down, he said. Pending completion of its military programme, the German Army was likely to oppose any action that might lead to an early war. Stalin's purges of the Russian officer corps had weakened the hand of those German generals seeking an understanding with Russia, but at the same time had weakened Russia herself. Germany was now groping for an intermediate policy under the impact of economic strains. Adding to the confusion was the incalculable and emotional figure of Hitler, upon whom nobody could count for certainty. Under such conditions the memorandum of the Association of Heavy Industries, coupled with another supplied by Colonel Thomas, Head of the Economic Department of the War Ministry, were being used as a kind of peace anchor, an anchor which might have a decisive steadying effect on the German ship of state. If unable to add any weight to it, Sir Robert recommended after talking to Dr. Goerdeler that Britain ought to do nothing to weaken the anchor. If a contest between the German hotheads and the cooler minds was to arise, Britain should also not give the former any reason to hope that the forces of law and order in Europe would be weakened, or treaty obligations diminished.

The Goerdeler memorandum, as it may be called, though actually compiled by the Association of German Heavy Industries, estimated the deficiency of raw materials at 40-60 per cent of German needs, of food and fodder at 25-30 per cent, and German exports as one-third of the normal figure. The maximum home output in the next four years would not produce more than 50 per cent of iron and steel requirements, 70 per cent of zinc, 45 per cent of lead, and 15 per cent of copper. Home production of raw materials was not more than 25 per cent of Germany's needs. German commerce was taken up approximately 50-60 per cent with Government orders. There was a large foreign and internal debt. The memorandum recommended it as desirable that Germany should abandon its policy of economic and political isolation, and enter into a system of negotiated international agreements.

Dr. Goerdeler warned Vansittart in a summary of his conclusions. He wished to impress on any whom his words might reach that the worst disservice Great Britain could do to Germany and to herself was to base British treatment of her on false hopes and premises. If the British allowed themselves to imagine that prospects in Germany were quite other than they were, the shock of the inevitable disillusionment which would then certainly follow would expose his Fatherland to the gravest of political risks. Great Britain and other foreign nations would feel that they had been deceived and then nothing would be too bad for Germany. This would lead again to a violent revulsion among the Germans.

He added that he had been appalled at the facile optimism of an acquaintance of Dr. Schacht whom he had met in the City of London. This British businessman had assured him that Dr. Schacht was firmly in the saddle and would ensure that German obligations would be honoured. An Anglo-German understanding would soon make all well.

Goerdeler finally summed up that Germany was near State bankruptcy and only able to pay her way by the issue of uncovered bills of exchange. There was an intense moral crisis in Germany about which, he said, there was some self-deception in Great Britain. It would be most wrong to entertain easy illusions.

"The most helpful thing you can do," he emphasised, "is to get at the true facts so far as ever you can; base your dealings with Germany and your policy on a clear realisation of them. Let that policy be firm and clear. Above all let the world and Germany see that you know the truth. Let them see that your standards of morality, public conduct and respect for law are the old high standards to which the people of Germany still adhere in their inward hearts as well."

Dr. Goerdeler made it quite clear that nothing could be worse for Germany and Europe in the long run than an artificial Anglo-German understanding, founded upon illusions and unreal. He assured Vansittart that there was no imminent danger of a military adventure. At the same time Britain would have great difficulty in coming to an agreement with the present rulers of Germany.

To anyone who knew Germany, here indeed was valuable intelligence and advice. It showed that his own precarious situation was known to those around Hitler, that they wanted a firm attitude adopted towards him, that they were aware of their country's economic weakness. Vansittart began to draft these views into one of his papers to the Cabinet. In early July the mind of Chamberlain was already made up on the fatal course that he had chosen of giving way to Hitler. But it was not too late to unmake that decision, to prefer firmer counsels. To this end Vansittart bent his persuasive pen. And here a remarkable intervention occurred. I find on the rejected draft the words written:

Suppressed by Eden.

This then was to have been the last of his warning papers on Germany, but the one never to be presented to the Cabinet. Vansittart overcame his reticence in the last days of his life to mention this setback to me. How differently might not the British Cabinet have taken up their attitude to Hitler and to rearmament at critical moments if they had in 1937 sat down to study the views of this "weighty and wise" German, whom even Sir Robert Vansittart respected. Did Mr. Eden perhaps fear the amused smiles of his elder Cabinet colleagues which disconcerted him when he spoke strongly of Germany himself and they murmured "His Master's Voice"? I have discussed this paper and its "suppression" with Lord Avon who tells me that he has forgotten the circumstances in which the paper was withdrawn, but suggests that the views of Dr. Goerdeler were made otherwise fairly well known at the time. But by whom to whom? Here was a paper on which the fatal course of appeasement might have been arrested. It seems unlikely that Mr. Eden disagreed strongly with its contents. Another explanation has been suggested to me. It is that it would have been dangerous to circulate the views of Dr. Goerdeler to so large and so talkative a body as the British Cabinet, but to this perhaps valid objection it can be answered that by removing the name of Dr. Goerdeler the risks to his life could have been avoided.

It is my opinion that since both Mr. Eden and Lord Halifax had seen Dr. Goerdeler during this visit, though neither vouchsafe him a word in their memoirs, Mr. Chamberlain himself had already been made aware of his views, as Lord Avon hinted to me. The purpose of Vansittart, however, in wishing the warnings of Goerdeler to have wider circulation is evident. It would have brought the Cabinet—and not only the Inner Cabinet—facts and advice upon which to reappraise the British approach to the German problem. It will be seen how a year later in the full crisis of the summer of 1938, the Cabinet as a whole still had no opportunity for complete discussion of policy decisions before they were made.

A 1919 Treasury minute had extended the authority of the Treasury over appointments in all other Departments. A Foreign Office official, Mr. Frank Ashton Gwatkin, one of those to whom Dr. Goerdeler spoke in London, wrote in retrospect that this instruction gave to the Head of the Treasury* "the last word in the appointment of the official heads of the Government Departments, their deputies and their Chief Establishment Officers. He extended this authority so as to interfere in the appointment of British Ambassadors and in the submission and non-submission of Foreign Office advice to the Cabinet.

"This nefarious system was an important contributory cause of the weaknesses of Foreign Office authority in the thirties and one of the reasons Foreign Office warnings about Germany and the warnings from British Representatives abroad did not reach the Cabinet in an effective form."†

It was made impossible for Vansittart to confront the whole Cabinet with information and advice which some ministers did not want it to hear. There was still time in 1937 to adopt a more stubborn policy towards Germany, but the few kept to themselves this inconvenient advice.

* Sir Warren Fisher.
† *The British Foreign Office*, Frank Ashton Gwatkin, 1950.

CHAPTER IX

A MONTH OF DECISIONS

THE understandable Neville Chamberlain is the man who wrote to an American friend in Boston* that "in the absence of any powerful ally and until our armaments are completed, we must adjust our foreign policy to our circumstances". Less comprehensible was his conclusion in a family letter written in the fateful month of November 1937, in which he spoke this thought aloud: "I don't see why we shouldn't say to Germany —'Give us satisfactory assurances that you won't use force to deal with the Austrians and Czechoslovakians and we will give you similar assurances that we won't use force to prevent the changes you want, if you can get them by peaceful means.'" The proposition does not bear analysis.

But it was in his mind when Lord Halifax, Lord President of the Council, finally responded to suggestions that he should pay a visit to Germany. These had come to him from the Ribbentrop entourage early in 1937. Lord Avon tells us that "neither Chamberlain nor I had then thought it wise for him to accept", but on October 14th at a diplomatic dinner party in London Lord Halifax broached the subject to Eden "in a genial way" that Marshall Goering had invited him to an international hunting exhibition. Winston Churchill who witnessed the conversation thought that Eden looked surprised and did not like the idea.† Lord Halifax mentions some chaff from Eden about shooting foxes, a recognised sport in Germany, and adds that Eden seriously thought it might be an advantage to go. "My own recollection," wrote Lord Avon, "is that when I first heard of this proposal I was not eager, but saw no sufficient reason to oppose it." He had a meeting with Lord Halifax and Sir Nevile Henderson in London at the end of October and prepared the ground for a talk with Hitler that would take place during the visit. Halifax agreed that he would "listen and confine himself to warning comment on Austria and Czechoslovakia", Eden recorded: "I have impressed on Sir N. Henderson the need for doing all that we can to discourage German intervention in

* Mrs. Morton Prince, January 16th, 1938.   † *The Gathering Storm.*

these two States. We must keep Germany guessing as to our attitude. It is all we can do until we are strong enough to talk to Germany."*

It should be noted that when the talks between Hitler and Lord Halifax did take place, Sir Nevile Henderson was not present. This was partly because Hitler was irritated by his somewhat garrulous personality and partly because Lord Halifax wished to have opportunity to break new ground. Lord Vansittart has not preserved any record of his own disagreement with the idea of this visit, though there is a hint of protest in one of his comments in November 1937 to Eden that the Foreign Office ought not to block the prospect of a similar talk in Rome, for which Mr. Chamberlain had been hankering ever since his exchange of views with the Italian Ambassador, Signor Grandi, in July. Mr. Iain Macleod in his *Neville Chamberlain* tells us that he has found evidence in Mr. Chamberlain's papers at this period of his "high respect and regard for Eden, though not for the Foreign Office", and that the papers record that while Vansittart argued against Halifax's visit to Germany, Eden expressed himself as "quite happy". The Chamberlain papers are sealed for the time being and there is no opportunity to probe this divergence between Foreign Secretary and Permanent Head of the Foreign Office. It may be said that Chamberlain was apt to interpret the attitudes of his colleagues the way it suited him. Lord Avon recalls that he saw that both Chamberlain and Halifax were bent on the visit. Vansittart's views on the policy of "keeping Germany guessing", though written eleven months later, are relevant. "The policy of keeping Germany guessing," he wrote,† "is the policy that obtained in 1914. We did keep the Germans guessing, and they ended by guessing wrong; and war followed." In the absence of stronger evidence to the contrary, it may be assumed that Eden and Vansittart thought similarly about the Halifax visit, but regarded it with varying degrees of apprehension. As the date of the hunting exhibition approached, it became evident from Sir Nevile Henderson's telegrams that Hitler would not come to Berlin to meet Lord Halifax, and that the impression would thus be given that Lord Halifax in going to Berchtesgaden was running after Hitler. News of the visit leaked out in London

* *Facing the Dictators*, p. 509.
† September 7th, 1938. Vansittart Papers.

while these negotiations were proceeding, and led to a painful interview between Mr. Eden and M. Yvon Delbos, the French Foreign Minister, on November 13th in Brussels. M. Delbos said that it was unfortunate that his Government had not been informed of the project. Even more embarrassing was an article appearing that day in the *Evening Standard*, which greatly angered Mr. Chamberlain, alleging that at the coming meeting in Germany, Hitler would offer Lord Halifax a ten-year moratorium on colonial claims in exchange for a free hand in Eastern Europe. This caricature of the probing and abstract exchanges of views between Ribbentrop and his British contacts had a grain of truth in it. At least the Germans thought that some Englishmen thought in these terms. For at Lord Lothian's meeting with Dr. Schacht on May 5th, 1937, Professor Conwell Evans recorded Dr. Schacht as alluding "to Amery's* advice on Germany—you can't have colonies but Eastern Europe lies before you".†

The *Evening Standard* report so annoyed Mr. Chamberlain that he took pains to find out its origin, though as his Press Chief assured a German diplomat, he was satisfied that it was not inspired by the Foreign Office. He also let it be known that he was "exceedingly angry" at German press reports claiming differences between himself and Eden, though he proceeded to give his estimate of Halifax as "the most important statesman and politician that England had at the present time". Thus slightly damaged by its advance publicity, the Halifax-Hitler meeting took place on November 19th.

Three days before these talks Baron von Neurath had before him a report of a conversation that had taken place in London in October between Konrad Henlein, leader of the Sudeten-Germans, and Sir Robert Vansittart. Herr Woermann reported from the German Embassy in London on November 9th that "I hear confidentially that Vansittart is supposed to have shown himself extremely ready to support Sudeten-German claims for autonomy. This is in accordance with the British policy of eliminating points of friction in Europe in such a way as to avoid raising the major problems that lie behind them.

"A further subject of the conversation is said to have been the Austrian question. According to my informant Vansittart

---

* L. S. Amery, M.P., a former Secretary of State for the Colonies.
† Sir J. Butler, *Lord Lothian*, p. 352.

wished in this matter to hear from Henlein what further developments were expected in Germany. He gave him to understand that Britain considered a union of Germany and Austria as inevitable in the long run, but pointed out the dangers that would arise if the union were attempted by way of a *Putsch*."

There followed an obscure allegation that Vansittart surmised a military occupation of Austria by Germany to be more feasible than a *Putsch*—an unlikely sentiment if his strenuous warnings on Austria are remembered. Henlein regarded it as an attempt to entice him into comment. Another paper before the German Foreign Minister at this time was a report from the German Embassy in Paris giving textually the important pronouncement made by M. Yvon Delbos on Czechoslovakia at the end of October in Lille. "France, bound as she is under various forms to a certain number of countries, intends to give an example of the most scrupulous loyalty. In all circumstances, whatever may be the form of the aggression, if the aggression is clear, she will keep her engagement to them." This meant that France would act if a *Putsch* was made in Czechoslovakia. If Delbos could have known, as perhaps he suspected during his conversation with Eden, what thoughts Lord Halifax would speak aloud during his Berchtesgaden meeting, he would have been even more disturbed. For Delbos and Vansittart clearly warned against solving the Sudeten-German or the Austrian question by a *Putsch*. Whereas the ill-chosen words of Lord Halifax seemed to recommend just that form of solution.

There was a long and affable conversation at the Berghof in Berchtesgaden with Hitler, interrupted by lunch, and marked by one warning of some asperity by the English High Churchman. Hitler said that either "a free play of forces or higher reason" would solve outstanding questions in Europe. Halifax spoke of a four-power basis for European stability (i.e. an exclusion of Russia). The German record of the interpreter Paul Schmidt quotes him as saying that apart from such immediate questions as the authority of the League and disarmament "all other questions fell into the category of possible alterations in the European order which might be destined to come about with the passage of time". On Danzig, Austria and Czecho-slovakia "England was of course interested to see that any alterations should come through the course of peaceful evolution. . . . Methods should be avoided which might cause far-reaching disturbances." Lord Halifax records that he explained as to Danzig, Austria and Czechoslovakia, that "on all these matters we (Britain) were not necessarily concerned to stand for the *status quo* as of today, but we were very much concerned to secure the avoidance of such treatment of them as would be likely to cause trouble."* Did this mean that if either a *Putsch* or a swift military intervention solved a question without war, Britain would accept it? Lord Halifax did not actually say so, but his emphasis was not that which Eden had wished the now excluded Sir Nevile Henderson to use. Let us see how the Germans interpreted it. In an aide-memoire to Henderson the Halifax-Hitler conversations were carefully stated at fair length by Herr Schmidt, but to German Embassies abroad a summary version showed how the Foreign Ministry wished to understand Lord Halifax's abstractions.

> Halifax admitted of his own accord that certain changes in the European system could probably not be avoided in the long run. The British did not believe that the *status quo* had to be maintained in all circumstances. Among the questions in which changes would be made sooner or later were Danzig, Austria and Czechoslovakia. England was only interested in seeing that such changes were brought about by peaceful development. Halifax did not go into any further detail. The Führer likewise did not go any deeper into the problem.

Could Lord Halifax have envisaged that his words would be so interpreted? He noted in his diary that "as to the political value of the talk, I am not disposed to rate this very high. I dare say that it was all to the good making contact". Sir Samuel Hoare thought in after years that "the immediate sequel could scarcely have been worse. Within a few weeks Hitler occupied Austria." But other and significant events played their part in that, and when the visit of Halifax took place, Hitler had already laid his plans.

They are revealed in the now published minutes of a small conference in the Reich Chancellery on November 5th, 1937.

* *Fulness of Days.*

This conference lasted four hours and was attended by Hitler, Field-Marshal von Blomberg, the War Minister, General von Fritsch, Commander-in-Chief of the Army, Admiral Raeder, Commander-in-Chief of the Navy, General Goering, Air Minister, Baron von Neurath, Foreign Minister, and Hitler's adjutant, Colonel Hossbach, who wrote the minutes of the proceedings into a memorandum dated November 10th. After a preamble on the need to consolidate the position in Europe of 85 million Germans, Hitler turned to the acute economic situation, on which Dr. Goerdeler had based his memorandum to General von Fritsch as drawn up by the Association of Rhenish and Westfalian Heavy Industries. He did not mention that memorandum, but it may be assumed that its subject matter had been under discussion, and Hitler disarmed counter-argument by saying that he expected and accepted:

Limited self-sufficiency in raw materials.

Total self-sufficiency in coal.

A much more difficult position in metal supplies, though in the case of iron ore he did claim that home supplies would meet requirements (whereas Goerdeler's memorandum had stated only 50 per cent).

No permanent solution to self-sufficiency in textiles, and certainly not in the case of food.

Must Germany then pursue its aims by self-sufficiency or "an increased participation in world economy"? Even with the maximum increase in home production, participation in world trade was unavoidable. . . . But to this there were limitations which Germany was unable to remove. . . . "As our foreign trade was carried on over sea routes dominated by Britain, the problem was more security of transport than shortage of foreign currency, which would show in time of war the full weakness of the German food situation. The only remedy, and that might appear visionary, lay in the acquisition of greater living space. The space necessary to ensure it can only be sought in Europe, not . . . in the exploitation of colonies. It is not a matter of acquiring population but of gaining space for agricultural use. Areas producing raw materials can be sought more usefully in Europe in immediate proximity to the Reich than overseas. The solution thus obtained must suffice for one

162

or two generations. . . . The history of all ages—the Roman Empire and the British Empire—had proved that expansion could only be carried out by breaking down resistance and taking risks. Setbacks were inevitable. There had never in former times been spaces without a master, and there were none today. The attacker always comes up against someone in possession.

"Germany had to reckon with two hate-inspired antagonists, Britain and France, to whom a German colossus in the centre of Europe was detestable. Serious discussion of the return of colonies to us could only be considered at a moment when Britain was in difficulties and the German Reich armed and strong. The Fuehrer did not share the view that the (British) Empire was unshakeable. Beside the Empire there existed other states stronger than she. . . . How for instance could Britain alone defend Canada against attack by America or her Far Eastern interests against attack by Japan? The Empire could not maintain its position by power politics. Significant indications of this were:

The struggle of Ireland for independence.
The constitutional struggles in India.
The weakening by Japan of Britain in the Far East.
The Mediterranean rivalry with Italy.

"Germany's problem could only be solved by means of force and this was never without attendant risks. If those were accepted there remained the questions 'when?' and 'how?'"

Hitler spoke of the period 1943-45. That was the period after which only a change for the worse in relative military strength could be expected, he said. The equipment of the army, navy and air force, as well as the formation of the officer corps was nearly completed. German equipment and armaments were modern. In further delay lay the danger of their obsolescence, and moreover the secrecy of special weapons could not be kept for ever. The recruiting of reserves was limited to current age groups. Further drafts from older untrained age groups were no longer available. German relative strength would decrease in relation to the rearmament which would by then have been carried out by the rest of the world. "If we did not act by 1943-45, any year could, in consequence of a lack of reserves produce the food crisis to cope with which the necessary foreign currency was not available. That must be regarded as the 'point of decline of the régime'. It was while the rest of the world was still fortifying itself that we were obliged to take the offensive. . . . If the Fuehrer was still living, it was his unalterable resolution to solve the German problem of space at the latest by 1943.

"Action before that period would be necessary if France should be involved in such an internal crisis as to make the French army incapable of going to the assistance of the Czechs.

"The first German objective, in the event of being embroiled in war, should be to overthrow Austria and Czechoslovakia simultaneously." Hitler thought that Polish agreements with Germany would only restrain their forces as long as German strength remained unshaken.

"The Fuehrer believed that Britain, and probably France as well, had already secretly written off the Czechs. Difficulties in the Empire and the prospect of entanglement in another European war were decisive in setting Britain against participation in a war against Germany. . . . Germany must maintain strong western defences during its attack on Czechoslovakia and Austria. Their annexation would mean more foodstuffs, better frontiers, release of forces and the possibility of creating new units. Italy was not expected to object to the elimination of the Czechs, but it was impossible at the moment to estimate what her attitude on the Austrian question would be. That depended essentially on whether the Duce was still alive. Poland will have little inclination—with Russia at her rear—to wage war against a victorious Germany. Military intervention by Russia must be countered by the swiftness of German operattions. The Fuehrer·saw the possibility coming definitely nearer of France being involved in a war with another state. It might emerge from present Mediterranean tensions. He was resolved to take advantage of that whenever it happened, even in 1938. As he saw it, Italy would be so involved in the Spanish Civil War that Britain and France would be unable to tolerate her presence any longer. Germany would supply Italy in such a war, having an interest that it should be drawn out."

It seemed possible to Hitler that France—and presumably Britain too—would be at war with Italy in the summer of 1938; that this would be the time for the attack of Germany on

Czechoslovakia and Austria and that Britain would decide not to act against Germany. "The Fuehrer had in mind no military agreements with Italy, but wanted, retaining his independence of action, to exploit this favourable situation. Germany would have to fall upon the Czechs with the speed of lightning."

Thus Hitler held these five senior men with his glittering eye. The Hossbach memorandum shows that at the end of his monologue Marshal von Blomberg and General von Fritsch raised objections. They did not like it to be assumed that Britain and France would be in the role of enemies. Should they be, France would still have a superiority in the West, even if twenty French divisions were engaged against Italy. German fortifications in the West were of negligible value, said the generals. The four motorised divisions intended to defend West Germany were still more or less immobile, and in the south-east the Czech fortifications were strong. Baron von Neurath objected to Hitler that a conflict of France and Britain against Italy was not so measurably close as the Fuehrer seemed to assume. To the misgivings of the two Army men Hitler replied that he was convinced of the non-participation of Britain (in a Central European conflict) and therefore that he did not believe in the likelihood of aggressive action by France against Germany.

Since it appeared to Hitler that Italy was to be involved in a Peninsular war with Britain and France, Goering thought and said that Germany should consider liquidating its military engagements in Spain. Hitler agreed to a limitation but thought that he must choose the proper moment.

Colonel Hossbach certified his account as correct and consigned it to the secret archives. It is a matter of surprise to me that Mr. A. J. P. Taylor could ever have interpreted this account of the November 5th conference as an indication that Hitler was forced into war before he was ready.* He was plainly naming his latest dates for war, but showing no reluctance to face earlier risks. On the following day in Rome, Herr von Ribbentrop, arriving from London, had an audience with Mussolini, at which Count Ciano noted that the Duce said that he was tired of mounting guard over Austria: "Austria is German state number 2. It will never be able to do anything without Germany; far less against Germany. Italian interest

* *Origins of the Second World War.*

today is no longer so lively as it was some years ago. . . . According to the Duce the best method is to let events take their natural course."

Thus Hitler received in November 1937 expressions of a certain disinterest both from Italy and Britain in the ultimate fate of Austria. One further meeting should be noted in this ominous month, that which took place on November 29th and 30th in London of Neville Chamberlain and Eden with M. Camille Chautemps and M. Yvon Delbos. The British made use of this meeting to inform the French Prime Minister and Foreign Minister of their recent contacts with Germany—Lord Halifax told the French Ministers of his talk with Hitler. On the wisdom of that encounter Mr. Eden was beginning to have increasing doubts. "I wished that Halifax had warned Hitler more strongly against intervention in Central Europe."* According to the record, Halifax had not properly warned Hitler at all, and had on the contrary stated his belief in the inevitability of change. Mr. Eden admitted that "my loyal collaborators in the Foreign Office were proved right in the uneasiness which they had expressed about the visit from the start". This oblique tribute must include Vansittart.

The two Soviet newspapers *Izvestia* and *Pravda* began at this time, the Germans noted, to comment on the Halifax visit to Hitler. *Izvestia* thought the salient fact was that Britain was inclined to appease the demands of aggressors. About the same time the French press repeated the view that although Lord Halifax must have treated the London-Paris axis as a reality during his Berchtesgaden talks, his visit to Hitler warranted a certain uneasiness and even mistrust. There had been mistrust from the start in French minds, the German Ambassador in Paris reported. The subject of principal concern to the French was whether in the expected discussion of Austria and Czechoslovakia Halifax would have taken the French views sufficiently into account. France had a treaty with Czechoslovakia. Britain had none. The British record of contradiction to Hitler was not good. What were the visiting French Ministers told? The first morning was given up to an account by Lord Halifax of his visit to Hitler. To have given the French the British written record of the talks should have been sufficient. Mr. Eden may have thought as early as November 29th that Lord Halifax

* *Facing the Dictators.*

had failed to warn Hitler sufficiently against intervention in Central Europe, but Mr. Chamberlain wrote that: "The German visit was from my point of view a great success, because it achieved its object, that of creating an atmosphere in which it is possible to discuss with Germany the practical questions involved in a European settlement. . . ." He took it that Lord Halifax had discovered that Hitler and Goering wanted "as close union as they can get with Austria *without** incorporating her in the Reich," and no more than their due political rights for the Sudeten-Germans. There is no warranty for this in the German record that was handed to Sir Nevile Henderson.

The place in historical record of the Chamberlain-Halifax-Eden talks with Chautemps and Delbos is curious indeed. They lie practically at the end of the long process of publishing British diplomatic documents for this period which begins with the year 1930 and slowly traverses the years between to attain 1937 last of all. We are assured by the Editors of the documents that this was the sensible and convenient way to do it. It has left some deep enigmas long unanswered. The Chamberlain diary note for November 26th, 1937 shows what was in the British Prime Minister's mind when M. Chautemps was coming to London. It ends with that catastrophic surmise: . . . "I don't see why we shouldn't say to Germany, 'give us satisfactory assurances that you won't use force to deal with the Austrians and Czechoslovakians and we will give you similar assurances that we won't use force to prevent the changes you want, if you can get them by peaceful means'."

Was that the basis of his private discussions with Chautemps and Delbos? They discussed colonies, "a broad African scheme" Professor Feiling tells us.† "We should expect some arms limitation in a general settlement and no forcible change in Austria—though that, we implied, was rather an Italian interest than a British." Lord Avon in his memoirs says nothing of a dicussion on this occasion about Austria. Was it dismissed in a few words as indefensible? Was it agreed that neither Britain nor France could render armed assistance to Austria? From his account relations with Italy were discussed, but "Czechoslovakia was the main topic". Why then was Czechoslovakia being discussed in isolation? Was the assumption that the Austrian republic on its flank would have ceased to exist by

* Author's italics.   † *Life of Neville Chamberlain*, p. 333.

the time that the Czechoslovak problem arose? In denying the possibility of support for Austria surely lay the destruction of Czechoslovakia too. It seems that M. Delbos spoke strongly against the granting of autonomy to the Sudeten-Germans of Czechoslovakia, because that would in reality disrupt the Czechoslovak state and leave France an immeasurably weaker ally. And it seems that the British Ministers when they saw the French dismayed at the idea of autonomy for the Sudeten-Germans comforted them by suggesting that Hitler would not require as much as that as a solution. This was an extraordinary embarrassment. For autonomy had already been discussed by Vansittart with Henlein as a possible solution that would not disrupt the Czechoslovak state, whereas the French Ministers thought that it would have just that effect. It must have become plain to M. Yvon Delbos that his formula for resisting any movement *quel qu'il soit* was not accepted in London. It may have seemed that the British were accepting that there must be change. Vansittart attended the talks as did M. Leger, the Permanent Under-Secretary of the French Foreign Ministry. They discussed colonies and colonial restitution to Germany, the serious situation in the Far East, the Spanish Civil War. Sir Thomas Inskip, Minister for Co-ordination of Defence, came in and talked about British military aircraft production. Apart from an awkward reference to a common interest with Italy in the integrity of the country, nothing was said in full session about Austria. "Most of the important business, both in conference and in less formal discussions," noted the *Daily Telegraph* on December 1st, "has been conducted direct between Mr. Chamberlain and M. Chautemps, with assistance wherever necessary of their Foreign Ministers." Mr. Chamberlain went to Victoria Station to see his guests off, and the Paris press reflected with some satisfaction that the conference had decided in favour of an understanding with Germany in which no individual points would be settled in advance of a general settlement. "The participation of all countries concerned (including Austria, Czechoslovakia, Soviet Russia) and consideration of their interests were decided upon." So the German Ambassador in Paris reporting to his Government quoted the echoes of the London conference in the French Press. But there was a significant revelation for Herr von Ribbentrop when he called on Eden to hear what the results of the talks had been. Ribbentrop saw Mr. Eden on December 2nd in the Foreign Office. The Foreign Secretary said that he wished to inform him on the subject of the Chautemps-Chamberlain talks. He said that progress had been made on the colonial question. Ribbentrop reported that Eden emphasised that Britain and France would want a *quid pro quo* which would give both countries a greater feeling of security. Ribbentrop quoted his own reply that he deplored this sort of bargaining. "The answer of Eden was that 'England was a nation of shopkeepers and could not be blamed for wishing to obtain compensation for giving up colonies'." Eden mentioned particularly an agreement on limitation of armaments as desirable. Eden thought that it must be possible to achieve a qualitative limitation of air forces as in the Anglo-German naval agreement. After discussing a guarantee of peace in the West, Eden is reported as saying of Austria:

"He had told the French that the question of Austria was of much greater interest to Italy than England. Furthermore people in England recognised that a closer connection between Germany and Austria would have to come about sometime. They wished, however, that a solution by force be avoided."

This was indeed very little different from the reflections of Lord Halifax in Berchtesgaden. Once more no warning was given. Lord Avon quotes M. Delbos as arguing to Chamberlain in their talks three days earlier that "the absorption of Austria and part of Czechoslovakia by Germany would not be without consequence for the structure of Europe. It was also necessary that treaties should be respected, for this was the basis of the law of nations." Beside these words, those of Eden to Ribbentrop appear pale and without good purpose. He does not disclaim them in his memoirs. It seems that he bore at that moment a share of the responsibilities for the catastrophe that followed. The words of firm counsel for which Dr. Goerdeler had hoped were not forthcoming.

CHAPTER X

ACROSS DOWNING STREET

"THE old man wants to see you at Number 10. He has a proposal to make to you. I don't know if you will like it or not."

Thus Sir Robert Vansittart remembered hearing in December 1937 from the Foreign Secretary that a change in his appointment was intended. These were not easy days for either of them. Eden had been endeavouring to draw President Roosevelt and Mr. Cordell Hull out of isolationism into an aligned policy in the Far East. At the end of September he had drafted a telegram to Washington advocating to the United States Government a stronger line towards Japan—"some form of economic boycott". After sanctions against Italy had failed, perhaps thus under a new catchword the democracies could seize the initiative. He wrote that Britain would back "any action likely to shorten the war (in China) if we were convinced of its effectiveness". The Imperial Defence Committee ordered an intensive study of blockade possibilities by the Advisory Committee on Trade Questions.

It had been left to Vansittart to take Eden's draft telegram across to Neville Chamberlain for approval, and the Prime Minister had considerably altered the last sentence to read that Britain was not convinced that economic action would prove effective, but would be quite prepared to examine it further. Perhaps Eden felt that Sir Robert should not have dispatched this telegram without referring the amendments back to him, but by then the Foreign Secretary had already left his office for the day. Things often seemed to go wrong when Eden was not there; and it would soon appear so again. But even after he had exchanged Vansittart for his former adviser on League of Nations affairs, Sir Alexander Cadogan, the difficulties remained. Sir Alexander had been recalled in 1936 from the post of Ambassador in Peking to become Deputy Under-Secretary in the Foreign Office. Seventh son of the fifth Earl Cadogan, he was then 54; not the next in seniority for the post, but considered able and discreet.

"I don't know if you will like it or not." Eden had decided

that autumn to appoint Sir Alexander Cadogan as Permanent Under-Secretary and "in agreement with Chamberlain" to create a new post for Vansittart.

Vansittart knew of the plans to remove him during the autumn of 1937. Before his secretary Clifford Norton left to take up the post of Counsellor in Warsaw in late November 1937, Sir Robert had said to him:

"They are trying to get rid of me. They want a Permanent Head whom they can push around. They know that I am quite independent of them. But I won't go!"

Eight years in the key position at the Foreign Office, seeing five Foreign Secretaries and a procession of Under-Secretaries. Entertaining them at Denham and 44 Park Street. Games of tennis early on with Anthony at Denham, when the young man wanted to learn the arts of diplomacy, clashes of will on the respective menace of Italy and Germany. Faith in the League and disbelief in the League. The League in armour, the League a cripple. Make the Cabinet listen! His Master's Voice! Why won't they listen on Germany?

"During the last months of 1937 I again considered the position of Sir Robert Vansittart", wrote Eden. When speaking to me of it in retrospect Lord Avon still considered it as a departmental matter—"a man should go where he is sent. . . . He could have had an exceptional influence in Paris. . . . He was not being effective. . . . He was rubbing them up the wrong way. . . . I felt the time had come for a change that would strengthen my staff at the Foreign Office. . . ." Sir Alexander was patient, quiet in his manner, more of a civil servant than was Sir Robert Gilbert Vansittart.

Eden, having brought in Sir Alexander as Deputy Under-Secretary had used him in November for conversations with Mr. Norman Davis, the roving Ambassador of President Roosevelt, to discuss increasing economic pressure upon Japan. The American had remarked dryly that he "supposed we had had enough of sanctions", a remark which nettled Eden. Of Japan Mr. Chamberlain exclaimed on November 9th to Eden "on no account will I impose a sanction!" It was difficult for Eden to advocate a stronger line against Japan when he knew that his principal permanent official had a fixation about Germany and would not support him with enthusiasm.

On December 12th H.M.S. *Ladybird* was attacked and hit,

and the U.S. gunboat *Panay* was sunk by Japanese bombing aircraft in the Yangtse river.

Eden at once pressed for a combined Anglo-American naval demonstration, but without avail. As to Italy, Vansittart had been urging him to concede a British ministerial visit to Mussolini, and Neville Chamberlain in an artless fashion was listening to well-meaning encouragement from his step-sister Lady Austen Chamberlain, who was on a prolonged holiday in Rome, talking about Anglo-Italian friendship to everyone she met. All this was galling and frustrating to Eden. Yet it did not add up into a sympathy of views between Vansittart and Chamberlain. Although both abhorred the thought of sanctions and mistrusted the League of Nations; although both wanted to make a friend of Italy and weaken the Berlin-Rome Axis; although both were hesitant about displays of strength towards Japan, there was no real confidence between them. Chamberlain suspected Vansittart of exercising a far greater influence in politics than was proper in a civil servant. To this period probably applies a remark made to me by a senior Security official—"Van was too much concerned with serving his country ever to pause and think that they would have a man in his position followed." His friendships with Churchill and other strong Conservatives had long been a source of irritation to the Cabinet—"they cost me more than I knew", wrote Vansittart.* Locked in the breast of Chamberlain there was a resolution to deal with Germany in a manner more open handed than Vansittart would ever have accepted. In Number .10, Neville Chamberlain went straight to the point.

"I have decided, Sir Robert, to offer you a new post, as Chief Diplomatic Adviser to the Government," said Chamberlain. He explained it further . . . "just like Sir Horace Wilson, my Industrial Adviser. This will end your present appointment."

He said that he saw the need for a change. He suggested no alternative.

"I don't know whether I will accept or not," said Vansittart.

"What will you do then?"

"I may stand for Parliament."

"What? You can't do that!" The Prime Minister leaned forward, startled. "You know far too much."

"I will think it over, Prime Minister, and let you have my

* *Mist Procession.*

answer," said Vansittart, but as he crossed Downing Street again to the Foreign Office his mind was already made up.

"Anthony and I were divided and I fully understood his desire for a change."*

"I have to go, Anthony. I don't like it," he said when he returned to the Foreign Secretary's room. "If I go, you won't last long."

He told Sarita that evening the news that they had been expecting so long, the topic of open speculation at London dinner parties. As they sat resigned and downcast, a visitor burst in, Admiral Sir Hugh Sinclair, Head of the Security Service. "Quex", as he was called in the Navy, had retired in 1926 to take up this secret job after being Chief of Submarine Service from 1921 to 1923. An emphatic man who had also little regard for contemporary politicians he had once remarked† of an important report on German rearmament sent to Mr. Baldwin that "I know he read it, because I had a man watching him while he did so." Quex was notable among his fellow admirals for his flow of naval expletives. He walked about the drawing-room of 44 Park Street, clenching his fists and muttering: "Van, this is disastrous!"

Vansittart could see plainly that Eden did not want him any longer at his elbow, and set about making his plans to go quietly. It was his emphasis on Germany that had brought about his downfall, and so that a change of policy should not be guessed from the change of personalities, he set out carefully in a communiqué the outline of an appointment that had not yet been defined, even within the Department. His communiqué on himself was duly published on December 31st:

"The Secretary of State for Foreign Affairs, in consultation with the Prime Minister, has recently had under review the conditions which for some time past have placed an increasing strain upon the personnel of the Foreign Office.

"Apart from the international complications arising from the Spanish war and the conflict in the Far East, which require concentrated and unremitting attention, international affairs in general necessitate attendance either by Ministers or by permanent officials at conferences, committees, and inter-departmental meetings of all kinds, seriously reducing the time

* *Mist Procession.*　　† To his friend, Lord Lloyd.

available for the prolonged and careful consideration of questions of broad policy by those in the positions of greatest responsibility.

"After weighing up all the circumstances, the Prime Minister and the Foreign Secretary have come to the conclusion that the required relief can best be afforded by the creation of a new post in the Foreign Office, following the example of somewhat similar posts in other Departments. The Prime Minister has accordingly authorised the Foreign Secretary to appoint a Chief Diplomatic Adviser responsible directly to the Secretary of State.

"The functions of the new officer will be analogous to those fulfilled by the occupants of the similar posts attached to other Departments (Chief Industrial Adviser and the Chief Economic Adviser to the Government) and will include advising the Secretary of State upon all major questions of policy concerning foreign affairs remitted to him for that purpose, and representing the Foreign Office on any occasions, whether at home or abroad, on which the Secretary of State may wish to avail himself of his services.

"In order to give full effect to the purposes in view, it is necessary that the new post should be filled by a person of international reputation and authority, and accordingly Sir Robert Gilbert Vansittart, G.C.B., G.C.M.G., M.V.O., Permanent Under-Secretary of State for Foreign Affairs, has been selected to be first holder of the office.

"Consequently upon the above appointment, the Secretary of State for Foreign Affairs has appointed the Honourable Sir Alexander Montagu George Cadogan, K.C.M.G., C.B., Permanent Under-Secretary of State for Foreign Affairs.

"These appointments will take effect on January 1st, 1938."

In Foreign Office circles it was said that Sir Robert Vansittart was being moved out of the key position that he had occupied for so long. He asked to be allowed to keep the big room on the ground floor at the corner of the Foreign Office building, next to the Foreign Secretary's which belonged by right to the Permanent Head of the Foreign Office. He did so partly because he had come to regard it as his own, and partly because this suited the pretence that he was still in a key position of power. How little power in reality remained to him was only made clear to the Foreign Office on January 22nd in a memorandum, in which Eden defined the status of the Chief Diplomatic Adviser and his activities.

Eden laid down that in future all papers would be submitted by his Under-Secretaries to Sir Alexander Cadogan and by him to the Secretary of State. Papers on which the Secretary of State wished for the advice of Sir Robert Vansittart would be so marked by the Secretary of State. Papers would thus be seen by Sir Robert after action had been decided upon them, unless his advice was specially required. In the event of urgency he would not see papers until action had been taken.

An exception was made of correspondence relating to the Committee of Imperial Defence as defence had been one of his special interests. This would remain the direct concern of Sir Robert Vansittart, and he was to represent the Foreign Secretary at all meetings of the Committee of Imperial Defence. He was also to be sent directly papers relating to propaganda.

Thus a shadowy role of advice, political warfare and propaganda was allotted to him; but on matters of policy, in dealing with dispatches from abroad and receiving the foreign Ambassadors, it was Cadogan who took over. In this sham position of precarious dignity, Vansittart was to remain. In January 1938 the Establishment Officer took advantage of his absence in Monte Carlo to try to remove his papers from the great room to an upper office, an intrusion that was repelled by his personal secretary, Miss Dougherty. Until the war started he continued to occupy his old room.

In retrospect Vansittart sometimes wondered whether he ought not to have refused the change and resigned instead. A year later, after the Munich agreement, he was in correspondence with Lord Howard de Walden when the latter urged him to seek election to Parliament as a Conservative in the Marylebone seat; but he still declined to take the step in January 1939. Yet he knew in December 1937 the hollowness of his new appointment. For he wrote to Mr. Gladwyn Jebb, who had already been selected as his Private Secretary in succession to Clifford Norton, to tell him of this sudden change in their fortunes, saying that the new appointment did not warrant Jebb coming on to his staff. It would be in Jebb's own interest to go instead to the new Permanent Chief, Sir Alexander Cadogan, and Sir Robert could get on perfectly well in the meantime with Miss Dougherty.

His tenacity had another reason than the consideration that civil servants ought to serve. He was master now of a curious patchwork of special intelligence about Europe, and although he could no longer advance his opinions so forcibly on the basis of this network, it was still productive and valuable. There may have been some reluctance among his timid masters to dispense altogether with this out-of-period figure. As for Parliament, Vansittart continued to think of it, but in moments of exasperation with the Party quagmire he growled to Sarita, "I'd have to wear sewer boots."

Knowing that he was writing his last report of the year as Permanent Head of the Foreign Office, and aware that the force of his warnings were the main reason for removing him, Vansittart sounded a gentler note at the end of 1937 than in some of his previous essays on world affairs. He succeeded in disguising his impatience and the despair that erupted from so many of his minutes and letters. His conclusions were not startling and it is evident he thought Germany might find some subtle and defensible way to bring about an *Anschluss* with Austria. He continued to draw attention to German assessments of the Reich's shortages of essential strategic materials. He quoted from a German military source the opinion that: "Germany could only risk a war if a certain and very quick victory could be achieved by using the Air Force and a relatively small part of the Army: this will be made impossible if our potential enemies continue to grow stronger and stronger."

Vansittart's own conclusions at the end of 1937 were that the European picture was to some extent confused "but on the whole reassuring. We seem to be faced with a Germany feverishly preparing for war, but experiencing great difficulties in her preparation: leagued with powerful allies, but allies whom she does not trust; united in appearance, but in reality torn by deep divisions of policy, philosophy and religion. Above all one has the impression of a nation which is definitely not ready for action on a large scale in the immediate future. We can therefore contemplate our own position with reasonable calmness and without the panic and precipitation that seems to animate some of our publicists."

There was perhaps another reason for this calming assessment, in that the British Cabinet had at last awoken to the dire peril of the country, was fearfully aware of the rising superiority of the Luftwaffe and maybe prepared to sacrifice in panic much more than was strictly necessary. A military witness, General Sir Edmund Ironside, then a member of the Army Council, wrote in his diary on December 29th: "the Cabinet in a muddled kind of way are terrified of making an Expeditionary Force. . . . The Cabinet also thinks that the Air Force can finish a campaign. They are terrified now of a war being finished in a few weeks by the annihilation of Great Britain. They can see no other kind of danger than air attack and discount all other dangers." Having tried to rouse them to this peril since 1933, Vansittart probably saw it as his immediate duty to prevent complete paralysis in counsels ensuing as soon as the situation became clear to them.

It is instructive to compare British and German documents and see what the enemy was thinking at the end of 1937. The German counterpart of Vansittart, Baron von Weizsaecker, Under-Secretary of the Foreign Ministry, analysed the meaning of Lord Halifax's attitude during his November visit to Hitler and the substance of a talk between Eden and Ribbentrop on December 2nd and another between Eden and Grandi. He noted an official German report that Eden said of his talks with Chautemps and Delbos that "they were ready, as were the responsible leaders of British policy, to examine any revision and any arrangement which could be reached without war." "This can only mean," commented Weizsaecker, "that Germany is to be allowed freedom of action within certain limits."

Weizsaecker proceeded with caution to assess the German position. "We ourselves are not yet strong enough to engage in a European conflict and therefore shall not seek any. . . . England today is still undecided as to whether or not she should buy peace in Europe by making concessions to Germany. It must be doubted whether a suitable price can be agreed upon. . . . Keeping England in a state of vacillation as long as possible is certainly to be preferred to a condition of hostility."

Baron von Neurath noted in the margin "and not eliminating the present areas of friction in the Mediterranean and Far East too quickly."*

Here was a secret tribute to the policy of Vansittart of obstinately refusing to be drawn into the sideshows of international friction. Meanwhile Herr von Ribbentrop prepared his

* Documents on German Foreign Policy, Series D, Vol. II.

own assessment of the year 1937 and the outlook for 1938. He saw that his mission of seeking friendship with Britain was on the point of failure. The champagne salesman had therefore in mind that he should himself be in Berlin when his report was read by the Fuehrer, so that interpolations by von Neurath might be avoided. His objective was that he should be promoted from his brief and unsuccessful Ambassadorship in London to replace von Neurath as Foreign Minister of the Reich.

The Ribbentrop report was dated January 2nd. It is a curious, penetrating and impatient document, but among those of the professional German diplomats written at this time, it stands out as the work of a policy maker. Ribbentrop wrote: "With the realisation that Germany does not wish to be bound by the *status quo* in Central Europe, and that war in Europe is possible sooner or later, the hope for an understanding among the British politicians favourable to Germany . . . will gradually come to an end. The fateful question is thus raised whether in the long run Germany and England will of necessity be driven into separate camps and march against each other some day. . . .

"French intervention on behalf of her eastern allies is always possible and so, as a consequence, is war between Germany and England. . . . A war between Germany and England can only be prevented if France knows from the very beginning that England's forces would not suffice to guarantee the common victory. England would possibly deter France from intervening in case of conflict between Germany and one of France's eastern allies, in order to localise it, so that England would not be forced to fight under unfavourable conditions.

"As to England, our policy ought in my opinion to be aimed at compromise, while fully safeguarding the interests of our friends.

"If England with her alliances is stronger than Germany and her friends, she will fight sooner or later.

"An unequivocal British concession regarding the Austrian-Czech question in accordance with our views would clear the air a little."

He summed up British thinking as follows:

"1. England is behind in her armaments. She is playing for time.
2. She believes time is on her side, owing to her command of material resources.

3. The visit of Halifax was a manœuvre in which a German-ophil personality was used.

4. England and her Prime Minister, in my opinion, see no possible basis of agreement with Germany.

5. We must therefore:

    i. Outwardly continue understanding with England,

    ii. Quietly but determinedly establish alliances against England.

"Only in this way can we confront England, who will be a tough and determined foe." He gave it as his view that

"Today I have no longer faith in any understanding . . ." and said, perhaps by way of excuse for his diplomatic failure, that:

"Edward VIII had to abdicate because it was not certain whether he would co-operate in an anti-German policy. Chamberlain has now appointed Vansittart, one of our toughest and most important foes to a position where he can play a leading role in the diplomatic game against Germany.* Henceforward, regardless of tactical interludes, every day that our political calculations are not actuated by the fundamental idea that England is our most dangerous enemy would be (a day) gained for our enemies."

From this dispatch germinated the decision of Hitler to bring Ribbentrop home as his Foreign Minister and to promote von Neurath out of the way to the post of Chairman of the Cabinet Council. Early in January, while Eden took a holiday in the Riviera sun, in occasional company with Winston Churchill and Lloyd George, the inner balances were shifting in Germany towards sole political and military power for Hitler. This process was made easier by a sort of Profumo affair involving the War Minister, Field-Marshal von Blomberg.

The affair is well told by Sir John Wheeler-Bennett in *Nemesis of Power*. Field-Marshal von Blomberg, most sub-servient to National-Socialism of the senior Army officers, wished to remarry after six years as a widower, and became

---

* The German diplomat Baron von Stumm wrote to the new German Am-bassador in London, Herbert von Dirksen, on May 2nd, 1938 a better assessment of Vansittart: "He is not so anti-German as he is always said to be. But to the Cabinet he seemed, as I definitely know, too pro-French, that is, he was too much under the charm of the French style of diplomacy and of handling European affairs. For that reason he was, so to speak, removed from the Foreign Office and can no longer rely on its apparatus. But since he is extraordinarily intelligent and in addition enormously industrious, his influence as a political adviser is not to be underrated." (Dirksen Papers.)

attached to a typist-secretary in his own War Ministry. When he consulted General Goering, the Air Minister saw no social obstacle to such a marriage in a time when the old Prussian caste system was being broken down by the National-Socialist revolution. Both he and Hitler consented to be witnesses at a quiet ceremony of marriage between Field-Marshal von Blomberg and Fräulein Erna Gruhn on January 12th, 1938. Soon afterwards a police dossier was circulated, which went from the hands of Count Helldorf, President of Berlin Police, to the desk of Major-General Keitel in the Army office with the suggestion that it be destroyed. It contained the case history of the early life of Frau von Blomberg, documented by police records, and showed her to have been of dubious morality. Keitel, as son-in-law of von Blomberg, felt it was too delicate for him to dispose of the dossier, and Goering to whom he took it, passed it to the Fuehrer. Hitler was appalled by the implications, and sensed the ridicule to which he was exposed. He was also disturbed by a visit shortly afterwards from Colonel-General Baron von Fritsch, Commander-in-Chief of the Army, who, supported by Goering, demanded that Blomberg should be retired. The peril to National-Socialism in this crisis lay in the reserved attitude of von Fritsch towards the Party and its leaders. It seemed essential to Heinrich Himmler, Chief of Reich Police and S.S., that von Fritsch should not gain power from the fall of von Blomberg, or create an unbalance in favour of the Army. Accordingly a similar accusation, this time of homosexuality, was laid against von Fritsch himself, and a perjured witness was found who by convenient coincidence had been involved in homosexual relations with a Captain von Frisch. Hitler was in a frantic mood and ready to act on an unsubstantiated case against his Commander-in-Chief. He suspended General von Fritsch after a short confrontation with the false witness, refusing the General even his inalienable right to a court martial. During the three weeks of disarray in the military hierarchy caused by this ruse and its aftermath, Hitler reorganised the political and military structure of the Reich to give himself supreme power. On February 4th, 1938 he issued a special decree that: "I exercise henceforth the immediate command over the entire armed forces. The former Wehrmacht Office becomes the High Command of the Armed Forces and comes immediately under my command."

He transferred to the High Command the functions of the War Ministry and appointed General Keitel as Chief of the High Command.

The Military Intelligence Service, or Abwehr, under Admiral Canaris, was entrusted with clarification of the von Fritsch case and worked with thoroughness, but not fast enough. It detained some witnesses in military camps, out of reach of the Gestapo; but the General Staff was inclined to be legalistic and not tempted to act on impulse or indignation. Although the campaign to rehabilitate General von Fritsch dragged on for five weeks after that, the battle was lost to the Army. The resignations of von Blomberg and von Fritsch were simultaneously announced, as if these were both cases of proven turpitude, and sixteen generals were relieved of their commands, though when the fever pitch of military anger against the Party had died down (after the successful invasion of Austria) most of them were reinstated. In the German Foreign Service, Baron von Neurath was on February 4th nominated to the Chairmanship of a Cabinet Inner Council. Ribbentrop was nominated Foreign Minister instead. Three senior Ambassadors Herr von Papen, Herr von Hassell and Herr von Dirksen were recalled from their posts in Vienna, Rome and Tokio.

This crisis was almost the last occasion on which the Army could have faced up to the Party, and it failed to do so; partly because it was thrown out of step by Hitler's timing of the court martial proceedings which could only begin after the invasion of Austria; partly because even when intolerably provoked by the calumny towards von Fritsch, the General Staff simply lost its nerve. The most indignant of the German intelligentsia, of whom there were many, felt hereafter obliged to work in secret against Hitler, and though they did so with thoroughness and sincerity, conspiracy was not the way to deal with him. An old East-Prussian squire, Herr von Oldenburg-Januschau, had once said that the Kaiser must at any time be able to send a Lieutenant and ten men to dissolve the Reichstag. All the Kaiser's men, though they toasted him in secret, could not bring themselves to stand together in January 1938 against Hitler and the Party. In the reorganisation that was thus initiated after February 4th, Himmler gained for his S.S. troops their divisional formations and a share in the military equipment that the Army had hitherto withheld. The well-armed S.S. presence near the army garrisons of Berlin ensured that no military *Putsch* would ever be a light-hearted affair.

So while every change in Berlin made war easier and reaction more difficult, the reshuffle in London made caution and compromise the main lines of British policy.

On January 12th while Eden was still on the Riviera, the same day in fact as the unsuspecting Hitler appeared at the wedding of Field-Marshal von Blomberg, an important dispatch reached London from Washington. It was the long-awaited Roosevelt initiative in European affairs. News came in a telegram from Sir Ronald Lindsay, British Ambassador in Washington, who asked Mr. Chamberlain to express himself on a plan that President Roosevelt had formed. He thought he might convene a conference to examine the political aims and claims of European states and see how far the hungry powers could be satisfied by equal access to the world's raw materials. In confiding to the British Ambassador the design of the President, Mr. Sumner Welles enjoined special secrecy. If he was supported by Mr. Chamberlain, the President would begin to work out tentative proposals with some of the small powers and announce his plan to the Diplomatic Corps in Washington on January 22nd.

This was a revival of President Roosevelt's idea for a world peace conference to be held in the spring of 1937. Eden had given cautious praise to the idea in November 1936, asking Vansittart to impress upon the British Ambassador in Washington that it was important for such a conference to be given thorough preparation after preliminary discussion with Britain.

Now in January 1938 there seemed to be more haste in the mind of Roosevelt. It is important here to note how his offer was handled in London by the new Permanent Head of the Foreign Office. Mr. Chamberlain, from his official country seat at Chequers, directed Sir Alexander Cadogan to discuss the Roosevelt plan with Sir Horace Wilson. Sir Alexander tells me that he did his best to alert Eden before Chamberlain's reply was sent to Washington. Sir Horace did not welcome the Roosevelt initiative, and Mr. Chamberlain declined to submit it to Cabinet discussion. From his biographies it is clear that the Prime Minister thought it would cut across his own lines of negotiation, make the dictators less anxious to talk with him, and perhaps reduce the bargaining power of Britain who still controlled more of the world's raw materials than any other nation.

Cadogan therefore drafted a reply suggesting that the President might defer his initiative, though Britain would give whole-hearted support if he decided to go ahead immediately. Chamberlain modified this telegram, insisting that despite the dangerous international outlook, "it may be possible to look forward to some improvement in the immediate future". He outlined his intended concessions to Italy, including possibly *de jure* recognition of Italian Ethiopia perhaps with the authority of the League of Nations, and expressed his hope that Britain might begin conversations before long with Germany too. He did not wish the draft to be sent to the South of France for the approval of Eden, and with that view of the way business should be done it is possible to have some sympathy. Sir Alexander, after telephoning to warn Mr. Eden, attempted to forward some secret papers to him via the Consulate-General in Marseilles, but the timing did not work and the Foreign Secretary was back at Folkestone before he could be met with the true facts by Sir Alexander Cadogan. He went on to Chequers to argue with the Prime Minister the merits of the plan of President Roosevelt to avoid a general war. Lord Avon in retrospect saw in the Prime Minister "a streak of ruthlessness, reminiscent of his father Joseph Chamberlain". Eden found Chamberlain reluctant to agree to a Cabinet meeting on the Roosevelt plan. It is in the diary of Neville Chamberlain that Eden suggested resignation on this issue, but Chamberlain pointed out to the Foreign Secretary "that Roosevelt had enjoined complete secrecy upon us".* The contribution of Sir Horace Wilson to this wrangle was made next day when he described the Roosevelt initiative as "woolly nonsense".

Eden re-read the Foreign Office file on the Roosevelt plan on returning to London from Chequers. On January 17th he wrote a letter to Chamberlain with further proposals for reactivating Roosevelt after the first cautious British reply.

The result was an immediate call from Sir Horace Wilson, who knew about the letter, and said that it would be sent on to the Prime Minister as he had just left again for Chequers.

* Chamberlain Diary.

He then delivered to Eden a short lecture on foreign affairs, which drew a sarcastic retort from Eden. The Foreign Secretary reflected afterwards that perhaps his sarcasm had been imprudent. Even for a Cabinet minister, it was unwise to cross swords with this powerful civil servant.

The Marquess of Salisbury, who as Lord Cranborne was then Under-Secretary in the Foreign Office, told me in 1963 that he thought this rebuff to President Roosevelt would have been the right issue on which to resign. Resignation would certainly have been difficult to avoid if Eden had not been on holiday. That slightly weakened his claim to have been ignored and circumvented. Eden realised an additional awkwardness—the Roosevelt initiative was still a confidential plan and a matter of high British policy. It would have been hard to explain to the House of Commons the reasons for such a resignation.

Signor Grandi on January 19th provided a second and more acceptable occasion for Eden to resign. The Italian Ambassador in a contrived interview with both the Prime Minister and Eden, brought out their full differences on Anglo-Italian relations.

In the British Cabinet and the Foreign Affairs Committee of the Cabinet the argument went to and fro. Could Britain persuade France to agree to *de jure* recognition of the Abyssinian conquest, so argued Eden, and yet keep France in the dark as to the disapproval felt by President Roosevelt towards such recognition? Ought there to be any question of according *de jure* recognition before Mussolini had withdrawn forces fighting in Spain?

It was plain that some of the Cabinet were for an alignment of Britain, France and President Roosevelt, even a Roosevelt encumbered with the Neutrality Act. Others thought of cultivating relations with Italy, or with Italy and Germany simultaneously, or with Germany to the exclusion of Italy. The unwritten rule that haunted these Cabinet sessions was that Britain could not make war in 1938. How right or how wrong these men were is no easy matter to judge. For the Cabinet does not offer its inner differences to public scrutiny.

CHAPTER XI

THE BEGINNING OF CATASTROPHE

The Cabinet wrangle over the Roosevelt initiative in January 1938 was followed in February by a determined attempt by Neville Chamberlain to get his own talks with Italy moving instead. Lord Avon remembers that Vansittart, back from a short holiday and in the comparative inactivity of his new appointment, received and brought to him a message of warning on February 7th. One of his Foreign Office colleagues had heard a Cabinet minister saying that Sir Robert had been "kicked upstairs", that the Prime Minister would now run foreign affairs and that Eden, if he did not fall in with the wishes of the Prime Minister's foreign affairs committee, would soon follow Vansittart.

Eden did not fail to repeat this story to Chamberlain, and the Prime Minister seemed astonished. Chamberlain, sensing estrangement and conflict of opinions, took pains to note in retrospect in his diary on February 19th the mounting differences between himself and Eden, as he remembered them. His memory scoured the past. In July 1937, he had sent a friendly letter to Mussolini through Signor Grandi without showing it first to Eden. He wrote that he did not think Eden minded. Of the Roosevelt initiative and his own reply in January "there was no time to consult Anthony". He asked his diary naïvely whether the amateur diplomacy of Ivy Lady Chamberlain in Rome had annoyed Eden. "This episode seemed to produce in Anthony only further suspicion."

Lord Avon in his version of their dispute over the procedure to be followed in negotiating with Italy makes the issue this: whether by open or secret talks, whether withdrawal of troops from Spain first, or first a *de jure* recognition of the conquest of Abyssinia.

"At last there came another surprise from Germany . . ." wrote Chamberlain, "Schuschnigg the Austrian Chancellor was suddenly summoned to Berchtesgaden, where he was outrageously bullied by Hitler." This was on February 12th. Lord Avon notes that "we did not know it until a few days later"—a curious commentary on the efficiency of British diplomats in Vienna. Eden hoped that President Miklas of Austria might not ratify the surrender of Dr. von Schuschnigg but recorded that this was no more than a faint hope. By February 16th enough of the danger to Austria was known for Mr. Bellenger, a Labour member, to ask the Secretary of State during question time in the House of Commons "whether in view of the fact that the integrity and independence of Austria are declared objects of British policy, he has any information concerning the week-end conversations between the Austrian and German chancellors; and, if not, will he ask to be informed of the purport of those conversations?"

Mr. Eden replied that the talks were held about the Austro-German agreement of 1936 and that a new agreement had been reached at the Berchtesgaden talks. A communiqué had outlined what happened, and the reorganisation of the Austrian government had been announced. There was reason to believe that there were other undertakings, "but until the actual text of the agreement is published, I am not in a position to make a statement".

Hitler had already insisted on Dr. Artur Seyss-Inquart, the Austrian Nazi leader, joining the Austrian cabinet in the key post of Minister of the Interior. Mr. Bellenger asked whether Mr. Eden "would give an assurance that the policy of His Majesty's Government in relation to the integrity and independence of Austria remains the same as stated by him on a previous occasion in this House?"

Mr. Eden replied: "My recollection is that what I said then was that His Majesty's Government desired in Central Europe, as elsewhere, peace and good understanding. That is certainly our policy."

Mr. Arthur Henderson, former Socialist Foreign Secretary, continued the probe. "Will His Majesty's Government stand by the joint declaration of February 1934 to the effect that they reaffirmed the interest of this country in the integrity and independence of Austria?"*

"I take it that the Hon. Member is referring to the Stresa declaration," replied Eden. "That is quite true. Of course that was a declaration by three Governments—Britain, France

* He referred to a tripartite declaration of February 17th, 1934 which was without military obligations for Britain.

and Italy. Italy has not, as yet, consulted His Majesty's Government on the matter."

By confusing the 1934 declaration with the Stresa declaration of 1935, Eden drew attention to his repeated affirmation—that the independence of Austria primarily concerned Italy. This ended the question and answer on an uncertain note. There was no firm warning to Hitler, though by now a full account of Dr. Schuschnigg's ordeal in Berchtesgaden must have been in the hands of the Foreign Office.

No move by President Roosevelt was to be expected in this diplomatic tangle. Events moved next towards a meeting between Chamberlain, Eden and Count Grandi on February 18th. Grandi and Eden had met on February 10th to discuss recognition of Italian-Ethiopia and a withdrawal of Italian volunteers from Spain: but as ever Eden was unwilling to give recognition other than through League procedure. As soon as the summons of Schuschnigg to Berchtesgaden, and reports of his intimidation there became known, Count Grandi began to avoid meeting Eden again. "I wanted Eden . . . to understand clearly that I did not wish to go to the Foreign Office and confer with him at a time when international politics seemed to be dominated by news of the events in Austria."*

Eden insisted, but without avail, Grandi even pleaded a golf engagement, and until a meeting was arranged for him with both Chamberlain and Eden for February 18th, he persisted in being elusive. A meeting of the three men was only made possible, we shall see, by a call on Count Grandi from "Chamberlain's confidential agent".

This meeting has become famous through the Ciano diary, in which Grandi's long dispatch of February 19th was published in full. It contains playful allusions to Mr. Chamberlain and Eden as "two enemies confronting each other, like two cocks in true fighting posture". Eden thought that Hitler was about to march into Austria with a nod from Mussolini. In support of his mistrust of Italy, Eden had quoted in a note to Chamberlain the opinion of Vansittart "who, as you know, has always been a strong partisan of Anglo-Italian conversations . . . agrees [with me] . . . and is now very doubtful whether Mussolini is sincere or whether he may not be 'playing

* Grandi dispatch to Count Ciano February 19th, 1938.

us along'." There is no indication in the Vansittart papers that Sir Robert was involved in this policy discussion. When Sir Alexander Cadogan indicated subjects as perhaps suitable for Sir Robert's expert advice, he usually found the Foreign Secretary unreceptive to the suggestion. Chamberlain seems to have been buoyed up by his own hopes that Britain might at this last moment reconstitute the Stresa Front.

Grandi began his dispatch to Ciano by reporting that there were two sharpened trends in the British cabinet, one for agreement with Italy (Chamberlain), the other against it (Eden). He related these to British anxiety about Austria. It was Chamberlain who first broached the Austrian question, saying that "the German action against Austria is evidently intended to change the European balance of power, and one must ask today, or in a short time, what remains of Austrian independence". Grandi referred to his most recent instructions from Rome not to discuss the problem of Austria, whereupon Eden interjected that "Italy had never denounced the Stresa agreement which provided for consultation between Italy, France and Britain on the Austrian problem." This drew forth a tirade from Grandi. After all, Eden was the man for economic sanctions against Italy in 1935 and now he was invoking Stresa.

"Grandi detailed one grievance after another," noted Eden in his diary and Chamberlain "nodded encouragingly", as much as to say—"there, you see, Anthony". At the end of that morning's talk, and when they were alone, out came the Prime Minister's emphatic "Anthony, you have missed chance after chance. You simply cannot go on like this."

There is a slight difference in the Grandi dispatch and Eden's own record. For Grandi wrote to Ciano that he refused to discuss Austria, whereas the British record was that "Count Grandi was asked what effect the opening of Anglo-Italian conversations might have on the Italian attitude towards Austria. Count Grandi replied that it was difficult for him to answer that, except to say that it would give his people more courage." The British version then adds that Grandi said he was unable to exchange views on the basis of the Stresa agreement—"indeed he said he had no instructions at all to mention Austria".

The Grandi dispatch contained in its latter pages **an**

illuminating hint to Count Ciano in Rome that "I would not wish . . . to leave Your Excellency the impression . . . that Chamberlain has in mind any plans for resisting Germany over the Austrian question. The British attitude . . . will remain . . . that of indignant resignation. In any case, it is not Germany or Austria which is the battleground between Chamberlain and Eden at present. It is Italy alone."

This appears to have been true, to judge by the record. A remark by Count Grandi to me in 1954 that "he preferred the attitude of Eden over Austria to that of Chamberlain, because it was stronger", still does not alter the essential fact. There was no British plan for anything beyond an immediate reaffirmation of the Stresa policy, and Grandi had convinced them that such a sudden gesture was not possible. The gulf that had formed since Stresa, and after the collapse of the Hoare-Laval initiative, was too wide to be easily bridged.

So it remained for Chamberlain and Eden to argue in Cabinet on the merit of seeking a *rapprochement* with Italy, and that was what happened on Saturday, February 19th. First Eden asked Sir Alexander Cadogan for his advice, which was to begin conversations in some form in Rome. But Eden decided that this would be too humiliating for him and that he would resign if the Cabinet disagreed. Sir John Simon and Mr. Malcolm Macdonald suggested to him that it was less a matter of principle than one of timing. In the Cabinet the two views were heard, Chamberlain asserting that he believed Grandi when he said that there existed no agreement between Italy and Germany over Austria. Why else should Italy be so anxious to have conversations with Britain? Eden argued the opposite case. He thought that Italy wanted British concessions over Abyssinia and Spain without giving anything in return. He declared himself unable to support such a policy. The Foreign Secretary spent that evening with the Secretary of State for the Dominions, Mr. Malcolm Macdonald, who warned him that he thought Neville Chamberlain wanted to get rid of him.

On Sunday 20th, the Prime Minister sent for his Foreign Secretary and asked whether he had changed his opinion of the night before. Eden replied that he had not. Chamberlain then said that with great reluctance he had come to the conclusion that it was in the national interest that they should part. Thus it might be said that Eden was told that he would have to resign. Eden accepted this view "as confirming my own decision". That afternoon the Cabinet sat again and argued it over. During an adjournment a small sub-committee tried to reconcile the conflicting proposals. In vain. The ubiquitous Sir Horace Wilson suggested to Eden's private secretary that the Foreign Secretary should give reasons of health for his resignation and go on a long voyage. That evening the issue was settled, the resignation reaffirmed; and a last proposal to avert it, by vacating another Cabinet seat to Eden, brushed aside by the Prime Minister who reiterated:

"Then, you will send me your letter?"

The letter was sent. Lord Cranborne also resigned, faithful to his friend and his principles.

There was an additional reason for Eden to resent the Prime Minister's handling of foreign affairs, the question of underhand diplomacy.

On the Sunday morning a reply from Mussolini, accepting the Chamberlain proposals for withdrawal of foreign "volunteers" from Spain, had reached 10 Downing Street direct. This was news to the Foreign Secretary when it was told to Eden by Chamberlain himself. Eden showed his surprise. "During those weeks I had neither knowledge nor suspicion of any contact between the Prime Minister and the Italian Embassy," wrote Lord Avon on this aspect of their quarrel.*

The allegations are plain in the Grandi dispatch that there had been contacts between himself and a "secret agent of Chamberlain".

Alfred Duff Cooper then still First Lord of the Admiralty, accepts that Chamberlain was simply acting behind the back of his Foreign Secretary.† The Grandi dispatch of February 19th mentions that "purely as a matter of historical interest I inform your Excellency that yesterday evening after the Downing Street meeting, Chamberlain secretly sent his agent to me (we made an appointment in an ordinary public taxi) to say that he sent me cordial greetings, that he had appreciated my statements, which had been very useful to him, and that he was confident everything would go very well next day!" This bizarre incident of secret diplomacy may indeed be of historical interest, if it is true. Lord Avon thinks that the full

---

* *Facing the Dictators.*   † *Old Men Forget,* Lord Norwich.

story will never be known. Mr. Iain Macleod in his biography of Neville Chamberlain defends the Prime Minister against imputations of a furtive and possibly disloyal habit of diplomacy. He points out that Sir Joseph Ball, Head of the Research Department of the Conservative Central Office, sometimes identified as the confidential agent, denied having met Grandi in a taxi cab, or anywhere else, on February 19th. However, Mr. Macleod also refers to a letter in which Sir Joseph Ball in the summer of 1937 thought fit to inform Mr. Eden's secretary, Mr. J. P. L. Thomas, that he had a contact with the Italian Embassy named Dingli, who was legal adviser to the Ambassador. Mr. J. P. L. Thomas acknowledged this letter and asked Ball to pass on to the Foreign Office any information that he might derive from it. The existence of these letters does not necessarily make all subsequent contacts of Ball with Grandi unobjectionable.

Mr. Macleod explains that on the 20th February Mr. Chamberlain knew of Mussolini's favourable answer to his approach before Eden did, because Mr. Dingli had been in touch with Ball in the country, so that the good news from the Italian Embassy might be quickly used to dissuade Eden from resigning—an account, says Mr. Macleod that "squares with Ball's reputation as a man of honour and distinction".

Lord Avon comments on this that he never at any time had even a remote suspicion that Sir Joseph Ball might be an intermediary between the Italian Embassy and 10 Downing Street, nor could Thomas have suspected it.* Yet on February 16th, after Eden's attempts to get Grandi into talks had failed, Chamberlain had told Eden that Grandi had asked for an appointment with the Prime Minister. Lord Avon records that he does not know whether "intermediaries" had conveyed this request. Grandi wrote that "the confidential agent of Chamberlain" came to see him on the 17th. His dispatch relates that the "agent" told Grandi not to avoid a conversation with Eden further, as the Prime Minister himself would most probably take part.

The "confidential agent" could again have been Dingli, acting through Ball, whom Vansittart mentions among Baldwin's staff as "round Joe Ball, his Intelligence Corps, of whom more was heard in the days of Chamberlain".† It could

---

Facing the Dictators, p. 577.   † *Mist Procession*.

not have been possible for Dingli, who had no access to the Prime Minister, to know what were Chamberlain's wishes. I have had an opportunity to elucidate this shaded chapter of diplomacy a little, having long known Sir Joseph and having met Signor Grandi in 1954. After playing a role in the capitulation of Italy in 1943, the former Italian Ambassador revisited England in 1954, a bedraggled figure, haunting the scenes of his pre-war distinction. His explanation to me of the taxi-cab incident was this. There had been no such assignment in a cab, and the intermediary to Sir Joseph had been Dingli, not himself. This did not much alter the picture.

"My dispatch was ornamented a little to impress them in Rome," said Grandi. "Of course I knew Sir Joseph. He is a friend. I will see him and perhaps compare our versions of what happened then."

"Of course, I knew Grandi, but we did not meet in a taxi-cab," Sir Joseph told me. When Sir Joseph heard that I had a written account of my conversation with Grandi, he several times asked to see it in ensuing years; but as Sir Joseph always seemed to be himself on the point of telling his own version of the story, I saw no sense in confusing him with the account of Dino Grandi. Sir Joseph used in his later years to tell me that he was writing a book of his own about his Downing Street activities. He came and went between his Wiltshire fishing lodge and the Flyfishers' Club in London, a tubby man with a dark twinkling eye, persistent but elusive. He claimed to have taught Chamberlain how to fish. He sometimes gave out mysterious hints on the contents of his book, and seemed always a little anxious to know what Grandi had said. Before the end he burned many of his papers and after his death in 1960 nothing more was heard of his book.

The resignation of Eden was a sensation of a kind that had not affected the country since Sir Samuel Hoare had been forced out on the Abyssinian issue two years previously. It had been forecast and yet it came as a shock of surprise. Winston Churchill saw him as a strong young man lost in a critical hour. Eden was cheered as he entered and as he left Downing Street. But his speech on resignation was thought by many to be hesitant, and the issues not clearly put. The resignation speech of Lord Cranborne was generally thought to be valid for them both, and Cranborne answered the criticisms of those in the Cabinet and the House of Commons who questioned their reasons.

"It has been suggested in some quarters," he said, "that this is a question not of principle but of detail, and that on questions of detail Ministers should not resign. I cannot agree with that assessment. I think it not a matter of detail, but a matter of fundamental principle. That is not to say that I accept the thesis that we should not enter into negotiations with authoritarian States in any circumstances whatever. That, I suggest, would be the negation of our whole creed of liberty of thought. Other nations are entitled to their political ideas and political systems, however much we personally may disapprove of them. We in this country should oppose any attempt to impose other ideas upon us, and we must concede the same right to others. The principle which, in my view, is involved in the point at issue between my right hon. Friend and his colleagues is quite a different one. It is the principle of good faith in international affairs. In the international sphere, the very existence of civilised relationships is dependent on a high standard of good faith.

"Unless nations are able to trust each other, any agreements that they may make with each other will not be worth the paper on which they are written. It is, therefore, to my mind, an issue of the widest character. It is no question of detail as to the time at which conversations should take place or the method by which they should be carried on; it is a question of the conditions under which any negotiations between any countries can be carried on at all with any useful results.

"I fully recognise that in respect of the proposed agreement with Italy, Members of the Government quite sincerely believe that this is the beginning of a new chapter; that the new agreement will not be the same as the old agreement; that it will be observed; that it will be the beginning of a new era of close and cordial relations such as existed happily between the two countries in the past. If the Government believe that, in my opinion they are absolutely right to go straight ahead at the earliest possible moment; but, perhaps because I have been in closer and more constant contact with these matters, I cannot share that confidence. I think that, at any rate, before entering on official conversations, we should have some concrete evidence that the attitude of the Italian Government has changed, and that they are really animated by friendly feelings towards this country. That, when all is said and done, is all that my right hon. Friend is asking for, and has asked for."

"You won't last long, Anthony, if I go," Vansittart had said. Eden rang him up on the night of February 20th to say that he had resigned. He explained his reasons about the Italian negotiations.

"Why are you going over that, Anthony?" asked Vansittart. "There is worse to follow, you know. There's Austria."

His recollection of Eden's reply was:

"They will not be able to stand it."

But Chamberlain and his elder men were able to stand it. It became a question of whether Eden, alone, without office, could continue to command public support. He did take the issue to his Leamington constituents on February 25th and they gave him a unanimous vote of confidence. Then he went to the South of France for a rest.

What if Eden had swallowed his pride and kept his convictions for a later day, as Vansittart had hoped? It would probably not have affected the Austrian issue, which was too close upon them. The trial of strength over foreign policy came in those Cabinet meetings from September 14th onwards, in which those who saw the issues as Lord Cranborne had so admirably stated them were very much outnumbered. Suppose then, that these two had not resigned in February, how different the prospects would have been early in September? The opponents of surrender to Hitler in Central Europe would have been Eden, Cranborne, Duff Cooper, De la Warr, Walter Elliott, Oliver Stanley and Winterton. Other ministers might have left the fence. Hore-Belisha was sitting on it rather unhappily. If the Fleet had been mobilised at an early date before all was lost, history might have taken a different course.

As it was, Chamberlain found a more amenable Foreign Secretary in Edward Halifax. The Prime Minister struck an ominous note when he resumed his talks with Grandi on February 21st, the day after Eden's resignation. There is an account of this meeting in the analysis made in November 1943 of captured Italian diplomatic documents by Herr Strohm the German Consul-General in Rome, who studied the documents dated from the beginning of 1938 until May 1940 to determine how close to Britain Italy had stood then, despite the Berlin-Rome axis. He noted that:

"Already on February 21st, 1938, Chamberlain explained to the Italian Ambassador, Grandi, that the British Government looked upon Austria as a lost cause and had no intention of making proposals or suggestions to other states in relation to the Austrian situation."*

Despite the suspicions of Eden that they were in agreement, Mussolini appears not to have betrayed to Hitler this British confession of weakness. To some extent the assessment of Mussolini by Chamberlain was correct at this time. There is another good witness of the attitude of Mussolini then, who saw that he had not already sold Austria to Germany. Three weeks after the first intimidation of Schuschnigg by Hitler, Colonel Joszef Beck, Polish Foreign Minister, visited Rome and noted a conversation with the Duce on March 7th. This was five days before the invasion of Austria.

"After several pleasant remarks about Poland, Mussolini quickly turned to the subject that seemed to make him anxious, the Danube basin and Austria in particular. He asked me at once what I thought of the Austrian problem. I replied that this of all those problems of common interest to our two countries was doubtless the most grave. . . .

"Mussolini asked me: 'How long do you believe that it can last?'

"I replied: 'Perhaps a year. Perhaps forty-eight hours.'

"The expression of Mussolini changed visibly. He leaned his head on his hand and said with obvious anxiety: 'You believe then that things are so far gone.' He reflected a little and added in a decided manner: 'If Britain and France imagine that I am going to pull their chestnuts out of the fire in this affair, they are wrong. To have Germany as a neighbour is certainly not convenient, but it is probably inevitable, and I cannot imperil the vital interests of the Italian people if these gentlemen in London and Paris won't take them into account in other parts of the world.' "†

On March 4th Sir Robert Vansittart, seeing the rising tensions in Europe, wrote an earnest reminder to Lord Halifax based on two telegrams from the British Embassies in Berlin

---

* F. W. Deakin, *The Brutal Friendship*, p. 834.
† *Dernier Rapport*, Editions de la Baconnière, p. 146.

and Paris. Sir Nevile Henderson submitted early in March 1938:

"Hitler is prepared to risk a general war if foreign countries resist his pretension to safeguard the interests of Germans living outside the Reich." Sir Eric Phipps pointed out in a dispatch from Paris that if Germany interfered beyond a certain point with Czechoslovakia "France will faithfully and unhesitatingly carry out her engagements to the letter". This was the reiterated pledge of M. Delbos given in the previous autumn, and Vansittart thought that it might lead to a situation of war from which Britain could not keep aloof.

Vansittart disagreed with Sir Nevile's estimate that Hitler was ready to risk war over Austria. He thought the attitude of Hitler contained a great deal of bluff. Germany was in no condition to risk or endure general war. Nor could she endure a long war. The risk was rather that she would bluff *herself* into big adventure and general conflagration by thinking that she could bluff everyone else. Vansittart concluded:

"I submit therefore very earnestly that we are incurring an enormous responsibility in not speaking to Hitler a great deal more firmly and explicitly than we have yet done in this matter. At present he is being allowed to rave and threaten without restraint. If he is not checked by being brought up against hard reality, he may carry himself and everyone else into disaster. I urge that we should take the proper step to obviate this before it is too late.

"That step is the plain speaking at Berlin which Hitler's hard absence of response to our overtures renders desirable."

"Almost every day I would receive unsolicited advice to take some action," wrote Lord Halifax of this period.* He thought that action would make it "rather more likely that if bluff did not succeed the issue must be war". No warning was sent.

On March 10th a courier reached Berlin from Austria to tell Hitler that Dr. von Schuschnigg had attempted to outwit him by making his peace with the Austrian Socialists, and that a plebiscite arranged for the following Sunday, March 13th, would not include the issue of the *Anschluss*. Hitler summoned his generals and told them that he would not accept such a stratagem. General Keitel advised him of operation Otto, an existing plan for an invasion of Austria, intended to be used if

* *Fulness of Days.*

a Habsburg restoration was imminent. This plan had been outlined in a strategic directive of June 24th, 1937, by Field-Marshal von Blomberg and elaborated since. Hitler declared that Special Operation Otto applied to this situation. There was to be a march on Vienna, he said, and all resistance was to be broken. It was to be an isolated action without simultaneous deployment on other fronts.

On March 11th the Austrian Nazis on instructions from Hitler, presented an ultimatum to Schuschnigg, who thereupon decided to cancel the plebiscite. News of his decision reached Germany only after Hitler had ordered at 1 p.m. on March 11th that the forces detailed should be ready for 'action by noon on March 12th. Goering heard at 2.45 p.m. that the plebiscite was cancelled, but felt instinctively that the situation had become so fluid that he and Hitler could get what they wanted. Nothing was countermanded. It was decided to demand Schuschnigg's resignation and a choice of Nazi names was sent from Berlin to Vienna to be presented in the new cabinet list. The evening of Friday 11th brought a crisis over the Chancellorship of Austria. Schuschnigg had resigned, but President Miklas would not accept Seyss-Inquart as head of Government. Hitler became nervous of the consequences to Italy and feared that she might succumb to Allied influences even at this late hour. He sent off his emissary, Prince Philip of Hesse, with a special message to Mussolini.

Meanwhile a damping answer from Lord Halifax to an appeal from the Austrian Government had been received. He said that the British Government "cannot take the responsibility of advising the Austrian Chancellor to take any course of action which might expose his country to dangers from which His Majesty's Government are unable to guarantee protection." France asked in vain in Rome for a joint discussion of the Austrian appeal. Count Ciano told the French Chargé d'Affaires abruptly that there was no point in holding talks.

On the main road from Munich to the Austrian border on Friday, March 11th, the British Consul General in Munich, Donald St. Clair Gainer, and his French colleague, M. de Vaux St. Cyr watched the German armour rolling up to the frontier. That night Gainer telephoned the news to Sir Nevile Henderson in Berlin, whose immediate comment on the telephone was:

"It cannot be true. General Keitel assures me that there are no troop movements."*

That Friday Mr. Chamberlain was giving a luncheon party in honour of the departing German Ambassador. Telegrams were brought in reporting the German ultimatum to Austria, and after mastering his discomfiture and courteously seeing Frau von Ribbentrop to her car, the Prime Minister returned to his other guests and read the telegrams to Herr von Ribbentrop. The German Ambassador appeared puzzled but said that this might be a peaceful solution to the problem that he had recently discussed with the British Government. The Prime Minister replied tartly that it appeared to be far from that. The party broke up in awkward confusion. Lord Halifax took the unusual step of calling at the German Embassy at 5.15 p.m. and acquainted Ribbentrop with dispatches from Vienna, in which it appeared that German troops would be set in motion within an hour if the ultimatum was not accepted. Ribbentrop "seemed frankly mystified", but when a message reached him from Berlin that Schuschnigg had resigned and that Artur von Seyss-Inquart, the Austrian Nazi leader, had replaced him as Chancellor (the latter report was still premature) Ribbentrop declared that this was much the best thing that could have happened. He listened attentively to Lord Halifax's expostulation that this was "an exhibition of naked force". Yet since there was plainly no threat of action in the Foreign Secretary's reproaches, it became even clearer than before that the German forces could cross the border. Six hours remained during which the strongest language that the British Government could muster in a letter delivered to Baron von Neurath was "a protest in the strongest terms" against an action which "is bound to produce the gravest reaction of which it is impossible to foretell the issues".†

This suspense of six hours and the use made of it by Britain, was instructive to Hitler. The German troops did not actually move in until the morning of Saturday, 12th March; and even then Goering covered the way for a possible retreat by "giving his word" to Sir Nevile Henderson that the troops would be withdrawn as soon as the situation was stable. Sir Nevile reported that he had made "violent protests", but as on future

* Sir Donald Gainer to author, 1963.
† Documents on British Foreign Policy, Series III, Vol. I.

occasions he seemed only too ready to see the German side of the case, conceding that "Schuschnigg had acted with precipitate folly". This drew on him from Lord Halifax a stinging rebuke for having weakened the force of his protest. Herr Hitler motored cautiously into Austria next day, and both he and Goering let it be known that the idea of a full union between the two countries only dawned on him when he saw the enthusiasm of the Austrian welcome. It is surprising that this version should continue to get some credence since the publication of the German documents.

To the Prince of Hesse who returned from Rome with a friendly message from Mussolini, Hitler babbled his relief that this time Italy had not reacted:

"Tell the Duce I will never forget this. Never, never!" And a good deal more of the same sort.

It was over with Austria, and now Czechoslovakia lay half-enclosed in a hostile grip.

CHAPTER XII

BLUFF AND COUNTERBLUFF

U PON the mind of one man in 1938 the future policy of
Great Britain now depended. "To suggest that the Cabinet's
action was dictated by the Prime Minister" . . . wrote Lord
Templewood, who was then Home Secretary . . . "is a travesty
of the facts." Nevertheless that was so, and impressions of
the cold grey power of Neville Chamberlain in that year
remained long with those who had to do with him. Sir Horace
Wilson gained in influence also as Eden fell. Lord Halifax
found it necessary in after years to deny the repeated assertions
that when he was Foreign Secretary, "Chamberlain interfered
unduly with the work of the Foreign Secretary and of his office
through the unwelcome intervention of Sir Horace Wilson.
I can only say . . . that I had no such experience. So far from
feeling that Horace Wilson interfered and made things difficult
between Prime Minister and Foreign Secretary, I always
found him extremely helpful when the pressure of work was
heavy, in ensuring that I was fully acquainted with the thoughts
of the Prime Minister, and vice versa, and that neither was
unconsciously drifting into any misunderstanding of the other's
mind."* This use of the Chief Industrial Adviser outside his
terms of reference was to have evil consequences. The new post
created for Sir Robert Vansittart might have been adapted
to fill the vacuum to which Lord Halifax alludes. Had chance
been a little different Halifax and Vansittart might have
formed a partnership strong enough to assert Foreign Office
influence. Their early life had thrown them together. They
were born in the same year, and had been contemporaries
at Eton, but their proximity had served only to show a distinct
contrast in promise and outlook. For when Vansittart was in
Division II, Edward Wood was in Division IV, and when
Vansittart reached the VIth Form in 1898, Wood was no
higher than Division II. Vansittart carried off four prizes and
many distinctions, and became a member of Pop and Captain
of the Oppidans; whereas Edward Wood left without academic

* *Fulness of Days.*

distinction, and began to shine later at Oxford University. In the years thereafter by effortless degrees he had risen on the rungs of politics through Parliament to become Viceroy of India, several times a Secretary of State, and finally Foreign Secretary. His style of writing was as dry and casual as Vansittart's was scholastic and ornate. No doubt Edward Halifax mistrusted brilliance as many Englishmen do. Vansittart mistrusted mediocrity. Neither found anything particular to say of the other in his memoirs, though both worked in the same office for three years. Vansittart mentions Halifax as a crony of Baldwin, and Halifax recalls that Vansittart once helped him to organise a masque during the 1939 state visit of the French President.

Could anyone in distant Eton days have thought that the insignificant Edward Wood one day would be censuring the friendships of the Captain of the Oppidans? One of Vansittart's first encounters with Lord Halifax as Foreign Secretary was over Winston Churchill. It had long been constitutional custom for the Secretary of State to direct that the Leader of the Opposition should be briefed on foreign affairs by the Permanent Under-Secretary or one of his officials; but this powerful back-bencher was being told a great deal at the discretion of Sir Robert and was speaking in the House with an authority that was uncomfortable to his own Party leaders. Of course Mr. Churchill had other sources of information, but probably none so authoritative as Vansittart.

"I want you to cease seeing him so much," asked the Foreign Secretary. He explained that in his view the advice and knowledge of the Chief Diplomatic Adviser were for the Government and not for individual members of the Commons.

"I can't end a friendship of twenty-four years just like that," retorted Vansittart. "I shall continue to see him." But the warning had been given, and though there could be no objection to a dinner party at 44 Park Street, the sight of a particularly shaped black bowler and the lingering aroma of cigars around the big corner room at the Foreign Office were sometimes a subject of embarrassment, even if Winston had dropped in to read a passage from a proposed speech.

"These visits . . . cost me more than he knew," wrote Vansittart.*

* *Mist Procession.*

Lord Templewood went into some detail in his defence of the Chamberlain Government against the accusation of abuse of procedure. He denied the charge of dictation by Chamberlain to the Foreign Policy Committee of the Cabinet. This body met about fifty times between 1937 and 1939, he tells us, in close contact with the Chiefs of Staff and took decisions in a "regular and methodical" way. He explains that Chamberlain's "great influence in the Committee came from his convinced belief in the wisdom of the policy that he had set before himself for many months, and from his skill in explaining it". Sir Robert Vansittart was not called into the Foreign Policy Committee, though Sir Alexander Cadogan, when he became Permanent Under-Secretary, was often asked to attend.

Thus Mr. Chamberlain did not always have an expert witness to his skill at explaining foreign business. Sir Alexander Cadogan related me the eccentric reason for this lack of balance in Cabinet counsels. Lloyd George once asked Sir Eyre Crowe from his own experience as Permanent Head of the Foreign Office, to say whether his successors in the post ought regularly to attend the Cabinet.

"No, sir," replied the Great Man with emphasis.

The Prime Minister asked Sir Eyre what was his reason for this advice.

"Because," replied Crowe, "I don't want my men to see what sort of things go on in the Cabinet."

His contemptuous reply was accepted for a long time as a ruling and out of it, as well as the much discussed Treasury minute of 1919 which created the post of Head of the Civil Service, this unbalance arose. The Office of the Prime Minister evolved its own foreign policy.

In many works of history there has been no reference to the important question which Mr. Chamberlain addressed to the British Chiefs of Staff immediately after the invasion of Austria. He asked for a report on the military implications of an alliance with France and other European States to resist by force any German attempt to attack Czechoslovakia. That much has been revealed by the Head of the Admiralty Historical Section, though Chiefs of Staff papers are not ordinarily published or available for scrutiny. Without this valuable clue neither the diplomacy of Britain, nor indeed the history of these years is intelligible. The reply of the Chiefs of Staff to Mr. Chamberlain was categorical—that the country was not ready for war, that no measures of force, whether alone or in alliance with other European countries, could now stop Germany from inflicting a crushing defeat on Czechoslovakia, and that any involvement in war with Germany at this period could well lead to the ultimate defeat of Britain herself through unpreparedness.*

This pessimistic opinion was founded on the weakness of Britain in the air and in air defence. It could be argued that these were the answers which Mr. Chamberlain expected from the Chiefs of Staff, that they strengthened his belief in his own policy of appeasement, and that they would have offered such advice with much more trepidation to Mr. Churchill, had he been Prime Minister in 1938. By way of exchange the Chiefs of Staff added a demand that the Treasury ruling against rearmament programmes interfering with normal trade should at last be rescinded and arms production go full ahead. The Cabinet agreed to this. Lord Templewood does not agree with the assertion that it was British military weakness that was the principal cause of the Munich agreement. "The over-riding consideration with Chamberlain and his colleagues", he wrote, "was that the very complicated problem of Czechoslovakia ought not to lead to a world war and must at almost any price be settled by peaceful means." Professor W. N. Medlicott, who is sympathetic to Chamberlain, takes the opposite view that military weakness determined the policy of Britain in 1938.† He has presumably in his role of official historian seen enough in the Chiefs of Staff papers to warrant such an opinion. For the contention of Lord Templewood that it was decisive with the British Government that Czechoslovakia was not a good cause for war and geographically beyond rescue, does not take into account—though the Wehrmacht appreciation obviously did—that in a naval blockade of Germany Britain possessed a potent weapon. "Nothing short of a world war could prevent the annihilation of the Czech military forces," argued Lord Templewood.‡ He did not examine the further question whether the alternative policy of concession would avoid a world war.

How justified was the pessimism of the Chiefs of Staff? If we compare their assessment with that of the German High

* P. K. Kemp, *Victory at Sea*, p. 26.
† *The Coming of War in 1939*, W. N. Medlicott, Routledge and Kegan Paul.
‡ *Nine Troubled Years*.

Command we find another opinion. In 1937 a German Wehrmacht directive stated that, if Germany was to engage in operations against France and Czechoslovakia, with the effort against Czechoslovakia, "the neutrality of England is to be regarded as indispensable". . . . Furthermore that "if either England, Poland or Lithuania, or all three of these countries side with our enemies from the outbreak of war, our military situation would be worsened thereby to an unbearable, even hopeless, extent."* Since the war it has been forcibly argued by apologists for the British diplomacy of 1938, among whom are some of those diplomats whose judgment was in question, that Britain had no other course than to play for time and avoid war. The Chiefs of Staff professed to think so, and their conclusion affected the whole conduct of the British Government in these months. That the German Chief of General Staff thought differently appears not to have become known until too late to enter into the British calculations. A curiously dissenting opinion was offered from Berlin in August 1938 by Sir Nevile Henderson who wrote that, "I believe if we saw any utility in war, now would be the time to make it rather than later."† But from a man of so many hesitations, this opinion carried no great weight and was overlooked in the general anxiety for peace. Moreover, on March 20th, 1938, when the gravest decisions were in the balance, Henderson in one of his many personal letters to Lord Halifax, insinuating advice that he wished to escape the prior comment of Vansittart, Orme Sargent and others, professed himself ready to warn Hitler that his next "rough house" would bring Britain and the Empire in arms against him, but "I cannot regard the Sudeten as a just motive". In another dismal letter on May 3rd Sir Nevile wrote that, "I admit that personally I am only too glad to wish that she (Germany) should look eastwards instead of westwards. I only see one good point about the extra sixpence on the income tax. It may possibly induce the British public to be in favour of an agreement with Germany which is aimed at taking it off again."

Sir Robert Vansittart had at this time better information and advice to offer. He was able to report in March 1938 that Field-Marshal Goering on February 8th had delivered a lecture to senior German Air Force and Army officers declaring that

---

* Stragetic Directive of German War Minister, June 24th, 1937.
† Dispatch No. 647. August 19th, 1938.

the situation of Germany had become economically so critical that the annexation of Austria and the conquest of Czechoslovakia, and subsequent economic domination of Central and Eastern Europe seemed the only solution. Goering had recommended an early Blitzkrieg against Czechoslovakia, and had been applauded by the Luftwaffe officers but treated with some reserve by the Army generals. Hitler was not convinced that France would honour her obligations and still less convinced that Britain would aid Czechoslovakia. The moderate elements in Germany, Vansittart reported, begged Britain to define her position while there was yet time. In view of this circumstantial information, the dogged faith of Sir Nevile Henderson in Goering in ensuing months appears an error of judgment.

Much more compelling than the advice of Sir Nevile Henderson was the outcome of a meeting on March 15th, 1938, of the French Conseil Superieur de la Defense Nationale, the equivalent to the British Imperial Defence Committee. M. Leon Blum attended as Prime Minister, and M. Daladier, as Minister of Defence presided. The Services ministers, the Chiefs of Staff and the Foreign Minister attended. The latter post was occupied by M. Paul-Boncour, the Chautemps cabinet having fallen just before the annexation of Austria. Their first concern was to find an answer to a blunt question from Chamberlain in reply to their attempts to draw Britain into a defence commitment towards Czechoslovakia. M. Paul-Boncour repeated this question to the French ministers:

"You say that you will go to the aid of Czechoslovakia, but what in fact will you do?"

M. Daladier declared that France could not go directly to the aid of Czechoslovakia. The question was whether Germany, in view of the number of troops that France could pin down, would risk an attack on Czechoslovakia. Blum thought that Russia would intervene, but Gamelin interposed that a Russian mobilisation might deter Poland and Rumania from supporting Czechoslovakia. M. Paul-Boncour made a subsequent comment that as long as Colonel Beck was Polish foreign minister, not only could Czechoslovakia expect no assistance from Poland, but Poland might herself try to profit from a German aggression. The answer to Britain proposed by M. Blum was that France could pin down German forces by operations (in the West), that France could not prevent an attack on Czechoslovakia, and that Belgium and Rumania should be urged to give military co-operation to France and Russia. But when the uncertain attitude of Italy had been appraised, M. Leger for the Foreign Ministry emphasised that France should "react" to a German attack on Czechoslovakia, rather than take an initiative. (This might mean simply manning the Maginot line.)

Mr. Chamberlain laid down his cautious line of policy in a speech to the House of Commons on March 24th, 1938, in which he said that Britain would fight in fulfilment of her engagements to France, Belgium, Portugal, Iraq and Egypt, in case of aggression. He then came to the question of assisting a victim of aggression under the provisions of the League of Nations Covenant which might cover Czechoslovakia, though no automatic military obligation could be accepted. At the same time "where peace and war are concerned, legal obligations are not alone involved, and if war broke out it would be unlikely to be confined to those who have assumed such obligations. It would be quite impossible to say where it might end and what Governments might become involved. . . . This is especially true of two countries like Britain and France with long associations of friendship." In a family letter he was alarmingly frank, writing to one of his sisters on March 20th that he studied the idea of a grand European alliance long before Winston Churchill mentioned it to him. "I talked about it to Halifax, and we submitted it to the Chiefs of Staff and the F.O. experts." But they had found it unpracticable. . . . "I have therefore abandoned any idea of giving guarantees to Czechoslovakia, or the French in connection with their obligations to that country."* Lord Halifax sent to Sir Eric Phipps in Paris on March 23rd an enclosure in which was set forth the British view of their obligations to France, making it plain that it would not cover a situation in which Czechoslovakia assumed a defiant attitude against making a settlement of the Sudeten-German claims.

Dr. Goerdeler, with the connivance of Dr. Schacht and General von Brauchitsch, returned conspiratorially to London and in April had two secret meetings with Vansittart, at the first of which he unfortunately asserted the right of Germany to have the Sudeten-German territories of Czechoslovakia ceded to her. His argument was that Britain should follow a course of *Realpolitik*. Vansittart said Britain would at the most concede

* Keith Feiling, *Life of Neville Chamberlain*, p. 348.

local autonomy to the Sudeten-Germans. "I declared the territory was German and must therefore be joined to Germany, not Czechoslovakia. Vansittart rejected this."*

It was easy for the British to conceive the suspicion that these secret German opponents of Hitler wanted to reap the first fruits of his policy without going the whole way with this dangerous man.

It was therefore not surprising that at their next meeting, when Goerdeler spoke earnestly of the hostility of the senior German generals to Hitler, Vansittart seemed to him inclined to attach little importance to this "treasonable talk".† Alas, Goerdeler had warned frankly enough in the previous summer. The subsequent hesitations of Britain and France had since become apparent to him. He suffered the compunctions of a German nationalist. He was ultimately to pay for his aberrations by hanging from a meat hook after the revolt of July 1944.

I gleaned a straw of evidence myself that Neville Chamberlain had made up his mind against involvement with Czechoslovakia when I returned to London early in May 1938 from Berlin, where I had for three years been Central European correspondent of the *News Chronicle*. Lord Lloyd, Chairman of the British Council, to whom Mr. Chamberlain and Lord Halifax listened on many questions, had asked me in March whether reasons could be advanced to the Prime Minister for risking war with Germany in 1938 rather than later. To my mind, an obvious reason not to avoid war at any cost in 1938 was that France still had many more trained reservists than Germany, though with its superior manpower and now conscription Germany would with each passing year overtake France in this respect. In March Lord Lloyd wished me to present these views to the Prime Minister and offered to arrange a meeting. When in May I reminded him of the proposed meeting, Lord Lloyd said only—"he is no longer interested".

The next move was a series of discussions in London with the French Government, on April 28th and 29th, at which the precarious position of Czechoslovakia was the principal concern, and the British Government repeated its caution that "His Majesty's Government found it difficult to commit themselves at this stage to sending even a comparatively small force to the continent in certain eventualities. The Government of the day

---

Carl Goerdeler and the German Resistance.   † Ibid.

might decide to do so or might not." M. Daladier made the shrewd observation that "he felt it would be wrong to believe that Germany was today in a position to meet every kind of military requirement". This was, as we shall see, a correct estimate, but the British insisted that military action in defence of Czechoslovakia was impossible. Instead a form of warning to Germany was drawn up which might be used in a crisis by the British Ambassador in Berlin if the situation became acute. Meanwhile the opinion gained ground in British official quarters that Herr Henlein might be used to procure a settlement with the Czechs on the basis of autonomy—a settlement against which M. Delbos had protested in the previous November as unreal and perilous to the Czechoslovak state.

Early in May Sir Robert Vansittart "received indirectly a feeler" from Konrad Henlein that "he would like to come to London and see me again". They had already met in October 1937, and there was then some hope in the minds of the British Government that Henlein might be used to find a solution to the Czechoslovak dilemma. The feeler came through Mr. Robert Hadow, as First Secretary in Prague, who was convinced that Henlein could be used in this way.

It is evident now from the published German documents that on May 12th Henlein visited Ribbentrop in Berlin, discussed his mission to Britain with the Foreign Minister, and informed him that he intended to see Vansittart and "certain other personalities". These included Winston Churchill. Baron von Weizsaecker noted in a secret memorandum that "Herr Henlein will deny in London that he is acting on instructions from Berlin," and would say that his Karlsbad speech demanding Sudeten-German autonomy was not known in Berlin before its publication.* Since Winston Churchill made a note of his conversation recording that Henlein offered "his word of honour" that he had never received orders or even directives (Weisungen) from Berlin, it is worth noting that Henlein was signing letters to Ribbentrop in 1937 as "Your obedient servant," and that he told Hitler on March 28th, 1938, in the presence of Hess, Ribbentrop and others that he could "only be a substitute" for the Fuehrer, whereupon Hitler exclaimed:

"I will stand by you: from tomorrow you will be my Vice-Governor."

* Documents on German Foreign Policy, Series D, Vol. II.

It is further recorded by Henlein in a memorandum among the German documents that "the Fuehrer appreciates the great success which Henlein has had in England and has requested him to go again to London, as soon as he possibly can, and to continue to use his influence with a view to ensuring no intervention by Britain".

A minute by Ribbentrop on March 29th attached to the German record of the Hitler-Henlein meeting refers to "the necessity of keeping the . . . discussion strictly secret" and mentions also "the principles imparted to Konrad Henlein yesterday afternoon by the Fuehrer personally". These quotations should dispose of any doubts about the *word of honour* of Konrad Henlein to Winston Churchill.

Both Neville Chamberlain and Lord Halifax thought that it would be wise to respond to the overture from Henlein and accordingly Sir Robert invited him to dinner at 44 Park Street on May 13th, together with Group Captain Malcolm Christie former British air attaché in Berlin, an active colleague of Vansittart in intelligence matters. They discussed the Sudeten-German problem for four hours. It was clear that even under seal of secrecy Henlein could not be allowed to meet British ministers. He soon dropped any pretence of secrecy about his visit and exploited it, though he avoided questions from the British press with an air of discreet mystery. Sir Robert recorded in a report on this visitor that he thought Henlein had behaved well and been discreet, but he began his conversation by telling the Sudeten-German leader that of late "he had been no longer ostensibly the moderate Henlein that I had known and appreciated in previous years. . . . He was now going too far and some of his demands exceeded the bounds of the possible. . . ."

Henlein in reply argued that when he had been moderate, nobody had listened to him. Sir Robert urged upon him another effort on the side of moderation and, to his doubts as to serious offers being made by the Czechoslovak Government, rejoined that he was sure serious offers would be made. Herr Henlein would get a very large measure of satisfaction without the risk of war, but it would be quite unworkable to set up a Nazi state within the boundaries of a democratic country, and other means must therefore be found of satisfying his legitimate requirements.

"I retained the general impression . . . from the whole

conversation . . . that I was, as in previous years, speaking to a wise and reasonable man . . . I found Herr Henlein far more reasonable and amenable than I had dared to hope, and I am sure that he will desire to remain so, unless he is too much interfered with by German pressure from across the border, for it is certain that there is a very strong party in Germany which would like to block any agreement, and would stop at nothing to achieve this dead end. . . . We parted on as friendly terms as ever. He repeated again that he was still out for a policy of conciliation, but said most definitely two or three times that this would be the last occasion. . . .

"If only the Czechoslovak Government will take its opportunity . . ." reflected Sir Robert, "we shall be helping both Herr Henlein and ourselves by putting really strong pressure on Berlin not to interfere with any acceptable solution; but it is certain that the pressure will have to be strong to be effective. . . . If for any reason the opening thus created could not be utilised, I fear that the day will be carried in Berlin by the party that aims at nothing but the dismemberment of Czechoslovakia with a view to facilitating Germany's eastward drive for which the complete domination of Europe is a prerequisite. If such a domination were established we should be confronted with a position which we have for centuries endeavoured to prevent with the instinctive knowledge that any lasting hegemony in Europe must of necessity reduce this country to a second-class power. I feel, however, that there is some slight chance of avoiding this fatal consummation by means other than the alternative method of preventing it, which would probably mean a European war."*

It is impossible to avoid the criticism that Vansittart and the Secret Service ought to have known of Herr Henlein's close association with Ribbentrop and Hitler, though Sir Alexander Cadogan tells me that "Van was soon cured of his illusion". Had he been fully aware of it, Sir Robert might have used stronger and more effective words and esteemed his guest a little less. This time Sir Robert was for a short time deceived, since autonomy was clearly to be no more than a stepping stone to the destruction of Czechoslovakia. Within a few days of his meeting with Henlein in London, events in Central Europe gave a new and fateful impetus to the crisis over Czechoslovakia. The

* Vansittart Papers.

British *démarche* of May 21st took place and Sir Nevile Henderson used the warning formula that had been drawn up with the French in London on April 29th.

Sir Nevile Henderson was an emotional man. Tall, lean, fastidiously dressed, he had the outward points of a British diplomat without any inner strength. His staff complained of him that he showed a bullying temper to his subordinates and he had left behind him an unpopular reputation in the Argentine. I had met him once or twice between November 1937 and the spring of 1938 when his main theme was that German aims were limited. His Services staff were more impressive than he was. Colonel F. N. Mason-Macfarlane, his military attaché, Captain Thomas Troubridge, the naval attaché, and also Sir George Ogilvie-Forbes, the Minister and sometime Chargé d'Affaires, did not share his widespread opinion that as soon as Germany had obtained its demands on behalf of Germans abroad, Herr Hitler would settle down as a peaceable European. But such was the conviction that Henderson put forward to me before and after the invasion of Austria. Not one of the British and American journalists who then observed the Berlin scene shared the view of the Ambassador, and none of his staff supported it. When I wished to discuss events in Germany with a British diplomat, I preferred to call on Sir George. In his room in the Chancery of the British Embassy we met regularly and discussed the situation with lowered voices. I was told that listening devices had been detected implanted in its walls from the adjoining premises of the Hotel Adlon.

Early in May 1938, I made such a visit and discussed with Sir George a conversation with a German acquaintance which I had memorised just after the fall of Austria. This German, a landowner in Pomerania known for his past monarchist activities, had given me some curious information.

As I sat in a quiet and little-known club in the Bendlerstrasse of Berlin, he had approached and spoken a few short sentences, any one of which would have been enough to send him to instant execution. A short greying figure with hard eyes and precise gestures, Ewald von Kleist-Schmenzin, Head of the Monarchist League spoke like a man with no words to waste:

"You do not believe this is the end, do you? Hitler has his plans against France, Holland, Belgium, Denmark, Russia, against England and the new world. He wants to annex Canada and Siberia. That is by the way. Mad? Yes, he is mad, but he is in command of his faculties.

"Now let us think of the situation as it is at present. Czechoslovakia is the next step. The army insists that this is a real military venture and must be entirely organised by the army. Hitler and his supporters reply that the Party can deal with the Czechoslovak problem and that the army has only to obey instructions. One thing I know for certain. If England says no, if only through diplomatic channels, the adventure must be put off. Hitler has admitted this, and what he fears like the plague is that England will caution him. For he must give way, and that will be a grave blow to his prestige in Germany. Tell your friends in London that we cannot make war yet. The army has few reservists and no reserves of material. The people are against war. The fortifications in the West are not half completed. The Nazis bluff. Their bluff carries them far, but in the end there is only one possibility, defeat. Do not publish anything that I tell you, but let them know in England that the General Staff needs a sheet anchor. The British Government alone can throw it to them by a firmly spoken word."

Hitler feared a British diplomatic intervention, *Wie die Pest*, like the plague, was the phrase that he had used. Then the Head of the Monarchist League abruptly left the room and I had not seen him since. A month and more had gone by since that conversation, and what prompted me to discuss it with Sir George was a Berlin rumour that the National-Socialist Motor Cycle Corps was about to attempt a mass unarmed ride into the Sudeten-German areas of Czechoslovakia in order to create incidents. Sir George carefully wrote out the sense of the conversation. He forwarded it to London, and though it is nowhere reproduced in the published documents, I have no doubt that it reached Sir Robert Vansittart in the first week of May or soon thereafter.

Sir Nevile Henderson is shown to have warned Lord Halifax on May 18th that German "extremists are pressing for an immediate showdown in the confident hope that the Western powers will once more accept a *fait accompli*. . . . This is confirmed by the French Consul General in Munich who was told by a highly placed person in the Brown House that the Czechoslovak question would be settled next month. There is some hope of my being able to exercise moderating influence, if I keep in touch with the German Government as continuously and as closely as possible."*

On May 19th the British acting Consul in Dresden reported "strong reason to believe German troops are concentrating in Southern Silesia and Northern Austria". Mr. Newton reported from Prague that "it is obvious that the Czechoslovak State cannot afford to allow its authority to lose all respect in the German and mixed areas". On the same day the British Consul-General in Vienna reported a convoy of German lorries moving towards the Czechoslovak border, and on May 20th the Czechoslovak Ministry of Foreign Affairs reported concentrations of German troops in Saxony. On the following day the Czechoslovak General Staff was reported as believing in a German general plan for provocation and intimidation. Mr. Newton cabled that "the Minister of Foreign Affairs is very uneasy and I fear with good reason". These samples show that both the Ambassadors in Prague and Berlin were alarmed, and though not convinced of a big military plan Colonel Mason-Macfarlane probably estimated the picture correctly on May 24th that "as long as German units continue to be moved about so much as they are being moved this spring, it will be difficult in moments of great tension to avoid sinister conclusions being drawn".

Sir Nevile made urgent enquiries of Baron von Weizsaecker on the evening of May 20th, but was told that the reports of German troop concentrations were "utter nonsense". The Ambassador had the spirit to ask the German Under-Secretary to remind General Keitel, the source of these denials, that he had given similar assurances to the British military attaché on March 11th, though the German troops had then already received orders to move into Austria.

Only a pale version of the pressures exerted by Britain on Germany this week-end is reflected in the published British documents. For Lord Halifax heightened the impression of alarm in direct telephone conversations with the British Ambassador on the open line, and there was some question of a special railway coach being ordered to take British families out of Berlin. Of this feature of the nerve war there is no trace in the official dispatches since published.

Sir Nevile Henderson reported on the morning of May 21st

* Documents on British Foreign Policy, Series III, Vol. I.

that he had called on Herr von Ribbentrop as instructed and "found him in a highly excitable and pugnacious frame of mind. He began by complaining that without previous agreement of the Ministry of Foreign Affairs I had informed Reuters last night of the German denial as regards military preparations." The German minister then flourished telegrams alleging 100 incidents in Czechoslovakia, and said that "Germany could not wait much longer" before going to the help of the Sudeten-Germans.

The instructions of Lord Halifax to Sir Nevile Henderson were that "you should add that if in spite of His Majesty's Government's efforts a conflict arises, France has obligations to Czechoslovakia and will be compelled to intervene if there is a German aggression. In such circumstances His Majesty's Government could not guarantee that they would not become involved." Henderson read these words slowly to Ribbentrop at a second interview that evening, and mentioned the speech of March 24th in which Mr. Chamberlain had defined British obligations. Ribbentrop listened carefully and took notes. Sir Nevile reported that the German Foreign Minister "was clearly perturbed by my reference to the Prime Minister's speech . . . but said that if the worst came to the worst, Germany would fight again as in 1914."

M. Georges Bonnet, the new French Foreign Minister, heartened by this British grit, called a press conference in Paris next day and reaffirmed that the French Government would honour its treaty obligation. This was almost too much for Lord Halifax for he quickly alerted Sir Eric Phipps that "His Majesty's Government have given the most serious warnings to Berlin, and these should have a prospect of success in deterring Germany from extreme courses. But it might be highly dangerous if the French Government were to read more into those warnings than is justified by their terms." Sir Eric read this message slowly to M. Bonnet, who listened carefully and also took notes.

By the 23rd May the heat had largely gone out of the crisis. There was no violence and no military action. There was an embarrassing strain of jubilation in the British and French press comments, it being asserted that "Hitler had climbed down". The truculence of Ribbentrop and the many reports of German troop movements were forgotten as the partisans of Anglo-Nazi understanding sought to establish that there never

had been any German intention to move that week-end. There
are a few unexplained points in the German documents, such as
Colonel Zeitzler's reply from the Supreme Headquarters of the
Wehrmacht on May 21st, recorded in a Foreign Ministry
minute, that "the movements in Austria which had been
intended for May 20th had not yet begun. . . ." Neville
Chamberlain on the 28th May wrote to a relative that "the
more I hear about last weekend, the more I feel what a d——
close thing it was". He seems in retrospect not to have shared
the obsessive regrets of Sir Nevile Henderson about the action
taken.

Had there been that farsighted wisdom which Sir Robert
had been led to imagine in Konrad Henlein, the Sudeten-
German leader would at this moment have started his
negotiations with Dr. Hodza, the Czechoslovak Prime Minister.
Instead he refused any further contacts with the authorities,
alleging that he would be negotiating under duress, since the
Czechoslovak Army had been mobilised in the heat of the crisis.
Indeed he seemed to insist that the Czech Army would have to
return to its normal footing before he would talk.

Herr Henlein began to play on his influence with Sir Robert
Vansittart in a series of messages sent through the British
Embassy in Prague, the first of which alleged there to have been
no progress in his talks with Dr. Hodza. He declared that the
"intense indignation of the Sudeten-Germans would soon
oblige him to make written demands, but not demands beyond
those stated in London."* In his talk with Mr. Churchill
Henlein had envisaged a plebiscite on the questions of the
status quo, autonomy for the Sudeten-German areas, or an
Anschluss with Germany.

In one way and another it soon became apparent to Hitler
and Ribbentrop that the British *démarche* of May 21st was in
reality no more than a restatement of Mr. Chamberlain's speech
of March 24th, that the diplomatic action was perhaps more
energetic than the actual wording warranted, and that Hitler
had lost considerably in his prestige by his attitude towards
Czechoslovakia. From a source with contacts in the German
Chancellery I noted at the time an infuriated exclamation of
Hitler:

"England, das werde ich Ihnen nie vergessen!" Nobody

* Documents on German Foreign Policy, Series D.

today vouches for the story that he rolled, like the Salian emperor, on the carpet and bit away at it, though that story was current in Berlin in May 1938. What was of great seriousness was that General Keitel on May 20th, the day before the British *démarche*, had happened to send to the Fuehrer the existing stragetic directives to the Wehrmacht with a reminder that they were valid only until September 30th, 1938, and would need renewal for the period October 1st onwards. The top secret draft submitted to Hitler contained as statement of intent that "it is not my intention to smash Czechoslovakia by military action in the immediate future without provocation, unless an unavoidable development in the political condition within Czechoslovakia forces the issue". Hitler in the fury of his diplomatic reverse altered this passage to read in the approved draft dated May 30th, 1938:

"Case 11, War on two fronts with main effort in the South-East.

"It is my unalterable decision to smash Czechoslovakia in the near future. It is the business of the political leadership to await or bring about the suitable moment from a political and military point of view."

Colonel Humphrey Stronge, the British military attaché in Prague, formed the impression that the Czechoslovak General Staff had exploited the May 21st crisis to force a showdown by mobilising. He was called to General Headquarters soon afterwards and invited by the Czechoslovak Chief of General Staff to inspect the frontier fortifications. For a week he toured the girdle of steel and concrete on the northern and western frontiers of Bohemia. In the south opposite Austria the ring was incomplete and the terrain open. Elsewhere the defences were impressive, and Colonel Stronge reported in this sense to Lord Halifax in June 1938 during a London conference of British military attachés from Europe. The Foreign Secretary asked him searching questions about the extent of fortifications. Lord Halifax must therefore have been aware that autumn that in transferring the Sudeten-German territories the rind of the Czech defences was being broken.

CHAPTER XIII

WHAT HAS BEEN DONE

"Nor did we know of the definite plans that Hitler had made with his Generals for an organised campaign of successive offensives," wrote Lord Templewood, who saw himself after the war as the apologist for British Cabinet policy in pre-war years. "At this time we were as much in the dark over Hitler's real intentions as we were over Stalin's. Very little military intelligence slipped through to us from the German side. Now as the result of the publication of the German secret papers, we know that Hitler was constantly planning acts of aggression. The Hossbach memorandum ... shows that as early as November 5th, 1937, he was preparing his future campaigns for the domination of Europe."*

This plea of ignorance was no more true than the assertion quoted in the previous chapter that the Chamberlain government did not depart from the constitutional Cabinet procedure in making its decisions about Czechoslovakia.

On the matter of intelligence enough has been published in the official documents to show how clearly Great Britain was warned. I now add some hitherto unpublished correspondence from myself to Lord Lloyd of Dolobran written in August and September 1938. This was communicated to Sir Robert Vansittart and to some members of the Cabinet. Compared with this information on German intentions, that upon which the British Cabinet had to act in August 1914 must have been scanty and uncertain. The first news appears to have been collected by the Central Department of the Foreign Office.

A letter from Mr. William Strang, Head of the Central Department, written to Sir Nevile Henderson in Berlin on July 21st gave an account of information reaching London that suggested a deliberate German plan to attack Czechoslovakia in the autumn of 1938. Colonel Mason-Macfarlane in Berlin studied the letter and admitted the possibility, but commented that "on the other hand I am continually coming across evidence that Germany as a whole is not ready for war this

* *Nine Troubled Years.*

autumn and does not want it. As far as the Army High Command is concerned, I am convinced that they are definitely opposed to war. Unfortunately the decision does not rest with the Army, and I have continually stressed the fact that under certain circumstances Herr Hitler will almost certainly march against Czechoslovakia without warning. But I am quite unconvinced that the military evidence now at our disposal indicates a clear intention to march this autumn."*

Sir Nevile Henderson reported in a letter to Mr. Strang on July 28th that, "I hear that a movement is on foot among the forward section of the Nazi Party to stage some sort of test mobilization on August 15th. . . . A demonstration is, I understand, all that it is intended to be. The Army leaders are . . . strongly opposed to the idea. . . . Its scope may have been greatly exaggerated. . . ."

The Ambassador pinned some hopes on the mediation mission to Prague of Lord Runciman, and was disappointed that Ribbentrop regarded it without enthusiasm. On August 1st Sir Nevile reported to Lord Halifax the German explanation of its announced autumn programme of military exercises which included the calling up of reservists in September. He described it on August 3rd as an "unusual step, a mixture of bluff and real menace. . . . If force is to be used in the last resort, this means by October." But he concluded that "the German nation in general is just as frightened and I believe the army also is just as perturbed as anybody else at the idea of war".†

The conclusion of the Military Attaché was that "I think we can summarise matters by saying that, while it is reasonably certain that there is no intention or desire on the part of the Army to take action against Czechoslovakia, the possibility that the Government may have intentions in this respect is becoming much greater, and they are forcing the Army to take steps which may well produce a crisis." Sir Nevile on August 4th saw the possibility of Hitler using force against Czechoslovakia in the autumn as "more real".

Colonel Mason-Macfarlane had strongly emphasised in other dispatches that August 15th was a dangerous date. He was recalled to London and questioned by the Cabinet, particularly by Sir John Simon, who cross-examined the Military Attaché

* Documents on British Foreign Policy, Series III, Vol. II,
† Ibid., Series III, Vol. II,

in legal style. "It was hard to convince them," Colonel Macfarlane told me afterwards, "that if the crisis did not happen on
that day, it might very well do so on some subsequent date."

My own information in a report dated August 3rd and sent
in confidence to my friend Lord Lloyd gave the true date—
September 28th.

Highly Confidential   3.8.38.
                                                              Berlin.

The situation in Germany at present appears to me as
follows. Germany is willing to bide her time, while Lord
Runciman is negotiating with the Prague government. This
is expected to take a month. Early in September there is
party day at Nuremberg, which lasts till about September
15th. Several of the military attachés here fear that a coup
on Czechoslovakia will follow—that is, at the end of September.

I learn from a German source of absolute integrity that
September 28th has been chosen and fixed as "x-tag", which
can be said to be the equivalent of "zero day" in the British
terminology. This information came directly to my informants early last week (about July 26th) from one of the three
highest Generals in the German High Command. This
resolution is not yet known to the commanding Generals.

Almost simultaneously I heard from another German
source of a conference that took place on or about July 14th,
a rough sketch of which I include here. I cannot vouch for
the accuracy of the conversations, which I reproduce in
direct speech. But I am satisfied that the source had no
interest in or motive of embellishing the account.

To return to the date mentioned above. This date coincides
with the highest strength of the German forces this year. It
is no reason for placation to be told that Germany is not
indulging in big manœuvres this autumn. Rather the
opposite. Manœuvres will take place between Divisions, all
over Germany. About 400,000 reservists have been called
up, many of whom have done service either last year or the
year before, while numerous men of reserve ages who have
hitherto done no training, have not been called up. Moreover, the reservists are being formed into reservist divisions,
rather than mixed with the conscripts serving this year. This

measure, military observers tell me, is without precedent in peacetime. Journeys abroad for reserve officers have been forbidden as from August 1st without special permission. The conscripts of October 1936, who should be released at the end of September are to be kept under arms until October 26th. A ban on holidays for officials in posts important in case of war may be introduced on August 15th, unless the foreign situation clears up.

The extreme haste with which the Western Front fortifications are being completed, and innumerable small military precautions and orders could be quoted to bear out the theory that Germany intends business this autumn. I regard the rather spectacular law forbidding the active officers of foreign powers to visit German frontier zones to have been presented in a manner calculated to have a certain psychological effect on Germans and foreign Governments alike. It was announced suddenly in the press, even before the law had been drafted.

In April, observers here considered that a firm warning by Great Britain would be sufficient to deter Germany from aggression. Now behind any such warning would have to be an unmistakable preparedness to act. Otherwise the sharpest warnings will be ignored or met with brutal rejection. Only preparations of a definitely military nature of Great Britain can convince Germany that the politeness of the British is not a sign of weakness. It is believed in Berlin that during the royal visit to Paris, Lord Halifax and M. Bonnet came to the agreement that they would not intervene with arms if Czechoslovakia were attacked. This strengthened the warlike spirit here. Moreover Lord Halifax is thought of here as a man who is prepared to give Germany plenty of rope in the pious hope that at some not too distant date she will hang herself with it.

I understand that if France should mobilise, Germany would put herself on the defensive on the Western Front. If France should attack Germany, this defensive would be maintained. If, on the other hand, Great Britain joined France; or, *when*, the Germans would take the offensive, through Holland.

The conference of which I spoke earlier was held by Hitler about July 14th. Present were Marshal Goering, General

Keitel, Dr. Goebbels, Chief of Police Himmler, and one other man whose name I do not know. A resumé of the conversation follows. Hitler spoke:

No one was to blame for the state of affairs on May 21st, he said, which was regrettable, since it damaged the prestige of the Reich abroad. He had decided to partition Czechoslovakia with Poland and Hungary within the next six months. The German forces would have to do with a courageous enemy. Therefore, if the conflict was short, it would be bloody. If France attacked, and Great Britain joined in at once, Germany would be ruined. But he, the Leader, intended to choose his time and had arranged that Great Britain would in the first few days be so fully occupied in Palestine and elsewhere, that she would have no desire to intervene. As for the French, he would make the semblance of preparations for an attack on France on the Western Front, which would prompt the French to put themselves on the defensive.

Here General Keitel intervened and remarked that, as the Rhineland was full of French spies, the simulated preparations for an offensive would not deceive the French.

Hitler replied that it did not matter whether the French intelligence service in the Rhineland was deceived or not. They would not be believed, as the French nation was in that state of mind in which it would be very willing to adopt a defensive attitude, but extremely unwilling to attack. He would make it easy for the French to assume the defensive, and would expect Dr. Goebbels, with his machinery, to make the threat appear substantial.

General Keitel demurred and remained silent. Thereupon the conference broke up, and a courier was sent to Schwerin (I think) where General von Brauchitsch, General von Fritsch and General Beck were staying. General von Brauchitsch, when he heard the name of the courier, at first refused to receive him, saying that he had not ordered him to visit him. The courier replied that he had a special message from the Chancellor, whereupon he was received and discharged his mission.

With regard to this account, it is interesting to note two rumours: one, that both Keitel and von Brauchitsch quarreled with Hitler recently; two, that General von

Fritsch will be given command of the Western armies in the case of a war with France.

A plan exists for disabling Great Britain in the event of a general war, mainly by the use of aircraft.

I understand that the most serious aspect of a general war for Germany would be her munition supplies, which are already sufficient for a war on all fronts of three months duration, and could be made to last, at the same calculated rate of consumption, for one or two months beyond that.

I wrote in a covering letter of August 3rd:

I think you can make use of this paper. It would interest your friends in the Army. Not even the commanding generals here know about the date which I mention. It comes from the C-in-C himself. There are perhaps nine men in Germany who know it, or shall I say, are authorised to know it— Hitler, Goering, Goebbels, Himmler, the Chief of Supreme Command, the C-in-C, the Chief of General Staff, perhaps Heydrich.

The Espionageabwehrdienst (Counter-espionage service) of the War Ministry believes that a war would be disastrous to Germany. It has therefore asked a good friend of mine to go to London and see whether he cannot find material to support the theory that Great Britain will intervene. (They bother less about France.) He is a courageous and upright gentleman although suspect to the Nazis. Perhaps you can remember his name. It was his point of view which impressed you over the breakfast table in April. I think that pains should be taken to supply him with support for his opinions.

Yours
very sincerely,
Ian G. Colvin.

This letter reached Lord Lloyd and was passed on by him at a time when the attention of Vansittart had been focused on the increase of Italian military aid to Spain. On August 6th his attention came suddenly back to Germany and he wrote to Lord Halifax:

"It will not be safe to defer much longer a warning to

Germany on the lines of May 21st. A war spirit is being clearly whipped-up and every preparation is being made, both as regards fortifying the frontier and calling up troops. The warning may require a little more timing; but we must be very careful not to put it off until it is too late. The danger will obviously be there in September. I consider mid-August the latest date. Safety would be better served if we spoke earlier. Otherwise the military programme will have gone too far. Personally I feel most strongly that we should act now."

The visitor to London mentioned in my letter was the same Ewald von Kleist-Schmenzin, whose opinion on the fine balance between Party and Army over Czechoslovakia may have been useful to the Foreign Office at the time of the crisis of May 21st, 1938. I have related at some length in *Chief of Intelligence* his relationship with Admiral Wilhelm Canaris, Chief of German Military Intelligence, and how it was decided to send him to London in the middle of August to sound the British on their intentions in the light of certain information that he was able to impart. I have nothing to alter in that account, but now I am able to add the memorandum of Sir Robert Vansittart to Lord Halifax, showing what impression the German conspirator made on him and how emphatic his warning was.

It did not seem essential that Kleist and his mission should become known to Sir Nevile Henderson, though at the same time I could not expect that the Ambassador would not learn through British officials in Berlin of his identity and his purpose in London. Herr von Kleist was not an official person and in furthering his visit to London I was acting independently. But it was necessary for him to apply for a British visa, and at that stage British passport officials and the military attaché were interested to know from me the nature of his business in London. I told them that Herr von Kleist carried letters of introduction to Mr. Winston Churchill and Lord Lloyd; and was one of those Germans in secret opposition to Hitler. Perhaps because his name did not figure in the Embassy record of leading personalities in Germany there were doubts about him. For that matter neither did the name of Admiral Wilhelm Canaris, the Chief of German Military Intelligence, appear in the Embassy record, and quite a number of men of importance besides. The Embassy was not well informed in 1938 about the conspiracy that lay against Hitler.

On August 16th Sir Nevile Henderson telegraphed to London that according to information given to the Military Attaché, a Herr von Kleist would come by air to London on August 18th as an emissary of the moderates in the German general staff. Sir Nevile added that he understood that Herr von Kleist carried letters to leading politicians and would seek "material with which to convince *the Chancellor* [*sic*] of the strong possibility of Great Britain intervening should Germany take violent action against Czechoslovakia." This was not quite accurate, as the evidence of serious British intentions was sought on behalf of General Ludwig Beck, Chief of the German General Staff, who had said to him before he left for England, so Herr von Kleist told me afterwards:*

"Bring me certain proof that England will fight if Czechoslovakia is attacked and I will make an end of this régime."

His journey was not detected either by the Gestapo or the press. Kleist arrived at the Park Lane Hotel on the evening of the 17th August and made use of his letters of introduction. His arrival was instantly reported to Lord Halifax by Sir Robert Vansittart, who addressed to him a long note of their conversation which faithfully reflects the same views and the same personality as I had known in Berlin.

August 18th, 1938

I spoke to you this morning about Herr von Kleist. In the afternoon about 4 o'clock I received an application from him to see me. He said that I was one of the few people in this country with whom he wished to speak and would be able to speak freely. I had to decide at once whether I would see him or not and I came to the conclusion that it would be a mistake to refuse to see him, and I therefore did so. I need hardly add that I did not see him at the Foreign Office.

Herr von Kleist at once opened up with the utmost frankness and gravity. He said (and this coincides with a great deal of other information which I have given you from entirely different sources) that war was now a certainty unless we stopped it. I said "do you mean an extreme danger?" He answered: "No, I do not mean an extreme danger, I mean a complete certainty." I said, "Do you mean to say that the extremists are now carrying Hitler with them?" He said:

* In November 1938.

"No, I do not mean that. There is only one real extremist and that is Hitler himself. He is the great danger and he is doing this entirely on his own. He receives a great deal of encouragement from Herr von Ribbentrop who keeps telling him that when it comes to the showdown neither France nor England will do anything." (You will remember that I gave you the same information from an entirely different source this morning as to Ribbentrop's present attitude and influence.)

Herr von Kleist continued: "I do not want to bother to talk about Herr von Ribbentrop. He is nothing but an evil Yes-man and although his influence is now cast in the wrong direction by encouraging Hitler he is not of sufficient consequence to matter. Hitler has made up his mind for himself. All the Generals in the German Army who are my friends know it and they *alone* know it for a certainty and know the date on which the mine is to be exploded."

I said: "Do you mean that such people as Goebbels and Himmler are not pushing Hitler in that direction as well?" Herr von Kleist said, "I repeat that I discount them. Hitler has taken this decision by himself. I am doubtful whether Goebbels and Himmler are really pushing in that direction. In any case they do not really matter."

I said: "What about Goering?" Herr von Kleist replied: "Goering would sooner avoid war but he will not and cannot do anything to stop it and that goes for my friends in the Army also although they are much more opposed to war than is Goering." I said: "Do you mean *all* the Generals?" He replied: "Yes, all and without exception, and I include even General von Reichenau who has hitherto passed for being the most extreme and forward of them all. They are all dead against war but they will not have the power to stop it unless they get encouragement and help from outside. As I have already told you, they know the date and will be obliged to march at that date."

I said: "What, according to you, is the date?" He laughed and said: "Why of course you know it." I disclaimed any such knowledge. Herr von Kleist said: "Well anyhow, your Prime Minister knows it." I said I did not think he was right there and I added that I was questioning him about the date that he had in mind because it seemed to me a matter of some importance if, as he thought, the adventure could still be stopped, because a good deal must naturally turn in such a case upon the amount of time that we had ahead of us. Herr von Kleist appeared still very incredulous that we should not be more exactly informed as to Hitler's timetable, but when I questioned him again he said: "After the 27th September it will be too late." (You will remember that in a letter that Lord Lloyd sent to you he mentioned that a friend of his in army circles had told him that the 28th September was the date.)

I said: "If you feel really sure that the date you mention is the appointed time, up till what time do you think that any deterrent influence could be exercised? by which I mean by what time will the preparations for adventure have gone too far for us possibly to stop it, if, as you think, we could?" He replied: "I think you could stop it up till the middle of September, but it would be still safer to stop it before the Party Day."

I said: "What means do you recommend for stopping it?" He replied: "There are two. Firstly, since Hitler now believes that the attitude of France and England in May was entirely bluff, you must make him understand that this is not the case." I said: "The French have already proclaimed their intentions very clearly on at least half a dozen public occasions, and the Prime Minister spoke very clearly on March 24th in the House of Commons." He replied: "That is not enough. Those impressions have waned and, as I have already told you, Ribbentrop keeps telling Hitler that from sure sources he knows that England and France would do nothing." I said: "What is your second remedy?" He replied: "A great part of the country is sick of the present régime and even a part that is not sick of it is terribly alarmed at the prospect of war, and the conditions to which war will lead them. I have already told you that the army, including Reichenau, is unanimous against it if they can get any support. I wish that one of your leading statesmen would make a speech which would appeal to this element in Germany, emphasising the horrors of war and the inevitable general catastrophe to which it would lead." I said: "As regards the second part of your remedy I should have thought that the proposal would have the contrary effect, that any attempt on the part of any foreigner overtly to divide the country would be more calculated to unite it and would prove a handicap rather than an assistance to those who wish to avoid disaster."

Herr von Kleist did not abandon his idea in spite of this dissuasion and on the other hand he adhered very firmly and persistently to his first remedy which, as you will remember, is the same as that which I have been reporting to you as being the desire and the almost open request of a number of other German moderates who have been in communication with me during these past weeks.

Herr von Kleist is seeing Lord Lloyd tonight and Mr. Winston Churchill tomorrow. He does not wish to have any contacts with people influential in the press. He says that if Hitler carries the day and plunges his country into war he will anyhow be one of the first to be killed, and that he has anyhow come out of the country with a rope round his neck to stake his last chance of life on preventing the adventure. He added further that he did not wish to see any members of the Labour Party. He knew already what their feelings were and what they would say to him and he did not wish to take any additional and unnecessary risks as regards his own life which was already in extreme danger. He had already been imprisoned three times on various pretexts. He is going back to Germany on Tuesday and it is possible that he may ask to see me again between now and then, but he repeated that with the exception of myself and one or two others he did not wish to enlarge the circle of his contacts. He had come over here to give the warning that we were no longer in danger of war but in the presence of the certainty of it, and to risk his own existence in doing so. He talked a good deal about the general lines of the policy of the party he represented (he said that he was "a Conservative, a Prussian and a Christian") and the lines of the policy he would like to see pursued were essentially reasonable. I do not, however, think that it is necessary to burden this paper with them. He added that there was no prospect whatever of any reasonable policy being followed by Germany so long as Hitler was at the head of affairs but that he believed that if war was avoided on this occasion as it had been in May, it would be the prelude to the end of the régime and a renascence of a Germany with whom the world could deal.

In conclusion he said that his exit from Germany had been facilitated by his friends in the army on whose unanimity he had enlarged earlier and that he has long been on the most intimate terms with them. They had taken the risk and he had taken the risk of coming out of Germany at this crucial moment although he had no illusions as to the fate that awaited him if he failed; but he made it abundantly clear, as I have said earlier, that they alone could do nothing without assistance from outside on the lines he had suggested.

Lord Halifax sent the Vansittart memorandum over to Number 10 Downing Street, and next day the Prime Minister commented from Chequers. There was some shrewdness in his letter, but also the hard determination not to be drawn out of the fixed attitude that he had taken up on March 24th in the House of Commons. He wrote:—

> Chequers, Butler's Cross,
> Aylesbury, Bucks.
> August 19th, 1938.

My dear Edward,

Just before leaving London this morning my Secretary brought me Van's account of his talk with Von Kleist. After reading it through I decided to bring it along with me to think over it a little more.

Early this morning I received an urgent request from Hutch* who telephoned that he must see me as he had important information to communicate. I saw him at 9.30. He said he had contacts with many Germans and he named one in particular but the name was unknown to me previously. He said this man was "in" with various generals and had written to say that Hitler meant business this time and it was essential if he were to be stopped that we should approach him and come to some understanding with him forthwith. When I said that I doubted if Hitler had yet made up his mind what he would do Hutch said that that was also the view of his correspondent. But Hitler would have to make up his mind before he spoke at Nürnberg. After that it would be too late to intervene.

* Major-General Lord Hutchison of Montrose.

There was really nothing new in what Hutch had to say (he left a long memorandum of his views) but perhaps it may usefully be compared with Von Kleist.

I take it that Von Kleist is violently anti-Hitler and is extremely anxious to stir up his friends in Germany to make an attempt at his overthrow. He reminds me of the Jacobites at the Court of France in King William's time and I think we must discount a good deal of what he says.

Nevertheless I confess to some feeling of uneasiness and I don't feel sure that we ought not to do something. His second remedy, that one of us should make a speech or give an inter-view in which we should, to use Van's phrase, be "more explicit" than on May 21, I reject. At any rate at present.

The first remedy is less committal and there are various ways in which we might convince Hitler that the position is no less serious than it was in May. One, which rather com-mends itself to me, is to send for Henderson and take care that everyone knew it. The procedure I suggest for your consideration is as follows.

Inform Henderson now of the substance of what Van has heard without of course disclosing the source. Ask him to comment on it and tell him that we are sufficiently impressed to be inclined to make some warning gesture. That at present we do not propose going beyond sending for him. That the date on which we should wish to see him would be Monday 29th inst. and that on receiving final instructions to come he should let it be known that he was sent for to consult about the serious position in connection with Czecho.

I think it rather a bad sign that Hitler has made no res-ponse to our communications to him.

I shall be here till Monday morning when I return to Downing St. till Wednesday afternoon. Perhaps you would turn over my suggestion and let me know what you think of it either here or there.

Yours ever,
N. Chamberlain.

A second interview took place between Herr von Kleist and Mr. Winston Churchill at Chartwell, and he met Lord Lloyd, though without striking quite the same understanding contact with him. Mr. Churchill promised as an unofficial person to set forth his views in a letter, which for the sake of security was later given to me by a British diplomat in Berlin and handed by myself to Herr von Kleist. The weight of its message lay in two paragraphs, but Mr. Churchill struck first an emphatic note:

"It is difficult for democracies in advance and in cold blood to make precise declarations, but the spectacle of an armed attack by Germany upon a small neighbour and the bloody fighting that will follow will rouse the whole British Empire and compel the gravest decisions.

"Do not, I pray you, be misled upon this point. Such a war, once started, would be fought out like the last to the bitter end, and one must consider not what might happen in the first few months, but where we should all be at the end of the third or fourth year.

"As I felt you should have some definite message to take back to your friends in Germany who wish to see peace preserved and who look forward to a great Europe in which England, France and Germany will be working together for the prosperity of the wage-earning masses, I communicated with Lord Halifax. His Lordship asks me to say on his behalf that the position of His Majesty's Government in relation to Czechoslovakia is defined by the Prime Minister's speech in the House of Commons on March 24th, 1938. The speech must be read as a whole, and I have no authority to select any particular sentence out of its context.

"Where peace and war are concerned, legal obligations are not alone involved, and, if war broke out, it would be unlikely to be confined to those who have assumed such obligations."

Carefully read, the "authorised" statement went no further than previous declarations, even though Hitler's intentions were becoming plainer. Sir Nevile Henderson was recalled from Berlin to offer his advice on this grave issue. His visit appears to have been the direct result of Herr von Kleist's information.

The views of Sir Nevile were already scattered over a series of cipher telegrams, personal letters to Lord Halifax and irascible exchanges with Orme Sargent, who put penetrating questions to him about German protestations that the Reich had no control over the Sudeten-Germans.

Even before Herr von Kleist had impressed the seriousness

of the situation on Vansittart, Lord Halifax had decided that the information reaching him warranted a warning memorandum to Hitler, which Henderson had duly handed to the Minister of the Chancellery on August 13th for direct presentation to Hitler. This warning emphasised that military measures created a situation "in which the peace of everyone of the Great Powers might be endangered". Hitler did not himself acknowledge the note, and the Foreign Ministry accepted its copy with bad grace. Ribbentrop wrote to Lord Halifax that this memorandum "has given rise to the greatest astonishment".

The extraordinary thing about Sir Nevile Henderson was that he recognised in at least two of his dispatches that it was still possible to stop Hitler at this late date.

On August 12th he wrote to Lord Halifax in a letter that "I doubt if Germany would actually go to war this year with Czechoslovakia if she was *certain* it meant British intervention." On August 22nd in a long dispatch about the whole Sudeten-German question he again put his finger on the point.

"It stands to reason that Hitler himself must equally be prepared for all eventualities. But from there to say that he had already decided on aggressive action against Czechoslovakia this autumn is, I think, untrue. . . ." There followed an amiable suggestion that Hitler wanted "a Swiss cantonal system for the Sudeten" . . . "And he may threaten the Czechs with worse in future if they cannot see sense now. I cannot believe that he will do more if we tell him that we shall *certainly* fight him if he does more. But what do we gain? Mere postponement and a rising market. That is the policy that we have been following for years with our eyes tight closed to realities."

On the previous day, however, he had transmitted a different picture contained in the report of an informant to his Military Attaché. Colonel Mason-Macfarlane now heard of a meeting at Doberitz between Hitler and his Corps Commanders at which Hitler had imparted his intention of attacking Czechoslovakia at the end of September. It contained this appreciation: "If by firm action abroad Herr Hitler can be forced at the eleventh hour to renounce his intentions, he will be unable to survive the blow. Similarly if it comes to war immediate intervention by England and France will . . . bring about the downfall of the régime." Sir Nevile commented that the informant was clearly biased and his advice largely propaganda. The information, however, could be taken seriously.

But Sir Nevile believed in *evitability*. In his letter of August 22nd he wrote: "I feel so strongly about the big British issue. Have we or have we not got to fight Germany again? The followers of the Crowe tradition in your Department argue and have long argued that it is inevitable. I regard that attitude as nothing short of disastrous. . . ." He reiterated in his last paragraph: "Defeatism to my mind is saying that we must fight Germany again, when there is still a chance and a big one that we need never do so . . . I would fight Germany tomorrow for a good cause but I refuse to contemplate our doing so for the Sudeten. If they were Hungarians or Poles or Rumanians or the citizens of any small nation, all England would be on their side."

Sir Nevile appeared to forget that there was a German minority in Poland too. Why did Sir Nevile continue to write private letters to Lord Halifax? Apparently to avoid the devastating minutes that Sir Orme Sargent, Vansittart and others attached to his official dispatches.

Lord Halifax at this stage put an end to his interminable writings with a curt instruction dated August 24th. "The Prime Minister and I wish to discuss the German-Czechoslovak question with you. I shall be grateful therefore if you will arrange to reach London in time for a meeting on Monday, August 29th." The Ambassador visited both sides of Downing Street.

Sir John Simon had already been instructed to make a speech warning against the danger of war in Central Europe. Sir Robert Vansittart had been authorised to tell Herr von Kleist about this in advance, and to inform him of certain naval movements that Britain would make if the situation grew more acute. The Lanark speech of Sir John was careful to say that there was "nothing to add or vary in the context" of Mr. Chamberlain's declaration on Czechoslovakia of March 24th.

In these days the idea came uppermost in the mind of Neville Chamberlain that he should be prepared to go and visit Hitler. Sir Horace Wilson ascribes the idea to Chamberlain himself, and has told me that it was first discussed in an upstairs room at 10 Downing Street between Chamberlain, Sir Nevile Henderson and himself with only a secretary present. The date of this conversation appears to have been August 30th, though it may have been August 29th. "It was quite a surprise to Sir Nevile who did not know why he had been sent for," Sir Horace told me. If this version is correct, the idea was adopted without the advice of any competent adviser other than the Ambassador. For Sir Robert Vansittart had not been consulted. Sir Alexander Cadogan was away on holiday at Le Touquet and has told me that he had no recollection of such a plan before he left on his August holiday. Yet a form of code was agreed, in which Mr. Chamberlain was to be referred to as Mr. X, and according to Sir Horace the formula was typed by one of the secretaries and given to Sir Nevile, who by the evening of August 31st was back at his post in Berlin.

The subject of a visit to Hitler by Mr. X was not mentioned at the small meeting of Cabinet ministers who gathered at 10 Downing Street on August 30th to listen to Henderson. Moreover, from the full Cabinet the plan was kept for another fourteen days, until Chamberlain made his final decision. The plan appears to have been adopted in principle without Cabinet consultation, and was only divulged when it was too late for any other course.

At the meeting of Cabinet ministers on August 30th, which Lord Templewood remembers to have lasted "most of the day", Sir Nevile was "as profoundly intent upon preventing war as was Chamberlain. Unlike Chamberlain he was governed by his nerves."* The Inner Cabinet view, reached on the basis of Henderson's advice, was that Hitler had not yet decided on military action (contrary to the Kleist report), but that the Czechs would have to make large concessions. This attitude may be compared with that of the French Military Intelligence reported on that day from the British Embassy in Paris. "Germany is ready for immediate war with Czechoslovakia, and it rests entirely with the political side if it is to be averted."

I find my own appreciation of August 30th in a letter to Lord Lloyd, drawing attention to the rising tension between Party and Army.

* *Nine Troubled Years.*

Berlin, W.35,
Kluckstr. 12 i
30.8.38.

Dear Lord Lloyd,

I enclose a note for you, which you may care to pass on to others, containing the opinions of our friend after reporting on his mission. I hope to see him again in a few days and know more. His reports have, I understand, caused the greatest concern in the War Ministry and in the Foreign Ministry, as well as a letter which he has showed to important people here.

If you read in the British press soon of the resignation of a German General, should it be General von Rundstedt, General Beck, von Brauchitsch, or another of the High Command, you may consider the situation much aggravated.

Yours
very sincerely,
(signed) Ian G. Colvin.

Memo

30.8.38.

There is much to be said against forcing out of the Czechoslovak Government concessions that could be interpreted as another personal triumph for Herr Hitler. This does not mean "slamming the door", but it does mean a firm attitude, which would refuse a patchwork solution to be rushed through before Party Week (September 5th-12th). If the democratic press gives some support to the attitude of the Czechoslovak Government, and Herr Hitler is not allowed to stampede other powers into granting him concessions immediately, this will appear as another reverse to his foreign policy. The War Ministry would like to take advantage of this to gain the power in the Third Reich from the Party.

The opposite view, which the French and British embassies here support, that very large concessions should be given, is objected to by our friend on account of his personal knowledge of Herr Hitler. He says that concessions would be swallowed by the Leader and a pretext found to attack Czechoslovakia afterwards. Similarly, the wide concessions made by Schuschnigg were immediately turned against him.

Our friend, incidentally, is of the opinion that at the present, friendly visits, such as that suggested in the British press, for Sir Kingsley Wood, would certainly do harm. It would be right to decline such an invitation, on the grounds that the time is not opportune.

Herr von Kleist had meanwhile reported to his fellow conspirators on his London visit. He tried to stiffen the General Staff, and showed the Churchill letter to Admiral Canaris and Weizsaecker, who circulated an extract from it on September 6th in restricted circulation. But the verdict of Herr von Kleist, and I remember well his emphasis, was that "I found no one in London who is prepared to wage a preventive war."

Sir Alexander Cadogan was on September 1st alerted at Le Touquet and arrived back in London on September 2nd. He spent September 3rd "catching up with papers". Lord Halifax came down from Yorkshire and on Sunday, September 4th with Sir Horace Wilson, Sir Orme Sargent and Sir Alexander Cadogan discussed the position on Henlein. They also discussed the question of another warning to Hitler, Sir Alexander noted in his diary that he supported the idea of a private warning. This had already been the subject of a dispatch from Sir Nevile Henderson.

On August 31st, immediately after his return from London, he had dined with Baron von Weizsaecker. This dinner at the British Embassy was a strange reversal of roles. The Head of the German Foreign Ministry told Sir Nevile over the table that "war in 1914 might possibly have been avoided if Great Britain had spoken in time". Sir Nevile agreed but said how difficult it was to be precise and to avoid provoking the resentment of Hitler. Baron von Weizsaecker assented but asked whether the Ambassador might not have a personal talk with Hitler at Nuremberg.

"I commented on the improbability of getting such an opportunity," reported Sir Nevile.*

Next day Ribbentrop impressed on him that on no account

* Dispatch of Sir Nevile Henderson in Series III of Documents on British Foreign Policy, Vol. II, p. 216.

was the Fuehrer to be infuriated by repetitions of the diplomatic warning of May 21st. Henderson was only too much of the same mind. May 21st was written on his heart. He took the hint that had been given by Weizsaecker and asked Ribbentrop whether Hitler "might wish to speak to him at the Nuremberg Party Congress". Ribbentrop appeared doubtful but said that he would mention it to Hitler. With war and peace in the balance, Sir Nevile was not prepared to make a firm request for an audience at Nuremberg. He asked Lord Halifax for "your authority to make my plans as seem best to me?" A telegram of September 4th authorised him to act as seemed best in the circumstances. Even a private warning, then, was not insisted upon.

But on the following day, Monday, 5th September, the German Counsellor of Embassy in London, Theo Kordt, on instructions from his brother Erich in the German Foreign Ministry, called on Sir Horace Wilson and told him that a conspiracy against Hitler existed in Germany and that a firm and unmistakable attitude by Britain and France would give the conspirators their opportunity on the day that the German mobilisation was announced. Sir Horace tells me that he remembers several visits by Theo Kordt, and that he did take him to Lord Halifax to whom Kordt repeated his information. "The plot against Hitler must have been discussed, because if there were such a plot, it would have solved a good many troubles," Sir Horace told me.* "While we may have hoped for such a development we could not see what could be done to bring it to a head."

There is no mention in the published British Foreign Office documents of the visit of the German Counsellor of Embassy to Sir Horace, though other memoranda of slighter interest written by the Chief Industrial Adviser are included. In his memoirs Erich Kordt recalls it in some detail and seems able to quote Colonel Oster, deputy to Admiral Canaris, as saying to him "If the British Government gives us through an energetic declaration the sort of argument that is understood by ordinary people, you can declare to the British Government that the military with Beck at its head will know how to prevent a war breaking out. Then there will be no longer a Hitler. Do you understand?"

* In 1963.

236

General Beck, Colonel Oster and their confidant Erich Kordt, were aware that in the event of a war on two fronts in 1938 Germany would have unfinished western fortifications with no more than seven or eight divisions to spare for the whole Western Front. They imagined that this must be known to the British and French, but the Inner Cabinet were taking no such calculations into consideration.

I am indebted to Sir Alexander Cadogan for some details in confirmation of the Kordt visit. He noted on Tuesday, 6th September that "Horace Wilson came over and said that he had been visited by Herr X who had said that he put conscience before loyalty and told him that Hitler was preparing to act against Czechoslovakia on September 20th."* They decided that "Vansittart should get Neville Chamberlain down from Scotland".

On September 7th Theo Kordt returned to the garden door of 10 Downing Street at the instance of Sir Horace, who secretly brought him together with Lord Halifax. Sir John Wheeler-Bennett writes in the *Nemesis of Power*, though without quoting his source, that on this occasion Herr Kordt gave the date that Hitler would order a general mobilisation as September 16th with the object of attacking Czechoslovakia not later than October 1st. This agreed with the information of Herr von Kleist and with mine. Erich Kordt is not so explicit about his own conversation with Lord Halifax in the account printed in the Kordt memoirs,† but relates a good deal else that his brother told Lord Halifax about the German military opposition and the need for a British declaration "that could not be clear and unmistakable enough". If this were given, "Hitler and Ribbentrop would probably not dare to start a war". If they did, the political and military circles opposed to Hitler would, as he quoted from Shakespeare "take arms against a sea of troubles and by opposing end them". On September 7th Sir Alexander wrote in his diary that: Halifax saw Herr X "who repeated his story and wants us to broadcast to the German nation".

"That would be fatal," noted Sir Alexander, who favoured a private warning. He also noted that Georges Bonnet, the French Foreign Minister, "tripped in from Paris" with news

* Some uncertainty attaches to this date, which may have been noted in haste.
† *Nicht aus den Akten*, pp. 279-81.

that negotiations over the Sudeten-Germans had been suspended. "He urged us to utter that warning." Sir Alexander sat down that evening to draft a message of warning from Neville Chamberlain to Hitler, but after a telephone call to the BBC Sir Horace said that he thought the situation was better.

The oration delivered to Lord Halifax in 10 Downing Street, imprecise though it may have been, was spoken by a man well known to them, the accredited German Chargé d'Affaires. It created a situation which warranted a full Cabinet meeting, if taken together with the intelligence reports of the past month and the worsening situation in Czechoslovakia. For whatever since has been written to disprove or discredit these unofficial approaches the fact remains that Germans in positions of responsibility were actually encouraging Britain to challenge Hitler and create a situation in which they would themselves be in the front line of danger. They must therefore have felt themselves assured of considerable support in the situation which they envisaged. But when Chamberlain reached London he called a meeting of Sir John Simon and Lord Halifax only with Sir Horace Wilson and Sir Alexander Cadogan as their advisers. They met at 11 a.m. in the Cabinet room on September 8th.

"The P.M. thought a warning not a good idea," noted Sir Alexander, "and mentioned that he wanted to visit Hitler."

This note of Sir Alexander is the first reliable record that I can find of Neville Chamberlain bringing out his cherished idea in conference. This may have been the first time that Lord Halifax heard it. For he said that "he thought they should call for Van".* Thus the Chief Diplomatic Adviser to the Government was called into what the secretaries had begun to call "the huddle", and Sir Alexander's recollection is that Sir Robert Vansittart "was asked to come over to the Inner Circle about this time, was consulted about the proposal for the Prime Minister to visit Hitler and spoke strongly against anything of the sort. He mentioned the word Canossa.

"While Vansittart spoke, Neville Chamberlain put his elbows on the Cabinet table and his head between his hands and never said a word."

As for his own views, Sir Alexander in furnishing these

* Sir A. Cadogan's notes.

details about **Vansittart**, added: "I confess I spoke for the visit and am still not entirely convinced that I was wrong." That afternoon Cadogan and Vansittart drafted a warning to be taken over to Number 10.

"The P.M. didn't like it," noted Sir Alexander. Of their respective attitudes as senior advisers on foreign affairs he noted:

"Van wants a warning. I want to prevent Hitler committing himself irretrievably."

Vansittart suggested summoning the British press and declaring that the British Government stood behind the new Czech proposals made by Dr. Hodza on September 7th, which went a long way to meet the eight points of Herr Henlein's Karlsbad speech. This was put forward to Mr. Newton in Prague, to Lord Runciman and to Sir Nevile Henderson in Berlin all of whom deprecated such a British attitude as likely to act as an irritant to Hitler. Yet the German Military Attaché in Prague confided in his British colleague on September 8th that "Herr Hitler's policy was at the moment largely one of bluff and that he would not now risk a world war," an opinion that matched with that of Leon Blum who told Sir Eric Phipps on September 9th that if Britain adopted a firm attitude, "il y a des actes de folie que meme un fou ne commet pas". Sir Eric Phipps had sent a long dispatch from Paris on September 8th representing the French Prime Minister as in a resolute mood, satisfied with the spirit of his people and prepared to meet his military obligations to Czechoslovakia.

On September 9th the deliberations of the Inner Cabinet resulted in a carefully phrased warning being drafted not to Hitler but to von Ribbentrop. It contained once more the well worn formula that in the event of a German attack on Czechoslovakia "France having become involved it seems to His Majesty's Government inevitable that the sequence of events must result in a general conflict from which Great Britain could not stand aside."*

This was cabled to Berlin and sent down on the night train to Nuremberg.

It was not, I think, the sealed envelope which Sir George Ogilvie-Forbes handed to me about this time for the Ambassador when I called on him in the British Embassy.

* Documents on British Foreign Policy, Series III, Vol. II.

For my notes are that I travelled to Nuremberg on the night train of September 7th and saw Sir Nevile Henderson on the 8th September. Everyone was writing letters to each other then, Sir Horace, Lord Halifax, Sir Alexander and Sir Nevile; the latter, having forgotten his stationery, on the fly-leaves of detective novels, which Sir Horace received with scribbled appeals not to be asked to deliver warnings. But my reception by Sir Nevile was characteristic.

The ancient city of Nuremberg was crowded with truculent Nazis roaring against the Czechs. I found my way on September 8th to the railway siding of Schweinau where the Ambassador had been installed in a wagon-lit, because the best hotels of Nuremberg were fully booked for the Nazi party. Henderson was without any kind of Staff. He let me into his cramped compartment and sat on the bunk in his maroon silk dressing gown, reading the letter. Then he spoke to me freely, as if I were aware of its contents.

"They don't understand, Colvin," he said, "I can't warn the Führer and talk policy to him at a Party occasion. If I did, he wouldn't listen, wouldn't understand it. It would have the wrong effect and send him off the deep end. They must start with the Czechs."

He began one of his interminable attacks on Dr. Benes, the Czechoslovak president, culminating with the exclamation, "Benes is a traitor, a traitor to his people." He had already said the same to others at Nuremberg. The blue official envelope was thrust deep into the pocket of his dressing gown. I never saw a man less prepared to act on his instructions.

On September 10th at 8.30 a.m. Sir Nevile Henderson managed to telephone from Nuremberg to Sir Alexander Cadogan in London. "He was violently against a warning," noted Sir Alexander. Henderson said that he could get his message in reply to his instructions as far as Cologne. Cadogan promised to send a plane to meet the messenger. By 4 p.m. on the 10th September the message was received in London. Two such dispatches were sent by Sir Nevile Henderson on that day. In a letter retransmitted by Sir George Ogilvie-Forbes in Berlin he saw that "the most fatal thing would be any repetition or appearance of repetition of May 21st threat. . . . It is essential to keep cool as atmosphere is electric. As it is, the tale of a London aeroplane is enough to start stories of another May 21st and that must be avoided at all costs. It will drive Hitler straight off the deep end."*

In the rather calmer dispatch sent via Cologne for the Cabinet he began "many good authorities believe Hitler is convinced Great Britain will not move if he resorts to force against Czechoslovakia. All are convinced that any warning in nature of *démarche* of May 21st is likely to be fatal to prospects of peace. . . . My conviction is that in the unbalanced state of mind in which I think Herr Hitler is any solemn warning, which he will regard as repetition of May 21st, however worded, will drive him to the very action which we seek to prevent." He had therefore decided not to present the warning and had told Herr von Weizsaecker, who was apparently expecting it, that "I have instructions of a kind but I have been told not to carry them out unless circumstances alter." It is difficult to think of a situation in which British diplomacy was more mistaken.

On Saturday, 10th September, it was still the Inner Cabinet that dealt with affairs of State. Neville Chamberlain first saw Sir Samuel Hoare who had come in to the Cabinet room to give him some news from Balmoral. The Prime Minister divulged his plan to visit Hitler to him, and finding his reactions favourable asked him to stay on when Lord Halifax and Sir John Simon entered the room. Lord Templewood records that besides the four ministers Wilson, Cadogan and Vansittart attended the meeting and that Chamberlain dealt with the question of another warning to Hitler before his speech of September 12th in Nuremberg. They decided against it as being more likely to excite him and push him into war. "Chamberlain then raised the question of his personal visit. The Ministers present were all agreed that it should be made, and that the Cabinet should be asked to approve it."†

Sir Alexander noted of the warning that "the Ministers decided to hold their hand. I think it right. Van furious."

He noted also that the calling up of some Royal Naval reserves had impressed the German naval attaché, who had hitherto been unable to believe that Britain would intervene in any circumstances. As the four Ministers came out of the Cabinet room, they found Winston Churchill waiting outside.

He asked for an immediate open warning to be sent to Hitler. He was the only one of them who understood.

Horace Wilson sought out Sir Alexander after dinner on the 10th September and discussed with him the planned visit to Germany (Plan Z). He had written a draft announcement of it. Sir Alec began to rewrite it next morning and discussed it with Lord Halifax. The Inner Cabinet "jiggered it about". At 5.30 p.m. on the 11th the Inner Cabinet met again and approved the re-draft. (Eventually Neville Chamberlain threw it aside and used an announcement of his own.)

They then decided not to take any further precautionary measures with the Royal Navy. "I say this is right," noted Cadogan, "though it gave Van apoplexies. . . . To increase naval moves might add to irritation."

There were more Ministers at the Cabinet room on September 12th, the day of Hitler's speech, but still no full meeting. Duff Cooper pointed out that they were meeting at the worst possible time, too late to take the advice that everybody had been offering Britain—to speak a firm warning. Too early to consider the new situation that the Nuremberg speech might create."* The Government were listening only to the advice of "the hysterical Henderson". Chamberlain rejoined tartly that Henderson was "the man on the spot".

Hitler made his speech in Nuremberg. It was full of menace, but guarded. It "pulled no triggers", wrote Sir Alexander. "We decided to sleep on it." Mr. Chamberlain had meanwhile kept the stratagem of his visit to Hitler from any wider discussion.

On September 13th the Inner Cabinet met in the morning, and in the afternoon it met again with the Services Ministers, the Minister for Co-ordination of Defence (Sir Thomas Inskip) and the Chiefs of Staff.

Sir Alexander thought "the Prime Minister quite rightly won't mobilise, but is ready to take precautionary measures". There were reports of widespread disorders in the Sudeten-German areas of Czechoslovakia. The Services Ministers were got rid of. That afternoon the decision was taken on the basis, or pretext, of two extraordinary dispatches from Sir Eric Phipps in Paris reporting the collapse of Georges Bonnet. Bonnet had approached him confidentially, he reported on

* Lord Norwich Diary.

September 10th, and asked to be told whether Britain would march with France if Czechoslovakia was attacked. Sir Eric had answered that this would depend on the nature of the German aggression. On the following day Sir Eric had read to M. Leger, Head of the French Foreign Office, the contents of a statement by Lord Halifax to the French Ambassador in London—"Whatever we might feel about any action that Germany might take in Czechoslovakia I did not think British opinion would be prepared, any more than I thought His Majesty's Government would be prepared, to enter upon hostilities with Germany on account of aggression by Germany on Czechoslovakia."* M. Bonnet, who had been told on September 11th in Geneva by Mr. Butler that Britain would probably not send a joint note to Germany with France and Russia, seemed to Sir Eric on the 13th in a state of "sudden and extraordinary collapse". Sir Eric decided to seek out M. Daladier himself, and found him still ready "but with evident lack of enthusiasm" to answer force with force if Germany invaded Czechoslovakia. "M. Daladier of today was a quite different one to M. Daladier of September 8th, and tone and language were very different indeed. I fear French have been bluffing." Sir Alexander noted that Daladier was shown to be "somewhat stiffer than Bonnet, but still very little backbone".

Daladier had told Phipps that he wanted to telephone to Chamberlain, but he was asked to communicate through Sir Eric, and so suggested to him a three-power conference, but repeated that "entry of German troops into Czechoslovakia must at all costs be prevented. If not France will be faced with her obligation, viz: automatic necessity to fulfil her engagement."

What led to the collapse of Bonnet? He told Sir Eric that he had just had a visit from Colonel Lindbergh, the American Atlantic flier, who had just arrived from Germany and told him that Germany possessed 8,000 warplanes, was building 1,800 a month, and could pulverise British and French cities. These figures were greatly exaggerated as post-war studies have shown that Germany in October 1938 had 3,200 first-line aircraft and was only producing about 700 aircraft a month in 1939. Yet this chance visitor, fed with Nazi propaganda, may have been the last straw on the nervous hump of

* Documents on British Foreign Policy, Series III, Vol. II, p. 292.

the French foreign minister. Chamberlain was not interested in analysing the "collapse". He accepted it at its face value.

It was these impressions from Sir Eric that decided Chamberlain to dispatch his private message to Hitler "in view of increasingly critical situation I propose to come over at once to see you with a view to trying to find peaceful solution. . . ."

It remained for Mr. Chamberlain to inform the King, the Cabinet, the Commons of what he had done. He hastened to explain himself to King George VI the same day in a letter, pointing out that:

"On the one hand, reports are daily received in great numbers, not only from official sources but from all manner of individuals who claim to have special and unchallengeable sources of information. Many of these (and of such authority as to make it impossible to dismiss them as unworthy of attention) declare positively that Herr Hitler has made up his mind to attack Czechoslovakia and then proceed further East.

"On the other hand Your Majesty's representative in Berlin has steadily maintained that Herr Hitler has not yet made up his mind to violence.

"In these circumstances I have been considering the possibility of a sudden and dramatic step which might change the whole situation. The plan is that I should inform Herr Hitler that I propose at once to go over to Germany and see him. If he assents, and it would be difficult for him to refuse, I should hope to persuade him that he had an unequalled opportunity of raising his own prestige and fulfilling what he has so often declared to be his aim, namely the establishment of an Anglo-German understanding preceded by a settlement of the Czechoslovakian question. After sketching out the prospect of Germany and England as the two pillars of European peace and buttresses against Communism, I should suggest that the essential preliminary was the peaceful solution of our present trouble. . . ."

A full Cabinet meeting was summoned for the morrow, September 14th. Sir Alexander closed the 13th in his diary, the day of collapse, with the significant remark:

"Cabinet to be told what has been done."

CHAPTER XIV

SOUNDING OUT POLAND

POLAND was a lesser known factor in the mounting crisis of summer 1938. General Rydz-Smigly, the Polish Commander-in-Chief, had been approached by General Gamelin, the French Commander-in-Chief, after the Rhineland crisis of 1936 with an overture from President Benes. Apart from a friendly answer to the enquiries of Benes—that the Czechoslovak Government "need not bother to extend their fortifications along the frontiers of Poland, that is, unless they have the money to waste,"* no progress had been made in drawing the two countries together. But if Poland in a moment of crisis stood by the side of Czechoslovakia and France, the situation envisaged as "hopeless for Germany" in Field-Marshal von Blomberg's directives of June 1937 would have been produced. It was not easy for Britain to sound the Poles on this delicate matter. Over the years France had met checks and setbacks in its policy of bringing Poland and Czechoslovakia into one camp. With Britain the relations of Poland were friendly but remote. Eden and Beck had met in Geneva on January 26th, 1938, but they had discussed nothing fundamental and not one important diplomatic document seems to have passed between the two countries in the first eight months of 1938. Such was the position late in August 1938, when I visited Warsaw and found Mr. Clifford Norton, the Counsellor, in charge of the Embassy in the absence of the Ambassador on leave. He regarded the question that I wished to ask the Polish Government, as to its attitude in the event of a German attack on Czechoslovakia, as an extremely delicate one, and one that he could not ask without instructions.

Sir John Simon had not yet made his warning speech at Lanark, and the full danger was not generally realised, least of all by the Polish Government, so it seemed to me on visiting Warsaw. The Poles thought of their country as a power able to stand on its own feet, and although they did not estimate highly the German assurances given to any of their neighbours,

* *Servir*, p. 234.

they still somehow placed reliance on the German-Polish Agreement of 1934.

Meanwhile another visitor, the First Lord of the Admiralty, Alfred Duff Cooper, had sailed along the coast of Poland to take soundings. For two days he had been in the company of Colonel Joszef Beck, the Foreign Minister, and had discussed this very subject.

The danger was apparent but its urgency was not completely realised when Mr. Duff Cooper sailed with Lady Diana Duff Cooper and a party of friends from Portsmouth Command in the Admiralty yacht *Enchantress*. With them were Mr. Brendan Bracken, M.P., Lord and Lady Gage and Lady Elizabeth Paget. They touched at Kiel, taking on board Captain Thomas Troubridge, the British Naval attaché in Germany. After exchanging courtesies with the Admiral commanding at Kiel, they set course along the Baltic coast to Gdynia. The autobiographies of Lord and Lady Norwich give little inkling of a serious mission. The holiday atmosphere in which these London society women encountered both Germans and Poles is reminiscent of the giddy thirties; but there was nevertheless a purpose in the meeting with Colonel Beck, who had suddenly become a key figure in Europe.

Joszef Beck had been one of Pilsudski's young men, and had distinguished himself in battle against the Bolshevik armies. He did not enjoy a good reputation in Paris, where he was remembered as a former Polish military attaché, of whom the Head of the Deuxième Bureau had once complained that a confidential document had vanished from his desk after he had left Beck there for a moment alone. In the First World War Beck had served in a German Uhlan regiment, and though M. Lipski, the Polish Ambassador in Berlin, and others told me that there was no doubt of his patriotism, there was equally no doubt of his preference for the German friendship. General Gamelin and the French Ambassador in Warsaw, M. Leon Noel, had sought to draw General Rydz-Smigly into a discussion of the case of Colonel Beck in September 1936, and even asked the French Foreign Minister, M. Yvon Delbos, to raise the subject of his removal with the Polish military leader. But General Rydz-Smigly had argued that "Beck is necessary for us to be on good terms with Germany. He is himself in relations with the entourage of the Fuehrer. And we have to play for time there." Rydz-Smigly's officers explained later that "the General had not a blind faith in M. Beck, but he remains necessary to us. To get rid of him would risk the appearance of wishing to break with Germany."

Such was the man to whom Lord Halifax sent to enquire on the attitude of Poland just before the high crisis of 1938. Flashily handsome, talkative, vain, somewhat debauched in habit and manner, he struck Lady Diana as "an ancient Pistol and a weak tipsy Pistol at that" . . . But he struck himself in much more favourable light and when he wished to condescend to less successful politicians than himself, his favourite descriptive was: "Ce n'est pas un Colonel Beck!" Of August 9th, their second day in company, she wrote that, "I don't believe he was once sober." The First Lord does not mention in his memoirs the nature of these talks with Beck, and Beck for understandable reasons made no reference whatsoever to them or to Duff Cooper in his *Last Report*. I am indebted to Lord Norwich for some lines copied out of the diary of his father which take the matter a little further. On August 8th, after a dinner given in his honour in Gdynia, Duff Cooper had a long conversation with Beck. "I found him very difficult to follow, tedious and very repetitive. The gist of what he said was that the Baltic States were as one—that all they desired was to be left alone, that he believed this policy coincided with that of England and that he was most anxious that I should convey all this important information to my colleagues. I came back to the ship as soon as I could escape him and Brendan came with me. I wrote an account of what Beck had said for Edward Halifax to see and went to bed soon after one. The others all went on to a night club with Beck and the other Poles. Beck drove the car and nearly drove it into a lamppost. He sang continually, drank more, and became less coherent." On August 9th Duff Cooper noted that "I never knew a man who repeated himself so often. Last night I attributed it to drink, but I find him just as bad this morning." This was an odd partner with whom to discuss the balance of power in Europe. There is no sign of the Duff Cooper report of August 8th in the Foreign Office documents published for this period, nor yet in the papers of Lord Norwich, so that the biography of Lord Halifax must be awaited before anything is added to this side chapter of British diplomacy. Colonel Beck gave

Mr. Norton a bare resumé of his talks with Mr. Duff Cooper during an interview which the British Chargé d'Affaires reported to Lord Halifax on August 30th. At the same time as assuring Lord Halifax of his sympathy for the Runciman mission of mediation, Beck restated the interest of Poland in the Polish minority in Czechoslovakia. Had President Moscicki of Poland given some indication of interest in a common military front with Czechoslovakia, it would perhaps have altered the course of events. But Sir Howard Kennard, the British Ambassador in Warsaw, did not report an encouraging impression on his return from leave on September 2nd. "M. Beck said that he was still of the opinion that Herr Hitler had no wish to precipitate a general conflagration. I fear that he did not display any more sympathy with the Czechoslovak Government than on previous occasions." On September 10th Sir Howard reported "there is little sympathy here with the Czechoslovaks as a people or with the Czechoslovak Government in its present predicament. Nor do the Poles feel the same horror of Nazism as is felt in democratic countries. . . . At the same time the Poles by racial instinct and historical experience dislike Germans. . . . The one eventuality which might throw Poland into the German camp would be any attempt by the U.S.S.R. to send help to Czechoslovakia across Poland." There was only confirmation in such dispatches for Mr. Chamberlain of his secret purpose. For although Sir Howard held out the probability that if Britain and France were involved in a war, Poland would be drawn in on their side, this was not clear enough for the tidy mind of Chamberlain. He stated to three Cabinet Ministers on September 10th, the same day as this dispatch was sent from Warsaw, his intention of going to see Hitler. He sent his message to Berlin on the 13th and called the full Cabinet on September 14th "to be told", as Cadogan put it, "what has been done".

"Ich bin vom Himmel gefallen. . . . I was knocked flat."

This exclamation has been uncritically accepted by W. Shirer, Keith Feiling and others as the reaction of Hitler to the Chamberlain telegram. But it was an afterthought of Hitler to say that he had said this, and there is no evidence that the visit was not something upon which Hitler was calculating all the time. Sir Nevile Henderson passed the message to Baron von Weizsaecker at 9 a.m. on the 14th and mentioned it to

Goering at 2 p.m., reminding him "that he had several times suggested to me a meeting of the Prime Minister with Herr Hitler".* In a letter from Nuremberg to Sir Horace Wilson on September 9th, Henderson had already mentioned Goering as saying "again to me yesterday (September 8th) Chamberlain and Hitler must meet". Sir Horace Wilson has told me that he does not think that Henderson imparted the plan to Goering in advance. Certainly he did not do so to Baron von Weizsaecker who at 9 a.m. on the 14th September questioned him about the origins of Mr. Chamberlain's plan; but in his relations with Goering the idea at least had been sufficiently discussed for the Prime Minister's message to have caused rather less surprise to Hitler than he professed. Indeed it seems likely that he was expecting something of the sort, since the suggestions of Goering to Henderson must have been made with his knowledge.

I find evidence at this date that the Munich Four Power conference was already being considered even before the sending of Mr. Chamberlain's first message to Hitler. Lord Halifax mentioned to his friend Lord Lloyd "very confidentially"† on September 12th the idea of solving the Sudeten-German crisis by a Four Power conference. Lloyd on the same day wrote to him an emphatic letter of protest that to concede a plebiscite would "smash Benes". Vansittart wrote a similar letter on September 13th, but dwelled upon a more significant point that had escaped Lloyd. The Four Power idea was meant to exclude Russia from any part in the solution, though she had treaty obligations to Czechoslovakia. In a vein of prophetic warning, he traced out to Lord Halifax the probable outcome of such a policy:

"I am strongly opposed to the idea of summoning a Four Power conference in present circumstances. It would be the thin end of the wedge for driving Russia out of Europe, and would be completely playing the German game at every point. It can be supported on no adequate ground; indeed there is far more ground for the presence of Russia than of Italy, seeing that three-quarters of the population of Czechoslovakia are Slav. The argument about correcting the Treaty of Versailles is specious; we are not revising Versailles but trying to correct the grievances of the Sudeten-Deutsch.

* Documents on British Foreign Policy, Series III, Vol. II, p. 322.
† Letter. Lord Lloyd to Lord Halifax, September 12th, 1938.

"If there were any immediate prospect of abating Germany's claims by these round-table methods, it might be worth while to consider swallowing our more ultimate objections. But so far from this being the case, it is only too probable that Italy would stiffen Germany at such a conference. On this ground there would be no objection to a meeting between England, France, Germany and Czechoslovakia, omitting both Russia and Italy. I have suggested this before.

"If we deliberately exclude Russia and include Italy, there will be considerable dissatisfaction and even protest in this country, which would be unfortunate at this moment. But this would be the more unfortunate in that there are good grounds for such criticism on any long view.

"If the German spirit were fundamentally changed, there would be no objection to any form of conference or pact which tended to a solution of any specific question. But that spirit has *not* changed. In fact every hour that we live demonstrates more clearly that it is Germany, not Russia, that threatens the physical existence of every country and of its individual citizens.

"So long as this is the case, it would surely be an unpardonable folly to assist Germany in driving off the map an associate whose weight we may need. It is precisely for this reason that Germany is trying to exclude Russia. If we lend ourselves to the beginning of this process, the future is fairly obvious—in two stages. In the first Russia will be evicted and retire into sulky isolation. In the second she will be penetrated by Germany, and Bismarck's traditional policy of close Russo-German relations will follow. The consequences to Europe are too obvious to need enlargement here.

"The conclusion must surely be that there could be no possible justification for embarking on such a course, unless we could be sure that it would dissipate the present danger. We cannot be sure. Indeed I think it is a definitely wrong method. We should discard it immediately, seeing that we have a better one of our own, which—though open to challenge at some points—certainly presents none of the ultimate disadvantages and dangers of the suggestion for a Four Power Conference."

But Chamberlain and Halifax would not hearken, and it is still unclear from the published British documents on what advice or authority Russia was to be excluded from a question in which she had treaty interests.

The British Cabinet meeting of September 14th could do nothing but take note of Hitler's acceptance of Mr. Chamberlain's proposal. They proceeded to elaborate plans for an orderly plebiscite in the Sudeten-German areas of Czechoslovakia. The secret continued to be kept until that evening, and Sir Reginald Leeper tells me that as Head of the News Department of the Foreign Office he was only informed of it by Lord Halifax late that afternoon. Leeper went on to dine with Eden, and had some difficulty in avoiding his questions until the 9 o'clock news gave the information to the world. Up jumped the infuriated Eden and rang Winston Churchill from the next room to discuss it. My own recollection of September 14th is that on that day I was informed in Berlin that General Ludwig Beck had resigned from his post as Chief of the German General Staff, and had submitted his resignation in writing in one short sentence:

"As I am unable to accept the responsibility for a war on two fronts, I request to be relieved of my appointment."

It was my good fortune that a colleague, Denis Weaver, was able to take a dispatch to London based on this information which was prominently published in the first edition of the *News Chronicle* of September 15th, but less prominently in the subsequent editions since the news of Mr. Chamberlain's initiative had by then become known. It had seemed to me that the obedience of the German military to Hitler had by then almost reached breaking point, and that between September 15th and September 28th anything might happen. "Anything" was, alas, not satisfactory to the meticulous Chamberlain mind. I related this coincidence of news to Sir Alexander Cadogan in after years, and he remarked that "if I had been told on the 14th September that General Beck had resigned, I would still have advised Mr. Chamberlain to go to Berchtesgaden."

What I did not know, and no other foreign observer knew, on the morning of September 14th, though I was given hints of a plot among the reserve officers, was that General Franz Halder, the acting Chief of General Staff, had already formed a plan with the Commander of the Berlin garrison, General von Witzleben, Major-General Hoeppner, commander of the Third Panzer Division, and Count von Helldorf in command of the Berlin Police, to arrest Hitler, Goering, Goebbels and Himmler. General Halder went at midday on the 14th to complete his plan with General von Witzleben on learning that Hitler was in Berlin and thus within reach of the conspirators. But news of Mr. Chamberlain's intention of flying to meet Hitler was received by General von Witzleben at 4 p.m., and the plotters therefore decided that Hitler was succeeding in his bluff, and no basis existed for a military revolt against him. Had the nerves of Chamberlain been stronger, had he listened less to what Phipps told him about Bonnet, had he understood what he had been plainly told by Vansittart and Lord Lloyd —that the end of the month was the time for anxiety—had he waited and taken the advice of Vansittart to put up a strong front, the history of the world might have taken a different turning. As it was, his mind was already fixed on what became the Munich conference.

Chamberlain thought that the impulses of Hitler were uncontrollable and that it was highly dangerous to leave him in an overwrought condition any longer. A year later after meeting Hitler three times the Prime Minister still adhered to this view. There seems to have been inadequate study of this phenomenon; for when General Sir Edmund Ironside saw the Prime Minister in July 1939, "I told him [Chamberlain] that I had seen and talked with Hitler (in 1937), and I told him that I was not sure whether Hitler blew up spontaneously or whether he did it to impress his listener. Chamberlain thought he did it spontaneously."*

Chamberlain should have taken Sir Robert Vansittart with him as the senior Diplomatic Adviser. Sir Robert spoke perfect German and was not so disliked by Ribbentrop and others as Chamberlain cared to believe. But the word "Canossa" spoken in their discussions at 10 Downing Street on September 8th had visibly upset the Prime Minister, and probably he resented the criticism of his plan for a Four Power Conference. Sir Horace Wilson was taken instead. He spoke no German. There was no British interpreter. They were brusquely refused the German record of the Berchtesgaden Conference by Herr von Ribbentrop. The Cabinet was thus at a great disadvantage when the Prime Minister returned to report to his colleagues on the 16th September.

While he was away the Inner Cabinet met at 5 p.m. on the 15th September to discuss the plebiscite proposals. Lord Halifax,

---

* July 10th, 1939, *The Ironside Diaries*.

Sir Samuel Hoare and Sir John Simon were present with Mr. Edward Bridges and Sir Alexander Cadogan, who noted in his diary "Van deliberately excluded."

"Halifax used to turn to me and ask—'should we have Van in?'" Sir Alexander remembered. "It was monstrous that I should be asked this, and I told them that they had created his post and the decision lay with them."

The vehemence of Hitler made a deep impression on Neville Chamberlain as they sat and talked in the Berghof on September 15th. He set down afterwards his own "bare record", which has been published. Their meeting culminated in Hitler saying: "Well, if the British Government were prepared to accept the idea of secession in principle and to say so, there might be a chance then to have a talk. . . . If you tell me the British Government cannot accept the principle of secession, then I agree it is of no use for us to proceed with our conversations. . . ." Chamberlain said, ". . . I think the only thing I can suggest is that we should adjourn our conversation, that I should go back and consult my colleagues and that we should meet again when I have heard what they have got to say."

"That is a possible course to take," said Hitler, "and in the circumstances that is the best thing to do."

Chamberlain: "Supposing we agree to do that, can the situation be kept as it is now, or will not something further happen that will upset it?"

Hitler: "Well the German position is that they have a great military machine and once that military machine is put into operation, it would be impossible to stop it. But I am willing to go as far as this: I will give an assurance that I will not give an order for that machine to begin to operate if I can help it: but I am bound to say that if further incidents occur it might be impossible for me to refrain from giving the order."

He then added that it would help if the Czechoslovak Government would recall their State police from the Sudeten-German districts, confine their soldiers to barracks and withdraw mobilisation. This would obviously have "helped", since the steady process of German mobilisation towards X-tag would continue. Indeed, ten days later I was informed that German reserve officers were receiving their call-up papers for the 28th, and told this to Colonel Mason-Macfarlane as we both watched Neville Chamberlain and Sir Horace pacing up and down the gravel outside the Hotel Petersberg between their meetings with Hitler, while A.A. guns mounted on railway trucks were driven past them in the Rhine valley below. Perhaps the Military Attaché thought that they had already been sufficiently alarmed. For his answer was: "That's just the sort of news they don't want to hear."

The Prime Minister arrived back in London from his visit to Berchtesgaden on the evening of Friday, September 16th, during which day the handful of dissidents in his Cabinet discussed "pressing their views to the point of resignation" as Lord Winterton put it. Oliver Stanley thought none of them should leave London in case a Cabinet should be called. But it was not, and late on the 16th Chamberlain imparted his impression of Hitler to the inner few only, calling the full Cabinet at 11 a.m. on Saturday the 17th and again at 3 p.m.

Lord Runciman was with them again, but as Duff Cooper noted in his diary, "his views were quite unhelpful as he was unable to suggest any plan or policy. . . . Then the P.M. told us the story of his visit to Berchtesgaden. Looking back upon what he said the curious thing seems to me now to have been that he recounted his experiences with some satisfaction. Although he said that at first sight Hitler struck him as "the commonest looking little dog" that he had ever seen, without one sign of distinction, nevertheless he was obviously pleased at the reports he had subsequently received of the good impression that he had made. He told us with obvious satisfaction how Hitler had said to someone that he had felt that he— Chamberlain—was a "man".

"But the bare facts of the interview were frightful. None of the elaborate schemes that we had discussed in Cabinet, and which the Prime Minister intended to put forward, had ever been mentioned. He had felt that the atmosphere did not allow of it. After ranting and raving Hitler had talked to him about self-determination and asked the P.M. whether he accepted the principle. The P.M. had replied that he must consult his colleagues. From beginning to end Hitler had not shown a sign of yielding on a single point. The P.M. seemed to expect us all to accept that principle without further discussion, because time was getting on. . .

"I said and others agreed with me that we must have further time for discussion and that it would be better to take no decision until discussions with the French had taken place, lest they should be in a position to say that we had sold the pass without consulting them."

When the Cabinet met again at 3 p.m. the view was heard that according to the principles of Canning and Disraeli, Great Britain should never intervene unless her own interests were directly affected, and unless she could do so with overwhelming force. Duff Cooper took this up, saying that "we were now faced with the most formidable power that ever dominated Europe and resistance to that power was quite obviously a British interest. As for 'overwhelming force', it was quite true that we had not got it, but it was also true that we had no means of acquiring it. So if we held to . . . that . . . doctrine . . . it meant that we could never intervene again, that we were in fact finished. If I thought surrender would bring lasting peace, I should be in favour of surrender, but that I did not believe there would ever be peace in Europe so long as Nazism ruled in Germany.".

Did he then favour war? Duff Cooper spoke of the fearful responsibility of incurring a war that might possibly be avoided and thought it worth while to avoid it in the very faint hope that some internal event might bring about the fall of the Nazi régime. But there were limits to the humiliation he was prepared to accept. He thought that the least that he could accept was a plebiscite under fair conditions of international control. Others spoke, some at great length, some more weakly, though several took the same line as the First Lord. But it was not a distinct line. They had only registered conditions as to the plebiscite. Nobody spoke for war. Duff Cooper noted that "no conclusion was recorded", but Sir Alexander Cadogan noted that "Cabinet decided on an orderly transfer by plebiscite", and that afterwards Lord Halifax had to receive the Trades Union Council and the American Ambassador, Mr. Joseph Kennedy, and do some explaining.

M. Daladier flew over next day and the Inner Cabinet met with the French at 11 a.m. on September 18th in the Cabinet room. Once more it was the cabal of British ministers, Chamberlain, Halifax, Simon and Hoare. Daladier brought Bonnet, Alexis Leger and his London Ambassador, Charles Corbin. Sir Robert Vansittart attended, as did Cadogan, Bridges, Horace Wilson and Mr. William Strang, Head of the Central

Department. Mr. Chamberlain retold the story of his Berchtesgaden talks at great length concluding that "it must be recognised that Herr Hitler had it in his power to bring about a general catastrophe. It was possible that he might not wish to attack Czechoslovakia unless he thought he could do this safely. But if he did decide to take the risk of a general war, or if he felt he had got into such a position in Germany that he felt some definite gesture was necessary, then nothing could be done to stop him."

It is noteworthy that Mr. Chamberlain did not impart to M. Daladier that the German Chargé d'Affaires himself had been imploring Lord Halifax to stand up boldly to Hitler. But Daladier had brought his own information and commented that "we knew that the majority of Generals of the German Army were in favour of peace". He expressed his concern at the idea of a plebiscite. "If we followed Germany in her present claim instead of negotiating a peaceful solution to the present incidents, we should only be encouraging a policy which must in the long run lead to war." He argued, and Mr. Chamberlain admitted, that the claims of the other minorities in Czechoslovakia would follow those of the Sudeten-German.

Then Chamberlain "drew attention to a secret paper which had just been put into his hands showing that German military preparations, far from slackening off after his visit to Herr Hitler, had intensified." Daladier rejoined by reaffirming the obligations of France. Then Halifax spoke. He acknowledged the obligations of France, but "whatever action were taken by ourselves, by the French Government or the Soviet Government,* at any given moment, it would be impossible to give effective protection to the Czechoslovak State. We might fight a war against German aggression, but at the Peace Conference which followed such a war he did not think the statesmen concerned would redraft the present boundaries of Czechoslovakia. The British Government, like the French Government, had to face hard facts. They were concerned with the French Government to find some means to save Europe from destruction and catastrophe."

The British suggested a luncheon adjournment, but M. Daladier continued. He could not help recalling, he said, that not very long ago the British and French Governments had

* At this time the views of the Soviet Government had not yet been sought.

agreed on the principle of maintaining the unity of Czecho-slovakia.

The record shows that the conference adjourned late for lunch, though Sir Alexander noted that he thought they had by then "brought the French back to earth". After lunch at the Carlton, they drew M. Daladier into discussion of secession of territory. He countered by asking for a British guarantee of the remaining Czechoslovak state. Lord Halifax demurred, saying that it was "quite impossible to allow the direction of British policy to be placed in the hands of any other country". Mr. Chamberlain tried to convince Daladier that Czecho-slovakia was "also a potential liability".

They paused at 5 p.m. when Mr. Chamberlain "suggested that the meeting should now adjourn to consider separately the question of a guarantee". But again he did not assemble his own full Cabinet to consider the grave commitment to which Lord Halifax had objected. Instead he used the adjournment for another purpose. "Our party started drafting a message to Benes telling him to surrender," noted Cadogan. He also noted that in the afternoon figures of French Air Force strength had been produced by the British in their attempt to persuade the French to see reason as the British saw it. He described the figures as "frightful". The French were said to have only between 21 and 28 aircraft equal in performance to the standard German types. Daladier had no Services experts with him and had brought no military statistics to London with which to answer these criticisms.

When the French reappeared at 7.30 p.m. Mr. Chamberlain explained that he and his colleagues had thought it best to draft a joint message. If Benes accepted it, "His Majesty's Government was prepared to join in the suggested guarantee". (He told the British Cabinet afterwards that there had been no time to consult it before deciding on the guarantee.) He asked the French ministers to consider the British draft over dinner. They did, and after dinner Daladier said that he found the proposition "very distressing"; but he undertook to have a reply from his own Cabinet by midday on the 19th. After discussing ways and means of taking the sole decision over peace or war out of the hands of Benes, the Anglo-French meeting adjourned just after midnight and the French ministers returned to France.

What became known hereafter as the Anglo-French proposals were accepted by the French cabinet on the morning of Monday the 19th. At the same time the British Cabinet met and, noted Duff Cooper, some "dithered at the thought of a guarantee". The proposals as drafted by the Inner Cabinet read that Britain would take part in an "international guarantee". If that term were stretched to include Germany and Germany refused to participate, could the obligation be maintained? At this meeting Hore-Belisha spoke with the critics, seeing no means whatever of honouring such a guarantee. During Tuesday the 20th, the Czechs continued their hesitations over the Anglo-French proposals and decided to call Parliament. But this delay jeopardised Chamberlain's next appointment with Hitler, which was provisionally arranged for Wednesday, September 21st, and so an Anglo-French *démarche* in Prague was decided upon for Tuesday night to bring the Czechs to compliance, at which the British and French Heads of Mission would meet President Benes himself. Much was made in the parliamentary debates after the Munich Agreement of an infamous telegram or ultimatum, said to have been delivered to the Czechoslovak Government at this meeting. Viscount Cecil of Chelwood quoted its four points in the House of Lords and Hugh Dalton in the House of Commons. Lord Stanhope and Sir Samuel Hoare denied that any such telegram or ultimatum had been sent. Such a document, published at the time by Professor R. Seton-Watson, has been published since the war from the archives of the Czechoslovak Foreign Ministry. It read (with a contradiction in the last paragraphs):

"Britain and France have the duty to prevent a European war, if humanly possible, and thus an invasion of Czechoslovakia.

"They wish the Czechoslovak Government to realise that if it does not unconditionally and at once accept the Anglo-French plan, it will stand before the world as solely responsible for the ensuing war.

"By refusing, Czechoslovakia will also be guilty of destroying Anglo-French solidarity, since, in that event, Britain will under no circumstances march, even if France went to the aid of Czechoslovakia.

"If the refusal should provoke a war, France gives official notice that she will not fulfil her treaty obligations."

The official British telegram to Mr. Basil Newton, British minister in Prague, was written very differently. Mr. Chamberlain gave it immediately to both Houses, and it was read to the Commons by Mr. Butler. It was rather longer, and it urged the Czechoslovak Government to withdraw its previous reply asking for arbitration and accept the Anglo-French proposals as "the only chance of avoiding an immediate German attack". After this somewhat hysterical, or perhaps calculated, assessment of the military situation—for Hitler could not just press a button in the German military machine like a juke box —the British telegram concluded that:

"If on reconsideration the Czech [sic]* Government feel bound to reject our advice, they must of course be free to take any action they think appropriate to meet the situation that may thereafter develop."

Mr. Butler told the House that the third and fourth points of the publicised version were particularly incorrect. Lord Stanhope, while denying just as emphatically that such a four-point telegram had been sent, defined the British attitude in terms not widely differing from the alleged document. The use of the words "Czech Government" in the genuine telegram suggests that even this was not drafted in the Foreign Office. Let us then look at the circumstances in which the joint *démarche* was made. President Benes received the two envoys about 2 a.m. on September 21st. "My French colleague read from his telegraphic instructions and I followed by reading your telegram," reported Mr. Newton to Lord Halifax. "President Benes made full notes. We left no written communication."†

The interview lasted till 3.45 a.m. and Benes said towards the end that he took the joint *démarche* to be a kind of ultimatum. The two diplomats agreed that "our *démarche* had the character of an ultimatum . . . but only in that it represented the final advice of our Governments". In the course of one hour and three-quarters they had plenty of time to convince Benes that his country would stand alone if he refused to co-operate. Mr. Newton was in no doubt of the impression created, since he communicated to London the same day the text of a Czechoslovak communiqué, in which there was reference to "the

* Hansard, H. of C., Vol. 339, Col. 450-51.
† Documents on British Foreign Policy, Series III, Vol. II, p. 449.

communication in which the two Governments express their attitude in regard to Czechoslovakia if she refused to accept the Anglo-French proposals and was as a result attacked by Germany." If indeed there was no written communication, it seems probable that the four points were a summary by President Benes made in their presence of what they were telling him. Thus the appearance of an ultimatum was contrived without much trace remaining on the record.

Although Mr. Hodza accepted the ultimatum at 6.30 a.m., his Government fell, and General Syrovy, a veteran of the Czech Legion, succeeded him. When the British Cabinet met at 3 p.m. on the 21st, Chamberlain had become a little stiffer. Some argued for "a decent interval" before the Germans marched in, or the Czechs and German democrats who wished to do so would be unable to leave the occupied territory. Duff Cooper in a stirring oration said that the limit had been reached, that the Prime Minister should tell Hitler that he had fulfilled his undertakings and rather than retreat further would prefer, if necessary, to risk war. The country would be solid behind him and he would later have the assistance of the United States. "I think what I said produced an effect", noted Duff Cooper in his diary. "Nobody contested it." One of the Inner Cabinet even whispered to him that he was in agreement, and that the Prime Minister had said earlier that morning that he was equally convinced.*

When Chamberlain met Hitler next day at the Hotel Dreesen, Bad Godesberg and began to explain to him the Anglo-French proposals for orderly transfer, drafted by Cadogan and Vansittart, he found a different attitude than in the previous week at Berchtesgaden.

Hitler said curtly:

"I am sorry, but all that is no use any more."

Instead of "all that" he propounded the claims of the Poles, the Hungarians and the Slovaks and envisaged occupying the Sudeten-German territory as marked on his own maps immediately, and holding a plebiscite afterwards. This preposterous attitude and the excitability of Hitler's talk prompted Chamberlain to remain withdrawn on the afternoon of Thursday, the 23rd. Until Friday evening they had no second meeting and sent frosty and fiery letters to each other across

* Duff Cooper Diary, 21st Sept.

the Rhine. In London, at last aware of the Anglo-French predicament, Lord Halifax sent a telegram to Mr. R. A. Butler in Geneva, asking him to sound M. Litvinov for any indication of Soviet action if the Czechoslovak Government resisted German demands. Mr. Butler received the Soviet Foreign Commissar's reply that evening. But it was only dispatched from Geneva to London at 10.45 a.m. on the following morning, a strangely dilatory procedure indeed at this anxious time. M. Litvinov said that "despite the Franco-British-German ultimatum to Czechoslovakia", if France honoured her obligations to Czechoslovakia and fought, Russia would fight too. He suggested transferring their conversations from Geneva to Paris "to show that we mean business". He said further that Russia had warned Poland that if Poland invaded the Teschen area of Czechoslovakia, the Russo-Polish non-aggression pact would lapse and Russia would take action. Considering how Russia had been cold-shouldered throughout the negotiations of September 1938, this reaction was not so weak as some have since suggested, or as M. Bonnet made it out to be at the time. It put the Poles in check. It offered an immediate diplomatic front of three powers, which had so far been lacking. But while the Litvinov offer lay overnight in Geneva, Chamberlain with his advisers Sir Horace Wilson, Sir Nevile Henderson and Mr. Ivone Kirkpatrick argued over the terms of the German demands on Czechoslovakia, finally agreeing to forward them to Prague after Hitler had here and there softened the wording. He retained in the memorandum his insistent demand for a withdrawal of Czechoslovak forces from the territories claimed by October 1st, the date to which the German clockwork mobilisation had already been set.

I flew back to Berlin on the morning of Saturday, September 24th with Colonel Mason-Macfarlane in a Lufthansa plane from Cologne. He was gripping a small black dispatch case containing the German ultimatum. I showed him a cartoon in an American newspaper of Benes carrying a desk block marked "President" into a pawnshop. He grimaced. In Berlin his car was waiting for him and he motored down to the Czechoslovak frontier, crawled through the Czechoslovak barbed wire at a frontier post and delivered the German memorandum to the British Embassy in Prague soon after 11 p.m.

Sir Eric Phipps was continuing to send dispatches from Paris reflecting the more defeatist views of Frenchmen. One such dispatch on September 25th claimed that "all that is best in France is against war at almost any price", and described the others as "a small but noisy and corrupt war group here". For several days Sir Eric had been reflecting the opinions of such men as the lank and perspiring M. Bonnet and M. Caillaux, President of the Finance Commission of the Senate, and echoing the panic spread by Colonel Lindbergh among French ministers. The Foreign Office irately directed him to make a rather wider canvass of French views, and on September 26th Sir Eric was able to report "a complete change in the French attitude" after Hitler's latest demands on the Czechs had become known.

Sunday, September 25th, was taken up with a full British Cabinet meeting in the morning and in the afternoon by talks between the "Inner Cabinet" with M. Daladier and M. Bonnet. In the morning each Cabinet minister stated his views, and Lord Halifax surprised them by saying in a low voice and speaking with some emotion that whereas hitherto his views had been in entire accordance with the Prime Minister's, there was now some divergence between them. In the night he had gradually come to change his mind. He thought that Britain could not advise the Czechs to accept the ultimatum, and that if France went to their help, Britain should go to the help of France. Duff Cooper and his few diehard colleagues were greatly surprised. One of the elder waverers produced a copy of the *Daily Telegraph*, read out a list of the already broken pledges of Hitler and said that he came to the same conclusion. From those most faithful to Chamberlain came the argument that Czechoslovakia was "strategically doomed"; but two other ministers appeared rather firmer. Duff Cooper thought that nine Ministers were against the German ultimatum, perhaps ten; and ten in favour of supporting it, with two Ministers adopting the "broad bottom" policy of sitting on every fence within sight.

In this quandary Mr. Chamberlain decided that he would send a messenger to Germany with a message for Herr Hitler. His letter did not reflect a very great resolution and neither did his choice of a messenger. Those who knew Hitler well, such as Weizsaecker, were in favour of imposing envoys. The

Baron once advised that "some general with a riding crop" should be sent. To hand Mr. Chamberlain had Sir Robert Vansittart, a broad six foot one inches and with perfect German. He chose Sir Horace Wilson, a slim five foot nine and no German at all. That afternoon he interrupted his meeting with the French ministers to announce this move and release a Press communiqué. The letter told Herr Hitler that the Czechs had refused his terms, which he already knew, and suggested that Hitler should negotiate direct with them on "the way in which the territory is to be handed over". A solemn warning was also in Wilson's pocket, which was meant to be read out to the Fuehrer.

Vansittart attended the afternoon meeting with M. Daladier and M. Bonnet. The record shows that Daladier began by making the same observations that the firmer British Cabinet Ministers had made in the morning, and that Sir John Simon, as the Cabinet cross-examiner, was soon put on to find out exactly what the French would do in case of war. He plied the French Prime Minister with questions. Daladier pointed out that already one million Frenchmen had joined the colours, in good heart, he said. These would at first hold German divisions in the West and so give relief to the Czechs, and later go over to the attack. His Air Force, though criticised by British M.P.s, would give an account of itself, and Russia had 5,000 planes and would also fight. But all that Daladier had been trying to say at the outset was that Hitler ought not to have immediate occupation of the demarcated territories and must be told to return to the Anglo-French proposals.

"Surely we need not accept every demand that he chooses to make and encourage him still further to regard himself as divine. . . . If Herr Hitler puts forward certain demands must we agree to them? He would then be Master of Europe and after Czechoslovakia would come Rumania and then Turkey. He might even turn to France and take Boulogne and Calais." But the British Inner Cabinet did not want to hear French historical logic. They wanted to hear from General Gamelin that he was not able to save Czechoslovakia. For next day, Monday the 26th, a meeting between the British Prime Minister and the French generalissimo was arranged. On this same day Sir Horace met Hitler.

The Cabinet was worried about a speech to be made by

Hitler at the Berlin Sports Palace on September 26th. Once more Lord Halifax sought to moderate it, and sent an urgent telegram adding to the Chamberlain warning a suggestion that Russia would also intervene. Once more his instructions were not properly carried out. Sir Horace, with Sir Nevile at his elbow, decided "that it seemed better not to deliver the special message". This was the omission of Nuremberg all over again. By shamming a rage and shouting that "Germany was being treated like niggers", Hitler managed to sound out the British visitors without seeming to be listening to what they were trying to tell him. He greeted the offer of direct discussion with the Czechs with the exclamation "Incredible, amazing!" October 1st, he cried, on October 1st he would have Czechoslovakia where he wanted. Henderson, Kirkpatrick and Wilson thought it impossible to continue the interview with a man who walked out of the room. Next day Sir Horace Wilson returned to see Hitler and began by congratulating him on the applause that had greeted his speech. This was a curious compliment. For I had listened to the speech of September 26th and found Hitler hesitant, given to long pauses, uncertain of himself; and the applause fitful, savage but uneasy. He seemed like a man at the end of his tether, and the mood of the man in the street in Germany was no more for war than it was in France.

Sir Horace then endeavoured to deliver his warning of the previous day, a carefully formulated statement about France honouring her obligations and Britain feeling obliged to support her. Once more Hitler resorted to his tactics of fury, interjecting that this meant that France would attack Germany and that Britain would also. The protestations of Sir Horace that he was being misheard must have again weakened the effect of this warning and reassured Hitler that no attacks were intended. This inexpert diplomacy was of no value. The important part of his message had been delivered, much weakened in form, a day late.

I find among my Berlin notes that on the afternoon of the 27th September I passed on to Sir George Ogilvie-Forbes a reliable report reaching me that since the interview between Hitler and Sir Horace Wilson that morning all Luftwaffe plans had been changed. The Luftwaffe would now concentrate the weight of its attack solely on Czechoslovakia with no offensive preparations against Britain or France. At the time I was unaware what had taken place between Hitler and Sir Horace. The record is now open. It shows that Hitler and Ribbentrop fiercely pressed him to say whether if Germany attacked Czechoslovakia, France and Britain would attack Germany. "Sir Horace Wilson demurred." Such feeble replies convinced them that they need not fear offensive operations in the West.

There remained the visit to London of General Gamelin. This was handled in the Chamberlain fashion. He first saw Gamelin alone.

General Gamelin had been asked the question on September 12th by M. Daladier whether he could go to the assistance of Czechoslovakia in the event of a German attack. His reply then was that Germany could not be defeated before Czechoslovakia had lost an important part of its territory; but this had been the case with Belgium, Serbia and Rumania in the war of 1914–18. He and his staff expected to make offensive probes against the Siegfried line soon after the tenth day of war. On September 16th Lord Lloyd visited him and explained the situation as he saw it—that a resolute attitude of Great Britain beside France would halt Hitler short of war. Gamelin noted this opinion and inserted a question mark after it.*

Lord Lloyd told me that the French Commander-in-Chief on this occasion expressed great contempt for the hastily constructed German fortifications in the West, saying: "Bah! C'est de la marmalade!" On the 22nd General Gamelin learned that Lord Halifax shared the misgivings of the French Foreign Ministry about restraining the Czechs from mobilising any longer. Early on the 25th Daladier told Gamelin that Bonnet was threatening to resign. That night Gamelin was summoned to join Daladier in London. Next morning the French Prime Minister presented him to Mr. Chamberlain and asked him to speak for the French Armed Forces. The French Ambassador acted as interpreter. Lord Halifax remained outside, ostensibly for the purpose of keeping M. Bonnet from going in too and infecting all with his own defeatism. Gamelin did not lightly describe the Siegfried line as "jam" to Mr. Chamberlain. Instead he pulled some maps out of his dispatch case and gave a careful professional account of the military situation—a French army of five million men, 100 divisions for a start, an air force inferior to the Luftwaffe, but able to give the Army

* *Servir.* The question mark may have been inserted at a later date.

short-range support. He named the German weaknesses, a High Command aware of the dangers, an unfinished system of fortifications, a shortage of military formations and reserves, a shortage of raw materials, especially petrol.

He thought that thirty Czechoslovak divisions would be faced with forty German divisions. (The French General Staff did not believe that Hitler would leave less than fifty in the West, whereas Hitler reckoned to hold it with a screen of nine or twelve divisions.)

Sir Thomas Inskip, Minister for Co-ordination and Defence, took Gamelin on to a meeting with the three Services ministers and the British Chiefs of Staff. They appeared to Gamelin unready for war, except for the Navy, and not to relish the idea of a Russian attack on Poland. Gamelin left London that evening and discussed with Daladier next day Hitler's Sports Palace speech ("these are my last territorial demands"). Gamelin argued that to let Czechoslovakia be crushed without intervening would have the immediate result of freeing thirty German divisions for action against France or Poland, and "one day Germany will have sixty active divisions which she can treble when she mobilises".

Meanwhile his exposé to Mr. Chamberlain had been misconstrued. For on September 27th a telegram from Lord Halifax to Sir Eric Phipps in Paris quoted General Gamelin as having "made it plain to us . . . that if German forces now invaded Czechoslovakia, Czech resistance is likely to be of extremely brief duration."

The Foreign Secretary coupled this with an opinion given by Colonel Mason-Macfarlane to him personally—but nowhere since printed—that "Czech resistance will prove to be feeble." The only written opinion of the British Military Attaché in Berlin that has been published was contained in a telegram of September 26th after his hurried journey to Prague with the German ultimatum. Then he "gained general impression Czechs' morale not very good. Certainly not if forced to fight alone." The Halifax telegram to Phipps urged therefore that M. Daladier should not take immediate action in case of German aggression against Czechoslovakia but first consult with Britain.*

* *Servir.*
† Documents on British Foreign Policy, Series III, Vol. II, p. 552.

Once more the evidence was bent one way. Colonel Mason-Macfarlane was not the competent authority on the Czechoslovak army; and Colonel Humphrey Stronge, the British military attaché in Prague described the Czech army as "confident in their cause, their leadership and their equipment".* Not only this, but his recollection of Colonel Macfarlane's impressions did not agree with those ascribed to him by Lord Halifax. It was to Colonel Stronge at breakfast on September 25th that Mason-Macfarlane, his face and clothes torn by Czech barbed wire retailed his first impressions of the Czechoslovak armed forces, and these were mainly of annoyance that he could not make himself understood to the Czech frontier guards in German.

Incredibly, no written record was kept of the Gamelin interview with Chamberlain, though some notes of Gamelin's talks with the Chiefs of Staff showed that he declined to give a definite estimate of the period that the Czech Army could be expected to resist; and described it as "a good army, good personnel, excellent morale of people fighting for their lives and an efficient command".† Gamelin protested to Lord Halifax in November 1938 that what he had said in September in London was that the Czech army could not defend Bohemia and would have to fall back on Moravia. This military conception had been already accepted by General Syrovy, the new Czechoslovak premier.

Gamelin's visit, though he avoided defeatist expressions, did not increase the resolution of the British. However, in the next two days two actions were taken in the nerve war which, if decided earlier, could have had a salutary effect. Both were at last in line with the recommendations of Sir Robert Vansittart. Mr. Reginald Leeper issued a Foreign Office press communiqué in the afternoon of September 26th that "if in spite of all efforts made by the British Prime Minister a German attack is made upon Czechoslovakia the immediate result must be that France will be bound to come to her assistance and Great

---

* Documents on British Foreign Policy, Series III, Vol. II, p. 581.

† Mr. Newton, the British Minister in Prague, drew the attention of Lord Halifax on November 1st, 1938 to the opinion of the German military attaché in Prague which was that "the morale of the Czech Army was excellent when they mobilised". "This view is in striking contrast with the opinion which was formed by Colonel Mason-Macfarlane and impressed with such force upon the French Government at the height of the crisis." British Documents, Series III, Vol. III, p. 253.

Britain and Russia will certainly stand by France." Thus Russia was mentioned for the first time in a British communiqué on the crisis over Czechoslovakia. At 8 p.m. on September 27th Duff Cooper obtained that the Fleet should be mobilised, and as Mr. Chamberlain did not object, let an announcement be sent to the B.B.C. It was not broadcast until midnight, and it was the morning of the 28th September, the day of the completed German state of readiness, before these two single acts of resolution could have their combined effect on the calculating Hitler. Meanwhile Sir Horace Wilson, in his second audience with Hitler on the morning of the 27th, had missed his great opportunity for quoting the communiqué in which the names of Britain, France and Russia were joined, despite the special telegram from Lord Halifax. His last words to Hitler had been a promise to "try and make those Czechs sensible".

The Chief Industrial Adviser took home an offer from Hitler to Chamberlain of a formal guarantee of the rump state of Czechoslovakia. Wilson reported to the Cabinet the same day. He thought that the only thing to do was to advise the Czechs to evacuate the territory, and had actually drawn up a draft telegram containing this advice. Duff Cooper criticised it, and to his surprise, so did others. One minister asked Sir Horace to explain what difference there was between his plan and Hitler's ultimatum, and Sir Horace seemed unable to find any difference. Ministers began to disown the Wilson telegram. But Halifax startled them next by producing a new British plan for a phased Czechoslovak withdrawal to begin on October 1st. This too had not been submitted to the Cabinet, though it had already been sent to Berlin. The Cabinet was once more asked to approve after action. A few protested, but as often before there was nothing to be gained. Not to be outdone, M. Bonnet devised a French plan, similar to the British, but even more accommodating to Hitler. It was submitted by the French Ambassador in Berlin on the morning of the 28th. The Czechoslovak agony was near its end. A message from Chamberlain to Hitler offered to take part in further talks with France and Italy, but Hitler replied that another visit by the British Prime Minister might not be necessary. He was already in touch with Mussolini. The intervention of the Duce had been sought that morning on instructions from London, Count Attolico had been told to make urgent representations in Berlin, and by 3.15 p.m.

Sir Nevile Henderson was able to telephone to Sir Alexander
Cadogan that Hitler invited Chamberlain to a conference in
Munich with Daladier and Mussolini. The historic moment
lives in the memory of many present when in the House of
Commons a sheet of paper was passed along the Government
benches at a moment when Neville Chamberlain in weary flat
tones was describing the seemingly hopeless deadlock with an
adamant Hitler. The Prime Minister first brushed the paper
aside when Sir John Simon handed it to him, then took it and
read it. As he did so, he turned pale and his hand shook. He
then announced in the same flat tones the nature of Hitler's
invitation. As soon as the House of Commons understood, it
drowned his speech in cheers.

A question mark hangs over this dramatic moment. It seems
to have been the product of no chance inspiration. Lord Perth
in a subsequent dispatch to Lord Halifax* ascribed to his own
démarche that morning the invitation that averted war. But was
this really the first time that Mussolini and Hitler heard the
idea of such a four-power conference? Sir Horace Wilson, in
whose mind the German official Dr. Fritz Hesse thought he had
implanted the idea on September 25th, told him that he would
discuss it with Grandi.† Yet even further back there is the evidence of Lord Lloyd in his letter of September 12th that Lord
Halifax was already planning it, and the vehement protest of
Vansittart on the 13th at the intention to exclude Russia.

Such was the obscurely managed and questionable end of
Czechoslovakia, the end of the balance of power in Europe, the
end of an era in diplomacy and international obligations. Those
whom I knew in Germany told me that it was not the end of
Hitler's demands. To Munich came the Czechoslovak emissaries
to hear their fate, like the burghers of Calais.

The International Commission worked in a spirit of surrender.
The British member, Sir Nevile Henderson, wrote to Lord
Halifax on October 6th, 1938:

"In my humble opinion we did the best thing possible by
agreeing to the 1910 map as a basis for the predominantly
German areas which the German Army can occupy by
October 10th."‡

* Rome Dispatch, September 30th, 1938.
† *Hitler and the English*, Wingate Press.
‡ Documents on British Foreign Policy, Series III, Vol. III, p. 615.

He recalled the frontier revision of the Versailles Treaty as a precedent.

Vansittart noted on October 11th when the Munich conference was over, and the German troops inside the Czech fortifications: "in my opinion the proceedings of the International Commission have been scandalous. It never even made an attempt to get a compromise between population figures . . . as instructed. It has simply reproduced Godesberg after we had flattered ourselves publicly on having got away from it. Over three-quarters of a million Czechs are now apparently to be under German rule. It is a shame."

CHAPTER XV

THE MEANING OF MUNICH

"Come inside the Embassy gate, so that these Germans can't see our faces, and I will tell you how unprepared we are."

Thus Major Kenneth Strong, Assistant Military Attaché in Berlin continued a conversation begun in the Wilhelmstrasse on the morning of September 27th, 1938. He started with the accusation that I was one of those who wanted war with Germany. He pursued the subject inside the big Chancery door. Although specialising at that time in the Wehrmacht, he was also well informed on the shortcomings of the British Army. It remains in my memory that he told me that Britain had some dozen anti-aircraft guns for the defence of the London area and a good deal else that was disturbing to hear. Less disturbing to me, however, than the aberration of policy into which our country had fallen. I remember also that after the crisis when I returned to Berlin from a voyage to Rumania in October 1938, and resumed this conversation, Kenneth Strong laughed shortly and said he thought that Hitler had been bluffing.

To unravel not only what happened in this crisis, but what might have happened is no easy matter. While the facts are fresh from my research I venture into this field of speculation because a number of Cabinet ministers, diplomats and historians have already asserted with emphasis that the Chamberlain policy was the only possible course. There is plenty of evidence of British unpreparedness. Lord Ironside records that production of 3·7 inch A.A. guns was only ordered in 1937; that he found two battalions at Dover on September 3rd, 1938 whose total strength was 320 men; that "we had no Army to send abroad . . . Chamberlain is of course right. We have not the means of defending ourselves and he knows it. He is a realist and any plan he could devise was better than war."* But Ironside was still complaining of shortages in December 1939, and there had to be a moment—assuming that Britain would never be ready for every eventuality—when the risk of war was said to be

* *Ironside Diaries.*

acceptable. According to the official historians, the safety point in British rearmament was thought to have been reached only in March 1939.* These official estimates do not, however, afford a blanket excuse for everything that was done in British diplomacy between August and October 1938, and on several points an analysis is worth while.

Should war have been made in September 1938 in defence of the Czechoslovak State? This question only arose after a series of delays and ineffectual warnings in August and early September failed to influence Hitler to cancel the gradual mobilisation of the German armed forces. The pertinent question was first—ought there to have been a firm and open warning to Germany in August committing Britain to stand by France? Of those whom I have met or whose documentary opinion is available, I find that those who were for careful and qualified warnings delivered secretly were Chamberlain, Simon, Halifax, Hoare, Henderson, Horace Wilson and Cadogan. I find among those who favoured an open warning spoken with unmistakable emphasis and backed by such measures as a timely mobilisation of the Fleet were Vansittart, Duff Cooper, Winston Churchill, Lord Lloyd and Reginald Leeper. They were not completely sure that Hitler was bluffing, but they shared the classic French conception of the balance of power. It was much easier to lose than to redress it. The case for an open declaration as we know was advanced by Dr. Theo Kordt in London on behalf of his brother Erich in Berlin, as well as by Baron von Weizsaecker, Under-Secretary of State in the Foreign Ministry. At least they wished Britain to make its attitude clear and unmistakable rather than risk a later misunderstanding. "British prestige was still high enough in 1938 for those in Germany not to have doubted British determination. I am still convinced today," wrote Erich Kordt in 1950, "that Hitler in face of British determination to fight would have recoiled from a war at the last moment."

What would have happened if Hitler had given the order to fight? Would he have found an obedient response from his military machine? I found Sir Alexander Cadogan positive that the German generals would not have disobeyed their orders. This was probably true of the period after September 13th, when Mr. Chamberlain took the decision to go and

* *The Coming of War in 1939*, W. N. Medlicott, p. 21.

negotiate with Hitler. Two British observers, Sir George Ogilvie-Forbes and Colonel Mason-Macfarlane shared the opinion after Munich, "that Hitler was determined after the rebuff of May 21st to gain his ends in Czechoslovakia even by warlike means".* But Mason-Macfarlane in his assessment of other than military matters in the interesting paper that he wrote on October 26th, 1938 was far wrong in several assumptions. For he accepted that Italy, Poland and Hungary would have fought beside Germany. We know now that under no circumstances was Italy prepared to make war in 1938, that Hungary stood aside and that Poland was only prepared to man her frontiers against Russia and march into a conceded area of Czechoslovakia if there was no general war. Mason-Macfarlane tried in retrospect to answer the question whether Hitler could have been stopped short of war and reached the conclusion that "the situation in Germany is now such that the Army Chiefs are not in a position to press their opposition to any policy of Hitler's without the practical certainty of dismissal". This does not, however, answer the question whether a sudden military *Putsch* was probable or capable of success. Moreover when it is remembered that Colonel Mason-Macfarlane fiercely advocated a preventive war against Germany on March 29th, 1939,† though he failed to give support to such an idea in August 1938, while there were 30 Czech divisions in the field and within their fortifications, there is room also to doubt his expertise and balance in political matters.

There is no published British document in which the prospects of an intended *Putsch* against Hitler and its chances of success were discussed. Mr. Chamberlain asked on August 19th in a letter to Lord Halifax that on this same subject he should seek the views of Sir Nevile Henderson. The Ambassador was not very well placed to know about conspirators. There is no published evidence of such a question going to him in Berlin. His own dispatches do not refer to the subject. He may have reported during his August visit to London and would certainly have counselled then against thinking of any such likelihood. Curiously he does make after the Munich conference allusions to this subject. In a little-known letter to Lord Halifax of October 6th, in which he confessed his inner thoughts at the

* Documents on British Foreign Policy, Series III, Vol. III, p. 622.
† Ibid., Vol. IV, p. 622.

height of the crisis, the Ambassador wrote: "In my blackest pessimism I tried to console myself with two thoughts: (*a*) that war would rid Germany of Hitler, and (*b*) that it [would] remove me from Berlin. . . . As it is by keeping the peace, we have saved Hitler and his régime. . . ."*

Much has been written to disprove the idea that a serious conspiracy against Hitler existed in September 1938. Sir Ivone Kirkpatrick has spoken with some hindsight as if there was never any such likelihood. I can only recall my distinct impression at the time that until it became known that Mr. Chamberlain would fly to Berchtesgaden, a real threat to the authority of Hitler and his whole Nazi party did exist. Sir Winston Churchill, well informed on Germany, has accepted the circumstantial story of General Halder which has many corroborations. In the latter days of the crisis over Czechoslovakia there was still some talk of an attempt to arrest him, but the moment had receded. Exactly how much tension the German generals needed to move them against their Feuhrer it is now impossible to say. What is correct is that the British had no intention of letting the tension run to such a dangerous pitch. But only when high tension had been reached would a *Putsch* have seemed justifiable to the German General Staff. There was no permanent coincidence of interest with Britain. The generals were ready to act against Hitler if he were seen to them to have totally miscalculated. He did not miscalculate this time. It seemed as if nothing could in 1938 make the British government understand anything but their own military inadequacy.

German weaknesses were ignored. At the time I was informed that petrol stocks in the Reich were sufficient only for three months under conditions of war or blockade, that the Siegfried line was not complete, that tests had shown its concrete to be of inferior quality, that the morale of the German population was poor and that of the High Command suspect. Yet the outlook of the few who decided the fate of Europe in these days was so limited, that to Sir Horace Wilson and Sir Nevile Henderson it actually seemed possible that Hitler might repulse the first Chamberlain overture altogether.†

---

* Documents on British Foreign Policy, Series II, Vol. III, p. 615.

† A letter of September 9th discusses this possibility. British Documents, Series III, Vol. II, p. 649.

When they returned from Bohemia the German reserve officers told me that they had found the Czechoslovak fortifications, "impressive and impregnable to our arms. We could have gone round them, perhaps, but not reduced them. As it is, we have left pioneers to fill them with earth and rubble."

"When after Munich we were in a position to examine Czechoslovak military strength from within, what we saw greatly disturbed us," said Hitler in August 1939 to Dr. Burckhardt, the League of Nations High Commissioner for Danzig. "We had run a serious danger. The plans prepared by the Czech generals were formidable." In fact the Czechoslovak Army among its 30 divisions possessed 14 that were armoured or mechanised. Britain and France together did not possess as many when they went to war in 1939. There was, moreover, the hope that if the Czechoslovak forces managed to retreat in good order into Moravia and Slovakia then under conditions of a British naval blockade they would effectively prevent Germany from reaching the frontiers of Rumania and the Ploesti oil fields. As for the threat of bombing to Britain, no serious attempt was made even in 1940 until seizure of the Low Countries and the Channel Coast made it possible to give maximum fighter protection to bomber formations.

"The limitations and deficiencies of Germany only became public knowledge in the official survey conducted by British and American economists immediately after the war," writes Professor Medlicott.* "Thus it was discovered that her aircraft production in the autumn of 1939 had been 675 a month, no more than that of Great Britain; her tank production was less; she had started the war with only three months' supply of aviation petrol."

Lord Halifax answering in the debate on the Munich agreement on October 3rd, 1938, admitted that "nothing has been more persistently pressed upon me during the last two or three anxious months than this: If only Great Britain would say clearly and unmistakably for all to hear that she would resist any unprovoked aggression on Czechoslovakia no such unprovoked aggression would be made. We never felt able to use that language."

On the second day of the debate, Lord Lloyd reminded him in the course of strong criticisms that "I was able to inform

* *The Coming of War in 1939.*

him in the very early days of August of the whole German plan which worked out to the actual day. He knows too where that information came from, and that there was counsel from that source that to save the situation there should be an immediate declaration. We had an assurance from an authority which has proved right in every other respect that if that declaration had been made before mobilisation, things would almost certainly have been saved. . . . Why did we not take our courage in our hands?"

Lord Swinton, no longer in the Government, made a speech of polite congratulation to his former colleagues after Munich with a warning that time must not be lost to make plans and pass necessary defence legislation. His speech was less interesting than the scene that preceded it in private. Chamberlain had asked to see Lord Swinton before the debate and had solicited his support. He counted on having this influential Conservative on his side. Their conversation on October 3rd illustrates the exalted frame of mind in which Mr. Chamberlain had come back from this third visit to Germany, this time with the sheet of paper jointly signed by himself and Hitler in the study of Hitler's flat in Munich on September 30th.

Chamberlain had drafted a formula that:

> We regard the (Four Power) Agreement signed last night and the Anglo-German naval agreement as symbolic of the desire of our two peoples never to go to war with one another again.
>
> We are resolved that the method of consultation shall be the method adopted to deal with any other questions that may concern our two countries, and we are determined to continue our efforts to remove possible sources of difference and thus to contribute to assure the peace of Europe.

Historians have discussed whether the Prime Minister seriously believed in the value of this pledge. Mr. Chamberlain waved it and read it out on arrival at Heston Airport. He waved it a second time on arriving at 10 Downing Street, exclaiming: "This is the second time in our history there has come back from Germany to Downing Street peace with honour. I believe it is peace for our time." Did he really regard it as "peace for our time"?

Lord Dunglass, his Parliamentary Private Secretary, memorised a breakfast table remark of the Prime Minister on September 30th before he showed the unsigned draft document to Hitler:

"If he signs it and sticks to it, that will be fine; but if he breaks it, that will convince the Americans of the kind of man he is."*

The Americans who mattered had no illusions by then, and Mr. William Bullitt had used to General Goering language that Lord Halifax had felt unable to employ. When Goering had in a heated moment reminded the American Ambassador to France that there were at least five million German-speaking Americans to be reckoned with, Mr. Bullitt had replied that there were also at least five million trees on which to hang them if that proved necessary.†

Lord Swinton set out to discover whether such were really his views before pledging his support on October 3rd. He called on Mr. Chamberlain in his room at the House of Commons.

"I will support you, Prime Minister," he said, "if you are quite sure in your mind that you have only been buying time for our rearmament."

To this trusted Conservative and Privy Councillor, Mr. Chamberlain could speak his innermost thought. What he did was to draw from an inner pocket the Chamberlain-Hitler declaration, wave the sheet of paper and exclaim:

"But don't you understand? I have brought back peace."‡

A week later on October 11th General Keitel reported to Hitler what reinforcements were necessary to break all Czech resistance in Bohemia and Moravia.**

What then had clouded the sky so quickly after the Munich Conference before the Anglo-German declaration was even crumpled in the pocket of Mr. Chamberlain? There was anger in Mr. Duff Cooper's resignation speech, in which he recalled that Hitler had paused when he knew that Britain had mobilised the Fleet. But he was resigning and as Herr Theo

* Lord Home to Iain Macleod, *Neville Chamberlain.*
† British Documents, Series III, Vol. II, p. 219.
‡ Lord Swinton to author 1963. Mr. Chamberlain half qualified his public gesture before the House of Commons on October 6th saying that he had spoken in "some emotion" and though he still indeed believed "that we may yet secure peace for our time . . . I never meant to suggest that we should do that by disarmament."
** International Military Tribunal Document No. 388—PS. 48.

Kordt pointed out in a dispatch to Berlin, even Duff Cooper expressed the hope that a new chapter in European history might have begun. The documents now show that in October 1938 German diplomats in London were trying to build upon the Munich Agreement, but that Ribbentrop sent repeated orders to German press correspondents to attack British rearmament, to attack Eden, Churchill, Duff Cooper and other critics of German policy. Lord Halifax on October 7th asked the German Ambassador to enquire about alleged ill treatment of those Sudeten-Germans who were not members of Henlein's party. Hitler's reply given in his Saarbrucken speech of October 9th was ominous. "We cannot tolerate any longer the tutelage of governesses."

Two of the British Cabal in the debates after Munich had answered the criticisms of Sir Archibald Sinclair and others by asserting that the Czechoslovak guarantee was open to Russia. Sir Samuel Hoare said on October 3rd "We do not in any way contemplate the exclusion of Russia." Sir John Simon said on October 5th that "it is our hope that Russia will be willing to join in the guarantee of Czechoslovakia. It is most important that she should do so. The Government have no intention whatever of excluding Russia . . . from any future settlements in Europe."

But they had already excluded her, as Vansittart expostulated so strenuously on September 13th and 20th.

Lord Halifax seemed to correct Simon, at any rate when speaking to Dirksen on October 7th. He said that Britain "did not wish to exclude Russia from the political life of Europe . . . would welcome it if Russia acceded to the guarantee, but Sir John Simon's speech did not mean that Britain wished to influence in that direction."* These tactful nuances failed to soften the harshness of the Saarbrucken mood.

On October 21st, Hitler laid down the future tasks of the Wehrmacht as:

1. Securing the frontiers of the Reich and guarding against surprise air attacks
2. Liquidating the remainder of the Czech State
3. The occupation of Memel.

* Documents on German Foreign Policy, Series D, Vol. IV.

He dictated on October 24th that "it must be possible to smash at any time the remainder of the Czech State, should it pursue an anti-German policy".

Hitler was cold with the Hungarians when they came to Munich to press their claims for Slovak territory, and unimpressed when Mr. Daranyi denied that Hungary sought a common frontier with Poland. At the Vienna Award conference on November 2nd he assigned to Hungary the rind of Slovakia containing nine towns, but not Bratislava. Thus he kept the slender province of Slovakia in being. He might need it as a military corridor into the Ruthenian province of Czechoslovakia, the frontiers of which bordered on Rumania, his nearest source of oil.

On November 8th a German diplomat in Paris, Herr Ernst vom Rath, was murdered by a Jewish youth, Herschel Grynspan. This unleashed widespread pogroms in Germany. A heavy strain was thus put on Anglo-German relations. It is difficult to know what the Inner Cabinet thought in private of peace prospects in these months. On October 31st, Dr. Dirksen reported to Berlin that "Chamberlain has complete confidence in the Fuehrer". Sir Samuel Hoare in discussing arms limitation with Dirksen had "let slip the observation that after a further *rapprochement* between the four European Great Powers, the acceptance of certain defence obligations, or even a guarantee by them against Soviet Russia, was conceivable in the event of an attack by Soviet Russia."*

This was a dangerous blandishment and unavailing. I find in my own papers a report of November 22nd, 1938 embodying the first indications that I received of Hitler's thinking after Munich. I print it as an interesting specimen of the facts and inaccuracies upon which Hitler made up his mind. There is also a certain interest in the sequence of aggressions forecast.†

November 22nd, 1938.

I.G.C.

MEMORANDUM

An exposé made by Herr Hitler in October of his future policy after considering the Munich Agreement. Attended by

* Documents on German Foreign Policy, H.M.S.O. Series D, Vol. IV, p. 321.
† Copies of this memorandum were sent to my Editor and to Lord Lloyd.

three or four of the highest functionaries of the Foreign Ministry, among them Herr von Ribbentrop.

It is difficult to approximate the date on which this speech was made. The source, which I am compelled to omit, was a person present. I have every confidence that his version is accurate and balanced. It agrees with all observations of the conduct and speeches of Herr Hitler since the beginning of October: some of the programme laid down in this speech has been fulfilled, the rest is in process of being fulfilled.

Herr Hitler began by producing a confidential report which had been brought to him. It was written by a Herr von Kries, correspondent of a German newspaper in London, and shown to the Leader by some interested person. He read the report to his listeners. The German journalist declared that on Monday, September 26th, the representative of Soviet Russia in London and Paris informed the British and French Governments that Soviet Russia was not able to take military action in a European war.*

Thereupon, Herr Hitler turned and rated the assembled few in wrathful tones, saying that he was surrounded by cowards and ignorant men. If he had been supplied with the report at the right moment, he would never have invited Mr. Chamberlain to Munich and would never have signed the Agreement. He then began to delineate his new policy.

It was necessary, he said, to devote attention to internal policy first. He wanted to eliminate from German life the Jews, the Churches, and private industry. After that, he would turn to foreign policy again.

In the meantime, Great Britain must be attacked with speeches and in the press. First the Opposition, and then Chamberlain himself. He had learned from the negotiations preceding Munich how to deal with the English— one had to encounter them aggressively (vor dem Bauch treten).

He would deal with England as he had done with France, where he had produced a confusion in political life. Flandin was for Germany and there were also such men in England. He named a rising British politician† as possible leader of a

* No such *démarche* is on record. Herr von Kries may have received a version of the Litvinov statement made in Geneva on September 23rd and received in London on the 24th.
  † Name omitted.

Fascist Great Britain. His (Hitler's) aim was to overthrow Chamberlain. The Opposition would not then be capable of forming a new government, and the same would occur as in France. The political strength of Great Britain would be paralysed. In England too, Fascism would gain the upper hand.

He did not want in the near future to brand as a lie his promise not to make more territorial acquisitions in Europe. Therefore he was turning to internal policy. But when Mr. Chamberlain was no longer Prime Minister, he would no longer consider himself bound by the Munich Agreement. Memel would at any time fall into the lap of the Reich; like a ripe fruit. Memel and Danzig were not urgent problems. Now it was for the Ukraine to be made into an independent State. He referred to the collaboration of Sir Henry Deterding in the German Plan. A vassal State was to be formed. Poland was to be squeezed (umklammert) as the Ukraine would be liberated against the will of Poland.

It may be commented upon this account, that evidently Herr Hitler was making a considered statement of policy, for he has held closely to it ever since. The socialisation of private industry is being prepared. I think it will not be long before Mr. Chamberlain is attacked. There are signs that the Ukraine is definitely the next objective, and that expansion eastwards will be carried out against the will of Poland, Hungary and Rumania.

A private understanding has been reached between the Governments of the Reich and Czechoslovakia that the new Czechoslovak fortifications shall not be built round Bohemia, as Germany will guarantee those frontiers, but along the narrow waist of Slovakia, so that the country can be held open for a German advance against the closing-up motion which Polish and Hungarian diplomacy still contemplates. The new forts are to be built out of the British loan.

It is worth remembering that in internal politics the plan against the Jews was sketched out by Herr Hitler himself, and left to Marshal Goering and Dr. Goebbels to work out, as is customary with the dirty work of the Reich, also that Hitler ordered personally the measures against the Confessional Church now taking shape. Apart from the newly emerged Ukraine plan, my outline of future aims remains unchanged in order–Memel, Danzig, Sleswig, Eupen-Mulmedy, Switzerland, Alsace-Lorraine.

This report has some points in common with documents since published. It was followed by more alarming information. The same German sources on November 27th reported to me that three Army Corps were to be mobilised within the next few days and march on Prague, the VIIIth Corps from Breslau, the XIVth from Magdeburg, the XVIIth from Austria. I arranged for a news dispatch without dateline to be published in the *News Chronicle* of November 29th containing this report. It resulted in a long and angry chorus in the National-Socialist press. Colonel Mason-Macfarlane reported that my source "was in a position to obtain accurate information", but could find no evidence of intention. He recalled recent military movements to deal with a crisis then threatening in Carpathian-Ukraine (Ruthenia). His analysis of German military intentions in 1939, forwarded on December 26th, was that an easterly (Poland) or south-easterly (Rumania) campaign by Germany was more likely than any move westwards, and that "military action for next year is contemplated and in preparation".*

General Keitel had meanwhile become nervous of military movements being detected. He realised that he could hardly carry out an orthodox advance on Prague without preparations. This led him on December 17th to issue a further secret directive, as the publication of German documents has since revealed. It instructed that, "The action (against Czechoslovakia) must be carried out only with the peacetime Wehrmacht, without reinforcement by mobilisation. Any units detailed to march must not leave their stations until the night before crossing the frontier."†

A curious pointer towards German intentions was received at this time by Lord Halifax through a British Embassy official in Berlin. The Foreign Secretary noted a December report forwarded to London that a German officer under cover of night and secrecy had revealed that Hitler had given instructions for plans to be prepared for an all-out air attack against Great Britain, for use in certain eventualities, such plans to be ready by the middle of March. This report had the effect of

* Documents on British Foreign Policy, Series. III, Vol. III, p. 544–45.
† Documents on German Foreign Policy, Series D, Vol. III.

accelerating British arms production, but the report itself was not accepted as evidence of a hostile disposition of Hitler, Lord Halifax recorded, until the seizure of Prague in March gave it added veracity.

The pattern of events in 1939 was shaped on October 24th, 1938, over a luncheon table in the Grand Hotel, Berchtesgaden, when the Polish Ambassador in Berlin, M. Josef Lipski, was the guest of Herr von Ribbentrop. The report of this conversation published in the German White Book of 1939 is significantly different from the version in the Polish White Book of 1939. In the German report written by Counsellor Walther Hewel, M. Lipski opened the proceedings by suggesting that the tail of Czechoslovakia, Ruthenia, should be chopped off and attached to Hungary in the interests of stability in the Danube Area.

He said this would be of great value in sealing it off against the East (Soviet Russia). Lipski too protested that the rumours of a bloc being formed against Germany were nonsense. M. Lipski's account to M. Beck does not reveal the Ruthenia plan, but he does mention a proposal of Herr von Ribbentrop for "a joint policy towards Russia on the basis of the anti-Comintern Pact".* Both versions agree that Ribbentrop proposed a general settlement of outstanding German-Polish problems. The Ribbentrop points were that:

> Danzig should be incorporated in the Reich. Germany should build an extra-territorial motor road and railway through the Polish corridor (Pomorze) to link Germany with Danzig and East Prussia.
>
> Poland would receive similar facilities through Danzig territory and a free port.
>
> Both nations would guarantee their common frontiers or each other's territories.
>
> The German Polish treaty to be prolonged by 10–25 years.
>
> Both countries to add a consultative clause to their 1934 Agreement.†

Ribbentrop brushed off a warning by M. Lipski that Poland could tolerate no change in the status of Danzig. He extended

---

* This proposition is not contained in the German Documents, doubtless in consideration of impending approaches to Russia, or was omitted because at the time of publication of the German White Book, Germany and Russia were on terms of understanding.

† Perhaps an Anti-Comintern Clause.

an invitation to Colonel Beck to visit him and discuss these ideas. Beck sent long and repetitive instructions to Lipski on October 31st, and these Lipski read to Hitler on November 19th. When Ribbentrop perceived how firm Colonel Beck was, he adopted a very friendly tone and appeared to waive the subject for the time being, adding that he had only vaguely discussed it with the Fuehrer. This did not prevent Hitler, when Beck visited him on January 5th, 1939 in Berchtesgaden from raising precisely the same points, saying that sooner or late Danzig must return to Germany and drawing attention to the need for greater freedom of communication between Germany and East Prussia. Beck was assailed again with these demands by Ribbentrop in Munich on the following day, and again Beck emphatically resisted them. He told Ribbentrop that the optimism that he had felt after previous visits to Germany had now given way to pessimism.

The Polish Foreign Minister was reticent about the German demands. Sir Howard Kennard was able to send only an uncertain report from Warsaw about them. In return Mr. William Strang forwarded to the British Ambassador early in November 1938 an alarming report from secret sources that Germany intended to abolish the corridor altogether and sever all minority territories from the Polish state. But since the diplomatic exchanges were taken no further after Beck's visit to Hitler, the menace to Poland remained invisible for the time being.

Early in December it appears that Ribbentrop sounded his British contacts on the acceptability of German claims against Poland. There is no record of such feelers in the published documents of the British Foreign Office, but other channels existed. For example the British Prime Minister's press adviser, Mr. George Steward, was in touch with the head of the Ribbentrop Office in London, Dr. Hesse, and had asked early in October for direct contacts between Ribbentrop and the Prime Minister's office, circumventing the Foreign Office, where, said Steward, "extremely bitter feeling" against Germany existed:

"It was important that all major questions should be dealt with direct, thus bypassing the Foreign Office and also Sir Nevile Henderson. . . ."*

Some such German approach had evidently been made, but

* Documents on German Foreign Policy, Series D, Vol. IV, p. 306.

at least the German proposals were put to expert British scrutiny. Sir Robert Vansittart commented on a secret discussion on December 7th, 1938:

"Not content with having dismembered Czechoslovakia, the Germans now wish to do the same to Poland and wish us to connive officially at their ambition by double-crossing the Poles beforehand. Such an attitude is impossible for any honourable nation to adopt, and the sooner it is dismissed the better. The answer that may be made to this is that Germany will soon take the corridor anyhow. That is pure defeatism in the first place, and in the second place such a consummation is unnecessary if Poland will readjust her relations sensibly with Russia, which she seems to be at present in train of doing. The Germans are so well aware of this that the Ribbentrop school is already bent on detaching the Ukraine from Russia and breaking up the present Russian régime from within. The Germans think they can overturn the Stalin State by the aid of the discontented elements in the Russian Army. We should then have in Germany a régime that had installed in Russia a régime favourable to itself, and had completely paralysed Poland by annexing the corridor. If that is not a total domination of Europe, I don't know what is. And we are apparently expected to be foolish enough not only to connive, but to consent to it in advance. In addition we are expected to make substantial colonial concessions. Besides colonies we are also to give them a large loan. . . . I ought to add, and it is an extremely important point, that by consenting to any further concession to Hitler whatever we shall be further sounding the death knell of the German moderates. . . . The Agreement at Munich almost extinguished them, as it was bound to do, and anything in the nature of a colonial concession, or some dirty dealing about the Polish corridor would complete the process."

The Munich Agreement was really stillborn. If Sir Robert's advice and the accompanying reports were being read by the Cabinet, they could hardly believe in any serious German intention to keep the Munich Agreement. Dirksen spoke in October of Mr. Chamberlain's complete faith in Hitler.* Lord Halifax asserts† that only after the March on Prague was that faith shattered. Chamberlain did not omit to announce an increased rearmament plan after the Munich Agreement, but

*In a political report to Ribbentrop.　　† *Fulness of Days.*

it was not the accelerated plan that the situation demanded.

The argument will long continue whether it was right or wrong to decline the risks of war in September 1938; and to have worked with such a large safety margin to British diplomacy—one which indeed made it difficult for Hitler to find a real pretext to go to war, even if he had wanted. I have sought the opinion twenty-five years afterwards of Sir Horace Wilson on Munich in retrospect. His summing up, after repeated exclamations that the Czechoslovak state was quite impossible and ought never to have been formed, was this:

"It was a very difficult situation. It was pretty clear Hitler had written off France, economically and militarily. You can add, of course, the decision of the U.S.A. on non-involvement. The Dominions said no war over Czechoslovakia. It was a perfectly English approach on the part of Mr. Chamberlain. He thought in foreign policy that if the situation was untidy, we should tidy it up, get the facts, put them in the right order and arrive at some conclusion."

The real issue in the summer of 1938 was not what Mr. Chamberlain wanted to do, but the way that he did it. In the estimate of his press adviser George Steward, "in the end the Prime Minister had not received assistance or support of any kind from the Foreign Office. . . . The final outcome was . . . exclusively due to Chamberlain who had however . . . ignored the provisions of the British Constitution and customary Cabinet usage."* Allowing for the fact that this opinion was given to a German in October 1938 in pursuit of dubious contacts, it is still the truth. Had the full Cabinet shared his knowledge in August and moments of decision in September, the flight to Germany would not have been so precipitate, the Fleet would have been mobilised sooner, the British attitude more tenacious, the anxiety to concede German demands less apparent. The irrefutable argument of Vansittart for bringing Russia into the deliberations would have received full and proper consideration. In short, had the wisdom of the British constitution been observed, British influence might have been used to an effective purpose.

In December 1938 I visited Mr. Winston Churchill in Chartwell and found him grieved and impatient at the inertia of Britain. He paced about like a giant who cannot use his strength.

* H.M.S.O. Documents on German Foreign Policy, Series D, Vol. IV, p. 306.

"The Czech should have fired their cannon," he exclaimed. To my question whether he in office at this time would have undertaken the same mission as Chamberlain—would he have gone to meet Hitler, he replied:

"Yes, but I would have invited Herr Hitler to come and meet me, in the North Sea, on board a British battleship."

CHAPTER XVI

THE GOLDEN AGE

The end of the year 1938 found Sir Robert Vansittart
greatly concerned at the dislocation between British military
policy and foreign policy. As he saw it, France had every
justification in asking Britain to share some of the military
burden on land. To fight "in the blue", that is on sea and in
the air, was no relief to France, which had just lost the aid of
40 Czechoslovak divisions and would soon be faced with nearly
150 German divisions and large Italian land forces. "The Germans are going to continue their drive for the domination of
Europe and will then turn West," he wrote to Lord Halifax on
December 19th, 1938. "All this will happen pretty quickly
now." He thought that Britain was being substituted for France
in the *Mein Kampf* doctrine as the main enemy, and that Britain
was still "basing her politico-military policy on assumptions
that have no chance of fulfilment, and the sands of time are now
running out very rapidly".*

The frozen calm maintained itself that winter, a tangle of
rocks hanging over Europe. Between January 11th and 14th
Mr. Chamberlain and Lord Halifax were in Rome on an
official visit, accompanied by Sir Alexander Cadogan and a
party of five advisers and secretaries. Sir Robert Vansittart was
not among them, though he had a standing invitation from
the Duce to return to Rome. His part in the visit, so I am told,
was confined to drafting security advice to the Prime Minister
and Lord Halifax, as it was suspected that behind the Raffaello
decorations of the official residence assigned to them, the Villa
Madama, there would be listening devices to record their
conversation.

Of this visit it is notable that the Duce told Mr. Chamberlain
that he desired peace to develop the Italian Imperium, the same
message as he had sent to Hitler during the Munich crisis. On
the second day of their talks at the Palazzo Venezia, January
12th, Mr. Chamberlain—asked by Mussolini whether he had

* Vansittart Papers.

any more points to raise—said that he would venture to ask
for the opinion of the Duce on a matter of some delicacy. . . .
He had hoped that after Munich . . . it would be possible . . .
to put relations between Germany and Britain on a better
footing. Unfortunately this had not been found practicable . . .
and the attitude of Germany was giving rise to a good deal of
anxiety and doubt. . . . Some thought that the massing of troops
might mean a move towards the Ukraine or Poland, or against
Poland and Russia combined . . . preceded perhaps by a sudden
attack against the West.

Mussolini shook his head and, speaking slowly and deliberately, said a German attack on the West was out of the question.
He did not believe that Hitler had any intention of setting up
an independent Ukraine. Hitler now desired to consolidate
his expanded Reich. Chamberlain thought these views . . ."not
quite sufficient to account for the uneasy situation" and asked
finally about a guarantee of Czechoslovakia. Mussolini began
ponderously to consider from which of her neighbours an
attack on Czechoslovakia might come—as for Germany, she
had shown that she regarded herself as "protector of Czechoslovakia". He thought therefore that there would be no attack
on Czechoslovakia from any side. . . . "Owing to the actions
of Germany and Italy, Central Europe would remain quiet."
To Mr. Chamberlain's enquiry whether Italy thought it
desirable to leave the question of the guarantee open for the
present, the Italian answer seemed to be emphatically yes.
However, the British Government took up certain points made
by Mussolini in this conversation concerning the constitution,
neutrality and frontiers of the new state and in a note of
February 8th asked for the German views on a guarantee of
Czecho-Slovakia. (The British had adopted the hyphen
introduced by the second republic of President Hacha in
deference to the egalitarian sentiments of the Slovaks.) On
February 15th Sir Nevile Henderson saw Ribbentrop but did
not press the guarantee question. It was not till March 3rd
that a German reply was received to the effect that Germany
preferred to await "a clarification of internal developments in
Czecho-Slovakia before any decision on a four power
guarantee." This cryptic reply appeared so unimportant to
Sir Nevile Henderson that he forwarded it to London by air
mail. He himself anticipated at this time "in the immediate

future a period of relative calm."* Mr. Chamberlain had two weeks earlier used calm language to the American Ambassador on the outlook in Europe. About that time reports reaching the State Department forecast a crisis in the middle of March, though indicating an attack on France as the likelihood. Thus the rumours at the beginning of March were few, and they did not point to a march on Prague. When Mr. Maisky lunched with Mr. R. A. Butler† on March 9th, Czechoslovakia was not discussed, though on March 6th Mr. Newton in Prague reported to the Foreign Office the relations between Czechs and Slovaks to be "heading for a crisis". Sir Nevile Henderson in a lengthy situation report dated March 9th reached the conclusion that absorption of Czechoslovakia would be "within a year or two". But on the evening of March 10th this leisurely survey was outstripped by a telegram in which he reported alarming views. His Vice-Consul in Dresden had information that "Slovak claims against the Czechs will be encouraged to the point of civil disturbance, whereupon Germany will send in troops to restore order. . . . If Herr Hitler seeks adventure, the most obvious form that it would take would be some *coup* in Czechoslovakia."‡ But before Henderson's dispatch had left Berlin the British Cabinet blundered into "the Golden Age".

The words are taken from a phrase in a speech by Sir Samuel Hoare. He had been preparing his annual speech to his Chelsea electors, "and as I wished to allude to foreign affairs, I consulted Chamberlain. . . ."§ The Prime Minister asked him to discourage the view that war was inevitable and Sir Samuel took his advice.

"Suppose," he told the electors of Chelsea on March 10th, "that political confidence could be restored in Europe . . . suppose that the peoples of Europe were able to free themselves from the nightmare that haunts them, and from an expenditure on armaments that beggars them, could we not then devote the inventions and discoveries of our time to the creation of a golden age. . . . Five men in Europe,** if they

* British Documents on Foreign Policy, Series III, Vol. IV.
† Under-Secretary for Foreign Affairs.
‡ His unerring senior Sir Orme Sargent, Deputy Under-Secretary, recorded on this dispatch that Henderson three weeks earlier had written his "definite impression . . . that Hitler does not contemplate any adventures at the moment".
§ *Nine Troubled Years.*
** Chamberlain, Daladier, Hitler, Mussolini and Stalin were intended. By the time he wrote *Nine Troubled Years*, Lord Templewood's memory had reduced them to four, omitting Mussolini.

worked with a singleness of purpose and a unity of action, might in an incredibly short space transform the whole history of the world. . . . The world could look forward to a golden age of prosperity." *Punch* appeared at this time attuned to the Prime Minister's optimism and its famous artist Bernard Partridge, who after years of patriotic service deserved better guidance, drew a cartoon for publication on March 15th of the grim spectre of war vanishing out of the window. The Prime Minister did more than brief Sir Samuel. On the evening of of March 9th he briefed the lobby correspondents in the House of Commons without consulting Lord Halifax. The speech of Sir Samuel was made on a day when Westminster political commentaries were reflecting official optimism. The *Daily Telegraph* Political correspondent, writing of Anglo-German relations and European problems—with attribution to Cabinet circles—reported the opinion that "unofficial and semi-official contacts have recently shown, it is thought, a point of view much nearer to the truth than official statements. The visit of Mr. Oliver Stanley, President of the Board of Trade, to Berlin this month will lead to another step in the settlement of outstanding differences in Europe."

Sir Alexander Cadogan traced this commentary to its source. Chamberlain had also spoken of disarmament and Franco-Italian relations. "He really shouldn't do this," noted Sir Alexander, "or at least he should consult Halifax beforehand."

The Foreign Secretary wrote a reproachful letter to the Prime Minister, and a most apologetic reply reached him from Chequers dated Saturday, March 11th. The Chamberlain reply, since published in the Halifax memoirs, was that "I promise faithfully not to do it again, but to consult you beforehand if they ask for anything on foreign affairs."* By the time he wrote this letter, Mr. Chamberlain (and Lord Halifax) had been apprised of what was likely to happen in Europe. The senior Intelligence Officer came that Saturday to Sir Alexander Cadogan's office, "to raise my hair with tales of Germany going into Czechoslovakia in the next 24 hours." "Maybe", Sir Alexander noted, and "told Halifax, but let him go off to Oxford. Warned P.M."†

Sir Alexander retained his doubts. My own notes show that

* *Fulness of Days.* By 1957 Lord Halifax appears to have forgotten the incident to which this letter alluded.
† Sir A. Cadogan, Diary.

a very similar warning reached me in Berlin on March 11th, with the advice not to publish, as that would have meant certain explusion for me, but to "let it happen, so that Mr. Chamberlain can see what sort of man Hitler really is". Having in mind that the *News Chronicle* forecast of a similar move on November 29th had not been confirmed by action at that time, I risked no open forecast. The German press that morning was full of reports of Czech terror against the Slovaks. What was unknown, except perhaps to the informants of my informant, was that General Keitel on March 11th sent to the German Foreign Ministry a Most Secret document (by hand of officer) containing Hitler's military conditions for the ultimatum to the Czechoslovak Government. The Czech Army was to lay down its arms, ground its aircraft and return to barracks.

Sir Nevile Henderson reported the press excitement in his dispatches. The Czechoslovak Government had either to act, or see the country split in two by Slovak separatism. The German press reported that Monsignor Tiso, premier of Slovakia, had appealed to Germany for support against repressive measures.

Henderson decided to let the Italian Ambassador do any inquiring at the Foreign Ministry about this critical situation. Sir Nevile suggested to Lord Halifax the least offensive possibility—that Germany might decide to man a demarcation line between Czechs and Slovaks, and compel a withdrawal of the Czechoslovak army from Slovakia. "But I doubt whether Hitler has taken any decision and I consider it therefore highly desirable that nothing should be said or published abroad during the weekend which will excite him to precipitate action." On the afternoon of Sunday, March 12th Sir Nevile still had "no evidence that the German Government intend to exploit the present unrest in Czecho-Slovakia". The Italian and Belgian Ambassadors had visited the Foreign Ministry and came back with the impression that "the German government are viewing the whole question calmly". On Monday the 13th the Ambassador reported German mechanised troop movements from Breslau and Vienna, but "German government is keeping its secret as to its exact intention". He now tried for an appointment with Baron von Weizsaecker, but was told that the Under-Secretary was away in the country with Herr von Ribbentrop. He could have sought out the next senior German official, but did not do so.

On the evening of March 13th Hitler received Monsignor Tiso, and declared his indignation that Slovakia had not yet proclaimed its independence. "Germany does not intend to take Slovakia into her Lebensraum and that is why you must immediately proclaim the independence of Slovakia, or I will disinterest myself in her fate." Tiso thanked the Führer, flew back to Bratislava and proclaimed Slovakia's independence. He accepted protectorate status three days later. On the evening of the March 14th it was the turn of President Hacha and M. Chvalkovsky to be summoned to Berlin. Hitler confronted the President and the Foreign Minister with a document making Bohemia and Moravia German protectorates. It was useless, he snarled, for the Czechs to expect support or intervention by Britain or France. Hitler signed the documents with a flourish and strode out, leaving the infirm President in the charge of Goering and Ribbentrop, who hunted the two Czechs round the table, thrusting pens into their hands and threatening that if they did not sign, Prague would be bombed into ruins. President Hacha fainted twice and was revived. At 4.30 a.m. Ribbentrop established telephone communication with the Cabinet in Prague so that his Ministers could give their assent to the signature. The broken man signed. German troops had already crossed the frontiers of Czechoslovakia. They seized a booty of 1,500 planes, 469 tanks, 500 anti-aircraft guns, 43,000 machine guns and a million rifles with ammunition and the vast Skoda arsenals as well.

The British Government came to grips with this crisis on March 13th, but no Cabinet was called. Lord Halifax went off to Sunderland on a false scent and made a speech in which he solemnly warned General Franco not to interfere with British merchant shipping.

"The Slovak situation is still very obscure", noted Sir Alexander. He showed intelligence reports to the Prime Minister repeating that the Germans were prepared to move in, but commented that there was still nothing definite to show that the Germans had decided to act—still less *when*.

Vansittart declared that the visit to Berlin by Mr. Oliver Stanley must be stopped. "Van in a neurotic state", noted Cadogan, but he too recommended to the Prime Minister that "if there is an *Einmarsch* in the next two days we should have to consider that particular question".

Lord Halifax arrived back from Sunderland on the morning of March 14th. Sir Alexander told him of his talk with the Prime Minister. Lord Halifax agreed that in the case of German "direct action", Oliver Stanley should not go to Berlin. Sir Alexander noted "all sorts of reports of what Germany is going to do—march in tonight etc. . . . Probably true. Talk with Halifax, Van, Orme Sargent and Malkin. If Germany has taken the decision, there is probably nothing we can do to stop her now."

M. Charles Corbin, the French Ambassador, called that afternoon to say that his Government was thinking of making an enquiry in Berlin. "That did not impress me very much," noted Cadogan. Lord Halifax telephoned to Sir Alexander from Parliament after 5 p.m. and asked for telegrams to be drafted to Berlin and Paris. Sir Alexander commented that the proposal to draft a telegram to Berlin was "quite useless, and the P.M. realises that, but wants to be 'on the record' ".

The Resident Clerk of the Foreign Office telephoned to Cadogan early on March 15th to say that the Germans were marching into Prague. Sir Alexander walked to the Foreign Office with Lord Halifax discussing the news and set about drafting statements to be given to both Houses that afternoon. Meanwhile the Cabinet met, summoned as usual too late for any effective action.* No doubt the intelligence reports were examined, and certain of them found to have been correct. At 12.30 p.m. Sir Alexander took his draft statements over to 10 Downing Street and discussed them with the Prime Minister, Halifax and Wilson till 2 p.m. Then the trio went to lunch and left Sir Alexander to put the draft in order over a sandwich in the Cabinet room. Sir Horace Wilson in retrospect told me that

---

* The bewilderment of the British Cabinet in 1939 was mystifying to Mr. Churchill.

In the debate of April 13th, 1939, he said: "We have seen both in the case of the subjugation of Bohemia and in the case of the invasion of Albania that apparently Ministers of the Crown had no inkling, or at any rate no conviction, of what was coming. I cannot believe it was the fault of the Secret Service. Several days before the stroke at Bohemia Nazi intentions were known in many countries. The whole timetable was laid down. The whole programme was known beforehand. We sneer at the Press, but they give an extremely true picture of a great deal that is going on, a very much fuller and more detailed picture than we are able to receive from Ministers of the Crown."

Sir John Simon expostulated: "What had to be remembered is that we do not get one set of information saying that one thing is likely to happen, but we get a whole series of messages stating all sorts of alternative developments, which have to be sifted out. After the facts are known it is easy to assume that the course of events was equally clear and certain beforehand." This was plausible, but not the full truth.

it was "when Hitler marched into Prague and broke his word to an Englishman, that Chamberlain said—'you don't do that to me'". That moment of awakening had not been reached on March 15th. For provided with the draft, Mr. Chamberlain told the House of Commons that Czechoslovakia had "become disintegrated . . . I have so often heard charges of breach of faith bandied about, which do not seem founded upon sufficient premises, that I do not wish to associate myself today with any charges of that character." He said also that Britain had no treaty liabilities to Czechoslovakia . . . "I bitterly regret what has now occurred. . . . But do not let us on that account be deflected from our course. The aim of the Government is now, as it always has been, to substitute the method of discussion for the method of force in settlement of differences."

The last words must have been of his own authorship or borrowed from Sir Horace Wilson. For Sir Alexander Cadogan noticed that although the Prime Minister had based himself on the drafted statement, he had decided to go beyond it. He made a diary note that the Prime Minister "added that he would go on with his policy ('appeasement'?). Fatal!"

On Tuesday March 16th an angry reaction was brewing in Parliament and up and down Great Britain. The French Ambassador came to ask for a joint protest. Lord Halifax and Sir Alexander went into earnest consultation that morning. "I don't know *where* we are," noted Sir Alexander. "We ought, I suppose, to make a stand (whatever that may mean), but after the P.M.'s speech, can we?" Two wartime biographies of Lord Halifax* recorded that the Foreign Secretary then persuaded Mr. Chamberlain to greater firmness in his long expected Birmingham speech of March 17th. This view is shared by Sir John Wheeler-Bennett† and Sir Alexander's last entry for March 16th recorded that he thought the Prime Minister had been "binged up to be a bit firmer". Sir John Simon had not been "binged up", however, and made a speech of miserable weakness on March 16th, saying that "it is indeed impossible to suppose that in these circumstances the guarantee to Czechoslovakia can have any meaning". Lord De La Warr, who had lost the office of Lord Privy Seal over his Cabinet attitude towards appeasement in September 1938, stood up as Minister of Education that

* *Lord Halifax*, Stuart Hodgson. *Viscount Halifax*, Allen Campbell Johnson.
† *Munich: Prologue to Tragedy.*

night and corrected Simon in a speech that described the events of the previous day as "naked and arrogant aggression".

Another positive move by Lord Halifax on March 16th was to send Sir Robert Vansittart to M. Maisky to tell the Russian Ambassador of the change of policy that the Birmingham speech would bring. M. Maisky was heartened, though in his reminiscences* he prefers to dwell on the perfidy of Sir Samuel Hoare's "golden age" speech than on the efforts of Sir Robert and Lord Halifax to stiffen Chamberlain.

Mr. Chamberlain in Birmingham on March 17th made a speech that upon analysis seemed only to mean that Britain would fight for its own liberty but would not enter into new and unspecified commitments. But the Prime Minister concentrated entirely upon the breach of the Munich Agreement that had been committed. "Public opinion in the world has received a sharper shock than has ever yet been administered to it, even by the present régime in Germany." Of the day on which German troops entered Czechoslovakia he said that "the Government were at a disadvantage, because the information that we had was only partial; much of it was unofficial. We had no time to digest it, much less to form a considered opinion upon it." For this reason his first exposition to Parliament had been cautious, he said. "I hope to correct that mistake tonight." He then proceeded to defend his policy of the previous year—"the peace of Europe was saved"—he repeated the assurances of Hitler and spoke of hopes that had been wantonly shattered. Was this the end of an old adventure or the beginning of a new? "Is this, in fact, a step in the direction of an attempt to dominate the world by force?" "There is hardly anything I would not sacrifice for peace, but there is one thing that I must except, and that is the liberty that we have enjoyed for hundreds of years." He ended, after some qualifications, with the assertion that the nation had not so lost its fibre that it would not resist an attempt to dominate the world by force.

Two comments by Vansittart mark the march into Prague. He reflected sadly that "there seems to be no longer any strength in our loins or capacity for moral indignation in our natures, and I fear that we shall be judged accordingly". In an outburst against Henderson, he exclaimed that "Our Ambassador in Berlin never warned his Government that the occupation

* *Who Helped Hitler?*, Ivan Maisky, 1964.

of Prague was imminent, and an extraordinary and incomprehensible official optimism was in consequence being disseminated on the very eve of this catastrophe. I cannot think how the Ambassador can have failed to foresee this event. I myself received and transmitted three separate warnings nearly a month before the event happened. I had hoped that sufficient action might be taken at Berlin to serve as a deterrent, although it was clear that Hitler's mind was already made up." He ended with a desperate "nothing seems any good; it seems as if nobody will listen to or believe me".

There is some confirmation of Vansittart's complaint in a diary note by the Permanent Under-Secretary ten days later, March 26th. "I must say it is turning out at present as Van predicted and as I never believed it would."

For his speech on the golden age Sir Samuel Hoare was vehemently attacked from all political quarters. It looked as if he might resign again. "I felt that my part in the Government was finished and that I had better retire from public life." Lord Beaverbrook gave him some encouragement to carry on, and this time Lord Beaverbrook's advice was accepted. But while the Cabinet were trying to assess what to do next, and what Hitler would do next, the State visit of the French President came full upon them. It was due on March 21st, and the pomp and protocol "has made this week a nightmare", wrote Sir Alexander. "It has rendered anything like an orderly conduct of affairs almost impossible."

They went through with the haunted charade. Upon Vansittart had fallen the task of managing theatrical entertainments written by Sacha Guitry and Sir Seymour Hicks. These were performed in a temporary theatre under the glass roof of the India Office courtyard. Sir Philip Sassoon found 18th century liveries for the footmen at the Foreign Office banquet, held in the Locarno room. The Goldsmiths Company lent its plate. Portraits of the Kings of England, with additions brought from the National Portrait Gallery, hung round the walls. Azaleas, roses and lilies were massed around the pillars of the Foreign Office and the India Office. The Duke of Buccleuch had lent tapestries. Lifeguards were posted in the corridors beside the busts and statues of Secretaries of State. "It all looked well and was amusingly original", thought Lord Halifax, and the Lord Chamberlain wrote to thank Sir Robert Vansittart on behalf of King George VI.

Sir Robert attended with a thousand other guests the reception after the State Banquet at Buckingham Palace which was followed by a smaller reception by special invitation. This must have been a painful function for him. The War Minister, Mr. Hore-Belisha, to please the French, had just spoken of creating a British land force of nineteen divisions. It was a response on paper to the policy that Vansittart had been advocating. But there was nothing like it in immediate prospect. That morning also there was confirmation in the telegrams that Lithuania had accepted an ultimatum from Germany and was evacuating its troops from Memel. Lithuania had also agreed to abandon any thought of union with Poland. Another British project gone! Rumania was signing away its mineral resources to Germany. Even the Dutch behind their neutral dykes feared a German ultimatum. Europe seemed to be crumbling away. The banquet took place in the white and gold ballroom of Buckingham Palace. Vansittart put on court dress, the riband and star of a Grand Cross of the Bath and the Grand Cross of St. Michael and St. George. The royal plate of gold and silver gilt decorated the table under glittering chandeliers. The Lords, the great Commoners, the Ambassadors, the High Commissioners were there. The Guards and the Black Watch played light music. Georges Bonnet, the lank haired, strolled among the French guests. His unclean image remained so vividly in the distressed mind of Sir Alexander Cadogan that he fancied a striking resemblance to Bonnet in a bedraggled young pigeon that was hatched that spring outside his window on the Foreign Office balcony—a likeness so disagreeable to him daily that he finally sent for the Clerk of Works to have nest and bird removed. Bonnet himself was less easy to dislodge. That night a chosen few danced at the Palace, and as Sir Robert and Lady Vansittart saw the tall spare figure of Lord Halifax bobbing round the floor with Madame Lebrun, blue garter sash and the garter badge itself around his calf, they thought of the fugitives of Europe and the war that was to be. For a King just dead, or a President, there would have been Court mourning, but who could order mourning for the death of a State? They left the gaiety and splendour and went back to 44 Park Street, overcome with foreboding, and found in the refrigerator for supper instead a slice of cold pie. They had witnessed the end of the golden age.

CHAPTER XVII

THE ANGLO-POLISH AGREEMENT

THERE had been little opportunity indeed to warn before the march into Prague. I can remember only sending a cryptic telegram to Winston Churchill's secretary, and wondering in the train that took me from Berlin to Prague on March 16th whether there would ever again be a clear storm signal as in the summer of 1938, or a series of lightning moves instead. I turned over in my mind one piece of information received in January from a reliable source. A victualling contractor to the German army had then received instructions to provide the same amount of rations as he had supplied in September 1938, and to have them ready by March 28th, 1939. They were to be delivered to forward dumps in an area of Pomerania that formed a rough wedge pointing towards the railway junction of Bromberg in the Polish corridor.

I was not able to follow the German troops from Prague into Slovakia, having instead to take a train to Kaunas and belatedly report Hitler's seizure of Memel. On March 24th I arrived in Kaunas. The Lithuanian capital was in the first panic of political capitulation. It would not be long before this pleasant pastoral State ceased to exist, never to be reconstituted by the victors. On March 26th I was in Berlin again, where there were some reports of troop movements in the direction of Poland, and Colonel Mason-Macfarlane was in a high state of activity. He kept on repeating to me that the German Army now had its "pants" down, by which he meant that they were strung out between Slovakia and the West without their reserves mobilised, and with Austria and Czechoslovakia in a state of unrest. Such was his appreciation of military dispositions. The Military Attaché gave an opinion of some weight when he said that the danger was that Germany would attack and quickly defeat Russia, and then turn West with that vast hinterland of resources at her command. This was to my mind a very different outlook* from the complacent attitude of some Conservatives

---

* The Polish Ambassador in London, Count Raczynski, noted this change of outlook in a dispatch of March 29th, 1939, in which he told Colonel Beck that "it used to be predicted that war between Germany and Russia . . . would weaken both, not without affording indirect advantage to the Western Powers. The rapid succession of events has showed the weakness of these arguments. . . ."

in the Cliveden circle that Russia was a convenient outlet for the frustrated energies of Germany. He embodied his views in a paper which Sir George Ogilvie-Forbes forwarded to London on March 29th with the observation that "the military attaché is in a very warlike mood". Sir Nevile Henderson was on recall in London and doubtless Mason-Macfarlane felt freer to air his views. "Germany", he wrote, "is at the moment capable of mobilising a total of little more than 100 Divisions all told—Active Reserve and Landwehr. Can she under existing circumstances embark on a war on the Western Front simultaneously with war against Poland and Yugoslavia, if she is forced to fight for and hold Rumania and part of the Ukraine to give her even a temporary respite from the effects of the blockade to which she would be immediately subjected?" He also thought that Britain must fight to avoid eventual elimination. This was the argument that some had used—but not Mason-Macfarlane—before the crisis of 1938.

I related to him my information of January about the ration dumps close to Bromberg and pointed out that the German newspapers of that morning, March 27th, had contained reports of incidents involving the German minority in Bromberg. These mentioned German houses being daubed with tar. It appeared to me that such reports had been written in the German Propaganda Ministry like some of those issued about the casualties of the Sudeten-Germans in the previous summer. Mason-Macfarlane agreed that a rapid move to cut the Polish corridor might be intended, though he had no positive information. He advised me to take my imformation to London myself. To both of us it seemed that written reports were largely discounted in London, if indeed they were read at all. These were the circumstances in which I flew to London on March 28th and found myself invited to talk with three members of the Inner Cabinet.

The first tremor after the fall of Prague was felt by Rumania. M. Tilea, the Rumanian Minister in London, saw Lord Halifax on the afternoon of March 17th and told him that German economic demands on Rumania amounted to something like an ultimatum. He thought that by forming "a solid block of Poland, Rumania, Greece, Turkey and Yugoslavia with the support of Great Britain and France, the situation might be saved". This conversation took place just before Mr. Chamberlain's

Birmingham speech, but the speech contained no hint of willingness to accept new commitments, and perhaps for this reason M. Tilea found himself admonished by M. Gafencu, his Foreign Minister, and obliged on March 18th to deny formally the story of an ultimatum, though still repeating it privately to Sir Alexander Cadogan. Rumania signed a secret economic agreement with Germany on March 19th. Meanwhile M. Tilea's sudden action, taken on his own responsibility, set up a chain of diplomatic activity. British envoys in Central and Eastern Europe were directed to sound friendly governments as to their attitude and willingness to stand together in the case of a German aggression. The answers began to come in on Sunday, March 19th, and to the British question "what will you do?" they returned the natural answer "what will you?" The Prime Minister told Sir John Simon and Lord Halifax that he had foreseen this, and had an idea for a declaration of intent with France, Poland and Soviet Union. A draft was begun in the morning and completed that afternoon, to be sent to Warsaw, Moscow and Paris. But after postulating a definite German policy of domination against which no State in Europe would be safe, and calling for mutual support, it simply concluded that in case of a threat to the independence of any European State, "our respective governments hereby undertake immediately to consult together". When Sir Alexander Cadogan showed this to M. Corbin, the French Ambassador protested that this draft would dishearten M. Beck and "would have a much worse effect than publishing nothing at all". Sir Alexander took the draft back to Chamberlain and Halifax and gave them Corbin's warning. They "toned it up", but without altering the cautiously formulated commitment.

"I am afraid we have reached the crossroads," wrote Cadogan in desperation.* "I used to say that if (Hitler) proceeded to gobble up other nationalities, that would be the time to call 'Halt'. That time has come, and I must stick to my principle because, on the whole, I think it right." He then summarised the British dilemma as he saw it—"if we speak plainly, we risk goading Hitler into launching an attack on us. But that is a risk that must be taken. This country has taken risks before."

Mr. Chamberlain decided to write another letter to Musso-

* The Cadogan Diary.

lini. Sir Alexander struggled with one draft after another, all of which seemed to him too like asking for another Munich conference. He professed himself satisfied on the evening of March 20th with the final draft which contained an emphasis of Anglo-French solidarity and a hint that Italy could not bully France. But the letter actually sent contained no such warning. It complained instead against Hitler and implored Mussolini to help restore the shattered confidence of Europe. The Editor of the Foreign Office documents in 1951 in publishing this letter came to the conclusion that "it appears not to have been drafted in the Foreign Office".

Sir Alexander believed that after another weary day between the Foreign Office and Downing Street, he had seen the final draft of the letter to Mussolini. They were, however, beginning to treat him as they had treated Vansittart.

On March 22nd Mr. Chamberlain presided at a meeting in his room at the House of Commons. He and Lord Halifax, with Sir Alexander Cadogan and Sir Eric Phipps met M. Bonnet and M. Corbin. To and fro they discussed how to bring Poland and Rumania into a common attitude of defence with each other and Soviet Russia. Mr. Robert Hudson, Secretary for Overseas Trade, had reported from Warsaw that Colonel Beck was evasive as to Poland's attitude to Rumania and inclined to guarantee her aid only against a Russian attack. Beck did not seem alarmed about his own country or any other, and Sir Eric Phipps had heard the view in Paris that Beck would not greatly care for a British declaration of aid and was only waiting for an opportunity to lean more towards Germany. The Polish Ambassador in London told Lord Halifax on March 21st that if Germany attacked Rumania, Poland would "come in". It was to clarify the meaning of these words in the mind of Colonel Beck that Lord Halifax anxiously awaited him in London. Halifax on March 22nd was reversing the argument that he had used so eloquently in September 1938 to disabuse M. Daladier and "bring him back to earth". Then he had opposed firmness because no direct military assistance could be given to Czechoslovakia. But on March 21st his argument to M. Bonnet was that "the primary question would not be: can we give direct assistance to Poland or Rumania? but: can we conduct a successful war against Germany?"*

* Documents on British Foreign Policy, Series III, Vol. IV.

The debate on the Eastern "bloc" in the Prime Minister's room on March 22nd brought out a sense of bewilderment in their minds. They were determined to do something, but not sure what. Lord Halifax said that Poland might expect the same assistance from Great Britain, France and Rumania as it was now proposed that Great Britain, France and Poland should extend to Rumania. Mr. Chamberlain opined that it was important to remember that Poland had a common frontier with Germany while Rumania had not. The British statesmen seemed to leave Russia out of their final reckoning. Bonnet thought that she might still be brought in and indeed had thought it better to talk with other Polish representatives than Colonel Beck, on whose decision their whole proceedings still hung fire. Bonnet thought that Poland could not refuse to co-operate, but Beck's first idea was for a secret agreement with Britain—one that would absolve him from seeming to exclude Russia from the system of alliance. They felt they must ferret him out into the open.

There was a meeting on Saturday, March 25th of Foreign Office senior officials, Vansittart among them, and on Sunday March 26th more telegrams showing the little States in a mood of fear "even Turkey", noted Cadogan in his diary, but "if we want to stem the German expansion, I believe we must try to build a dam *now*. Of course, as to whether if Germany really does gobble S.E. Europe, she will *really* be stronger to attack us I still have some doubts. But Mason-Macfarlane thinks she will, and he ought to know more about it than I. If we are set on this course, we must set about it quickly and firmly. It might act as a deterrent to avert war."

After dinner on March 26th the Prime Minister met Halifax, R. A. Butler and Cadogan and discussed a form of guarantee to both Rumania and Poland. The Foreign Policy Committee of the Cabinet met on the draft guarantees at 5 p.m. on March 27th and approved them without strong objection, not even from Sir John Simon. That night the British military attaché in Warsaw reported that half a million Poles had been called to the colours and Poland's Western frontiers reinforced, though there was no sign of unusual activity in the northern part of the Corridor.

Sir John Simon called for copies of the telegrams next morning and read them through again. Sir Alexander wondered if

Simon was getting cold feet. It was proposed that Britain and France guarantee both Rumania and Poland, provided that both countries assist each other in the case of a German aggression. Anthony Eden went to lunch with Cadogan and said that the Cabinet should be broadened. On this day I visited the Foreign Office and found Sir Reginald Leeper receptive to my news from Germany. He arranged that I should see Sir Alexander Cadogan and Lord Halifax on March 29th. Winston Churchill wanted to hear from me over lunch how near the threat of war was to Poland, and listened to me on the subject of Colonel Beck. I had been told in Berlin that Beck had accepted German money. The source of this information was a German officer well placed to know, the Head of the Eastern Section of the German War Ministry. Mr. Churchill accepted this suggestion with calm:

"Paid but perhaps not bought," he suggested.

On the morning of Wednesday 29th I saw Sir John Simon at the Treasury. I knew him slightly. When I told him that we should be firm in support of Poland, he joined his fingertips and asked me dryly:

"How shall we be firm?"

I said by a naval blockade of Germany.

"That means war?" "Yes, sir."

He asked me whether I had been in the last, which was a disconcerting question. Finally he smiled a smooth smile and assured me that whatever decision was reached, it would be the product of complete agreement between himself the Prime Minister, and Lord Halifax.

From Sir John I went to Sir Alexander Cadogan, who had walked into Leeper's room when I was speaking to the Head of the News Department on the previous day. Sir Alexander took me down to the room of Lord Halifax, who listened with attention. He seemed to be inspired and borne along by his pursuit of an alliance for peace. He let me talk at much greater length than Sir John had done, and I told him the story of the past summer in Berlin, and how the enemies of Hitler had conspired to bring him down over the Czechoslovak crisis. This appeared to be a completely new aspect of the German problem to Lord Halifax. He had been that morning expounding to the Cabinet the British policy in regard to Poland and Rumania, and had seemed to carry his points. But perhaps he may have felt that he had not completely convinced that obdurate man, the Prime Minister. For he seized the telephone that afternoon and spoke to Chamberlain at the House of Commons. Would the Prime Minister see me if Halifax brought me over? About 6 p.m. there was a gathering in secret in the Prime Minister's Gothic room, the same room in which Baldwin had tossed the telegrams in the air exclaiming—"tell them we want more aeroplanes".

Chamberlain fitted into the architecture. He was exactly like his photographs and wore a black jacket and pinstripe trousers with a heavy gold watch chain. As I spoke, I noticed that he plucked away at the loose skin of his throat in deepest indecision.

"Tell the Prime Minister what you have just told me," said Lord Halifax. The Foreign Secretary stood and only the Prime Minister sat. Beside me were Rex Leeper, Sir Alexander Cadogan, Lord Halifax, and a future Prime Minister of England, Lord Dunglass,* the Parliamentary Private Secretary, was in attendance.

A seventh person I took to be the Head of the Secret Service. Vansittart, who of all men knew my subject best, was not there, but from notes taken by Sir Alexander Cadogan it is plain that in the view of Sir Robert at this time there should be an open declaration warning Hitler, even if the Poles did not join in an Agreement.

I began with the information that I had gathered, indicating that an attack could be made very quickly on the Polish Corridor, severing Poland's access to the sea. I repeated the story of the ration dumps and the German reports of excesses by Poles in Bromberg, that seemed to suggest an agitation campaign. I added what else I knew.

Every now and then Lord Halifax would draw my attention to some point that had struck him in my previous narration and ask me to repeat it.

What amazed me about this conversation was that important information which I had carefully passed on to the British Embassy in Berlin seemed entirely unknown to these Ministers. Some details of great importance that I could not have included in my press dispatches I had carefully related to several members of the British Embassy weeks before, and made what I knew common knowledge with them. Yet all the information

* Sir Alec Douglas-Home.

which the two senior members of the Cabinet seemed to have in mind was a brief message from the American Ambassador, Mr. Joseph Kennedy, to the effect that his information was that Ribbentrop was pressing for an early liquidation of the Polish problem. That agreed with my information that Ribbentrop had described Poland as "soft" and easy to defeat at any time.

I find that I summarised it all in a letter to Lord Halifax written to him that night before returning to Berlin, and in quoting from it now, I am quoting what in substance I told the Prime Minister four hours earlier:

"Now relating to this date, the 28th March, I add the following: A German Colonel in touch with the War Ministry related to friends of mine three weeks ago the whole German Army was to be in a state of preparedness on March 28th 'down to the last waterbottle'. Further, a high S.S. official told another friend of mine that it was at the end of March that they had to be ready, and that at the end of March one could expect great events. Another point which I forgot to mention during my interview with yourself and the Prime Minister is an utterance of one of the lieutenants of Rudolf Hess, the deputy of the 'Leader'. He told a German friend of mine for whom he had a certain regard that he would do well to be outside the Reich in the next few months. He spoke perhaps ten days ago, and he was not thinking, in my opinion, of the Czechoslovak business which was merely a side issue.

"All my information has pointed to a crisis at the end of March, and in this sense I have written repeatedly to my friend Lord Lloyd. There are two interesting observations to be made. I know that Poland was originally put on the German programme of conquest for this summer. Only in the last few days has it been advanced to such extraordinary pre-eminence that we may expect an attack on the Polish Republic in twelve hours, three days, a week or a fortnight. Although the Operations Department of the German War Ministry has been working for the past month on plans of attack against Poland, I have not heard that an ultimate date for attack has been fixed, as it was last autumn against Czechoslovakia. I have not heard that Hitler has said to his military underlings: You must be ready to attack Poland at this and that date. My judgment of the situation, with which your own information from Mr. Kennedy agrees, is that it is Ribbentrop who has hustled Herr Hitler into immediate action. Therefore I consider that the plans of Herr Hitler are not irrevocable, although he may have seen the force of Herr von Ribbentrop's arguments that they must strike now rather than wait until the 'democracies' have summoned up their courage and mobilised their forces for war in the summer.

"In a few words, the intention is present. The Germans believe that the democracies are infirm in their purposes. They are likely to strike.

"Now I come to the subject which interests you most as far as my influence can produce anything of use to the British Empire. Our friend went back to his country estate last October disillusioned and despairful, with the thought in his mind that his world and your world, and the world of all those who give their word as something worth keeping and worth fighting for had collapsed under the pressure of this strange new world that had broken all the laws of morality and got away with it. In November the revolutionary tendencies that are latent in the Nazi party broke surface in the anti-Jewish pogrom. How un-justified that persecution and that massacre were will be clear to all, or rather to those few, who know what actually the relation-ship was between the dead man and the Jew Grynspan. I do not want to enlarge upon those depressing occurrences or what caused them, except to prelude my judgment that the outcome of these excesses was gravely detrimental to the prestige of Herr Hitler and the Third Reich. The faith in the Leader that was shaken by these occurrences which were so obviously ordered by the Government of the Third Reich was still further shaken this spring among those who knew what Herr Hitler intended. What did Herr Hitler intend?

"May I repeat the gist of those three eventful speeches which he held in his new Reich Chancellery during the end of January and the beginning of February? First, he called up the lieuten-ants of the German Army, several thousand young men, and told them that this year was the decisive one in the history of the Third Reich. He expected sacrifices from them. Second, he called up those commanding Generals who had been so bold as to offer their opinions last autumn on the advisability of his campaign against Czechoslovakia. Your secretaries will find the dates for each of these meetings in the daily press; but they will not find the essential contents of his speeches. To the generals he said, and I think I may without distortion put the following in quotations, 'It must not occur again that a German General shall say to me as one of you said last autumn, "I cannot take responsibility for this or that". I tell you that he who utters such a sentence now is a traitor to the Third Reich. He will pay for such an utterance with his life. Whoever of you does not like this may go. But I abjure you to accept my supreme responsibility in everything that concerns the Third Reich by giving me your hands one after another.' There were present every commanding general, eighteen in number and perhaps more; the Commander-in-Chief of the Army, the Chief of the Supreme Command, the Commander-in-Chief of the Navy, Field-Marshal Goering commanding the Air Force, the generals of the Air Force. In all they were thirty strong. Not one of them declined his hand. There were many of them whose thoughts, if I estimate rightly, turned away from that compulsory gesture. Thirdly, we come to his interview with the Colonels. He called up every colonel commanding a regiment in the Third Reich. I am unable, in my present haste, to give you the date of this meeting. I think you will find it in the *News Chronicle* and in other newspapers, although the contents of this meeting was, if at all, only imperfectly known to the press. Herr Hitler demanded the same signs of loyalty from these officers as from the lieutenants and the generals. Of the lieutenants he felt sure because he felt that they recognised that the future of Germany lay in his policy and his command of the Third Reich. Of the generals he felt sure because he had browbeaten and bullied them and set them in the wrong many times when their own instinctive animosity had risen against him. The Colonels were men who had seen the last war, who had practical work to do and yet had command and authority over German troops. Some, loved by their regiments, had witnessed the excesses of the Party in small provincial towns, some perhaps from upbringing or from sentiment had reasons for declining to back Hitler's Government wholeheartedly. To them he appealed on the pretext of aggression from his most hated enemy, England. May I quote again at the risk of being a few words out but not of missing the essential: 'I expect an attack from England in 1940 at the earliest. We will act on the dictum of Frederick the Great—"I will attack the very first".' This show ended about February 10th. Hitler held receptions and banquets and put before them all the splendour of his new chancellery. He tasted the savour of a number of his plans in night Councils. He gloried in the fall of Barcelona, and marvelled at the complacency of his 'enemies'. He said to one of his lieutenants in these days, thinking of how much the Western Powers were giving away to him, 'How can they be so stupid?' The 'stupid' were Great Britain and France. He kept Baron von Neurath in February in ignorance of his intentions that were to ripen in March. The Baron was optimistic to his own closest friends that peace would be maintained. High personages of the Chancellery went to the French Embassy in February and explained to them that Germany wanted peace. Germany had only acted so rapidly against Czechoslovakia, they said, because Hitler was exasperated by the 'slanders' of May 21st. The French were inclined to believe this, not because they trusted the Germans but because they still held to that last forlorn hope that the gleams of sunshine might last. The action against Czechoslovakia came with remarkable rapidity. There is no doubt that it was to be expected by anybody who knew what the ordeal was to which Monsieur Chvalkovsky had been subjected in February when he called in Berlin, but the astonishing march over the mountains in snowy weather, the occupation of Prague, the push into Slovakia, were only the prelude for this preparedness at the end of March, to which I now return.

"German preparations are such that they can mobilise in a matter of forty-eight hours their whole effective military strength which is about one hundred and twenty divisions in the opinion of our military attaché in Berlin. There has been as yet no final order either for marching against Poland or for mobilising. The army has been instructed to practice secret mobilisation without the knowledge of the civil population. That again may be a symptom. The Germans, we know, move secretly, swiftly, and, outwardly to all appearances, in unison. They may attack the Poles tomorrow, the next day, the day after, in a week. They are in their deep souls cowardly because they are not convinced of the justice of their cause, therefore they may postpone, but I believe the German game to be so desperate that they will push ahead."

"Tell the Prime Minister," said Lord Halifax, "what you have just told me about these people in Germany who do not believe in Hitler."

I recapitulated the story of the men in Berlin who thought

Hitler mad, and that he was leading their country to eventual ruin. I spoke of the frame of mind of the generals in 1938, of the defamation of von Fritsch and the resignation of General Beck. I spoke of the sceptical many and the influential few.

"What have these people to offer us?" asked Neville Chamberlain dryly. He tugged away at his throat, did not look at us, stared at one gloomy corner of his room.

"I do not know now. I should have to find out," I replied. "Last year they had something definite to offer, but that possibility since the Munich agreement, since the overthrow of Czechoslovakia no longer exists."

It was difficult to say this, but Chamberlain seemed to understand it. What was also so curious was that their listening gave me the distinct impression that they were hearing these facts for the first time with a somewhat naïve astonishment. Yet Vansittart had written reports on these subjects, and Cadogan's diary records that he too reported on the German opposition and its warnings.

"What would the German people say," someone asked, "if Lord Halifax were to exchange places with Mr. Chamberlain?"

I was taken aback by this. Personally I should have liked to see the change, though in the light of after knowledge I think it would have meant no difference to the history of the world. But it was my concern to impress Neville Chamberlain and get him to act, and by saying that he ought to stand down, I thought I would perhaps weaken my arguments in his mind. For every man is vain of his own ability. So I said very stoutly that he ought to stay and shoulder the burden, and that a great many people in Germany remembered him with respect. It was not for me, at the age of twenty-six, to give opinions on the premiership. Looking back, the promise of Lord Halifax did not prove equal to the task, though at this moment he was acting the man and the leader.

"How would it affect people in Germany if we gave a guarantee to Poland?" asked Cadogan.

This struck me as an extraordinary step. I thought of the Czechs abandoned in the year before. I hadn't thought of a Polish Agreement as something remotely probable. All I could suggest was:

"It would help."

There was silence, a shuffling of feet. Someone kindly said:

"You will take care of yourself when you return to Germany."

I offered afterwards to try and find out whether there was still a possibility of reaction inside Germany, but when I reached Berlin I found a note already waiting for me to say that "it would be unwise if Mr. Colvin gave anyone in the Reich the impression that the British Government wished to enter into relations with them".

"In the evening Ian Colvin of the *News Chronicle* came and saw Halifax and me with Rex Leeper", recorded Cadogan. "He gave hair-raising details of imminent threat of German thrust against Poland. He made a good impression, but I am not entirely convinced. I get so many of these stories. But Halifax was also impressed and we took Colvin over to the P.M. about 6 and he repeated his story."

He noted further in his Diary that:

"Halifax who had stayed behind with the P.M. came over later and said that the latter had agreed to the idea of an *immediate* declaration of support of Poland, to counter a quick *Putsch* by Hitler." Sir Alexander sat up with Lord Halifax and R. A. Butler till 1 a.m. on March 30th drafting it out. Next day the Cabinet saw the draft declaration and it was approved by the Foreign Policy Committee that afternoon. Telegrams were sent to Warsaw and Bucharest requesting agreement to an immediate declaration. On the morning of March 31st the Cabinet again saw the declaration and the Foreign Policy Committee approved a revised version. Cadogan thought it a *frightful* gamble, but also thought that "we must challenge Hitler . . . and stop the rot". They went to tell Maisky and Joseph Kennedy, so that the Russian and American governments should be informed. Kennedy rather ungraciously commented that the declaration would be regarded in America as a "subterfuge". That drew a hot retort from Cadogan. This step was far ahead of any undertaking that Britain had ever yet given to any country except Belgium.

In a declaration to the House of Commons on March 31st, Mr. Chamberlain made the surprising announcement that "in the event of any action which already threatened Polish independence, and which the Polish Government considered it vital to resist with national forces, His Majesty's Government would feel themselves bound at once to lend the Polish Government all the support in their power."

My appearance was thought to have been useful to Lord Halifax in accelerating his purpose. Winston Churchill growled afterwards that all the objections to aiding Czechoslovakia applied in this case, with the additional disadvantage that we had lost the Czechs. "But never mind, you were right to get it."

I had at this time no direct contact with Vansittart. He was like a man seen in another field ploughing a straight furrow. There seemed to be no occasion to speak to him, though I watched him once or twice in action. When towards the end of his life I related the story to him of my part in the Polish Agreement, it was new to him, and he smiled and said:

"Well, at least you accomplished something with them. I never could."

CHAPTER XVIII

A WALL HALF BUILT

Maxim Litvinov, for twenty-one years in charge of the Commissariat for Foreign Affairs, drew a prophetic picture of Europe at war during an interview on March 23rd, 1939 with Mr. Robert Hudson, Secretary for Overseas Trade. The British minister explained the Munich Agreement to him as a settlement on which Britain had "no option" for political and military reasons. Litvinov then reviewed the state of Europe as he saw it. He described France as "practically done for . . . full of German agents, disaffected and disunited, at the mercy of certain leading politicians whom he profoundly distrusted. . . . He foresaw in the not far-distant future a Europe entirely German from the Bay of Biscay to the Soviet frontier and bounded . . . simply by Great Britain and the Soviet Union. Even that would not satisfy German ambitions. . . ."

As a picture of Europe in the summer of 1940 this was indeed accurate. Litvinov was not any happier after the Anglo-Polish declaration of March 31st. He stated the Soviet preference for a conference of powers and states threatened by German expansion. On the obstinacy of Colonel Beck this proposal was defeated.

President Roosevelt stepped in with a vigorous warning message to Hitler (and Mussolini) on April 14th, but in substance it was no more than a rhetorical exercise. The President named some 30 countries for which he invited German assurances of non-aggression. Twenty of these countries were in fact traversed, invaded or defeated by Germany in the next five years, but nevertheless the President's intervention savoured of sarcasm. It had no practical effect. American neutrality legislation remained unaltered. Hitler's answer before the Reichstag on April 28th was a massive performance in which he poured withering scorn on the Roosevelt accusations.

The British moves, if long overdue, were of a more practical nature. A Ministry of Supply was set up and on April 26th a Conscription Bill introduced, though even at this late stage in their country's destiny the British Labour leaders bitterly opposed it. Dolefully Henderson sat about in Berlin with instructions to inform Ribbentrop that the Bill was not a measure of encirclement or aggression. The Ambassador was finally fobbed off with Baron von Weizsaecker, who received the message coldly and referred to the Anglo-Polish declaration. Of this Hitler exclaimed in his Reichstag speech:

"An intention to attack [Poland] on the part of Germany, which was merely invented by the international press, led, as you know to a so-called guarantee offer. If . . . fresh unrest has broken out in Europe during the last few weeks, responsibility lies solely in propaganda at the service of the international warmongers. . . . I know nothing of . . . threats to other nations. . . . Every day I read of German mobilisations . . . all these with regard to States with whom we are . . . living . . . in deepest peace."

It is instructive to compare these protestations with what has since become known of the Wehrmacht planning at the time. Armies in all countries lay plans for various eventualities, usually for defence; but copies of these plans, produced before the International Military Tribunal at Nuremberg in 1946, show that on April 3rd, 1939 a series of military directions began to be issued from the High Command, some under the signature of Hitler and others signed by Keitel which laid down the actual timetable for aggression that summer and elaborated "Operation White", the destruction of the Polish Republic. "The political leadership has the task of isolating Poland as far as possible and limiting the war to Poland," declared the preamble of this Most Secret document. "A growing internal crisis in France and a consequently reserved British attitude could lead to such a situation in the not too distant future." This was followed by a characteristic aside:

"An intervention by Russia, if she is capable of it, will according to all forecasts not help Poland, as it would mean its destruction by bolshevism." This was a paraphrase of Hitler's belief that Colonel Beck would not accept an alliance with Russia. The Plan continued: "The main object in building up the German Wehrmacht remains the enmity of the Western democracies. Operation White is only a precautionary completion of the preparations, but should not be regarded as the pre-condition of a military conflict with the western opponents. The aim of the Wehrmacht is to destroy the Polish Army. A surprise attack is to be aimed at and prepared. . . . The preparations are so to be made that (they) can be executed at any time after September 1st, 1939 . . . The High Command is to make a timetable for Operation White between Services. Intentions and Plans of the Services are to be handed in by May 1st."

It is pertinent to reflect whether these nation-wide preparations could have been decided without becoming known to the Western Allies. A correct appreciation of the events of 1938 would have shown that Hitler's rages were carefully timed to his military programme, and therefore any evidence of military intentions in 1939 was of high importance.

The explanation of Lord Templewood that the Cabinet did not know of Hitler's plans seems less acceptable than that of Vansittart—that they did not read the reports or were unable to believe them. That there was any paucity of information about the aggression of 1939 seems unlikely. The published British Foreign Office documents give indications, but do not include the intelligence reports that should have been presented to the Foreign Affairs Committee of the Cabinet regularly and read by them. It is however possible to divine from the gravity of Sir Robert Vansittart's commentaries what information he commanded. An incident related* about him gives a clue to the vacuum. He used to send in the customary red morocco boxes from the Foreign Office to the Cabinet those papers and reports which he considered of special interest. Lack of response prompted him once in 1939 to interleave separate reports, so that they could not be removed and read without becoming separated. When the box returned to him, the papers were nested exactly as they had left him, like an uncut book. He concluded that they had not been read. Foreign Office authority had been divided in January 1938 between himself and Sir Alexander Cadogan. The arrangement may have worked after a fashion, because Cadogan was an imperturbable and conscientious man, but it did not work without some friction and the split responsibility for advice and direction of 1938 and 1939 has since been discarded.

It is perhaps some indication of the extent to which knowledge of Hitler's intentions was available in the early summer of 1939 if I mention the secret German directive of May 10th, 1939 "for Economic Warfare and Security of Industry". "The

* Lady Vansittart to author.

Commanders-in-Chief of the Services will report to the High Command of the Army by August 1st, 1939 the measures taken on the basis of these directives." Could war preparations in German industry with a completion date have failed to come to the notice of Dr. Goerdeler, to name only one leaky vessel among the bitter opponents of Hitler? I have no notes of my own information in May, but recollect that August 1st was mentioned to me early in June by German informants as a crucial date, and find corroboration in some notes written by me on July 10th, 1939 after a visit to Germany that "the determination of Hitler to have a showdown on or about August 1st has been altered. The date now quoted to me was August 25th, and that this postponement had taken place there seemed to be complete certainty in the minds of those with whom I spoke. But since the German armed forces have been working to the date August 1st for at least two months past, it is reasonable to suppose that they will have reached an advanced state of preparedness by that date, so that an event of major importance such as the seizure of Danzig becomes increasingly likely from July 31st onwards."

I have it also in recollection that the Reich Under-Secretary of State for the Four Year Plan, in an address to Economic directors (Wirtschaftsfuehrer), said in April 1939 that Germany was so near bankruptcy that a war seemed inevitable, while a private paper shown to me in the handwriting of Count Schwerin von Krosigk, the Finance Minister, listed the internal indebtedness of the Reich since Germany had ceased to publish its budget in 1934 as 65 milliards of Reichsmarks in the shape of industrial credit bills, a report considered so disturbing by the City Editor of the *News Chronicle*, Sir Oscar Hobson, that he asked for publication to be withheld. All this I recount as indications received at the time not of the certainty of war, but of its high probability and its timing. The final estimate of the German moderates in July was that the Anglo-Polish Agreement could only be effective in keeping the peace if the British attitude were unmistakable, if Russia was drawn into the alliance and if the United States altered its Neutrality Act.

Of Chamberlain the German moderates said to me in July 1939 that "we suspect he still has some contact with Hitler. We don't know what it is, but as long as this suspicion exists, it will be hard to raise opposition here against Hitler." They said that the Anglo-Polish Agreement by itself had not shaken Hitler's authority, and the youth of Germany believed in him fanatically.

In May 1939 I recall a final and ominous piece of information received before leaving Germany—a new weapon was in the first stages of study that seemed peculiarly suited to the methods of Hitler. It was, an informant said, a project that would require few ingredients, but it would produce a bomb capable of destroying the British Fleet in harbour. The apparatus would be an electrical device worked with radium and water. This struck me as such an extraordinary claim that I asked to have it verified. The informant returned with an apology. He had misheard his source the first time; for the metal in question was called uranium, and there was something else that he himself could not explain but which had been described as heavy water.*

I have quoted at some length from the sources upon which British press correspondents in Berlin founded their mistrust of Hitler's policy. Sir Nevile Henderson disliked our pessimism.

"The Press is making diplomacy impossible. Whatever one tries to do is frustrated by the press," wrote Sir Nevile to Lord Halifax on April 26th. ". . . Is it not possible to give the whole of the British Press a grave warning of its heavy responsibilities. . . . ." It is quite possible that this divergence of outlook was precisely because the Press had a better idea of what was to happen than the Ambassador did.

There is no clear forecast in the British Embassy dispatches of the spring and summer of 1939. Mr. Ivone Kirkpatrick who had "never known him to be wilfully misleading" reported that General von Reichenau "assured me earnestly (on June 8th, 1939) that there was not the slightest chance that Hitler would plunge into a reckless attempt to solve the Polish problem".†

Henderson, with whom Baron von Weizsaecker dined on June 11th, seemed to have heard that Hitler was prepared to wait at least "till September" and thought he might wait

---

* In a circle of West German atomic scientists in 1954 I heard well-meant protestations that Hitler had never been told of the dangerous possibilities of atomic fission. That may be, but when Hitler in April 1939 received the Rumanian Foreign Minister, Mr. Gregori Gafencu, on his way to London, the Chancellor said that "not only had Germany the strongest Army in the world, but her technicians and physicists had not been idle. Things would be seen that had never been seen before. German towns would no doubt not escape, but on the other side not a single town would continue to exist."

† Documents on British Foreign Policy, Series III, Vol. VI.

longer, though Weizsaecker was unable to reassure Henderson on that point.* On July 24th Henderson wrote in a letter to Halifax "in spite of all rumours I cannot discover any concrete evidence to indicate that Hitler is contemplating anything at the moment except a waiting game". On July 28th he wrote "if I had to put all my money on one thing, I would put it on Hitler not wanting war",† but to this he added "my estimate is that Germany will be at its readiest at the end of August". The hottest clue in this guessing game was mentioned in a letter to Sir A. Cadogan of May 16th in which the Ambassador spoke of Baron von Weizsaecker being "very confident about a two or three months' pause". But a systematic German plan and time-table appears nowhere to have been visualised in the dispatches of Sir Nevile Henderson.

In May I was in London again and went down to Chartwell to find Mr. Churchill pacing about his study, full of anxiety that the Munich Agreement had brought no improvement in British armed strength in relation to Germany. If Britain had filled some dreadful gaps in her armaments, the overall balance of strength was still shifting towards Germany, he said. In London Lord Lloyd thought I should see Lord Halifax again and telephoned to him in my presence. It was five weeks since the Foreign Secretary had taken me to see the Prime Minister and discussed with him the German threat to Poland. After a considerable pause Lord Lloyd put down the telephone with a grimace of extreme displeasure. The Foreign Secretary did not wish to see me, he said. Maybe Lord Halifax thought it too late, or of no purpose, to listen further on the internal position in Germany. The violent reactions of Hitler may have moved him once more to counsels of caution. The rebuff of Lord Halifax was to me a straw showing the way the wind blew. In some quarters it was said that Mr. Chamberlain had been advised that he had really nothing to hope from the German moderates, and was already chafing under the European commitment that he had assumed. His mounting problems may have made him regret assuming a commitment in Eastern Europe.

It was seventeen years before I spoke again with Lord Halifax and that was on alighting from the Leeds express in London when I found myself standing at the same carriage door. I reminded him that we had together helped to contrive the

* Documents on British Foreign Policy, Series III, Vol. VI.   † Ibid.

Polish guarantee. With thoughtful serenity he agreed that this
was so, and together we walked to King's Cross station taxi
rank, finding no other words. He asked me then whether the
House of Lords lay at all in my direction and I replied that I
was on the opposite way to Fleet Street. Very courteously he
raised his bowler hat and we parted with much unsaid.

The documents now reveal that the talks of Chamberlain and
Halifax with Beck early in April 1939 did not go well. I had
strongly advised in the Prime Minister's room on March 29th
against dealing with Beck alone, because of his known bias
towards the Germans in the past. I suggested that the Prime
Minister of Poland should be invited to accompany Beck to
London or that there should be simultaneous talks with
President Moscicki. The British ministers demurred at the idea
of going behind the back of Colonel Beck. That would have been
no easy thing. There was an additional handicap to the London
talks of April 4th and 5th. Sir Howard Kennard in Warsaw had
most definite views on the necessity to bring Russia into the
alliance, but he sent his dispatches by hand of King's Messenger
in a railway train, and so they arrived five days after the
London talks had ended. Sir Howard advised that "at least
twelve months will be required before the Polish Army can in
any way rely on home production of armaments on a large
scale, and after the outbreak of war, the raw material supplies,
which are near the German frontier, are likely to fall into
German hands . . . for Poland . . . a friendly Russia is thus of
paramount importance."

Beck did not seem to think so. He did not reveal the nearness
of the peril either. He said nothing of the harsh demands that
had been made upon M. Lipski by Ribbentrop on March 21st
—for Danzig and a motor road across the corridor. He said the
Polish government had not noticed any signs of dangerous
German military action. He said that any pact of mutual assistance between Poland and Russia would bring an immediate
hostile reaction from Berlin, and would probably accelerate the
outbreak of a conflict. An Anglo-Polish agreement would be "a
very important matter for Germany, though not so important
as a Polish-Russian agreement". The Polish Government had
"not a very high opinion of Soviet Russia (either from a
military point of view or as a means of transit)". He was

evasive when Chamberlain suggested that Russia was necessary at least for the transit of war materials. He was even reluctant to have a mutual defence arrangement with Rumania against Germany. He foresaw no catastrophe for Poland in Germany attacking Rumania and closing the Polish frontier with Rumania—though his own Ambassador in London, Count Raczynski, on April 4th said that "an independent Rumania is absolutely vital to the existence of Poland". Beck told Chamberlain that Poland was "largely self-supporting in munitions", also exported arms, and even supplied guns to Great Britain. The puzzled British without the last dispatches from Warsaw, having obstinate prejudices against Russia themselves and nervous of a German *coup* on the corridor, gave Beck what he wanted—a bilateral guarantee of assistance. Soon there were misgivings in London about Colonel Beck. His own economic advisers complained that he had asked for no financial aid. Lord Halifax complained that Beck had been "less than frank" about recent German threats.* The Rumanian foreign minister complained that Beck was dilatory about talks with Rumania.

Some sort of hold-fast was necessary in Europe, but the Anglo-Polish declaration remained uncompleted, a sort of scarecrow of diminishing effectiveness, an object of diplomatic curiosity to the Russians and Germans. The puzzled Hitler, trying to assess these amateur British moves, sent one of his staff, Herr Hewel, to dine on April 22nd with Sir George Ogilvie-Forbes, the British chargé d'affaires in Berlin. The German repeated that "permanent good relations with Britain were one of (Hitler's) oldest and dearest ambitions. He has expressed the desire that some really prominent person with a fluent knowledge of German should come and have a man-to-man talk without the intermediary of an interpreter . . . as has hitherto been the case."† This seems like a hint that he wished to see Vansittart again, and talk with a professional diplomat. Vansittart was not sent. Lord Halifax was disturbed to note on May 9th that "Herr Ribbentrop and others still believe that His Majesty's Government are not prepared to implement their guarantee to Poland." Colonel Mason-Macfarlane was used to impress on the German Army Command that the guarantee

* The threats had been more serious than Halifax had been told by Beck.
† British Documents, Series III, Vol. V, p. 286-87.

would be honoured, but German military circles remained sceptical. Meanwhile in London and Moscow the British sought to devise an agreement with Russia to supplement the Anglo-Polish agreement.

When Stalin and Litvinov had weighed up the meaning of the march into Prague and the Anglo-Polish negotiations in London, they saw the need for some clear and definite act on their part. It came in the offer of a triple defence pact to Britain and France. Ivan Maisky presented the proposal himself to Lord Halifax on April 17th, and Sir William Seeds, the British Ambassador to the Soviet Union, forwarded the Soviet draft handed to him in Moscow on the 18th. It provided for all manner of assistance between the three powers in the event of aggression and direct aid to other states in Eastern Europe who might be the victims of aggression. Maisky noted in after years that Winston Churchill in his war memoirs wrote that this offer should have been promptly accepted. The official British re-action was to ask what military action would be taken under such a pact, and with the assent of which East European states. Meanwhile Lord Halifax thought it would be helpful if Russia, without entering into any commitments of a specific nature, made a declaration of intent to resist aggression similar to that of Great Britain. This struck the Russians as being an entice-ment into danger without a counter-guarantee.

On the morning of May 3rd Sir William Seeds was able to see Litvinov. The Russians had been pressing to know by what method the British would assist Rumania against aggression, and Lord Halifax directed Sir William to answer that Britain would "intervene" and to invite "the Soviet Governments for their part" ... to "make the declaration which I have proposed to them".

Litvinov listened and asked whether in the event of a German aggression against the states guaranteed, there would be a declaration of war by Britain.

Sir William said that "declarations of war were rather out of fashion these days, but ... an aggressor ... would find himself in at any rate a state of war with Great Britain". He concluded to Lord Halifax "I trust I did not go too far. If so, I can only plead that no good purpose would be served here by merely reiterating that His Majesty's Government would lend all support 'in their power'."

Sir William had not gone far enough. That afternoon Stalin saw Litvinov, the apostle of collective security, and removed him from the post of Foreign Affairs. He no doubt thought, as had Joseph Kennedy on March 31st, that he smelled subterfuge. Seeds a week later tried to assess the reasons for the dismissal of Litvinov, and arrived at no definite explanation. He thought that it might be for several reasons. On May 8th he had to call on a much more suspicious Molotov and object to a Soviet proposal that Russia should give automatic military assistance to Poland and Rumania in the event of German aggression. M. Molotov asked Sir William whether it was intended to start military conversations.

"I said this would depend on the course of events . . . only as a later development if events called for it." Such were his instructions.

M. Molotov reminded the Ambassador that Sir John Simon had (on April 13th) expressed British readiness for military conversations.* Sir William appeared to have forgotten that such a proposal had ever been made. Molotov thought Poland now "much more prepared to consider a closer association with Soviet efforts". Sir William thought the contrary. Thus the correspondence went to and fro with prompt and direct Russian questions and dilatory and involved British answers. There is no doubt that every British reply went through the creaking machinery of the British Inner Cabinet, endlessly reformulated, full of reservations.

"I am beginning to get very uneasy about the delay in coming to an understanding with Russia," wrote Sir Robert to Lord Halifax on May 4th. "If Russia goes into isolation, this will mean a period of the sulks, which may very well be succeeded, and indeed probably will be succeeded, by closer relations with Germany. That I regard as absolutely fatal." The special friendship of Vansittart for Maisky was thought by Lord Halifax perhaps useful in breaking the deadlock, and Vansittart was instructed to approach the Ambassador on the basis of their past friendship to find out what sort of terms would be acceptable.

Ivan Maisky lunched with him at 44 Park Street on May 16th. Vansittart had not neglected his friend in the ensuing years since their first talks about an Eastern Pact. He had

* In a somewhat hesitant reply to a question by Mr. Hugh Dalton.

informed him in advance of the new Chamberlain attitude defined in the Birmingham speech of March 17th. They now discussed for two hours the intractable problem of a defence system for Eastern Europe. Sir Robert reported that Maisky spoke for a full pact to include the Baltic states and Rumania, whereas he had argued that the main purpose was to get an agreement speedily concluded and to approach the reluctant Baltic states simply meant delay. He argued that "no German attack on Soviet Russia was conceivable except by the broader front of Poland and Rumania, and Maisky agreed to examine the British ideas. The Cabinet met the same day to consider M. Maisky's attitude and on May 17th Lord Halifax proposed a new formula: *a.* to leave out the Baltic States, *b.* to hold staff conversations. But if M. Maisky asked for a direct guarantee from Great Britain, Sir Robert was to allude to Polish and Rumanian objections to this course. Lord Halifax preferred that Soviet Russia should make a declaration similar to those of Britain and France and then concert future action. He reverted to the ambiguous phrase of rendering "all the mutual support and assistance in their power". Sir Robert sensed what was holding them back:

"We should not be deterred from any action which we think in our own interests," he wrote on May 15th, 1939, "by fear of what may be said or felt about it in Germany. This consideration has force in regard to the solution of our negotiations with Russia."

Sir Robert saw Maisky again on the morning of May 17th with the British proposals as approved by the Foreign Affairs Committee of the Cabinet. He saw him again that evening. M. Corbin also saw Maisky. But on May 19th Lord Halifax had to report to his colleagues that their proposals were rejected by the Soviet Government on the grounds that Britain and France did not contemplate a direct guarantee of assistance to Soviet Russia, but only wished Russia to guarantee others. Molotov had proposed instead a triple pact of mutual assistance between the three powers. He reverted to a formula published in *Izvestia* —an effective barrier against aggression must consist of Britain, France, the Soviet Union and Poland, or at least the first three of these powers. There upon the negotiations stuck fast. It was more than Chamberlain would swallow.

The evidence in the documents is that Britain was trying to

be fair to all, including those small states who did not wish for Soviet protection. There was more to it than that. Theo Kordt, Counsellor of the German Embassy in London, a hidden adviser on Germany to Sir Horace Wilson, at this time held the view that to conclude an agreement with Russia would perhaps push Hitler into a war. Dr. Kordt was misinformed, as Colonel Beck had been. Only in the second week of June did Kordt revise his opinion after a visit to Germany and became "convinced that an Anglo-Russian agreement may work to a great extent for peace". But when these second thoughts were communicated to Sir Nevile Henderson it became apparent that the British Ambassador in Berlin wanted no British agreement with Russia, and he vigorously contested them. "Up to a fortnight ago," he wrote to Lord Halifax on June 17th, 1939, "I wished (our negotiations with the U.S.S.R.) to end only one way. Now one cannot but be uneasy lest they drive us in deeper than it is prudent to go." Once more as in the previous summer the German moderates wanted the British to go forward and Henderson wanted them to retreat. On June 28th he pursued his idea. He embodied it in another letter to Halifax, meant to escape the penetrating criticisms of Sir Orme Sargent:

"I am sorry to say that I do not personally believe that Hitler is going to be much intimidated by an Anglo-Russian agreement."* Vansittart never doubted the necessity of such a pact.

On May 27th Mr. Molotov told Sir William Seeds that the Anglo-French proposals to Russia "produced the impression on his mind . . . that Great Britain and France wanted to continue conversations *ad infinitum*, but were not interested in obtaining concrete results". He added in a speech on June 1st that Russia "of course understood the difference between a verbal declaration and actual policy". Sir William told Lord Halifax on that date that he thought "Soviet assistance not worth purchasing at the price of extra hostility of the Baltic States". On the same day Lord Halifax answered remonstrances from the Polish Ambassador in London at delays in providing British financial assistance to Poland. The British pretext was that "in the event of war one of the strongest weapons in the hand of Great Britain must be that of economic staying power, which accordingly it was essential not to impair". The sum in question was not above £10,000,000. Mr. Chamberlain went further and told Count

* British Documents, Series III, Vol. VI, p. 706-10.

Raczynski on June 6th that "while it was very possible that the primary attack would fall on Poland, this was not certain, and even if it did, it was impossible for anyone to anticipate how long the war might last, and if it was a long war, it was essential that this country should not have weakened its economic strength . . . our financial position was not so strong as it was in 1914."* Mr. Clifford Norton in Warsaw expressed his concern on July 5th that the loan to Poland of £8,000,000 had conditions attached by the Treasury that there should be "fundamental readjustment of Polish economic and financial conditions".

During this period of faltering Allied policy, Germany and Italy signed on May 22nd the Pact of Steel, which provided for immediate military support in war. A week later, however, Mussolini in a secret memorandum reminded Hitler that Italy needed a preparatory period for war which "might extend to the end of 1942".

Early in June 1939, there were some indications that the danger foreseen by Vansittart of Russia and Germany coming together was a real factor. On June 7th Sir Eric Phipps reported that the French Ambassador in Berlin feared a partition of Poland by Germany and Russia. On June 13th Sir Nevile Henderson wrote, "I feel instinctively that the Germans are getting at Stalin." On June 15th Dr. Erich Kordt arrived in London and imparted the information "definitely that the Germans and the Russians are in contact as the result of an approach made by Herr von Ribbentrop to the Soviet Ambassador in Berlin". Dr. Kordt met Sir Robert Vansittart during this visit at a flat in Cornwall Gardens and discussed this development with anxiety.

"We have some reliable information that Hitler has already taken steps to open talks with the Soviet Union," declared Dr. Kordt, "and these steps have not been rebuffed."

He has recorded Vansittart as giving an assured answer: "This time Hitler will not find us asleep. Put your mind at ease. We are definitely concluding the agreement with the Soviet Union."†

The conspiratorial German diplomat claimed after the war to have warned Britain of Hitler's intentions; and though Lord Halifax supplied Kordt with a handsome affidavit at his trial before a war crimes tribunal, Vansittart in a differing statement

* British Documents, Vol. V, p. 779.   † *Nicht aus den Akten*, Erich Kordt.

declared that he had never received any information of weight from the Kordt brothers. His reserved attitude towards them may perhaps be explained by German documents which he kept in photostat, showing that Dr. Theo Kordt had in the course of his diplomatic duties furthered certain German espionage activities in Britain. This cold attitude after the war may also have reflected the vehement disillusion and rejection of all things German that characterised Vansittart in the war years and after. That he was emphatically warned by Kordt on or about June 16th of the German-Russian negotiations there is no reason to doubt. Had Mr. Chamberlain been informed of this danger ten days earlier, he might have chosen a more important emissary to Moscow than the Foreign Office official, Mr. William Strang.

On June 7th Mr. Chamberlain announced that it was intended to send a Foreign Office representative to Moscow. He had chosen Mr. William Strang, Head of the Central Department, since Sir William Seeds was indisposed and unable to return home for further instructions. Such was the reason given though the indisposition of Sir William Seeds was not of a serious nature. Chamberlain had noticed Strang during the negotiation over Czechoslovakia with Hitler in the previous autumn. He was the sort of average intellect that Chamberlain trusted. It did not occur to the Prime Minister that a man whose duty it had been to help demolish the Czechoslovak state might be an unsuitable envoy to send to Moscow. He for some reason preferred him to the Head of the Northern Department, which properly dealt with Russian affairs.* Lord Strang has since claimed that his was no special mission but simply a posting to render assistance to an overworked Ambassador. The fact remains that the Russians mistook him for an envoy and were offended at his relatively junior status. Their annoyance was quickly made known to Daladier, and has been accepted as genuine by Sir Alexander Cadogan. It was without doubt an apparent slight. The Russians were affable enough to Strang personally. But his arrival did not mend matters. Draft Anglo-French proposals grew lengthier yet, and more complicated

---

* It would have seemed altogether more appropriate that Sir William Seeds should be seconded by Mr. Laurence Collier, the Head of the Northern Department, which was concerned with Russia, or that the Deputy Under-Secretary in charge of the Northern Department should have taken over the negotiations in Moscow himself.

than ever. On June 22nd Lord Halifax cabled to Sir William Seeds: "you are doubtless as bewildered as I am by the attitude of M. Molotov". He had accused the British and French Governments of treating the Russians as simpletons and fools. Strang was not at ease in his negotiations since some of the defence arrangements devised with Colonel Beck were meant to be confidential and could not be discussed with Molotov—though apparently well known to him. Mr. Strang on July 20th reported from Moscow that "Molotov does not become any easier to deal with as the weeks pass. . . . He seems bored with detailed discussion, and the admirable argumentative material with which you supply us makes little impression on him. It took us for instance an inordinate time trying to make clear to him the difference between initialling an agreement, signing an agreement and bringing an agreement into force, and even now we are not sure that he has grasped it. Indeed we have sometimes felt that the differences that have arisen between us might perhaps be based on some colossal misunderstanding and yet we have usually come to the conclusion in the end that this is not so, and that Molotov has seen clearly the differences between the respective positions of the two sides."

On August 3rd, "M. Molotov was a different man from what he had been at our last interview," wrote Sir William Seeds. Molotov had been furious at what he took to be an insinuation by Mr. R. A. Butler in the House of Commons on July 31st that Soviet Russia might wish to annex the Baltic States.

The remarks of Mr. Butler had not been in the nature of a policy declaration. The Under-Secretary for Foreign Affairs made them in the course of a review of the world situation which was mainly concerned with tension in the Far East. But he said of the negotiations with Russia that "the main question was whether we should encroach on the independence of the Baltic states. We are in agreement with the Rt. Hon. Baronet that we should not do so, and the difficulty of reaching a formula on this point is one of the main reasons why there has been delay in these negotiations."

This statement will have seemed more sinister to the Russians if read together with a previous speech by Sir Arnold Wilson, to which Mr. Butler was referring. For Sir Arnold said that "I believe that . . . there is substantial difference of opinion between Russia and ourselves and France, and I much hope that the Government will not be driven by speeches in this House to conclude an agreement with Russia which would be interpreted in the Baltic states, Poland and Rumania as a betrayal of their interests in the interests of Britain and France. I have full confidence in the policy being pursued by the Prime Minister." How asked Molotov, could the formula prepared by the British and French prevent a repetition of the surrender of President Hacha in other guaranteed states? "I feel our negotiations have suffered a severe setback" concluded Seeds. They were speaking in terms so hedged and legalised that neither could trust the other. "Their distrust and suspicion of us have not diminished during the negotiations," wrote Strang to Sir Orme Sargent on July 20th. "Nor, I think, has their respect for us increased. The fact that we have raised difficulty after difficulty on points which seem to them un-essential has created an impression that we may not be seriously seeking an agreement. . . . We should perhaps have been wiser to pay the Soviet price for this agreement at an earlier stage, since we are not in a good position to bargain. . . ."

Russo-German talks had already been in secret progress for two months, though there is no mention of them in the published correspondence of the Foreign Office with its representatives in Moscow, and in a comprehensive Foreign Office memorandum of May 22nd on the Anglo-Soviet negotiations, a Soviet-German *rapprochement* is mentioned only as a possibility . . . "the worst possibility . . . which might arise from a breakdown of the present (British) negotiation". The memorandum adds that "anti-Soviet propaganda in Germany has been almost completely damped down: we know that certain members of the German general staffs are in favour of an understanding with the Soviet Union, and we have some evidence that they have lately again been advocating it".

Lord Strang writes that it was always present in the minds of the Moscow negotiators that the Rusians might come to an understanding with the Germans. He thinks the second week in August the time when the Russians veered that way. He says that he drew attention to this danger in two letters of June 21st and July 20th; but attentive reading of the first, published in the Foreign Office documents, discovers no such warning. As to the second letter of July 20th, he visualises it only if there was a final breakdown of his own mission, which "might drive the Soviet

Union into isolation or into composition with Germany".
Vansittart has left no written indication that the warning of
Kordt was regarded as important. No dispatch repeating it to
the British mission in Moscow has been published. My own
recollection is that a German visitor to London in July told me
of German-Soviet discussions actually in progress in Berlin, and
that knowing him to be a reliable source, I took care that he
should impart his information to Winston Churchill, Lord
Lloyd and others. Since we did not know how well these secret
talks were going, they tended to be forgotten and the report to
lose credibility. The Anglo-French military mission was to prove
a failure, because it had neither firm instructions nor powers of
decision. As Mr. Strang's talks dragged on, Sir Nevile Henderson in Berlin wrote on July 28th to Lord Halifax saying that he
was telling Germans that "if Hitler makes a gesture, I am sure
the P.M. will respond, and so little by little the door is opened
again". No doubt these utterances of his were made known by
Ribbentrop to Molotov. Baron Weizsaecker had requested his
friend, M. Karl Burckhardt, the League of Nations Commissioner for Danzig, to advise the British to adopt towards
Germany an attitude of menacing silence as the best tran-
quilliser in these circumstances. That was for Henderson an
impossibility. He wrote, he talked all the time. Vansittart wrote
little in these months, but to more purpose. He advocated an
early mobilisation of the Fleet in April 1939 and again in July
1939 just as he had done in August 1938. He thought British
guarantees largely held to be paper in Germany; and that the
Germans were well aware that the belated conscription
measure in Britain would take a long time to become effective.

I find written on a single sheet of foolscap paper dated July
10th, but without any address or classification, what must be his
final exhortation to mobilise the Fleet. "If we do not do this, I
consider that the odds are definitely and distinctly on war. I
trust that this will be most seriously and urgently considered.
The time before we are in the danger zone is very short indeed
—a few weeks at most."

CHAPTER XIX

THE FINALE

The same principal actors who in 1938 went through the grim dress rehearsal of war began to assemble again in July and August 1939 for the real performance. Lord Halifax found the crisis of 1939 much easier to endure, because the Government were committed. There seemed to be no room for doubt or manœuvre. This time it was very little use to utter open warnings or secret warnings, to edit and re-edit statements. Nevertheless Sir Horace Wilson, who was now styled the Permanent Head of the Treasury and Official Chief of His Majesty's Civil Service, still found it advisable to keep an attentive ear for his German visitors. He warned them too in a homely way after his fashion. To Herr Helmut Wohlthat, Reich Commissioner for the Four Year Plan, who came to London in June and July ostensibly for economic talks, he delivered himself of an admonition of such staggering simplicity that he was able to repeat it to me nearly verbatim twenty-four years later. It is enshrined in the British Foreign Office documents:

". . . the analogy that I . . . used about the residents in a street who were all willing to be neighbourly with one another, but did not like it if one of the householders made lots of nasty noises during the night and the next day went battering in the doors of some of the other residents. The rest of the people in the street could not stand that kind of bullying."* "I could not have been more outspoken than that," reflected Sir Horace in 1963. Herr Wohlthat listened and assured him that Hitler wished to avoid a war. Sir Horace records that he in turn said that this was quite understandable, as Hitler could not have overlooked the great increases in Britain's offensive and defensive power.

A much more effective warning was that of Robert Hudson who told Wohlthat curtly on July 20th that "it has always been this country's policy never to allow any Continental power to secure military preponderance in Europe". The secret talks between Hudson and Wohlthat were a last attempt to appease

* British Documents, Series III, Vol. VI, p. 340.

Germany economically if economic appetite was her real malady. Sir Horace sent a report of his own conversation of July 19th with Herr Wohlthat to the Foreign Office for the record. But this report conveys an impression of that particular conversation very different from that which Dr. von Dirksen committed to paper after going over the same ground with Sir Horace. Something said on July 19th made the German Ambassador wish to confirm personally what had been said to Wohlthat. He accordingly slipped round to visit Sir Horace Wilson, who with the privy approval of Mr. Chamberlain, held these talks at his home. Dirksen sought to ascertain whether some angry suspicion in Parliament of the Hudson-Wohlthat talks—there had been leakage of a reported offer of a huge loan to Germany—had undermined the basis for further negotiation. Sir Horace assured him, the German Ambassador immediately noted on August 3rd, "that the basis of the Wohlthat-Wilson conversation remained in force". Sir Horace Wilson confirmed that he had suggested to Herr Wohlthat the following programme.

    1. Conclusion of a treaty of non-aggression in which both sides would undertake to renounce unilateral aggressive action as a method of their policy. . . . Sir Horace Wilson (said) "that an Anglo-German agreement involving renunciation of aggression vis-à-vis third Powers would completely absolve the British Government from the commitments to which it was now pledged by the guarantees to Poland, Turkey, etc."

What could this have meant? What could it have been understood to mean? According to the Dirksen memorandum Sir Horace enumerated other points, an Anglo-German declaration, negotiations on trade and raw materials and "the British side would be prepared to make a declaration of non-intervention in respect to Greater Germany. This would embrace the Danzig question, for example. . . . Sir Horace Wilson expatiated at length on the great risk that Chamberlain would incur by starting confidential negotiations with the German Government. If anything about them were to leak out, there would be a grand scandal and Mr. Chamberlain would probably be forced to resign." In a memorandum of August 18th written for Herr von Ribbentrop Dr. von Dirksen put another piece into the jigsaw puzzle. "It is necessary to state as a general preliminary remark that Great Britain has not pledged herself 100 per cent to support Poland in *any* conflict. This would be contrary to the British disposition always to leave a loophole."*

Dr. von Dirksen continued "This assures a certain amount of elasticity . . . if the Polish side should stage a provocation, it would be of decisive importance in the determination of Britain's attitude." Further in the lengthy memorandum written after his recall to Berlin on August 9th, 1939, Dr. von Dirksen returned rather more sharply to his conversations of August 3rd with Sir Horace and repeated that "Wilson affirmed that the conclusion of an Anglo-German *entente* would practically render Britain's guarantee policy nugatory . . . would enable Britain to extricate herself from her predicament in regard to Poland."†
The Germans were on the fatal paths of error. Someone had blundered.

It should be said that at a later stage, when Hitler had invaded Poland on September 1st and Ribbentrop sent in his agent Dr. Hesse to make a specious offer of withdrawal, Sir Horace showed more mettle. But far too late. How had these extraordinary misconceptions about the British mood been allowed to arise? It seems that Chamberlain had still not entirely abandoned his idea of an *entente* with Germany, and that his diplomacy was not fully communicated to the Foreign Office. Only thus can the discrepancies between some British and German documents be explained.

Herr Ewald von Kleist, the man who reminded Mr. Chamberlain of a Jacobite, appeared no more on the stage. He had, he told me, nothing more to offer. Hitler hanged him in the end, after the Churchill letter was found in his desk.

Dr. Goerdeler appears to have sent a warning in August, though no date is given in his biography.‡ Sir Alexander Cadogan remembered that Goerdeler wanted Chamberlain to broadcast from a British battleship in the North Sea a peace appeal to the German people—an idea that caused Sir Alexander to doubt Goerdeler's mental balance, though to a German used to Hitler's reflexes it was not all that crazy. Admiral Canaris, Chief of German Military Intelligence Services, sent emissaries to London early in July, fearful of

---

* *Dirksen Papers*, Vol. II.   † Ibid.
‡ *Carl Goerdeler and the German Resistance.*

losing contact with the enemy of whom he had wished to make an ally. One of his agents, Lt.-Colonel Count von Schwerin, was received by Admiral John Godfrey, Director of Naval Intelligence, with whom the Count lunched on July 3rd and 6th emphasising the imminent danger of war and telling Mr. Gladwyn Jebb, Secretary to Sir Alexander Cadogan: "Take Winston Churchill into the Cabinet. Churchill is the only Englishman that Hitler fears. He does not take the Prime Minister and Lord Halifax seriously. . . . Hitler can only be convinced by deeds not words."* Von Schwerin told Mr. Jebb that he thought that there was still some reason why Hitler was genuinely convinced that "after Munich it was the British intention to surrender at any rate Central and Eastern Europe to Germany".

The misunderstandings may have arisen from the first talks of Herr Wohlthat with Sir Horace Wilson in June. They were almost certainly increased in the mind of Hitler and Ribbentrop by the Dirksen reports of August 3rd and 18th. It was not helpful that the Anglo-Polish agreement of mutual assistance had still not been signed when Parliament adjourned on August 4th. Leakages about the Wohlthat negotiations had heightened the feeling of mistrust. Duff Cooper bitterly attacked the Government. Churchill entertained terrible doubts to the very last day of peace that the Government would not honour its pledge to Poland. Early in August the negotiations with Russia appeared no nearer to agreement. Many feared that Chamberlain, with Parliament adjourned, would act on his own or allow himself to be surprised by events. They awaited his speech on the adjournment with deep suspicion.

On August 2nd Mr. Chamberlain moved the debate on adjournment "that this House at its rising do adjourn till 3rd October". His motion continued that the Speaker might recall the House at the advice of the Government in case of "unforeseen events". But many members knew enough, and thought that the Government knew enough, to appoint some special procedure for recall or even remain in session.

Mr. Harold Macmillan said of Mr. Chamberlain after hearing his speech, mindful how the Inner Cabal had misused the constitution in 1938, that "he [the Prime Minister] reserves to himself full powers for his judgment, and his judgment alone,

* British Documents, Series III, Vol. VI, p. 295-98.

to be exercised. . . . I still thought until his last speech, and particularly the last sentences, that he would give us some assurance . . . that if a radical change in the situation of Europe took place, he would then think it his duty to ask Parliament to meet, in order that it might freely express its opinion."

The dry answer from Neville Chamberlain was that "it is not possible for me by myself to give specific pledges now about conditions that have not arisen and cannot be foreseen. Such circumstances as those which he prescribes must necessarily be included in my view."

A young member, Ronald Cartland, Member for King's Norton, shaken by this obstinate refusal to perceive the obvious, exclaimed "personally I do not see why . . . the Prime Minister . . . could not come down and say 'we will decide to meet on 21st August, or on a certain date, and if, after consulting with all the Opposition leaders we are all agreed that there is no reason to meet, then do not let Parliament meet'." The crisis seized Cartland by the throat. He exclaimed: "We are in a situation that within a month we may be going to fight, and we may be going to die. . . ." There were parliamentary cries of "Oh!"; but as far as he was concerned both forecasts were to be fulfilled.

A Swedish business man, Birger Dahlerus, slid into the presence of Lord Halifax on July 25th and proposed himself as intermediary to Field-Marshal Goering, who though polishing his medals for war, was still anxious for private diplomacy with the British. Lord Halifax accepted this barren contact. Asked about Dahlerus, Sir Horace Wilson in 1963 laughed and told me "we used to call him the Walrus". The Swede involved himself and them to no purpose. Goering's aims were transparent. On August 8th he complained furiously to Dahlerus that Sir Robert Vansittart was secretly encouraging the Poles to resist German demands. The Dahlerus initiative petered out in a last telephone call from Berlin to Downing Street on September 3rd which ended in the ominous click of a replaced receiver. Others made "last attempts". Dr. Theo Kordt, left in charge of the German Embassy in London, busied himself with Cabinet contacts. He too was imbued with ideas of mediation.

After the British Parliament had safely dispersed Hitler

revealed himself a little to Karl Burckhardt, the League of Nations Commissioner for Danzig. Burckhardt told the British that the Reich Chancellor appeared to him on August 11th "white and old and nervous". Hitler said: "if each time I take a step necessitated by history, I find Britain and France in the way, what can I do?" He spoke longingly of Lord Halifax, a man who had understood him once, and again said he would like to meet an important Englishman who spoke good German for direct talks. Would not General Sir Edmund Ironside do, who had just visited Poland? The mood of depression passed. Another Hitler told Count Ciano next day that the question of Danzig would be settled one way or another by the end of August. A visit to Danzig by the German cruiser Koenigsberg had been arranged for August 25th.

Uncertainty seems still to have persisted in the minds of Halifax and the Inner Cabinet as to the timing of Hitler's intentions. Although the Head of the British Secret Service had taken his holidays in June, his expertise did not communicate itself to his masters. "We have in the course of the last six months had so many dates given to us," wrote Lord Halifax on August 19th to Neville Chamberlain, who had gone to Scotland for a short holiday, "that one is naturally sceptical about any repetition of them, and I do not suppose that we should exclude from our minds the possibility that all this this may have its place in the general nerve storm which we have been told was *designated to rage** during these weeks. On the other hand the information given seemed to me too circumstancial to ignore, and the actual dates given were, so it is alleged, given to the Italian Government, which obviously increases their significance. . . . If the appreciation is in fact a true one, it is also a black one, and there is no time to lose."

He was referring to the information given to him by Sir Robert Vansittart. Early in the third week of August, "Vansittart gave me a good deal of information which came from a reliable source, which he disclosed to me, and which I can disclose to you when I see you." This concerned Mussolini's cautionary memorandum to Hitler on the Polish question, and the subsequent bullying of Ciano by Hitler at their Salzburg meeting. "Vansittart told me last night that he had further information from his sources to the effect that . . . it was pretty

* Author's italics.

well decided in Berlin to take action against Poland any day after the 25th of this month. The actual dates given were between the 25th and the 28th."*

Neville Chamberlain was due to return to London on August 21st, and the Foreign Secretary pondered the draft of a letter to Hitler, which the Prime Minister might read in the train, and on the advisability of presenting it by the hand of General Sir Edmund Ironside, a man of impressive stature.

On August 11th the British and French Military Missions at last arrived in Moscow. Next day they were shown by the Russian delegation the names of five Soviet officers described as having full powers to sign military agreements. The French General, reported Admiral Sir Ernle Drax, replied that he had no powers to sign—only to discuss. Two days later Ribbentrop, after talks with the Russian Ambassador in Berlin, instructed the German Ambassador in Moscow, Count von der Schulenburg, to call on Molotov and announce to him that conflicts between Germany and Russia were a thing of the past. By August 19th the visit of Herr von Ribbentrop to Russia had been arranged.

The leisurely manner in which the Allied military mission proceeded to Russia by sea, instead of flying, helped to increase the impression of western nonchalance. I have since discussed this criticism with Lord Strang, who argued that the military delegates could not well have flown over Germany. It is, however, unquestionable that they could have flown via Stockholm or Bucharest. Lord Strang's own recollection is that by the time that the negotiations were broken off, all differences had been ironed out, except the definition of military aid in the event of indirect aggression. But the chasm over Poland remained apparently unbridgeable. . . .

August 20th was a fateful day for the Anglo-Polish alliance. "We have done our best both with M. Beck and with the General Staff to persuade Polish Government to agree to passage of Soviet troops," cabled Sir Howard Kennard from Warsaw to Lord Halifax. "Political objections appear to be overwhelming."

A strong and urgent telegram from Lord Halifax warned that Beck's obstinacy might mean a final breakdown in the Anglo-French talks in Moscow. They had in reality broken down

* Documents on British Foreign Policy, Series III, Vol. VII, p. 80.

already, although the delegations were still in attendance.

On August 22nd a last attempt to save the talks came from France. General Doumenc in Moscow received a telegram from the Quai d'Orsay in which the French Government declared that it considered that Russia should have the right to enter Polish territory as soon as Poland was at war with Germany. But, as M. Maisky commented what was the attitude of Poland? Sir William Seeds sent an enquiry to London. "Can we assume that you agree?" No reply was received to this, perhaps for the reason that while the Cabinet was considering in London, a further telegram from Sir William on August 21st reported the new Commercial Credit Agreement between Russia and Germany.

On the knotty question of passage through Poland, Mr. Strang wrote to Sir Alexander Cadogan that "the French government has gone ahead without consulting us, and now ask for our support. . . . It may well be that their judgment of the Polish attitude is the right one. . . . It is clear that we cannot disavow the French Government; nor can we, I think go so far as they have done. . . . We might, however, instruct Admiral Drax to say something in Moscow to the effect that H.M.G. have the conviction that if Poland were at war with Germany, Poland would be willing to accept the collaboration of Soviet forces." Next day this leisurely pace was broken, as the German success became evident. On August 23rd Lord Halifax asked Sir William Seeds to request the Soviet Government for an explanation of the reported German-Russian non-aggression pact—"His Majesty's Government find it hard to credit this report."

On the night of August 23rd Ribbentrop was sitting in Moscow chatting with Stalin and Molotov. According to the German documents, Stalin and Molotov commented adversely on the British Military Mission in Moscow saying that it "had never told the Soviet Government what it really wanted". Ribbentrop spoke of "a typically stupid British manœuvre" in another letter sent by Chamberlain to Hitler, "with certain allusions to 1914". Stalin seemed to know all about it. The letter presented by Sir Nevile Henderson at Berchtesgaden, read: "the announcement of a German-Soviet Agreement is taken in some quarters in Berlin to indicate that intervention by Great Britain on behalf of Poland is no longer a contingency to be reckoned with. No greater mistake could be made." But this firm sentiment was weakened by the expression of willingness to discuss "the questions arising between Germany and Poland", if confidence could only be restored, and even "concurrently to discuss wider problems". In the second of two angry interviews with Henderson, Hitler said that "England was determined to destroy and exterminate Germany. He was, he said, fifty years old. He preferred war now to when he would be fifty-five or sixty." An unyielding letter from Hitler to Chamberlain on August 23rd, asserted the German claim to Danzig and the Corridor. It threatened general mobilisation if Britain and France carried out their mobilisation measures, and ended with a dash of pathos: "I have all my life fought for Anglo-German friendship; the attitude adopted by British diplomacy—at any rate up to the present—has, however, convinced me of the futility of such an attempt. Should there by any change in this respect in the future nobody could be happier than I."

On the same day Molotov and Ribbentrop signed the German-Soviet non-aggression pact in Moscow. On the morrow, August 24th, the House of Commons reassembled to hear an account of the crisis from Mr. Chamberlain, who began: "When at the beginning of this month, Hon. Members separated for the summer recess, I think there can have been few among us who anticipated that many weeks would elapse before we should find ourselves meeting here again." His speech repeated that Britain was open to negotiations, but it ended on a sterner note than he had struck hitherto and spoke of a united nation ready to act in a critical hour.

For reasons upon which I have already touched, Hitler was not prepared to believe that he was serious. As soon as Ribbentrop was back from Moscow, noted Dr. Fritz Hesse,* Hitler gave the order for the invasion of Poland. "The order was given at 2.50 p.m. on the 25th August. The invasion was to begin at 4.45 a.m. on the 26th."

Two events on the afternoon of August 25th led him to change his mind. Mussolini sent a long telegram, declaring that he could not take part in a war upon which he had not been consulted. About 6 p.m. it was reported from London that the Anglo-Polish treaty of mutual assistance had been signed. It had been necessary for the Polish Ambassador to make a special

* *Hitler and the English*, Fritz Hesse, Wingate.

démarche. After some strong language by Count Raczynski, Lord Halifax's last doubts and objections had been dispelled. When he heard this news, Hitler asked Keitel whether operations could be suspended and, receiving an affirmative reply, countermanded his orders to the German Wehrmacht.

He thought at once that he had lost face with his warlords. He blamed Ribbentrop, and left him out of his next talks with Henderson. The crestfallen Ribbentrop could hardly believe that his triumph in Moscow would leave the British still determined to support Poland. He had the Dirksen reports from London with their account of the attitude of Sir Horace Wilson . . . the talk of an Anglo-German entente . . . of a Chamberlain policy of grand design. Maddened by doubts, he thought of Sir Robert Vansittart. He, the proclaimed enemy of Germany, would best know what these extraordinary British really intended. Theo Kordt in London was instructed to put out "a feeler", and Sir Robert appeared again at the flat in Cornwall Gardens, where brother Erich Kordt had first acquainted him with the secret of the Russo-German negotiations. Sir Robert was accompanied by Lady Vansittart, which gave the visit some camouflage. Theo Kordt repeated his questions: he had been told, he said, that Britain would not fight over Poland. Sir Robert said quite firmly that Britain would. It was the way that he said it that seemed to convince Kordt. The German at last understood. He broke down, sobbed a little and exclaimed:

"Why did you not make your decision last year? We could have prevented war over Czechoslovakia. You let Czechoslovakia go, and now you stand for Poland. We cannot stop it now." Sir Robert repeated what he had said already:

"Well don't attack Poland and there need be no war."

"It has gone too far," groaned the German. "Hitler will not draw back."

Hitler on August 25th played his last card in the diplomatic game—an offer to guarantee the British Empire and accept some arms limitation in return for a restitution of German colonies. "Immediately after the solution of the German-Polish question he would approach the British Government with an offer," reported Sir Nevile Henderson from Berlin. Sir Nevile thought this offer "could not be ignored". He accepted to fly to London in Hitler's aircraft and discuss it further. For two days the British Cabinet deliberated on the Hitler offer. Their response was a long communication affirming that no solution could be accepted that did not safeguard Poland's essential interests. The British reply was fairly firm. But it embodied the idea of direct negotiations between Germany and Poland. This may have seemed an essential suggestion in London. In Berlin it was liable to be misunderstood.

"In the end I asked him (Hitler) two straight questions," Sir Nevile Henderson reported after seeing Hitler again with the British note on the 28th. "Was he willing to negotiate direct with the Poles and was he ready to discuss the question of an exchange of populations?" This sounded ominously like a Munich solution. Henderson furthermore seems to have said that the crux was whether Hitler wanted a war with Poland *or* British friendship. "Generally speaking Herr Hitler kept on harping on Poland and I kept on just as consistently telling Herr Hitler that he had to choose between friendship with England, which we offered him, and excessive demands on Poland which would put an end to all hope of British friendship."

Herr von Ribbentrop intervened to ask whether Sir Nevile "could guarantee that Mr. Chamberlain could carry the country with him in a policy of friendship with Germany". Hitler asked whether Britain would be willing to accept an alliance with Germany. Henderson did not think this possibility excluded, "provided the development of events justified it".

In this conversation on the night of August 29th, Sir Nevile thought that he had made it quite clear to Hitler that Britain would fight for Poland "if her independence or vital interests were menaced". Mr. Kirkpatrick in London commented on his dispatch that Hitler might put Britain in a difficult position by accepting the British proposals, and would gain a lot simply by abandoning excessive demands on Poland. Sir Orme Sargent added that "if in fact Hitler does accept negotiations, we may be certain that he will endeavour to conduct them as far as possible in the same way as he conducted negotiations in Munich last year". Lord Halifax recognised the reality of these anxieties, but thought that even if no permanent settlement in Europe was possible with the Nazi régime, "I don't think this ought to be conclusive of not working for a peaceful solution and proper terms now."

Sir Robert Vansittart wrote to Lord Halifax on August 30th,

pointing out the danger of talking about an alliance with Germany. "Sir N. Henderson seems to have conducted his conversation with Hitler very well," he commented, "with one exception. That exception is the answer to Herr Hitler's question whether England would be willing to accept an alliance with Germany. . . . This I think is very dangerous indeed. It is the third German reference that I have seen to such a possibility. It is not of course practical politics. There is all the difference in the world between an alliance and a treaty. . . . If the Germans were clever enough to allow it to transpire that this question had been put to the British Ambassador, and that he had answered to it in the terms that he employed, I think that we would face a great deal of indignation and suspicion in this country. . . . An alliance means a military alliance if it means anything. And against whom should we be allying ourselves with such a gang as the present régime in Germany?"

"There is force in Sir R. Vansittart's minute,"* wrote Lord Halifax. Sir Nevile was instructed to avoid the topic. Parts of his interview certainly partook more of bargaining than of firm and solemn warning.

On August 29th, the Polish Government decided that it must order a general mobilisation next day, "provided the development of events justified it". Mr. Chamberlain reported to the House on August 29th, "little change—the catastrophe is not yet on us". That day Hitler accepted the British idea of "direct negotiation" with the Poles, but Sir Howard Kennard very clearly pointed out from Warsaw the unreality of the British Cabinet's proposal:

"I feel sure that it would be impossible to induce the Polish Government to send M. Beck or any other representative immediately to Berlin. . . . They would certainly sooner fight and perish rather than submit to such humiliation." On August 30th Lord Halifax told Henderson that Britain could not advise Poland to accept the proposed German procedure for negotiations which was that Polish plenipotentiaries be sent to Berlin. On August 31st, however, the Foreign Secretary instructed his Ambassador to tell the Polish Government that its Ambassador in Berlin should declare himself ready to transmit proposals. Colonel Beck replied that Lipski would not be authorised to accept any document as it might be

* Documents on British Foreign Policy, Series III, Vol. VII.

accompanied by some form of ultimatum and he himself "had no intention of going to Berlin to be treated like President Hacha". On September 1st at 12.50 a.m. Lord Halifax sent a petulant telegram to Warsaw asking that M. Lipski be instructed to receive a German document and pointing out that the latest German proposals sent to the British Government had not seemed like an ultimatum to Poland. Lipski had in fact called at the Foreign Ministry at 6 p.m. on August 31st, and was told haughtily by Ribbentrop that his visit was useless as he had no plenipotentiary authority. At dawn on September 1st began the German invasion of Poland. It was preceded on August 31st by a faked frontier incident, in which a small group of German storm troops disguised in Polish uniforms captured the German radio station at Gleiwitz after killing near the frontier several selected concentration camp inmates, who had been dressed in German uniforms. This was the ostensible "Polish act of provocation" that was meant to give the British their pretext not to honour their obligation to Poland. It had no such effect.

The British Cabinet met in the morning of September 1st. It drew up a briefer communication than usual. But it was not a declaration of war. It called upon Germany to withdraw promptly from Polish territory or His Majesty's Government would "without hesitation fulfil their obligations to Poland". That morning Mr. Chamberlain invited Mr. Churchill to join his War Cabinet.

In the House of Commons, Members asked Mr. Chamberlain what time limit there was on the British demand. There was none. Hitler meanwhile addressed the Reichstag. He said that he was "making a change in the relationship of Germany and Poland that will ensure a peaceful co-existence". The Luftwaffe bombed airfields, troop concentrations, towns and roads in Poland. Not until 9.30 p.m. would Ribbentrop consent to receive Henderson. He vouchsafed even then no immediate answer, saying that he would submit the British note to the Head of State. His design was to win time for the conquest of Poland.

Sir Howard Kennard transmitted a request on September 2nd from Colonel Beck for "some diversion as soon as possible in the West". His troops were fighting hard, but hampered severely by German air superiority. "I trust I may be informed at the earliest possible moment of our declaration of war." Mr.

Chamberlain gave a long account of events to the House but to his warning message "up to the present no reply has been received". There was anger and dismay in the House, less at Hitler's silence than at the inconclusion of the British Government. Delays in the French mobilisation were said to be the cause for the absence of any British action. The French, having their own misgivings, made an arrangement that day by which they would declare war six hours after the British. They pleaded evacuation delays. In the Cabinet on September 2nd pressure on the Government was heightened to the point of resignations. At 5 a.m. on September 3rd Lord Halifax instructed his Ambassador in Berlin to deliver a communication to the Minister of Foreign Affairs that was in the form of an ultimatum. It reminded him of the British note of September 1st and continued:

"No reply has been received but German attacks on Poland have been intensified. I have accordingly the honour to inform you that, unless not later than 11 a.m. British Summer Time today 3rd September, satisfactory assurances have been given by the German Government, and have reached His Majesty's Government in London, a state of war will exist between the two countries from that hour." Sir Nevile could not deliver this ultimatum to Hitler personally. Dr. Paul Schmidt, the interpreter, received it, and hastened to the Chancellery, where it was received by Hitler and Ribbentrop in disconcerted silence. At last Hitler asked: "What do we do now?"

The French ultimatum, as agreed, was notified to Germany shortly afterwards. The delay ascribed by the French to military reasons may well have been a precaution to make sure that France was not alone in her declaration. So war started, though directions to the Royal Air Force, for political and strategic reasons, forbade any attack on German ground installations. The Poles bled alone at the outset.

Vansittart paced about his big room at the Foreign Office that Sunday morning of September 3rd, reciting to himself and to a junior official, Mr. Harold Caccia, his story of failure. He had worked since 1930 with the object of preventing war, and war had now started. The last war had taken his friends. This would take the sons of his friends. As he spoke the ultimatum expired and Britain was at war. Mr. Chamberlain broadcast a short address from the Cabinet room in 10 Downing Street informing the nation that it was already at war. After he had finished speaking, a siren wailed and the balloon barrage of London began to rise slowly into the sky. At the House of Commons there were prayers and a statement by the Prime Minister: "this is a sad day for all of us . . . everything that I have worked for has crashed into ruins". When the House rose, he set about remaking his Cabinet, invited Churchill to take the Admiralty, took Sir Samuel Hoare for a walk in St. James's Park and offered him the Privy Seal instead of the Home Office, but with a seat in the War Cabinet. Sir Samuel reflected upon the dignity of his new office. It was a consolation in losing a Secretaryship of State to think that the office of Lord Privy Seal "stood very high in the hierarchy of political and social life and took precedence over all the Dukes".*

Upon the Poles who had for fifty hours endured alone, the news of Britain's declaration of war had a cheering effect. But the hail of fire and steel continued to fall upon them unabated.

Sir Nevile Henderson duly asked for his passports and left Germany with his staff. He was permitted to write a defence of his own diplomacy and that of the Government in a White Paper published on September 30th. It drew from Vansittart his final commentary on the Origin of Germany's Fifth War.

"The Ides of March (1939) constituted in fact the parting of the ways and were directly responsible for everything which happened thereafter", wrote Sir Nevile Henderson. He began by assuming some uncertainty as to the final issue.

"Up to the beginning of August . . . the situation remained serious but not immediately dangerous." He then referred to a Polish note of August 10th "denying the judicial right of Germany to intervene in the affairs between Poland and the Free City, and warning the German government that any future intervention to the detriment of Polish rights and interests at Danzig would be considered as an act of aggression."

"I have little doubt," wrote Sir Nevile, "that the latter phrase served more than anything else to produce that final brainstorm in Herr Hitler's mind on which the peace of the

* *Nine Troubled Years.*

world depended. . . ." A few paragraphs later, however, he wrote of the same Polish note that "Herr Hitler is a master of turning events to suit his own purpose. . . ." that "Herr Hitler's carefully calculated patience was exhausted . . ." and that the methods employed in 1938 and 1939 were "gradual mobilisation of the German army over a period of months and its secret concentration at the appointed positions". Yet he would not disavow the element of chance or accident. He spoke of Hitler's "premeditated impatience", the fact that he had never travelled abroad, and relied on Ribbentrop for his opinions of the British. It was a report that Sir Nevile might have written better at a greater distance in time from his recent ordeal.

Vansittart evidently realised this at once. For I have found in the big Dutch tallboy at Denham Place that contained most of his papers a foolscap commentary which he penned in sheer exasperation. This *aide-mémoire*, which he may never have intended for circulation, contains, however, his own profound reflections on the causes and origins of the Second World War and as such should be given to the nation that he served.

"From the point of view of propaganda it was doubtless wise to present to the world as a White Paper Sir Nevile Henderson's 'Final Report' of the 30th September. There is also no doubt that it will be read by posterity; and since it contains a fundamental misreading—and therefore misrepresentation—of history, I cannot allow it to pass as 'final' without placing on record the view of one who thought otherwise. In this, of course, there is nothing personal; indeed, Sir N. Henderson's view has been so widely and highly held in this country that I only call it 'his' for convenience of reference. In raising the point I have no desire to revert to past differences, least of all to recriminate. It is, however, essential to our future safety, indeed to our very existence, that the root-error of the past, with all its consequences, should now at long last be recognised.

"The error is this. Underlying the whole report is the suggestion that the war of 1939 was due to a series of incidents, and that it would not have taken place if only such-and-such another thing had not taken place. These other things vary in magnitude from the occupation of Prague to Blomberg's *mésalliance* with his 'typist'—a kindly euphemism. Sir N.

Henderson even goes so far as to say in paragraph 16 that a mere phrase 'produced that final brainstorm in Herr Hitler's mind on which the peace of the world depended'. In a word, Sir N. Henderson suggests throughout that the war of 1939 was accident not destiny.

"Nothing could be further from the truth. There was no brainstorm and no accident. From the advent of the Nazi régime on the January 30th, 1933, nothing could have happened other than what has actually happened; there never was the least chance that any course could or would be pursued other than that which was, in fact, pursued, step by step, with remorseless, systematic, calculated tenacity. This is destiny; and it is on this view that I have from the first differed fundamentally from Sir N. Henderson and from all those here who have been of his persuasion. For the theory of accident is implicit in the doctrine of appeasement, which is necessarily motivated by the idea that if only Germany could be satiated with instalments, she would become 'somehow good', and peace would be preserved. ('Satiated' is the word that Sir N. Henderson himself quoted before the absorption of the Sudetenland.) There was, unfortunately, never any such prospect, as the sequel has proved. The contrary view is represented by a minute which I wrote in May 1933:

" 'The present régime in Germany will, on past and present form, loose off another European war just so soon as it feels strong enough. Their only fear is that they may be attacked before they are ready.'

"Few will now be found to deny that this, written at the start, was the truth from the start. It is, however, entirely incompatible with the theory of accidentalism. And it is accidentalism to say, as Sir N. Henderson said in a speech to the press on November the 10th, 1939, that 'the megalomania of one man defeated the Prime Minister and me'. So slapdash a sketch bears only a superficial resemblance to reality, which is something both wider and deeper.

"The reason why there was nothing accidental about this war is a very simple one. Much has been, and more will be, written about the history of German psychology and the literature which illustrates it. No valid judgment of Germany can be formed without a knowledge of these signposts, which all point in the same direction.

"No country can dominate the world without first destroying the British Empire. The Soviets too recognised that from their start; and, since both Nazism and Communism have always desired, and always must desire, to 'liquidate' us, there is nothing surprising in their latest alliance. They have at least one common interest. I pointed out in 1936 that we, and not Russia, were destined to be Nazism's Enemy No. 1; and the inevitable, not the accidental, has happened. To believe for a moment that Hitler's Germany really desired an enduring settlement with us, that the attitude of Hitler himself in the past was that of 'a rejected lover'—to use the phrase in one of Sir N. Henderson's dispatches—was courting the disaster that came. It was just the same old technique, covering the same old skin-game, as was practised and vaunted by Tirpitz. To the very end, however, the delusion persisted; and as late as the July 26th, 1939, we find Sir N. Henderson writing: 'From the very beginning Hitler has always sought above all an understanding with Britain.' And as late as the end of August he was saying to Hitler that even an alliance between England and Germany was not 'excluded'. Germany's Fifth War and the concentration of her entire hatred—born of jealousy—on this country are the answer.

"And how has it been possible that all writings on the wall and on Foreign Office paper as to the real nature of the German menace produced so little effect, that Sir Eyre Crowe before 1914 and I before 1939 had almost identically dis-heartening and unpleasant experiences? (Telling the truth about Germany has always been an unpopular exercise in England: it involves immediate mental, and ultimate physical discomfort.) Here also the answer is a straightforward one, though it cannot be found on the surface.

"Firstly, those who have ruled this country in the twentieth century are necessarily products of the nineteenth, of that Victorianism that all but carried through the next reign, and assumed the necessity of Progress. Men were supposed to be continually rising 'on stepping-stones of their dead selves to higher things', because this was the destiny of Man—an abstraction that never existed. Nobody dreamed that Regress was equally possible, and that in five years—according to our artificial time-tables—'Man' might go back fifty or five hundred. Even now it is hard for the ruling generation to forgo the great ancient dreamlands, harder still to realise that the last is but a hedge behind.

"This led automatically and directly to the Second cause, which despite its antiquity has only just acquired a name: wishful thinking. The Church chimed in, of course: one must love one's neighbour and think the best of everybody. Cabinet Ministers inveighed against 'suspicion'. Wishful thinking became entangled with, and fortified by, our national religion and the slack good-humour of our national character. Things couldn't be as bad as that.

"The Third cause in the concatenation is that wishful thinking—directed naturally against upheaval and toward the maintenance of the amenities of life in approximately their present form—is necessarily strongest among those who have most to lose by change. And historically it is precisely these categories who have most do do with the direction of affairs, in politics, business and the press.

"The Fourth of these linked causes has been German propaganda. It has always had a mesmeric effect on this country; and it follows automatically that it has the greatest effect among those most addicted to wishful thinking, who have been automatically those possessed of most influence.

"These facts all lead to one conclusion, and from that conclusion there is but one escape. Providence has twice been kind to us. We cannot count on a third indulgence.

"These reluctant truths by the nature of things—for the nature of things political is peculiar—cannot have the same notoriety as the myth of accidentalism; but they should at least be known—lest once more 'the clouds return after the rain'."

When he had written it all and unburdened himself, he returned home to the old house that he had grown to love more and more, the big windows of Denham Place darkened, and mounted the Georgian stair beneath the eyes of the grave Vansittart portraits. They seemed to stand for the solid, immovable greatness of England; but among them moved another train of men, a mist procession of those whom he had served. The Marquess Curzon . . . "no such thing as great men". Ramsay Macdonald . . . "a' these people dependent on me". Baldwin . . . "the man who can see far into the future is a charlatan". Sir John . . . "another empty sack". Lord Halifax

who said to him when Vansittart offered to resign on his six-
tieth birthday: "I always thought, Van, you were the fifth
wheel of the coach" . . . Many more peopled the stair of his life.
There was still to be drama in Denham Place, fugitive spies
with news of Germany, papers to burn from all over Europe,
the unavailing warnings that one Power would one day be
too strong for any coalition to restrain. He accepted a peerage
on his retirement in 1941 and resigned as soon as he reached
retiring age, accepting a gruff rebuke from Winston Churchill
for going so soon. Lord Vansittart spoke with much force and
increasing bitterness in the House of Lords on the subjects that
he had so tenaciously studied, the German menace and the
emergent dominance of Russia. Because he minded so much
more than his political masters, he also spent much of his
remaining life helping the unfortunates of the vast displace-
ment of Europe who had been ground small between these
two millstones. He had unending patience and kindness in
forlorn causes. I see him still as we last met in 1957, a few weeks
before his death, surprised that I should wish to write a book
round him, insistent that he had altered nothing, saved nothing, averted nothing. "I have failed" . . . . Who can tell? He
made selections of his papers with the idea of writing one day
the story of his baffled diplomacy. But he was reluctant to go so
deep into it all again. It hurt him overmuch and only his
incomparably happy second marriage seemed to make life
still bearable. He failed to describe the climax of his efforts.
The pen had not proved the mightier weapon in his life time.
The decisive chapter would be traced by vapour trails in the
sky over his beloved England, in the snows of Stalingrad and
written indelibly in the sea. His pen had simply left the testimony of a great public servant, whose masters were unequal
to the high precepts to which he had so earnestly sought their
adherence.

BIBLIOGRAPHY
(British editions)

The Vansittart Papers.

The Cadogan Diary (extracts).

Documents on British Foreign Policy, Second and Third Series. H.M.S.O.

Documents on International Affairs, 1939-46. Oxford Press.

Documents on German Foreign Policy, 1919-39. H.M.S.O.

Survey, 1930-1939. Royal Institute of International Affairs.

Documents and Materials Relating to the Eve of the Second World War, Ministry of Foreign Affairs, the U.S.S.R.

German Foreign Ministry Archives, Bonn.

The *Daily Telegraph* Library.

Hansard.

The Mist Procession, Lord Vansittart. Hutchinson, 1958.

Lessons of my Life, Lord Vansittart. Hutchinson, 1943.

Munich: Prologue to Tragedy, Sir John Wheeler-Bennett. Macmillan, 1948.

The Nemesis of Power, John Wheeler-Bennett. Macmillan, 1953.

Life of King George VI, John Wheeler-Bennett. Macmillan, 1958.

The Gathering Storm, W. S. Churchill. Cassell, 1948.

The Brutal Friendship, F. W. Deakin. Weidenfeld and Nicolson, 1962.

Stanley Baldwin, G. M. Young. Hart-Davis, 1952.

The Life of Neville Chamberlain, Keith Feiling. Macmillan, 1946.

Neville Chamberlain, Iain Macleod. Muller, 1961.

Fulness of Days, Viscount Halifax. Collins, 1957.

Ourselves and Germany, the Marquess of Londonderry. Robert Hale, 1938.

Victory at Sea, Peter Kemp. Muller, 1958.

Retrospect, Viscount Simon. Hutchinson, 1952.

I Remember, Viscount Swinton. Hutchinson, 1952.

King George V: His Life and Reign, Harold Nicolson. Constable, 1952.

Le Livre Jaune Français, 1938-39. Paris Imprimerie Nationale.

Documents Concerning German-Polish Relations and the Outbreak of Hostilities on September 3rd, 1939. H.M.S.O., 1939.

Peace and War, U.S. Foreign Policy. The State Department, 1943.

The Polish White Book, 1933-39. Hutchinson & Co.
Dokumente zur Vorgeschichte der Krieges. Carl Heymann Press, Berlin 1939 (The German White Book).
Nine Troubled Years, Sir Samuel Hoare, Viscount Templewood. Collins, 1954.
The Narrow Margin, Derek Wood and Derek Dempster. Hutchinson, 1961.
Facing the Dictators, the Earl of Avon. Cassell, 1962.
Old Men Forget, Alfred Duff Cooper, Viscount Norwich. Hart-Davis, 1953.
The Duff Cooper Diary, unpublished.
The Light of Common Day, Diana Cooper. Hart-Davis, 1959.
Ciano's Diplomatic Papers. Odhams Press Ltd., 1948.
Diary with Letters, Thomas Jones. Oxford, 1954.
Lord Lothian, J. R. M. Butler. Macmillan, 1960.
The Fateful Years, Hugh Dalton. Muller, 1957.
The British Foreign Service, F. T. A. Ashton-Gwatkin. Syracuse University Press, 1950.
Failure of a Mission, Sir Nevile Henderson. Hodder and Stoughton, 1940.
Both Sides of the Curtain, Sir Maurice Peterson. Constable, 1950.
The Inner Circle, Ivone Kirkpatrick. Macmillan, 1959.
Home and Abroad, Lord Strang. A. Deutsch, 1956.
Ambassador Dodd's Diary, W. E. & M. Dodd. Gollancz, 1941.
Hitler and the English, Fritz Hesse. Wingate, 1954.
The Last Day of the Old World, Adrian Ball. Muller, 1963.
The Appeasers, Martin Gilbert and Richard Gott. Weidenfeld and Nicolson, 1963.
All Souls and Appeasement, A. L. Rowse. Macmillan, 1961.
In the Nazi Era, Sir Lewis Namier. Macmillan, 1952.
The Origins of the Second World War, A. J. P. Taylor. Hamilton, 1961.
Rise and Fall of the Third Reich, William Shirer. Secker and Warburg, 1960.
In Allied London, Count Edward Raczynski. Weidenfeld and Nicolson, 1963.
Dernier Rapport, Colonel Joszef Beck. Editions de la Baconnière, 1951.
Diplomatic Twilight, Sir Walford Selby. Murray, 1953.
Nicht aus den Akten, Erich Kordt. Union Deutsch, Stuttgart, 1950.

The Ironside Diaries. Constable, 1963.

The Ribbentrop Memoirs. Weidenfeld and Nicolson, 1954.

Austria, Germany, and the Anschluss, Jürgen Gehl. Oxford Press, 1963.

Bound for Diplomacy, Valentine Lawford. Murray, 1963.

Who Helped Hitler?, Ivan Maisky. Hutchinson, 1964.

Carl Goerdeler und die deutsche Widerstandsbewegung, Gerhard Ritter. Deutsche Verlag, Stuttgart, 1955.

Servir, General Gamelin. Librairie Plon, 1946.

Memoirs of Ernst von Weizsaecker. Gollancz, 1951.

Vom Anderen Deutschland, Ulrich von Hassell. Atlantic Press, Zürich, 1946.

Hitler's Interpreter, Paul Schmidt. Heinemann, 1951.

Account Settled, Dr. H. Schacht. Weidenfeld & Nicolson, 1949.

The Coming of War in 1939, W. N. Medlicott. Routledge & Kegan Paul, 1963.

The Foreign Office Documents and the Archives of the German Foreign Office, Sir Walford Selby. Article in the *Quarterly Review,* October 1951.

Reflections on British Policy Between the Two World Wars, Lt-Col. the Hon. Arthur Murray. Oliver and Boyd, 1946.

The Antique Collector, October 1962.

INDEX

356

940.5311   c 1d
COLVIN, IAN G.
   NONE SO BLIND.

SOUTH PUGET SOUND REGIONAL LIBRARY
        OLYMPIA, WASHINGTON

PLEASE KEEP CARD IN POCKET

TIMBERLAND
LIBRARY
DEMONSTRATION

OLYMPIA